Philippians
for today
Priorities from prison

Day One

© Day One Publications 2005
First printed 2005

ISBN 1-84625-000-5

9 781846 250002 >

British Library Cataloguing in Publication Data available

Published by Day One Publications
Ryelands Road, Leominster, HR6 8NZ
☎ 01568 613 740 FAX 01568 611 473
email—sales@dayone.co.uk
web site—www.dayone.co.uk
North American—e-mail—sales@dayonebookstore.com
North American—web site—www.dayonebookstore.com

Designed by Steve Devane and printed by Gutenberg Press, Malta

Dedication

To all who suffer in prison for Christ and His gospel; to all prisoners who now trust Christ and live for Him there; and especially to my dear Christian brothers, Alan and Steve, who I believe should not be in prison.

Contents

Contents

ENDNOTES APPEAR AT THE END OF EACH SECTION.

Doug McMasters is Senior pastor of Calvary Bible Church, Grass Valley, California, USA and a board member of the USA branch of the D. Martyn Lloyd-Jones Trust.

Ministering to a church that worships in three shifts in order to fit into the sanctuary, I've had the frequent experience of introducing members to others—even long-time members—who attend a different service. I've found the process of introducing two strangers to each other perfectly delightful. It begins with mentioning names and a short statement of each person's status, title, or relation to the introducer. That is typically followed by a longer, well chosen anecdote about one party, usually on a subject of known interest to the other, designed to bring the two into a discussion of discovery, with the hope that perhaps a long, lasting friendship is launched.

Gerard Chrispin has done the Church an excellent service by introducing believers to the book of Philippians. Even those who have enjoyed many conversations with the letter to the Philippians will find themselves learning new insights from him. Gerard Chrispin is an obvious student of the Word of God, and that coupled with his background in law, prisons and the incarcerated, makes him well acquainted with both the content of Philippians and the condition of the human heart. He holds an obvious love for God's Word and people, and through this commentary on Philippians, he strives to make them fast friends.

A skilled introducer will hold back some information—even the sweetest—knowing that relationships only develop when they progress beyond the information given about each social contact. Gerard Chrispin brings the believer plenty of information to stimulate interest in knowing more, and provides a series of discovery questions near the end of the commentary to ensure new discoveries will be the cherished possession of all who think through them. I'm convinced anyone reading—and using—Gerard's commentary will own an ongoing friendship with the book of Philippians.

Friendship with the letter to the Philippians is needed in our day. The days when truth was prevalent in the church and peace ruled have waned, and Paul's message to the Philippians of personal joy and doctrinal fidelity amid an onslaught of error within the church, and persecution without, is perfectly suited to today.

Doug McMasters
Grass Valley, California, USA

Philip Hacking is a leading evangelical Anglican, a former chairman of the Keswick Convention, England, a conference speaker, and author.

At a time when Europe is the only continent where the church is in decline, this is a timely insight into a letter written to the first church planted in Europe. In an age when the concept of suffering for the gospel is largely neglected in our western society we are introduced to a letter of joy, hope and love coming from an apostle in prison.

The author of this in-depth study has himself been involved in prison ministry with his legal expertise and as a Christian counsellor. This gives an added dimension to a very thorough and practical exposition of the book. I was privileged to expound this Philippian letter at the Keswick Convention some years ago under the title of *Prison Praise*. The book is a remarkable blend of deep theology but always bearing on the real world and often disturbingly practical teaching.

The layout of the book lends itself to personal and group study which will deepen understanding of profound doctrine and yet not allow it to remain as a merely cerebral exercise. So Paul in chapter two will introduce us to a mind-blowing view of the Person of Christ written not for exam purposes but to challenge a church in danger of dividing over personalities to discover the meaning and power of humility

Philippians is basically an extended thank-you note, with its reminder of the importance and joy of Christian giving. In the process, it highlights the deep meaning of fellowship in the gospel, a costly affair. With Paul's gratitude for these constant friends goes a longing for their growth in the faith not least under the attack of false teachers. What changes in this world?

This letter from prison is a beautiful example of how to blend personal testimony, of which the book is movingly full, with objective Christian truth. Preaching has been defined as 'truth mediated through personality' and Christian writing needs the same blend. People need to know how the truth helps in daily life and how daily experiences become the agency of truth learned and proclaimed.

A prisoner like Paul lived with death ever imminent. Mostly you would scarcely know it reading Philippians. Yet every now and again the resurrection hope shines brightly through its pages. This book helps us to look, at leisure, over Paul's shoulder, and learn to rejoice in hope whether in or out of prison.

Philip Hacking
Sheffield, England

This book on Philippians is a *devotional and discipleship* commentary. It seeks to draw out important principles and apply them to a Christian's daily life and service for Christ. The method used is to look at the meaning of the book in its biblical context, draw out the principles and then suggest areas of application. Because this is not intended to be an academic book, a number of examples and quotations from books which motivate discipleship and devotion are used. I hope that they help to put flesh and bones on the skeleton. This may be the main difference from more traditional Bible commentaries of an academic nature only. I hope that the lessons drawn will assist personal application—'where the rubber hits the road'—more than mere academic debate. But there are precious doctrines and key issues treated in the book of Philippians and so the comment in this commentary seeks to present those important truths faithfully, enthusiastically and logically.

Hopefully this book will be easy to read. Each chapter in Part 3 of the book is preceded by the text of the corresponding chapter of Philippians. Then the commentary on each verse in each chapter is preceded by the text of that verse. I have used my favourite translation, the New King James Version, which is published by Nelson. When a word or words need to be emphasised in the commentary, whether in quotes or not, the words are italicised. (Naturally, you will need your Bible to check cross-references to other parts of the Word of God.)

The book consists of four separate parts.

Part One is a bird's eye view of the letter, giving a general panoramic overview.

Part Two carries brief pen sketches of the characters encountered during the founding and operation of the church to which Paul writes. They are taken from Acts and Philippians itself. Some are of key Christian workers, including Paul himself, whilst converts and those in opposition to the gospel are also presented. I hope this will enable the reader to grasp that this letter is about real people in real life situations.

Part Three is the 'engine room' and is what the book is really all about, so anyone eager to get straight into the text of Philippians should start here! Each verse is looked at individually, but to give continuity and context there are mini-overviews provided where a more general heading covers a cluster of verses before each individual verse in that cluster is considered. The comment on the verses, unless inappropriate in a given situation, is written in the present tense, to underline its practical reality and relevance, not only to the Christians at the Roman colony of Philippi, but to third millennium readers wherever they live, work and witness in today's world.

Part Four poses two questions on each verse, which may be used for personal consideration, or provide an abridged personal commentary for those who wish to note their answers, or promote focused discussion in either large or small groups. This will be of help to adult Sunday Schools, church Bible studies, individual fellowships, Christian Unions, Young Life branches, Bible study team times on evangelistic outreach teams or to any similar group or informal fellowship hungry for God's truth from His Word. They can also be helpfully used in one-on-one discipleship training.

The source references for each chapter's consecutively numbered quotations or origins appear at the end of each section as 'Endnotes'.

This book is dedicated to all who suffer worldwide for the gospel, to all who are suffering greatly in many different ways whilst walking with Christ, and to prisoners in UK prisons who have come to know Christ and must learn to live for Him in an environment we would all shrink from. Specifically it is dedicated to Alan and to Mary, his loyal wife, and to Steve. Steve's wife has divorced him during his long imprisonment. Both Ian and Steve have trusted Christ whilst in prison. I believe both were wrongly convicted and imprisoned. Both have told me that, despite the hardships and injustices suffered, they thank God that He took them to prison because there they met the Saviour.

I am indebted to my dear friend and brother in Christ, David Harding, for his comments from time to time on what I have written. I have revisited nearly all of the areas where he suggested improvements could be made, but I do not blame him for the outcome! All I can say is that it would have been far worse if he had not been involved at formative stages. My wife, Phillippa, as well as arranging our busy itinerary to preach the gospel around UK prisons with Day One Prison Ministries, has used some of her precious and scarce 'free time' to make her criticisms and comments. I have appreciated her comments and acted on them (nearly always!). I am grateful to Doug McMasters, Pastor of Calvary Baptist Church, Grass

Valley, California, and to Philip Hacking, now President of Day One Christian Ministries, which is Day One's parent organisation, for their kindness in providing the Prefaces to this book. I want to thank Day One for their help and opportunity given to share the truths of this wonderful letter of Paul. I am grateful to John Roberts, whose idea it was to write another book, and to Steve Devane for his excellent cover design and Digby James for his expertise in doing everything necessary to convert my painful word processing into a book of the usual high quality that Day One produce. I am also very grateful to Jim Holmes for his encouragement and editing.

Most of all, of course, I am grateful to my crucified and risen Lord through whom 'I can do all things' as He 'strengthens me'.

Gerard A. Chrispin
Southampton, England
May 2005

AV = Authorised Version, or King James Version, of the Bible
NASB = New American Standard Bible
NIV = New International Version of the Bible
NKJV = New King James Version of the Bible
IB = The Interlinear Bible (Sovereign Grace Publishers)
PHILLIPS = J.B. Phillips 'The New Testament in Modern English'
RV = Revised Version of the Bible
RSV = Revised Standard Version of the Bible
TAB = The Amplified Bible

A bird's eye view of the letter

Who wrote it?
The apostle Paul.

To whom did he write it?
The young Christian church at Philippi, a Roman colony. This was where the first European church was founded. The colony was a military outpost and settlement of Rome which had been established in order to control the region of Philippi and make it a small replica of Rome.

When did he write it?
Estimates vary from AD 51 to AD 64. We may assume it was probably written in the mid to late AD 50s. (One's view of the time of writing is affected by whether the place of writing is understood to be Rome, as seems to be the case, or elsewhere.)

From where did he write it?
From prison, and almost certainly from Rome, although Ephesus and Caesarea are locations favoured by some.

Why did he write it?
1. To encourage the young church spiritually in the face of persecution that could bring suffering;

2. To combat doctrinal deviancy which encouraged the adoption of Judaistic legalism's insistence that circumcision was necessary for salvation. This error implied that faith alone, in Christ alone, by grace alone was not sufficient to save a repentant sinner;

3. To appeal for oneness in Christ because of the great example of humility that Jesus gave, and in the light of His continual presence and His imminent coming;

4. To stress the nearness of Christ as a vital factor influencing Christian attitude, action, service, suffering, and survival.

What to look out for

1. The need and priority to preach the gospel selflessly, and its true nature in practice;

2. The all inclusive nature of a loving church;

3. Joy and rejoicing;

4. Godly satisfaction;

5. The nature of God in the Trinity;

6. The example of Christ's humility to counteract personality clashes;

7. The Christian's certain hope;

8. God's help in Christian living and service;

9. Giving;

10. Christ's near presence and glorious second coming.

The characters

The people involved in the Philippian church

The Philippian Christians themselves are well identified in the letter, but there are other people involved, directly or indirectly, with the church at Philippi. They are found either in the letter itself or in Acts chapter 16 where Paul and his co-labourers in the gospel of Christ are involved in taking the gospel to the Philippians. Those in the letter are given brief pen-sketches in (1) below, and those in Acts chapter 16 similarly in (2) below. The apostle Paul features in both (1) and (2).

The background to the church in Philippi is found in Acts 16:6–40.

(1) Characters, in order of mention, appearing in the book of Philippians

PAUL (SEE ALSO BELOW UNDER (2), DEALING WITH ACTS 16:6–40)

Mentioned 158 times in the New Testament as 'Paul' and 23 times as 'Saul', the great apostle—who preferred to be known as the 'chief of sinners'—needs little introduction. Having Roman citizenship by birth, he was, nevertheless, a zealous Jew and a leading Pharisee, taught by the master Gamaliel. His hatred for the Christian church led him to persecute it and cause the death and imprisonment of many Christians. On the way to Damascus, with authority to imprison Christians there, the risen Christ appears to him and he is struck blind by the strength of the light that outshone the sun. Befriended by Barnabas, at the direction of God, Paul is taken into fellowship with new sight, not only physically but also spiritually. He becomes an apostle of Christ. He turns into a preacher and teacher of the gospel and of God's Word, a prayer warrior, an advocate for the truth, and a loving but firm founder of many churches. He is a disciple-maker. He writes more letters in the New Testament than anyone else. His absolute commitment to Christ and His gospel cause him to suffer much, including imprisonments, stonings, floggings and shipwrecks. Nevertheless, he is determined to preach the cross of Christ and His resurrection because he knows there is no other message that can save lost sinners. His care for all the churches gives him his greatest pain, as he seeks to bring backsliders back, protect young Christians, groom leaders and set a transparent example of devoted discipleship.

He writes this letter to the Philippians from prison, and with the likelihood of death and martyrdom not far away. His heart for God, His Word, the gospel, the Christian church, his brothers and sisters in Christ, and the lost is visible for all to see. He is only mentioned by name once, in the opening verse of the letter.

TIMOTHY

Timothy, mentioned twenty-four times in the New Testament and twice in the book of Philippians (1:1, and 2:19), was Paul's 'spiritual son'. Born of a Jewish mother and a Greek father, the seeds of the gospel were sown in his young life by his mother, Lois, and his grandmother, Eunice. But it is Paul who helps him to develop his discipleship and servant-heartedness into Christian leadership, as he takes a fatherly spiritual interest in him and in his welfare and service. Paul never loses that concern for his spiritual protégé and the two pastoral letters to him are a pattern of practical godliness and a guide to leadership for all who read them. Timothy becomes Paul's fellow worker, supporter, encourager, prison visitor, courier, messenger, trusted delegate to the churches, leader and disciple-maker. He usually works in a small team of dedicated servants of Christ, but is personally so trustworthy that Paul feels able to send him on his own to manage a crisis or to teach the church.

EPAPHRODITUS

All we know from the Bible about this remarkably selfless servant of Christ is found in two verses in this letter (2:25; 4:18). He is Paul's secretary and courier, probably writing by his hand the words dictated to him and then carrying them to the recipients. He is a man of great integrity who could be trusted with carrying financial gifts from givers to recipient. A disciplined soldier of Christ and co-labouring, caring brother of Paul, his attitude towards his own illness and sacrificial service is a notable landmark in this book.

EUODIA AND SYNTYCHE

Just once (4:1) do we meet these two ladies in the church. They are most often remembered as a warning that Christians can spoil the blessing for themselves and others by not being 'of the same mind in the Lord'. But we should charitably remember that this seems out of character for them, as they are mentioned as 'women who laboured with [Paul] in the gospel'. Like each one of us now, any gospel labourer then could be tripped-up in the question of interpersonal relationships. Praise God it does not prevent their, or our, names being recorded 'in the Book of Life' by God's grace.

CLEMENT

In the verse after we meet Euodia and Syntyche, we meet Clement. It is simply said of him that he also laboured in the gospel with Paul and those ladies. He too is in the 'Book of Life'. He is a little-known Christian who obviously impressed the apostle and was faithful to his Lord.

2. Characters, in order of mention, appearing in Acts 16:6–40

LUKE

Luke is one of Paul's co-workers in the gospel's advance to the Philippians. This is clearly shown by the way he includes himself in the 'we' of Acts 16. Luke is the author of the gospel that bears his name, and of the Acts of the Apostle, both of whom are addressed to Theophilus, with Acts referring to Luke's 'former account' written to him. Luke is a doctor, referred to as 'the beloved physician' (Colossians 4:14). He has an eye for detail, as his accounts show. On one occasion he alone was present to support the apostle (2 Timothy 4:11), who describes him as one of his 'fellow labourers' in Philemon 1:24. He appears to be an intelligent, loving, hard-working servant of Christ and His gospel. This man chooses to put others in the limelight rather than be there himself. He is mentioned only three times by name in the Bible, but has made a great impact on the world through God's working.

PAUL (SEE ALSO (1) ABOVE DEALING WITH THE LETTER TO THE PHILIPPIANS)

Paul, Silas, and, at times, Timothy and Luke (in the book of Acts that he wrote he says 'we ran a straight course') go to Macedonia in answer to a vision from God of a man needing the gospel to be preached to him there. They then sail, via other cities, to Philippi, the chief Macedonian city. In preaching the gospel there, they reach women at a riverside prayer meeting and Lydia is converted. Paul casts out the spirit of divination from a possessed slave girl and ends up in prison with Silas after they have both been beaten with rods. The girl's masters are furious that her liberty means they cannot use her as a paid fortune-teller any longer. In prison, Paul and Silas praise God and experience a remarkable and literal 'act of God' in a great earthquake. This results in their witness to the jailer. First he, and then his family, trust Christ and are baptised. For the good of the infant church's future, Paul insists that the magistrates must come to get them out of prison. Although forbidden on pain of death to authorise the flogging of a Roman citizen, they have illegally inflicted this on Paul. The magistrates do as Paul demands and now plead for Paul and Silas to leave! Paul and Silas return first for fellowship at the house of Lydia, where they encourage the new Christians, before they move on.

LYDIA

Lydia is referred to in Acts 16:14 and 16:40. Even before her conversion she was someone who believed in prayer and meets Paul when he goes to speak to the women praying together by the river. She worships God without knowing Him personally. She is a businesswoman from Thyatira, who sells purple used in making dyes. She has her own house, which is open for God's people and God's cause after she comes to know Christ. It was here that Paul and Silas go to meet the Christian brethren in Philippi after their release from prison and before their departure. It is very likely that the infant church at Philippi is nurtured there at the home of this lady, who appears to be single. We do not know if she is divorced or widowed, but she is in charge of the household. Lydia comes to salvation because God gives her an open heart to hear the Word of God preached by Paul. Her love for Christ and her influence is such that her witness brings her household to the Lord, leading to her and her household being baptised!

SLAVE GIRL AND HER 'OWNERS'

On the way to prayer with other disciples, a slave girl, possessed with a spirit of divination, follows Paul and his companions and declares them to be God's servants proclaiming His salvation. This she does for many days, until Paul casts the spirit out of her in the name of Jesus Christ. The masters of the delivered girl drag the Christian brothers into the market place and then before the magistrates where they are beaten with 'many stripes', handed over to the jailer, and put in the prison's stocks. Satan's servants do not like to see an oppressed young person delivered, especially when it hits their pockets. Acts 16:16–24 covers the events described above.

SILAS

Silas' name appears thirteen times in the Bible, all in the book of Acts, which records the lifestyle and evangelistic outreach of the apostles and those closely associated with them. Although he is, therefore, not mentioned in the letter to the Philippians, his willingness to sacrifice and suffer joyfully for Christ helps the apostle and his team to give a foundational example to the young Christians in that Roman colony. Remember that he is the one who sings hymns in prison with Paul after being flogged! He is a leader of the church, a trusted man to report what had happened, has the gift of prophecy, and works as a team member, often being named with Timothy. He is a prayerful spiritual man with a rugged, yet joyful, doggedness.

THE PHILIPPIAN JAILER

The jailer is told to keep Paul and Silas secure, and that is why they are in the stocks within his prison. We do not know if he witnessed the amazing event of flogged and wrongly imprisoned prisoners, doubly secured, praying and singing hymns to God at midnight, with the other prisoners a ready audience! He was asleep at some stage because a great earthquake roused him. The earthquake itself set the scene for a more amazing 'act of God'— the jailer's own salvation through Christ! Realising that the shaking of the foundations had resulted in the prison doors being opened, he assumes that the prisoners have fled and is about to commit suicide to avoid the shame and reproach at not having vigilantly achieved the task given to him. But Paul assures him that all the prisoners are still there. The man trembles and immediately asks how he can be saved. No doubt he has already heard why

Paul was in prison, namely because he had expelled a demon and taught people about God. He has noticed the difference between his inwardly liberated Christian prisoners and himself. Paul follows up his famous exhortation to 'Believe on the Lord Jesus Christ, and you will be saved, you and your household' by presenting God's Word to him and to everyone in his house. God blesses that biblical presentation of the gospel in that all his household, as well as the man himself, become believers and are baptised. We do not know the ages or number of the members of his household, but they all came to faith at this time. The evidences of conversion are clear: a loving care for suffering brethren, as the jailer washes the stripes of Paul and Silas; obedience to the command to be baptised; an open home and provision of food; and rejoicing! The jailer and his family are set free from their sins. Acts 16: 25–34 provides the narrative.

Open the letter!

Philippians Chapter 1

[1] Paul and Timothy, bondservants of Jesus Christ, To all the saints in Christ Jesus who are in Philippi, with the bishops and deacons: [2] Grace to you and peace from God our Father and the Lord Jesus Christ. [3] I thank my God upon every remembrance of you, [4] Always in every prayer of mine making request for you all with joy, [5] for your fellowship in the gospel from the first day until now, [6] being confident of this very thing, that He who has begun a good work in you will complete it until the day of Jesus Christ; [7] just as it is right for me to think this of you all, because I have you in my heart, inasmuch as both in my chains and in the defence and confirmation of the gospel, you are all partakers with me of grace [8] For God is my witness, how greatly I long for you all with the affection of Jesus Christ. [9] And this I pray, that your love may abound still more and more in knowledge and all discernment, [10] that you may approve the things that are excellent, that you may be sincere and without offence till the day of Christ, [11] being filled with the fruits of righteousness which are by Jesus Christ, to the glory and praise of God.

[12] But I want you to know, brethren, that the things which happened to me have actually turned out for the furtherance of the gospel, [13] So it has become evident to the whole palace guard, and to all the rest, that my chains are in Christ; [14] and most of the brethren in the Lord, having become confident by my chains, are much more bold to speak the word without fear. [15] Some indeed preach Christ even from envy and strife, and some also from good will; [16] The former preach Christ from selfish ambition, not sincerely, supposing to add affliction to my chains; [17] but the latter out of love, knowing that I am appointed for the defence of the gospel. [18] What then? Only that in every way, whether in pretence or in truth, Christ is preached; and in this I rejoice, yes, and will rejoice.

19 For I know that this will turn out for my salvation through your prayer and the supply of the Spirit of Jesus Christ, 20 according to my earnest expectation and hope that in nothing I shall be ashamed, but with all boldness, as always so now also Christ will be magnified in my body, whether by life or by death. 21 For to me, to live is Christ, and to die is gain. 22 But if I live on in the flesh, this will mean fruit from my labour; yet what I shall choose I cannot tell. 23 For I am hard-pressed between the two, having a desire to be with Christ, which is far better. 24 Nevertheless to remain in the flesh is more needful for you. 25 And being confident of this, I know that I shall remain and continue with you all for your progress and joy of faith, 26 and that your rejoicing for me may be more abundant in Jesus Christ by my coming to you again.

27 Only let your conduct be worthy of the gospel of Christ, so that whether I come and see you or am absent, I may hear of your affairs, that you stand fast in one spirit, with one mind striving together for the faith of the gospel, 28 and not in any way terrified by your adversaries, which is to them a proof of perdition, but to you of salvation, and that from God.

29 For to you it has been granted on behalf of Christ, not only to believe in Him, but also to suffer for His sake, 30 having the same conflict which you saw in me and now hear in me.

'Bridges to blessing'

Mini-overview: 1:1 to 1:11:

To all the saints: my prayer for you all.

After greeting the church at Philippi, Paul tells the Christians there how he thanks God for them, and what he prays for them.

1:1 From the slaves to the saints!

[1] Paul and Timothy, bondservants of Jesus Christ, To all the saints in Christ Jesus who are in Philippi, with the bishops and deacons:

SURPRISE, SURPRISE!

The early Christians were said to have turned the world upside-down.[1] In fact they had begun to turn it the right way up! The effects of the gospel so often reverse what men would expect. So it is at the very outset of this gem of a letter written by Paul. Here we see the *prisoner* writing to the church to encourage and help them! Usually the mail to help and encourage comes *into* prison. Here we see it going *from* prison to help set others free in a deeper and personal sense.

LOYALTY

Paul is in jail. Timothy, his son in the faith,[2] is named with him in what Paul has to say. Timothy is so supportive of his senior role model that his identification with Paul is permanently noted in Scripture. It is always good when Christians stand by their faithful brothers and sisters in Christ. This is especially so when they are outcast, criticised, persecuted or imprisoned. No doubt Timothy was a regular visitor to his imprisoned older brother in Christ. His close links with the Philippian church[3] would encourage readers and writer alike. So his name is linked with Paul's and Paul may even have dictated the letter to him. If that was so, Timothy was not only a prison visitor but also Paul's hard-working secretary. The failure of many of us to find time to write a letter to a missionary in another country is in sharp and searching contrast. Even as we read the traditional opening of the letter, which identifies the sender and the recipient, we are challenged about our faithfulness in visiting and writing and encouraging those in need.

SLAVERY MEANS LIBERTY

Is Paul depressed that he is languishing in a Roman jail? No, not at all. He is not a prisoner of sin, of circumstances or even primarily of Rome. Along with Timothy, who is not imprisoned, he states they are 'bondservants of Jesus Christ'. He goes to the first cause—Christ! Literally he is saying that they are slaves. But whose slaves are they? Paul gratefully adds 'of Jesus Christ'. In the adverse circumstances surrounding him, he reminds himself of this totally liberating fact: his ties to the love of God in Christ are closer and more permanent than any human fetters can ever be! George Mattheson's stirring hymn starts with the words

Make me a captive, Lord,
And then I shall be free.
Force me to render up my sword
And I shall conqueror be!4

I well remember a prayer I heard at school when I was very young. That phrase was 'whose service is perfect freedom'. I could never understand that, until I came to Christ and knew the liberty He gives to those who trust Him. How encouraging to remember that in earth's darkest hour we are 'slaves of Jesus Christ'! What blessed bondage is that!

THE CHURCH IN A NUTSHELL

Many people get too confused with externals and think the church is a building or a formal organisation or denomination. This first verse corrects that, simply yet deeply. What really is the church? It consists of the three types of people to whom Paul writes: saints, bishops and deacons! In fact it includes everyone at Philippi who had exercised personal saving faith in the Lord Jesus Christ, because Paul addresses his letter to 'all the saints in Christ Jesus who are in Philippi'. That is so wonderfully all-inclusive. He does not ignore some whose income is less or who have lower educational achievements than others. He does not overlook the newly converted, or favour men over women, or one race over another. No—'*all* the saints' are important to Paul, because they are all important to God. Are they all 'in Christ Jesus', who bore their sins and gave them new life through His resurrection? Do they all know the indwelling of the Holy Spirit? Yes! Then all are part of the body of Christ and equally precious to the God who had bought them. The same is true today. We must treat all fellow believers in Jesus with equal honour, respect and love.

STAINED GLASS WINDOWS?

What does 'saint' mean? 'Saint' has nothing to do with stained glass windows or lists of those whom the Vatican wishes to canonise. The word means 'set apart' and refers to every sinner who has repented from sin and taken Christ's substitutionary sacrifice on the cross as payment for his own debt of sin. He has thus received Christ by faith to be his only Saviour and Lord. He has been set apart from sin, Satan's dominion, and control by a polluted world system. He has been set aside to know, follow, honour, worship and serve his Saviour and Lord. He has been so set apart by divine grace that God sees him as already 'called', 'justified' and 'glorified' in Christ.5 That is his standing in Christ. His state needs to be set apart, in practical holy living each day, by the help of the Holy Spirit and by feeding on the Word of God.

BISHOPS AND DEACONS—WHO ARE THEY?

Yet equality in our standing in Christ does not mean that all have equal authority in the running of the work of God. Neither do we all have the same tasks to do. Thus, although his letter is to all the Christians in Philippi, Paul particularly singles out two groups of people. The 'bishops' together comprise the leadership and the 'deacons' have special responsibility within the church for particular areas of service. We are too conditioned by an ecclesiastical image of 'bishops'. An Anglican vicar friend of mine used to say that a 'bishop' is not someone who says, 'Call me father' whilst dressing like mother! Rather he is one of a team of spiritual overseers (which is how the NIV translates the word), or supervisors, in the church.[6] The words 'overseer' or 'elder' carry exactly the same significance: a more mature and spiritual man, meeting the biblical criteria for leadership.[7] Along with other like-minded Christian men of proven reputation, bishops are responsible for guiding and directing the affairs of that local church through the application of biblical teaching. 'Deacon' means 'servant'. The deacons in a church are those with particular aptitude and responsibility for areas of church work delegated to them by the church through the authority of the bishops (or elders). Francis Davidson has pointed out that the Greek word translated 'deacon' is found 'frequently in the Gospels and Epistles and is generally translated "servant" or "minister", which is its meaning. In a more technical sense "deacon" is applied to the class of church officers whose duty is concerned more with material things than with those directly spiritual (*cf.* 1 Timothy 3:8). This special office may have had its origin in the election of the Seven in Acts 6, although there this name is not given to them.'[8]

(One could question the use of the word 'office', as a servant does not hold office. Perhaps 'task' would be a better word.) Nevertheless, a deacon must also be a spiritual person; no doubt an appropriately gifted deacon, with the gift of teaching and preaching God's Word, could also be recognised later in the leadership role of bishop (or elder).[9] Thus the recipients of the letter from Paul constitute the church. They are spiritually 'in Christ Jesus', geographically in Philippi, but under the leadership of the bishops and served by the deacons.

1:2 'Have a nice day!'
[2] Grace to you and peace from God our Father and the Lord Jesus Christ.

WORDS ARE CHEAP
I heard about a New York mugger who took at knife-point the ring, gold chain, wallet, money, credit cards, laptop computer, and designer label leather coat and shoes from his well-heeled victim. He then departed with the sickly smooth words 'Have a nice day!' The insincerity of that is obvious, yet how often are we involved in the giving and receiving of superficial greetings? It is easy to wish someone 'A happy Christmas', 'A happy birthday' or to 'Have a nice weekend' when we do not really care too much

about the fulfilment of those wishes. Words are cheap. The Christian should seek to blend true sincerity with his or her admirable desire to be friendly.

PAUL'S GREETING
But Paul means his greeting! 'Grace and peace from God our Father and the Lord Jesus Christ' are his standard opening. We see identical words on nine occasions in the New Testament[10] and in very similar words also to the Romans, twice to Timothy, and to Titus.[11] The rest of what he writes in the New Testament makes it very clear that he means what he says.

GRACE
From start to finish we see that it is only God's unmerited grace that gives us the opportunity to be reconciled to God.[12] Grace literally means 'undeserved favour'. When we were far away from God in our sins, and deserving His punishment, God the Father devised a way by which sinful and rebellious men could be pardoned and justified and be the recipients of eternal life. That grace caused His eternal Son, the Lord Jesus Christ, to come to earth to redeem us by His blood. Having come to know Him, God then grants us His grace for our daily living. Mercy means I do deserve something from God (namely, His wrath and punishment) but I do *not* receive it: grace means I deserve nothing from God at all, yet I *do* receive it (namely, all His multi-faceted blessing in Christ). That grace includes God's mercy, of course. Well has William Clayton, the pioneer church planter with Belgian Evangelical Mission, explained grace: 'The grace of God is before all an attribute of His divine nature. We can speak of His grace, as we would speak of His love, His power, His holiness, as an aspect of His personal character. The grace of God is His attitude of love towards the wicked, the sinful, the rebellious—which we all are—to save them from the punishment they deserve and to give them favours which they do not deserve.'[13] More simply, 'GRACE' can stand for 'God's Riches At Christ's Expense'.

PEACE
Having become the beneficiaries and recipients of that grace, we profit from the peace that comes in its train. We have 'peace with God through

our Lord Jesus Christ'[14] and experience the 'peace of God which surpasses all understanding' in our hearts and minds.[15] 'Peace with God' deals with our position in Christ. We have become reconciled to a God with whom we were previously enemies because of our sinfulness. 'Peace of God' is our experience when, reconciled and indwelt by the Holy Spirit in our hearts,[16] we know that the Prince of Peace lives in us.[17] In every sense this double blessing of grace and peace are from the Father and the Son and are applied in our hearts by the third Person of the Trinity, the Holy Spirit.

SO?

If we have benefited from God's combined blessing of grace and peace in our lives, we will seek to live close to the Giver of that benefit. The evidence of such a lifestyle will be the ongoing influence of His grace and the increasing deepening of His peace, like a river, in our lives. We will be, as the Corinthians were,[18] letters 'known and read by all men'. The 'letter of my life' should make a lasting impression on others and introduce them to the new lifestyle of grace and peace which I have received. My deeds, words and demeanour should be easily read and point to Christ. The closer I live to the Lord, the stronger will be the impression I give of God's grace and peace.

1:3 'Thanks for the memory'

3 I thank my God upon every remembrance of you,

GRATITUDE FOR GRACE, NOT SENTIMENTAL SLUSH

The sentimental old love song of the 1950s *Thanks for the memory* was intended to pull nostalgically at the heart strings. But sentimental slush is not at the heart of Paul's words here. He is grateful for God's grace that makes the Philippian Christians what they are. Verse 5, below, tells us the specific reason for his giving thanks, but think for a moment on the wonderful example he sets of thanksgiving. This will recur in chapter 4, but here we see its first mention in the letter. His first memories of the Philippians are of a quiet riverside, soon followed by a nasty riot! After that scene of peace came the hostility, opposition, beatings and incarceration in a prison. But when he thinks back he gives God thanks for '*every* remembrance of you'! Imprisoned yet again, as Paul writes he still knows the joy and gratitude now that he had then! That really is God's grace in action!

IT IS A PRIORITY

The very first thing that Paul tells us he does is to 'thank my God'! We all should do that. No circumstances, even imprisonment, should quench this positive help to victorious living. No feelings of depression or opposition should become a wet blanket stifling the fire of grateful faith, sparked off by God's grace. Thanksgiving will chase away those negative feelings. God's grace will bear us along, rejoicing in His peace, if thanksgiving is our attitude and we simply say, 'I thank my God' in all circumstances. Test yourself! When you are truly thankful to God, are you easily overcome by the cares of this world? When you openly express your gratitude, do you not find that you are as far less critical of others and more content with your own lot? A nurse called Rachel Brown worked for years unstintingly and alone among London's prostitutes. She admitted that there were times when she did feel a little 'down', especially first thing in the day, but she had made it her practice to start her morning prayer time with thanking God for who He is and for what He had done for her. Her testimony was that God warmed up her heart with joy as she exercised herself in thanksgiving. No wonder she had such an amazing effect upon the ladies to whom she witnessed every day, and was such an encouragement to those invited to speak at her meetings in her flat.

IT IS PERSONAL

Note that Paul rejoices in a personal God. He says, 'I thank *my* God'. True thanksgiving to God starts with a personal relationship with Him and is promoted and enhanced only by a deepening of that personal tie with the 'Son of God who loved *me* and gave Himself for *me*'.[19] (All my emphases above.) The bondservant remembers again that the lover of his soul is God Himself, and that He is faithfully ever present with him.

IT IS PERPETUAL

Every time that the apostle remembers his faithful and loving Christian family in Philippi, he thanks God. Never, despite their undoubted faults and failures, does Paul fail to thank God upon remembering them. What a challenge to us as 'rememberers'! Do we dwell on the negatives of other Christians, thus forgetting that they are trophies of God's grace? Many have already come a long way by His grace—probably much further than we have. Are we positive about their good points that evidence the power of the gospel in their lives? What a challenge to us, too, as the persons 'remembered'! Have we been such a blessing and encouragement to others that when they think of us they thank God? (Or are they thankful that they are *not* like us!) Have we helped the cause of Christ and fellow Christians so that, even knowing our 'feet of clay', they will thank you God for us? Will missionaries always remember us with real gratitude to the Lord for the support they get in various ways, spiritually and personally, materially and financially, in communications and in sympathy?

'GIVE SOME OF YOURSELF AWAY'
Chuck Swindoll, President of Dallas Theological Seminary, suggests some practical ways that we can be the kind of 'blessing and encouragement to others' mentioned in the last paragraph. In a chapter entitled *The Gift That Lives On*, he urges us: 'That's right, give some of yourself away,' and writes: 'Give an hour of your time to someone who needs you. Give a note of encouragement to someone who is down. Give a hug of affirmation to someone who is in your family. Give a visit of mercy to someone who is laid aside. Give a meal you prepared to someone who is sick. Give a word of compassion to someone who just lost a mate. Give a deed of kindness to someone who is slow and easily overlooked. Jesus taught: "… to the extent that you did it to one of these brothers of Mine, even the least of them, you did it to Me" (Matthew 25:40)'.[20] We should never aim to be remembered for our sakes, but for His. I have a feeling that if Dr Swindoll's advice became a habit, God the Father would be thanked far more, Christ would be pleased more often, and we would be gratefully remembered by others more readily.

1:4 Joy accompanies the 'always', 'every' and 'all'
4 Always in every prayer of mine making request for you all with joy,

THE ALL INCLUSIVENESS

We have already noted that Paul writes to 'all the saints in Christ Jesus … in Philippi'. He now goes further and tells them that he prays 'for you all'. How encouraging to have such a faithful prayer warrior behind you, especially when he reminds you that his prayers are going up for you. A very elderly Christian lady living on the Wirral peninsula, Miss Bowra, had been blind from birth and rarely ventured out from her home. I felt so privileged when she told me that I was among those she prayed for every day. When she went to be with the Lord—a day she was greatly looking forward to as the time when she would see for the first time *and* see Jesus before she saw anything or anyone else!—I felt much poorer personally. I would rather have been in her prayers than in a millionaire's will. She had the spirit that Paul had: pray for them and tell them so! We cannot always spend a long time praying for each individual. But, as Paul with the Roman Christians, we can 'without ceasing … make *mention* of [them] *always* in [our] prayers'[21] (my emphases).

A GODLY HABIT

There are some who suggest that unless we feel the particular pull of the Holy Spirit to pray we are not being led by Him, and that we are merely being dutifully mechanical. Some go further and say that we should not pray at these times, but wait till we feel led and have liberty. The great apostle would disagree! Spirituality and feelings, whilst they can and do go together wonderfully at times, are not always necessary companions. Thus Paul reveals a habit of holiness. He makes it clear that, despite his amazingly crowded lifestyle, it has always been his practice, and implies that it will still be his aim, to make request for all the Philippian Christians 'always in every prayer of mine'. It seems that whenever he prays about Philippi, and arguably whenever he sets himself to pray, he prays for them all, without fail. No doubt there were times when he felt too busy or disinclined to do so, but he did it anyhow. Do not let anyone talk you out of the godly habit of prayerful support for others, either on your own or in the church or group prayer meeting, just because you might not feel like it or because you have other pressing things to do. Cultivate this faithful and godly habit of always praying for others as a priority, irrespective of your feelings. If prayer were only impulsive, neither the Thessalonian church, nor we, would be urged to 'pray without ceasing' or enjoined 'Brethren, pray for us.'[22] There would be no need for such exhortations; it would just happen automatically. So often we do not 'feel led' or we say we have 'too much to do'. Well did R. A. Torrey say: 'If there is anything the average worker in this hurrying age needs to have impressed upon him, it is the necessity of much prayer. By praying more, we will not work any less, and we will accomplish vastly more.'[23] I recall a very busy Christian man, who was at the top of his busy profession and investing his free time and sleep time for Christ, telling me that he was 'too busy *not* to pray.'

WITH JOY

It is no accident of grace that the self-denying discipline of faithfully praying for others combines so well with 'joy'. Joy is part of the fruit of the Spirit[24] and it is the Spirit of God who prompts Paul to the ongoing task of praying for his bothers and sisters at Philippi. As Paul relies on his Lord to keep him to his task, he is able to add those two words 'with joy'. Joy is a gracious benefit that God gives those who put Him first, even in seeking blessing for others. Remembering that 'JOY' is 'J' for Jesus, 'O' for others and 'Y' for yourself, in that order, you will find that a surrendered life is a joyful life. To do His will increases the inner joy we have, by His Spirit. And doing God's will includes praying for others.

1:5 The best fellowship available this side of heaven

5 for your fellowship in the gospel from the first day until now,

FELLOWSHIP OF FAILURES

To dwell above with saints we love:
Oh yes, that will be glory!
To live below with saints we know:
Well that's a different story!

So says the 'tongue in cheek' poem! Clearly, our fellowship in heaven, in the absence of sin, Satan and worldly temptations, and in the personal presence of the Lord Jesus Christ, will be infinitely and eternally better than even the best fellowship here on earth. The trouble with fellowship, worship and service down here is that everyone has the same sinful nature as we have ourselves! Those of us who rejoice in God's sovereignty can easily fail to submit willingly to His sovereign will for us. In underlining the work of the Holy Spirit, we must admit that there is not nearly as much spirit of holiness in our lives as there should be.

A DEEPER BOND?

Paul reveals the specific reason for his thanksgiving when he remembers his Philippian Christian brothers and sisters. He refers to 'your fellowship in the gospel'. The word 'fellowship' means 'sharing', 'partnership', or 'participation'. There often seems to be a uniquely deep bond of fellowship between Christians who are totally dedicated to work in harness, to share the gospel with lost sinners. That does not mean that sinless perfection characterises the Lord's servants pulling the plough of evangelistic endeavour together! In fact we become more aware of the faults of each other as we draw closer to each other in this soul-searching and often physically challenging work. Evangelistic service can put the preacher under great pressure, whether his service consists of public speaking or personal witness, or both. In those circumstances, our walk with the Lord can suffer and our eyes can be taken from Him and focus on the weaknesses of others. We can also leave our first love, and thereby cause our fellow-workers more problems still. Satan likes that.

MUTUAL INVOLVEMENT

Nevertheless, many Christian workers, seeking to walk in the light with the Lord and with each other, find that serving together in the gospel promotes a deeper level of sharing. The frontline battle for souls promotes a camaraderie not known by those who do not live to make Christ known. This is often experienced in the overseas missions, in open-air witness, door to door visiting, running evangelistic missions, sponsoring different evangelistic ventures, reaching unsaved holidaymakers, or offering Christian leaflets to 'the man in the street'. So it is with Paul: he is particularly thankful that these Christians have shared with him in making the gospel known.

IN AT THE START—AND STILL GOING STRONG!

Paul's thankfulness for their participation in the gospel is two-pronged. He recalls that this sharing in taking the good news of Christ to the Philippians was 'from the first day until now'. John MacArthur concludes, 'These believers eagerly assisted Paul in evangelising Philippi from the beginning of the church there'.[25] There was no church there when Paul started preaching the gospel, but the new converts stood with him from day one. You can appreciate why he was so affectionately grateful for and to them. To be involved in the coming to faith of previously lost sinners is a wonderful bonding privilege. To have those young converts willingly stand with you in reaching their friends and acquaintances with the gospel draws you even closer together. But better still, that initial enthusiasm for witnessing for Christ has not grown cold. At the time of writing the letter, Paul rejoices that this vibrant testimony is still being carried on 'until now'. To have the zeal of a newly converted Christian is tremendous. To keep on keeping on, in continual daily witness, really underlines Paul's thanksgiving. Verse 6 later explains why they are continuing in the work of the Lord: it is simply because the work of the Lord is continuing in them.

THE CHALLENGE

The example of the Philippian church puts us on the spot. Are we fully involved in positive evangelistic work, with others whose lives are dedicated to telling others about Christ? If we have been involved in such work in the past, are we still faithfully continuing in making Him known today? Are we as keen as we were? So often Christian soldiers break rank with one another because sin and selfishness spoil their fellowship. We cannot fight alongside those whom we are attacking, or those who cause us to defend ourselves against them! Do we need to 'clear the lines' of fellowship by asking forgiveness ourselves, or forgiving wrongs suffered from other Christians? If so, let these words of Chuck Swindoll stir our hearts: 'It isn't long before anyone who gets serious about serving others must come to terms with forgiving others as well. Yes, *must*—it's a required course in the servanthood curriculum.'[26] Let us be practical too. Do we regularly support by our efforts those who labour in the gospel, so that it can be said of us that we are participating as partners with them? Do we have fellowship on that level—not only in the fellowship of the Lord of the gospel but also in the fellowship of the gospel of the Lord?

1:6 God's ongoing work

6 being confident of this very thing, that He who has begun a good work in you will complete it until the day of Jesus Christ;

CONFIDENCE BECAUSE IT IS GOD'S WORK

We encounter an essential principle of the Christian life here. The only reason why Christians continue in their walk with Christ, or in their work for Christ, is that God is at work in them. Without God in our lives we fail. We can do literally *nothing* without Him.[27] God's ongoing work within gives Paul confidence concerning the church at Philippi. He does not argue that they will stand because of Paul. Although he is God's apostle and no doubt has presented the good news of Christ extremely clearly, that is not why they will last the course. Neither does he link their going on with their own abilities, aptitudes or experience. No! His confidence focuses on two aspects of the same wonderful truth. *God* is at work! And He is at work *in their hearts*. Not only that, but he reminds them that it is the Lord who *began that work*. And *He will complete* the work that He started in them. God never starts what He will not finish, be it the creation of the world, the atoning death on the cross which was heralded by the triumph cry of the victorious Gladiator, 'It is finished!',[28] or the work of salvation in the life of sinners who turn from their rebellion to Christ as Saviour and Lord. Philippians 2:13 takes up this theme a little later.

GOD'S WORK WITHIN

Which young couple, who realise they are to become parents, do not appreciate something of God's hidden work within? As a father and grandfather it always has amazed me! To think that a real live human being is growing (and kicking!) inside the mother's body is captivating! Of course, only the parents-to-be initially know that the miracle of human life is taking place inside. Only later will it become first noticeable to a few and then obvious to all. This principle of God's unseen working applies from planting sweet peas to the conception and growth of a baby. But the day comes when His work becomes obvious, and at last the flower appears or the baby arrives.

SEED IN OUR HEARTS

So it is with God's work of salvation. The seed of God's Word is sown in our hearts. It may have been loved ones or friends who shared with us what Christ meant to them personally. Or perhaps we heard a preacher urging us to turn our back on our sins and come to the cross for mercy and forgiveness. Or perhaps God's Spirit spoke to us directly through the book He wrote—the Bible. Or maybe, as we read a Christian book, the truth of its message shone into our darkened hearts. Through whatever means He chose, God the Holy Spirit showed us our sins and impressed upon us that we were lost, guilty, and condemned. He pointed us to the Saviour, and gave us His grace to put our faith in Christ. God began a spiritual and eternal work in our hearts. That seed took root. It began to grow, producing in us a new spiritual life. That life is eternal and indestructible. The work that God began will certainly be completed by Him 'until the day of Jesus Christ' when it will have reached perfection, all by His grace. On that day the Christian will see the final consummation of his or her salvation. God will graciously reward His child's faithfulness (which God enabled anyhow!) and every Christian will be glorified with a resurrection body![29] Well has the evangelist, Roger Carswell, succinctly commented: 'For all who trust Him there is the promise of His eternal presence. We have the promise of Jesus: "I am with you always, even to the end of the age." (Matthew 28:20). Again, we have God's promise: "I will not leave you or forsake you." (Joshua 1:5) He goes before His people and is behind them and beside them. He is beneath them and above them and has promised to abide with all who trust Him. The Christian has Someone who can ensure his eternal future.'[30]

1:7 You are in my heart

7 just as it is right for me to think this of you all, because I have you in my heart, inasmuch as both in my chains and in the defence and confirmation of the gospel, you are all partakers with me of grace.

LOOK AT THE EVIDENCE

Why is Paul so confident that God has 'begun a good work' in his Philippian friends? He says 'it is right for me to think this' of them all. He uses logic to reach his conclusion that God is working in them. But what logic is this? He again goes back to the abiding evidence of their salvation, that they are fully involved and identified with him in the gospel. We can learn from this that the real evidence of conversion can be measured by the degree of commitment to the message of salvation through Christ. If I claim to belong to Christ but am untouched by His priority of saving sinners, how do I know that my claim is based on fact rather than fancy or feelings? My wife has always been interested in each job I have held. She has always asked questions about any work in which I have been involved and encouraged me in it. Why? Because, amazingly, she loves me! That love for me means she is closely involved in the work I do. Similarly, if I claim to love Jesus, how can I not be intimately concerned in the work which is closest to the heart of the One whom I say I love? How can I fail to be involved in it?

HOW HAVE THEY SHOWN THEIR LOVE FOR THE GOSPEL?

There are three ways that they demonstrate their identification with the gospel which they have come to love. They own Paul in his chains; they partake in his defence of the gospel; they are his partners in the confirmation of the gospel. They are not like those who forsook Paul, possibly through fear, at the apostle's first defence of the gospel[31] or because a love for the world has taken over from a previous love for Christ and his mission.[32]

CHAINS OF METAL—CHAINS OF LOVE

Paul is in jail. That could embarrass the local Christians. They could feel ashamed of him, especially as some 'preaching rivals' of the apostle could ask if this is really the mark of a respected Christian leader who claims to be an apostle. (We will see more of this later in this chapter.) They may fear that any public identification with him may mark them out also for opposition and persecution. But they are not ashamed of Paul, who emphasises that they are 'partakers of grace' with him 'in my chains'. They are so committed to God's messenger and to God's message that their chains of Christian love for Paul are far stronger than the prison's metal chains that bind him. How important it is to maintain solidarity with our brothers in Christ who are unpopular, reviled, persecuted and imprisoned. How great is the priority to remain in fellowship with those faithful to our Lord even if there is a cost to be known as a sympathiser or supporter.

DEFENCE OF THE GOSPEL

In any football match, army engagement, or legal dispute, it is important to be able both to defend and attack. So Paul and all his Philippian partners in God's work are always ready to defend the gospel. This justifies Christians who today seek to argue apologetically for the truth of the message of the Bible. In fact we should all 'always be ready to give a defence to everyone who asks you a reason for the hope that is within you'.[33] The fact that 'faith comes by hearing, and hearing by the word of God'[34] does not mean, for example, that we should be ignorant of the strength and dependability of the grounds on which our faith is founded. For example, we should know, or learn soon, the arguments for the truth of the Bible, the basic evidence for the resurrection,[35] why a literal six-day creation is credible and foundational to the Christian faith,[36] and why we need to hold that Jesus Christ is the only way of salvation.[37] Our defence of these positions, both from Scripture and from logic, will not of itself win a sinner to Christ. However, the assurance given thereby to a seeking soul can be as compulsively attractive to him as a silver spinner is to a mackerel about to be hooked. Our willingness and ability to share what we believe, backed up by a gracious and consistent Christian lifestyle, may motivate an unsaved person to take a serious interest in spiritual things. That can lead to a thirst for God and finally the salvation of any such serious seeker.

CONFIRMATION OF THE GOSPEL

But although no team will avoid defeat without a good defence, in order to win, there has to be a positive attacking strategy and capability. In evangelistic and missionary terms, this calls for the clear, compassionate, compelling and faithful communication of the simple biblical gospel. As God aids in making His truth known, He will confirm its truth and validity, both in its presentation and in its effects. This is one reason why Paul loves the Lord's people at Philippi. They not only identify with him in his bonds and in his defence of the gospel, but they are also his partners in its 'confirmation'. They are eager to reach souls for Christ. We have to ask if we would have stood with them in their vulnerable situation. How many days go by without our personally having witnessed to someone about the saving work of the Lord Jesus, when we still have freedom to do so? But someone may say, 'That is only the task of the gifted in these things, and I am not led to witness to others.' Paul's commendation of the Philippians is that in this defence and confirmation of the good news of Christ, they are '*all* partakers with me of grace'. In fact, there is the key. Just as surely as God's grace is upon them *all*, they are *all* partners in his use of the sword of the Spirit, the Word of God, in the twofold witness of defending the faith and actively sharing the gospel with lost people.

IN HIS HEART

It is this wholehearted dedication to Jesus, to evangelism, to God's Word, and to his persecuted servant that endears these young but serious converts so deeply to Paul. They are more concerned with promoting the cause of Christ than with their own desire for ambition, pleasure-seeking, or maintaining a 'cool' reputation with outsiders. No wonder Paul says feelingly, 'I have you in my heart'. This is a particularly Pauline way of thinking. In his letters to the Corinthians, for example, he mentions 'heart' thirteen times and in 2 Corinthians 6:11 says, 'O Corinthians! We have spoken openly to you, our heart is wide open' and then urges them to be open to his rebuke and teaching about their compromised walk. Always Paul is an apostle with *heart*. Those loving the Lord and His gospel are always welcome there!

1:8 God knows!

8 For God is my witness, how greatly I long for you all with the affection of Jesus Christ.

IT'S TRUE AND IT'S POSSIBLE!

Paul is aware that his claimed affection for all his Christian friends in Philippi must pass scrutiny from his omniscient and omnipresent God! He knows that 'God is my witness'. Remember that, when we comment on our attitudes and activities affecting others, God knows if we really are telling the truth. But the apostle's affections for the saints in Philippi are so strong that he knows they come from their mutual relationship with, and love for, Jesus Christ. More than that, those very warm affections are themselves aglow with the reflection of the Saviour's infinite love for Paul and the Philippian Christians. Paul says it is 'with the affection of Jesus Christ' that he longs for them. That is a high and pure level of affection, no doubt enabled by the indwelling Saviour Himself. J. Sidlow Baxter remarks: 'Christ's heart had, as it were, become Paul's, and was beating anew in the apostle's bosom. The very feelings of Christ were moving within the consciousness of His servant.'[38] John MacArthur says the word translated 'affection' literally 'refers to the internal organs, which are the part of the body that reacts to intense emotion. It became the strongest Greek word to express compassionate love—a love that involves one's entire being.'[39] The *Tyndale Commentary* concludes: 'The compassionate regard of Jesus Christ on which Paul patterns his apostolic affection is either His love for men during His earthly ministry ... or His love for His Church. But many commentators see a more "mystical" meaning in the words: for example, "his pulse beats with the pulse of Christ" (Lightfoot), as though Christ were expressing His love through the personality of His servant.'[40] It is clear that because his close fellowship with Christ warms his regenerate heart, Paul can say, 'I long for you all'. And the affection of Christ demonstrated the Redeemer's love for all sorts and conditions of humanity as well as for the Church and for His Father, in all situations. So it is no surprise that each person in that church is included: no favourites here! And note that he does not just see them as co-labourers to be appreciated, but as brothers and sisters to be loved. How such an attitude amongst twenty-first century Christians would revolutionise the fellowship in our churches today! This is why the author of the letter to the Hebrews urges his readers to '... consider one another in order to stir up love and good works', and goes on to reinforce the importance of regular meetings together, mutual exhortation and an urgent realisation that time is running out.[41] For us as Christians to show that affection towards others today calls on a biblical view of how Christ loved, and a prayerful dependence on Him to perform the miracle of doing it today through us.

1:9 Abounding love must not be blind

9 And this I pray, that your love may abound still more and more in knowledge and all discernment,

PAUL'S PRAYER

Paul now tells the Christians at Philippi again that he is praying for them. But this time he tells them exactly what his prayer target is. He prays that the love they already have will get better and better. He wants it to 'abound still more and more'. The word 'still' is an encouraging word. It implies that their love has abounded already. What a good lesson in encouragement. When you want to urge others on to greater heights, show them that you appreciate what they have already done. Yet Paul's prayerful desire for them is that their already abounding love will carry on abounding 'still more and more'. His appreciation of what they, through grace, have achieved does not quench his appetite for further and better achievement.

LOVE FIRST

In 1 Corinthians 13, Paul compares love with faith and hope and concludes in verse 13, after thorough examination in that chapter, that 'the greatest of these is love'. Love is the single most important spiritual reality in the life of a Christian. It is the first-fruit of the new life in Christ and the goal of every Christian throughout the rest of his, or her, life. So it is that Paul, already recognising the Philippians' sterling sacrificial service in the gospel, reminds them that love is the quality that must keep on growing. As we grow in our love for God, so we also grow in our love for our fellow men. This moves us to self-giving service to other Christians, and in unstinting efforts to help those outside Christ and to share the gospel with them. As Paul prays for them, we ought to pray for one another and for ourselves, 'that [our] love may abound still more and more.' This love may be easier to pray for than to apply, but God's grace is always available.

'KNOWLEDGE AND ALL DISCERNMENT'

But biblical love is not just a sloppy feeling! Because it is a love essentially based on God, it is pure and wise, knowledgeable and discerning. Paul's concern is that the increase in love 'may abound still more and more in knowledge and all discernment'. However hot one's heart may be, God requires a cool head. In case unwise actions spring from the purest and warmest of emotions, he prayed for an increase in love to be matched by a growing knowledge and discernment. The same is true for us today. What better fount of knowledge than the Bible, God's infallible and inspired Word? That is why every Christian should study it carefully every day. What better way of improving progressively in discernment than by first asking God in prayer for His promised wisdom,[42] and then by applying that wisdom in trusting and obeying God and His Word? We are not asked to 'feel' if we are doing the right thing. Rather, motivated by God's love and applying biblical principles after prayer, we will express and apply God's love wisely. The *New Bible Commentary* concludes: 'Thus love would become not an unregulated impulse, but a guiding principle with the practical end that they may discriminate differences between moral qualities, thus choosing the best.'[43]

1:10 The reason and the goal

[10] that you may approve the things that are excellent, that you may be sincere and without offence till the day of Christ,

DOING AND BEING

Why does Paul pray that their love would increasingly abound with 'knowledge and all discernment'? He says it is a two-fold purpose. The first is that they may *do* something. The second is that they may *be* something. In *Gathered Gold*,[44] the British evangelist, teacher and writer, John Blanchard, quotes Hugh Latimer (my emphases): 'We must first *be* made good before we can *do* good; we must first *be* made good before our works can please God—for when we are justified by faith in Christ, then come good works.' The Christian life always consists of doing and being. There are many important things to do, or not to do, according to the Bible. But the aim of all these things is to *be* someone whose heart is constantly beating for the Lord. Doing for doing's sake can lead to hypocrisy and pride. Doing in order to be pleasing and useful to Him glorifies God and blesses others. In this case what Paul wants them to *do* is to 'approve things that are excellent', and he wants this so that they 'may *be* sincere and without offence' right until the time of the consummation of their salvation on 'the day of Christ'. At that point perfection will have taken over by God's love, power, grace and eternal plan.

APPROVING EXCELLENT THINGS

We can see now why knowledge and discernment are needed to guide their increasing love. Approving is to do with the mind. In the context of this letter it is to do with testing of coins to see if they are approved. They had to be carefully 'put to the test'[45] before a decision could be made on their genuineness. The Philippian Christians were urged to follow the same principle in exercising their love, otherwise it would be possible ignorantly but affectionately to endorse things that were wrong. How many well-meaning but untaught people have thought it marvellous, for example, that different denominations or even different faiths have come together in the nominal unity of the ecumenical movement, irrespective of the denial of biblical truths thereby, or in the 'with it' thinking of the so-called New Age religion, which is an international amalgam of many gross errors? For some, their hearts say, 'How nice to be friendly and unified. How can God be against that?' Yet love for the Word of God leads us to embrace its teachings which feed our knowledge and our discernment. As we study it we see that there can be no spiritual unity without truth and a common commitment to the Bible as God's faultless, inspired and only revealed will. So those who say that salvation is by faith alone, in Christ alone, cannot dilute or pollute that message by claiming to be one with those who substitute anything else as a means of knowing God. To reach a settled conclusion without God's Word would be arrogant and ignorant. But to arrive at that position because God has said so in the Bible is humble and authoritative, and gives us certain knowledge founded on absolute truth, and discernment flowing from heavenly wisdom. Note that our target is not just 'good' or 'better' things. We aim for 'excellent' things: nothing but the very best should be our aim for God. We should shun anything that is not commended by Him. Our love for Him should be as real as that, and our knowledge and discernment should be that well informed.

NO SINCERITY—NO PROGRESS

Paul wants the Philippian saints to 'be sincere'. Sincerity is a vital ingredient in the Christian life. But it is never enough to save anyone or to ensure that they go on with Christ in loving discipleship. Much less is it a guarantee that people are correct in the views they hold. In all these things, you can be sincere but sincerely wrong. Examples of mistaken sincerity range from the amusing to the tragic, all showing that one must be right as well as sincere. Many years ago, my grandfather rode his bicycle from Leeds to a small Yorkshire country town called *Ben Rhydding*, hoping to climb the (non-existent!) mountain which he had confused with *Ben Nevis*! Sincere, but wrong! Less amusing was the time when I got on the wrong train for Southampton, and ended up wasting two hours just to get back to where I had started. Again, sincere but wrong! Tragically, the newspapers have occasionally reported a child who ate forbidden 'sweets' to find they were medication that killed the child concerned. Once again sincere, but tragically wrong! The so-called 'friendly fire' in the wars in Iraq, which claimed lives of soldiers fighting on the same side, also illustrates the tragedy of mistaken sincerity. In spiritual and eternal matters, sincerity is not sufficient either and biblical knowledge and spiritual discernment are so important. We must be *right* as well as sincere. But without sincerity, we will never make progress towards Christ or with Him. Sincerity is essential: although it has no saving or sanctifying power of itself, we cannot be saved or sanctified without it. The *Tyndale New Testament Commentary* on Philippians says that the Greek word which is translated 'sincere' 'may possibly be derived from *heile*, "sunlight", which would continue the thought of testing, i.e. tested by the exacting standards of clear sunlight and shown to be unmixed, pure, genuine. Moffat translates this "transparent".'[46] John MacArthur helpfully develops that thought when he says, '"Sincere" means "genuine," and may have originally meant "tested by sunlight." In the ancient world dishonest pottery dealers filled cracks in their inferior products with wax before glazing and painting them, thus making worthless pots difficult to distinguish from expensive ones. The only way to avoid being defrauded was to hold the pot to the sun, making the wax-filled cracks obvious. Dealers marked their fine pottery that could withstand "sun testing" as *sine cera*—"without wax"'[47]. If we fill in cracks of our hypocrisy and self-centredness with the wax of superficial and deceitful external appearance, we lose our true spiritual value and can never be real before God or before men. We need to be genuine and to be open to God at all times. Am I really transparent? Are you? And is that transparent sincerity constantly being informed by biblical truth?

NO OFFENCE

Only by living in this open way before God, which calls for a selfless love for Him and a growing acquaintance with His Word, can our love, knowledge and discernment lead us to be 'without offence'. In his first letter,[48] the apostle John uses the illustration not of wax, but of darkness. He teaches, 'If we say that we have fellowship with Him, and walk in darkness, we lie and do not practice the truth. But if we walk in the light as He is in the light, we have fellowship with one another, and the blood of Jesus Christ His Son cleanses us from all sin'. If we are walking transparently with God and with one another as children of light we shall be 'without offence'. We need to have both the fire of God's holiness to melt away the wax filling of our insincerity, and also the light of God's truth to extinguish the darkness of our tolerated sins. Only in this way can we be 'without offence till the day of Christ'.

1:11 Fruitful righteousness—glorifying praise

[11] being filled with the fruits of righteousness which are by Jesus Christ, to the glory and praise of God.

FILLED WITH FRUITS

Sowing seeds or planting young plants usually results in future growth. In Genesis we read that 'God said, "Let the earth bring forth ... the fruit tree that yields fruit according to its kind, whose seed is in itself ..."'.[49] That seed produced further fruit trees, which brought forth more fruit, which in turn again yielded an increase of seed. So the cycle continued! Now we encounter the 'fruits of righteousness' which are to adorn the lives of the Christians to whom Paul writes. The seed that ultimately produces this fruitfulness in their lives is that gracious blend of ever-growing love, holy knowledge and spiritual discernment already considered. Consistent with the principle of the Genesis cycle, those very fruits of righteousness will yield further seeds of wise love and loving wisdom that, when sown in the witness of the gospel, will produce more fruit through the lives of converted men and women. Note that our spiritual ambition should be to be 'filled' with those 'fruits of righteousness'. Jesus told His initially small band of followers, 'By this is My Father glorified, that you bear much fruit; so you will be My disciples.'[50] The fruit to which Jesus referred no doubt included the 'fruits of righteousness' as well as the 'fruit of the Spirit'.[51] Unless there is evidence of the growth of this spiritual fruit, we should seriously question whether our nature really has been changed within by a new spiritual birth. Dr Martyn Lloyd-Jones put it this way: 'A true Christian must exemplify the Beatitudes, because you do not get grapes from thorns or figs from thistles. A good tree must bring forth good fruit; it cannot help itself, it is bound to. A man who has the divine nature within himself must produce this good fruit, the good fruit which is described in the Beatitudes. He is poor in spirit, he mourns because of sin, he is meek, he hungers and thirsts after righteousness, he is a peacemaker, he is pure in heart, and so on.'[52] Hopefully we will all also be looking, praying and working for fruit of another kind: the fruit of the gospel in seeing individuals turn in repentance to Christ.

BUT WAIT A MINUTE! NOBODY IS PERFECT!

Let me remind you that we are still considering Paul's *prayer* for his Christian friends that began in verse 9. It is *not* yet a recorded final achievement! I remember, as a little boy, planting some carrot seeds in our garden and going back the next day to dig them up to see if they were growing! My disappointment, although it knew no bounds, was not reasonable! Fruit does not come overnight. It takes time to grow. And when it comes it is seldom perfect—some is too small; some is diseased; there may well be the odd blemish here and there and some of it is out of shape. We all need patience and endurance to keep on keeping on. Remember God is at work in you if you have come to know Christ. He is not through with any of us yet! We are looking at what we should be in Christ, and what we can be in time if we trust and follow Him. But there is a long way to go for us all. I know of no effective Christian who would not say a heartfelt 'Amen!' to that.

WHAT KIND OF TREES ARE WE?

Nevertheless, we do glorify our heavenly Father when He sees these fruits appearing by His Spirit and by His grace in our lives. The world also will look at us then and know we are disciples of Christ. You tell a tree by its fruit. You expect apples on an apple tree and pears on a pear tree: simple logic! In the same way, if we are abiding in Christ, the visible fruits should demonstrate His righteousness in us. These 'fruits of righteousness' are indeed 'by Jesus Christ', as He alone can produce them in us through the Holy Spirit's work. It is through Christ alone—that is by His will, power, grace, righteous life, and redemptive work in the cross and resurrection— that such fruits can be produced. They will be 'to the glory and praise of God'—thus underlining the words of Jesus that 'By this is My Father glorified'. Have you ever witnessed someone seeing an exotic fruit tree for the first time, perhaps on a trip to a beautiful part of the world? Listen to the 'ooohs' and the 'aaahs'! How pleasant is that sight, scent and taste! Our righteous acts for His sake, like abundant fruit, should so adorn our lives that people can tell whose tree we are, and appreciate His work in us. Jesus said that men would 'see your good works and glorify your Father in heaven'.[53] But, in practice, what kind of trees are we? Perhaps more important, what kind of trees do we want to be?

RIGHTEOUSNESS RIDICULED

Righteousness is ridiculed today. In our modern world heterosexual immorality is regarded as the norm. Homosexual immorality is heralded merely as an acceptable alternative lifestyle, protected by politicians and now, sadly, endorsed by many denominational leaders. Greed and selfishness are indulged by some who would pride themselves as being free of those more obvious transgressions of God's law. Against this backdrop of ungodliness, there are millions of innocent, pre-born children being killed each year. Approximately two hundred thousand pre-born babies are butchered in the UK, two million in the USA, and over twenty million in China each year. Against this backcloth of rejection of God's standards, many find it easier to rationalise their sin and laugh at a righteous lifestyle rather than face up to a guilty conscience, turn their backs on their sins and ask God for forgiveness. And despite the fact that there are many sincere and genuine folks in our churches, it is a fact that not all self-confessed Christians are entirely free from this attitude. Just as Adam and Eve attempted to hide from God in the garden He made,[54] so, under the cover of being religious or church-going, some are chained to hypocrisy, self-righteousness and critical spirit and seek to hide religious observance and formality. Interestingly, many who ridicule the Bible's standards of righteousness as 'out of date' do not hesitate to complain when they suffer because of other people who break other laws of God. Even those who oppose God's moral standards recoil when the breaking of those standards hurts them. They do not like lies to be told about them, or burglars breaking into their homes to take their prize possessions, or being deprived of a spouse through someone else's immorality, or being unfairly dismissed from their employment. No doubt about it—our sense of righteousness can be extremely selective and selfish!

THE BLESSING OF RIGHTEOUSNESS

Yet our salvation would be impossible without biblical righteousness. We do not have any righteousness of our own as 'All our righteousnesses are like filthy rags'.[55] On the contrary, our hearts are 'deceitful above all things, and desperately wicked'.[56] Thus we need two things: first, to be forgiven for and cleansed from our unrighteousness, and, second, to have genuine righteousness put into our bankrupt moral account. This is exactly what Jesus has done for every sinner who has trusted Him. As we come in humble repentance and faith to Him who lived a perfectly righteous life and died on the cross for our sins, and honestly 'confess our sins, He is faithful and just to forgive us our sins and to cleanse us from all unrighteousness'.[57] We experience His forgiveness and cleansing! But at the same time the righteousness of Christ is put into our account. God's justice having been satisfied by Christ's substitutionary death for us at Calvary, we are seen as righteous because His righteousness is attributed to us in Christ. By His grace alone 'He has made us accepted in the beloved'![58] That is why God is not only 'faithful' to His promise to forgive us, but also 'just' in that the punishment for our sins has been paid for by Christ. Our lack of righteousness (or being 'just') is made up for us by His righteousness (or justness) which has been fully transferred into our bankrupt account and credited to us. That is why our righteous God continues to be 'just' in pardoning us. He has not *condoned* our sinfulness in Christ: He has *condemned* it on the cross. Because of that, there is no condemnation left for the sinner who has trusted Christ crucified. And we receive the righteousness that there is in Christ, that we could never produce by, or find in, ourselves.

RIGHTEOUSNESS—APPLIED AS WELL AS IMPUTED

Christ's righteousness counting for us is termed by theologians 'the imputed righteousness of Christ'. But the 'fruits of righteousness' stemming from that include 'the applied righteousness' of Christ. The evidence that we have benefited from His imputed righteousness is that the Holy Spirit now begins to change us from within and apply God's righteous standards to our lifestyle. Although our righteous acts cannot save us, the arrival into our lives of new deeds of righteousness are the evidence that we really are 'born again'. Our new righteousness will affect how we see and respond to God Himself. We will begin to worship Him in the way He has prescribed in the Bible. We will allow no idols, made by ourselves or others, to rival our love for Him. Our conversation will be clean, wholesome and worthy of Him. The Lord's Day will become increasingly important and precious to us and we will keep it to please Him. But our righteousness will grow as we grow in Christ. It will show in the way we treat other people. The list of changing values and conduct could go on for pages. Lies will be replaced by truthfulness, grumbling by gratitude, selfishness by an active concern for others, wanting to receive by willingness to give, and hatred by love. Materialism will give way to a desire to grow spiritually, dirty-mindedness to a desire for purity, taking parents for granted to a new concern to help them and see them blessed, and neglect of children's welfare to more time spent with them. Bad language and jokes in poor taste will go and wholesome words and a clean sense of humour will be established. Indifference, prejudice or opposition to strangers will surrender to an overwhelming desire to help and see all kinds of people coming to know Christ. Personal devotions will become important; prayerfulness will take over from prayerlessness, and doubtful, superficial or inconsequential reading will diminish as a serious searching daily study of the Bible becomes the norm and an appetite is encouraged for reading helpful Christian books. The more we go on with Christ, the more will we be 'filled with the fruits of righteousness which are by Jesus Christ, to the glory and praise of God.' And it will show to others, though we will feel increasingly unworthy.

Notes

1 Acts 17:6.
2 1 Timothy 1:2.
3 Philippians 2:19–24.
4 'Make Me a Captive Lord', *The Christian Life Hymnal* (National Young Life Campaign), number 254.
5 Romans 8:30.
6 1 Timothy 3:1–7.
7 1 Timothy 5:17–19.
8 **Prof. Francis Davidson,** *The New Bible Commentary: The Epistle to the Philippians* (Inter-Varsity Press), page 1034.
9 1 Timothy 3:8–13.
10 1 Corinthians 1:3 ; 2 Corinthians 1:2 ; Galatians 1:3 ; Ephesians 1:2 ; Philippians 1:2 ; Colossians 1:2; 1 Thessalonians 1:1; 2 Thessalonians 1:2; Philemon 3.
11 Romans 1:7 ; 1 Timothy 1:3; 2 Timothy 1:2 ; Titus 1:4.
12 Ephesians 2 :8,9.
13 Translated from the French text in **William Clayton,** *La Foi Evangélique* (Editeurs de Littérature Biblique), page 76.
14 Romans 5:1.
15 Philippians 4:7.
16 Romans 8:9; 14:17; 15:13.
17 Ephesians 3:16,17.
18 2 Corinthians 3:2.
19 Galatians 2:20.
20 **Charles R. Swindoll,** *The Quest for Character* (Hodder and Stoughton: A Hodder Christian Paperback Omnibus), page 161.
21 Romans 1:9.
22 1 Thessalonians 5:17; 25.
23 **R.A. Torrey,** *How to Work for Christ* (Pickering and Inglis), page 21.
24 Galatians 5:22.

25 **John MacArthur** (Author of commentary/notes and General Editor), *The MacArthur Study Bible, NKJV* (Word Bibles), note on Philippians 1:5, page 1820.

26 **Charles R. Swindoll,** *Improving Your Serve,* (Hodder and Stoughton: A Hodder Christian Paperback Omnibus), page 246.

27 John 15:5.

28 John 19:30.

29 1 Corinthians 3:12–15; 4:5; 15:42–44; 2 Corinthians 5:1,2; 9–10.

30 **Roger Carswell,** *Why me?* (OM Publishing), pages 92 and 93.

31 2 Timothy 4:10.

32 2 Timothy 4:14.

33 1 Peter 3:15.

34 Romans 10:17.

35 **Gerard A. Chrispin,** *The Resurrection: the unopened gift* (Day One), especially Chapter 1, which deals with the evidence for the resurrection of Christ.

36 **Dr Andy Macintosh,** *Genesis for Today: Showing the relevance of the Creation/Evolution debate to today's society* (Day One), especially Chapters 1 and 2.

37 John 14:6; Acts 4:12; Galatians 1:6–10.

38 **J. Sidlow Baxter,** *Explore the Book—In One Volume* (Zondervan), page 186.

39 **John MacArthur** (Author of commentary/notes and General Editor), *The MacArthur Study Bible, NKJV* (Word Bibles), note on Philippians 1:8, page 1820.

40 **Rev. Ralph P. Martin,** *Tyndale New Testament Commentaries: The Epistle of Paul to the Philippians* (Tyndale Press), page 64.

41 Hebrews 10:24, 25.

42 James 1:5.

43 **Prof. Francis Davidson,** *The New Bible Commentary: The Epistle to the Philippians* (Inter-Varsity Press), page 1035.

44 **John Blanchard** (compiler), *Gathered Gold* (Evangelical Press), page 148.

45 **Rev. Ralph P. Martin,** *Tyndale New Testament Commentaries: The Epistle of Paul to the Philippians* (Tyndale Press), page 65.

46 **Rev. Ralph P. Martin,** *Tyndale New Testament Commentaries: The Epistle of Paul to the Philippians* (Tyndale Press), page 66.

47 **John MacArthur** (Author of commentary/notes and General Editor), *The MacArthur Study Bible, NKJV* (Word Bibles), note on Philippians 1:9, page 1820.

48 1 John 1:6,7.

49 Genesis 1:11.

50 John 15:8.

51 Galatians 5:22.

52 Dr Martyn Lloyd-Jones, *Studies in the Sermon on the Mount Volume 2 (Matthew 6 and 7),* (Inter Varsity Press), page 258.

53 Matthew 5:16.

54 Genesis 3:8.

55 Isaiah 64:6.

56 Jeremiah 17:9.

57 1 John 1:9.

58 Ephesians 1:6.

Mini-overview: 1:12 to 1:18

I am in prison but the gospel is free!

Paul tells the Philippian Christians how his imprisonment has 'turned out for the furtherance of the gospel'.

1:12 The furtherance of the gospel

12 But I want you to know, brethren, that the things which happened to me have actually turned out for the furtherance of the gospel,

ENCOURAGED BY A PROPER UNDERSTANDING

Imagine the feelings of the 'insignificant' (from the world's viewpoint) band of Philippian Christians when the great apostle writes to them to say, 'I want you to know' and underlines his ties with them by calling them 'brethren' or 'brothers'. But involving your fellow-Christians by keeping them informed is, I am sure, not the only reason why Paul writes. He wants them to have a proper understanding that Christians who walk with God will go through unjust and undeserved suffering. He can illustrate this in a poignant way, because he is the sufferer in the case study before them. His concern is to demonstrate that God will achieve His perfect purposes in the dark, just as He can accomplish them in the sunlight. Paul also knows that these loyal supporters will pray and stand with him in his hour of trial. He trusts their heart for the gospel, their mutual concern, and their love for him. Open fellowship that enables you to take the lid off difficult situations for prayer is to be treasured and nurtured. We should be keen to share and encourage when we can. We also need Bible teachers who will step up to the fact that Christians will suffer, and that God is in it all. Trends of recent years have made Christians expect too much from superficial teaching which extols the always 'healthy, wealthy and successful' mentality that has done so much to damage the cause of true discipleship.

ACCEPTANCE

Some people are self-effacing and masters of understatement, when they are centre stage. Paul is one such person: he never seeks the spotlight for himself, yet he will never pass up an opportunity to seek to proclaim his

Saviour and glorify his God, even if it means that the focus is upon him. Here he almost casually mentions 'the things that have happened to me'. They are truly 'exceptional and amazing.' They include his having faced the hostile and wicked opposition of haters of his gospel, his Lord and himself, as well as his imprisonment with the imminent threat of execution. Whilst all this is going on, some self-centred Christians are belittling his apostleship and claiming that they are better leaders and preachers than the man whom they should be supporting wholeheartedly. Those are some of the things that Paul could say had 'happened to me'. Yet there is no hint of frustration or bitterness and, as we shall see later in chapter three, Paul is at peace. His spirituality is not only seen on the public platform, or when he again takes the lashes on his back, or in his Spirit-inspired letters. Here at 'ground level' we see the man, in all his vulnerability and weakness, accepting what looks bad for him from the hand of his God, who he knows nevertheless can and does make all things work together for his good.[1]

EVIDENCE OF GOD'S OVERRULING

Paul's confidence in the sovereign and loving purpose of his Lord and Saviour, even though he did not know the end of the unfolding divine plot, is fully justified. He can even now look back and effectively say that it 'has actually turned out' well. Sometimes God does encourage us by glimpses of what He can do for us and through us when the circumstances seemed to conspire against us. The current of life's sea that takes us off our planned course may well be moving us into the place of God's perfect choice for us. Next time that things seem to go sadly wrong for you, remember this: God is in control and knows what He is about to do in your life. And He loves you.

PAUL'S PRIORITY—THE GOSPEL

But what result has Paul already seen? What thrills his soul to the extent that he must share it with his friends in that Philippian church? Simply this: 'the furtherance of the gospel'. He seeks nothing other than that. His life is being lived out to promote the gospel, and his desire for personal comfort and safety is secondary to that. Warren Wiersbe's comment underlines this: 'Neither Paul's safety nor his comfort was the most important thing on his mind. The most important thing was that the gospel be proclaimed in Rome and that people turn to the Saviour.'[2] What an example he sets for them and for us. Have you lost out in some way? Stop and ask if the changed circumstances can lead you to further the gospel. Have you been bereaved and, quite rightly, feel the deep sorrow of that personal loss? Ask God to fashion your heart now, whilst it is soft, and show you the shortness of time and the need of other dying men and women. Have you lost your job recently? Use the humiliation and the uncertainty to knock away the props that so often can stop you trusting Him. Ask Him to make His strength and presence more real to you than ever before, so you can talk with conviction of a God you can know and trust in the dark, as well as in the sunshine of success. Do you want to escape a certain set of circumstances or a neighbourhood, but you seem chained there and feel frustrated? Recognise that God may well have someone there who has not yet heard His gospel and that is why He has placed you there. Have you been rejected by someone you love? Then reaffirm your trust in the One whose love hugely surpasses any other love and who will carry you through, despite the hurt. He will enable you to recommend Him to those who feel, and perhaps are, unloved by others. A prisoner trusted Christ whilst being in prison for a crime which vehemently he denies doing. (I am of the same opinion.) Released on appeal, and given bail for over eight months, without incident, he was surprisingly reconvicted at his re-trial after an alarmingly long deliberation by the jury. I spoke to him immediately after he was sentenced, when he was clinging to the verse 'I will never leave you nor forsake you.'[3] Accepting the injustice of his situation, he invested some of the small amount of money available to him in prison to buy chocolate biscuits to encourage other inmates to come to the Bible hour being taken by a Day One Prison Ministry Associate. Traumatised as he was by the unexpected verdict and sentence, this middle-aged man, who was a 'babe in Christ', accepted that 'The lot is cast into the lap, but its every decision is from the LORD.'[4] Another prisoner, Paul, knows that same confidence, though his incarceration is directly *because* of the gospel, of course.

BILLY BRAY

Billy Bray, the Cornish tin miner and former brawler and drunkard (though not a prisoner for the gospel) is a wonderful role model for us all in this question of furthering the gospel. His changed life, from blasphemy and godlessness, was known by all when he turned to Jesus Christ as his Saviour. But years passed by and serious illness forced him to call for his doctor. Let us listen in to their conversation: the italicised words are what the doctor said: '"Now, doctor, I have sent for you because people say you are an honest man, and will tell them the truth about their state." After the doctor had examined him, Billy said—"Well, doctor, how is it?" *"You are going to die."* Billy instantly shouted "Glory! Glory be to God! I shall soon be in heaven." He then added in a low tone, and in his own peculiar way, "When I get there, shall I give them your compliments, doctor, and tell them you are coming too?" This, the doctor says, *"made a wonderful impression upon me."*[5] The 'furtherance of the gospel' was more important to that Primitive Methodist Christian than the mere matter of dying!

'THE TITANIC'S LAST HERO'[6]

The latest *Titanic* film is sadly, and quite unnecessarily, contaminated by immodesty for box office appeal and thus not to be recommended to those who seek to combat unholiness of thought. However, one benefit from its immense popularity is the interest in the consequent and independent retelling of the dying efforts of John Harper to see drowning people come to Christ. This Christian preacher shared the gospel whilst he literally floated on the brink of eternity. Let me quote briefly from the start of the stirring book by Moody Adams: 'As the dark, freezing waters of the Atlantic crept slowly up the decks of the *Titanic*, John Harper shouted, "Let the women, children and the unsaved into the lifeboats." Harper took his life jacket—the final hope of survival—and gave it to another man. After the ship had disappeared beneath the dark water, leaving Harper floundering in the icy waters, he was heard urging those about him to put their faith in Jesus Christ.' No wonder that the book's tribute to this unsung hero declares: 'While the flames of other ambitions flickered and died, John Harper's burned even brighter as he sank into a watery grave. When death forced others to face the folly of their life's pursuits, John Harper's goal of winning men to Jesus Christ became more vital as he breathed his final breaths.' Here was the ultimate test of the 'furtherance of the gospel'. His brave and selfless soul-winning example graphically illustrates Wesley's deepest desire to:

Preach Him to all and cry in death,
'Behold, behold, the Lamb!7

1:13 Reality shines through

[13] So it has become evident to the whole palace guard, and to all the rest, that my chains are in Christ;

EVERYONE KNOWS WHY PAUL IS THERE!

Have you noticed that little word 'So'? Paul now tells us that people have noted that he is in prison because he is trusting and proclaiming Christ, or as he puts it here 'my chains are in Christ'. But that word 'So' is an important link. It tells us why everyone knows of Paul's Christian testimony. It is because of things working out 'for the furtherance of the gospel', with Paul's willing acceptance of the fact that this means he must suffer. Paul is universally recognised as a Christian who has been jailed for his faith in Christ. When we are totally committed to the gospel, opportunities to witness are never far away. How often does our fear of what people think of us, or losing our 'respectable' reputation, remove from us that total and utter dedication to make known the message of redeeming love? Are we not shamed by the comparative enthusiasm that today's fans will demonstrate publicly to show their liking for their favourite sports celebrities or teams, pop singers, or film stars? In prison, Paul's love for his Saviour burns brighter still. What, apart from his life, has he to lose except his testimony? And he is determined to see the influence of that testimony grow, not diminish!

MY CHAINS ARE IN CHRIST

Just a thought about the phrase 'My chains are in Christ': Paul is willing to accept imprisonment which almost certainly involved him being chained to individual guards. The likelihood is that he spends many hours chained to them. Not only does the 'whole palace guard' know they have a unique prisoner under their care, but very probably a large proportion of that guard has been on the other end of Paul's chains. It is inconceivable that the man who has 'become all things to all men that [he] might by all means save some'[8] will miss this opportunity to share the good news of Jesus Christ with those to whom he was chained. One imagines that he, the captive, relishes this unique opportunity to speak to a 'captive audience'! Because he knows 'the terror of the Lord', Paul is dedicated to persuading men to repent and turn to Christ, and encouraged the Corinthian church to do the same.[9] Surely there is some Spirit-aided persuasion by the prisoner, liberated from sin, to his guardians, who are miserable slaves of it. If only we could be 'flies on the wall' during those conversations! How hearing Paul at work would motivate and fashion our efforts at personal evangelism! No doubt, in similar circumstances, some Christians would grumble at their chains. Can we not hear Paul rejoicing that his chains give him the chance to proclaim the liberty in Christ that he knows? That liberty is 'where the Spirit of the Lord is',[10] and that Spirit is definitely with His faithful captive witness.

THE SPREAD OF THE GOSPEL

Paul's witness is 'to the whole palace guard, and to all the rest'. His gospel spreads from the soldier chained to him, to the 'whole palace guard' and then 'to all the rest'. Through him, the gospel is now a talking point. God's Word can spread like wildfire when one person shares his or her testimony with another. God will honour those desiring wisely to obey the command of Jesus to 'preach *and* publish openly the good news (the Gospel) to every creature (of the whole human race).'[11] Others, initially outside our knowledge or anticipation, also become interested and influenced. Rightly we should be concerned to take every individual opportunity presented to us to make Christ known. But we should also have the missionary heartbeat to present our message 'to all the rest'. Obedient Paul, though chained, touches many for his Saviour! How can he do that? Because he knows God personally and is strengthened by Him. This is such a reality to Paul that in other circumstances he writes: 'most gladly I will rather boast in my infirmities, that the power of Christ may rest upon me. Therefore I take pleasure in infirmities, in reproaches, in needs, in persecutions, in distresses, for Christ's sake. For when I am weak, then I am strong'.[12] Corrie ten Boom, who herself suffered in the prisons of concentration camps in World War II, quotes from those verses, and writes: 'In ourselves we are not capable of suffering bravely, but the Lord possesses all the strength we lack and will demonstrate His power when we undergo persecution. It makes no difference whether we have great or little power of endurance, or none at all. To Jesus Christ it is the same ... Thank you, Lord, that our strength is not important, for your strength will be demonstrated even in our weakness.'[13]

1:14 A godly example is infectious
[14] and most of the brethren in the Lord, having become confident by my chains, are much more bold to speak the word without fear.

ENCOURAGEMENT BY EXAMPLE
Paul now states, as a fact, what has happened in the life of 'most of the brethren in the Lord'. How encouraging, but how realistic, is that phrase 'most of the brethren'. His example of openly and straightforwardly proclaiming Christ has an enormous effect on 'most of the brethren' who are now following that example. Paul's ministry from God is not only preaching the gospel, or teaching the spiritual truths of the Bible. He is also a disciple-maker *by example*. Gospel preachers and Bible teachers do well to bear in mind that their hearers often look to see what the speaker actually does himself. To illustrate, we now will consider a few high profile individuals whose personal examples, away from the public gaze, still stir us on to be 'more bold to speak the word without fear'. They were not in prison at the time, but the principle of boldness to witness still applies.

D. L. MOODY
D. L. Moody's messages have stirred many to engage in personal evangelism. But so has his challenging example of earnestly seeking to speak to at least one individual each day personally about Jesus. He pursued this goal no matter how many he had preached to in public. Bearing in mind how often the fear of embarrassment can cause guilty

silence, we would do well to consider the account of Woodrow Wilson, then President of Princeton University, when Moody entered a barber's shop and unknowingly sat in the next chair to him. He records: 'Every word that he uttered … showed a personal and vital interest in the man who was serving him; and before I got through with what was being done to me, I was aware that I had attended an evangelistic service, because Mr Moody was in the next chair. I purposely lingered in the room after he left, and noted the singular effect his visit had upon the barbers in that shop. They talked in undertones. They did not know his name, but they knew that something had elevated their thought. And I felt that I left that place as I should have left a place of worship.'[14]

JOHN CALVIN

John Calvin has influenced nations by his writings proclaiming God's sovereign grace in the salvation of sinners. How much more urgent do those truths appear when you consider his personal example. Often unrealised even by those who quote him, he was doggedly faithful in prison visiting and in door-to-door visitation to urge sinners to turn to Christ. I quote from a superb little book, now out of print, about his work in Paris—'a French writer of the period gives the following striking testimony, the more remarkable because a Roman Catholic: "Devoted otherwise to his books and his study, he was unweariedly active in everything which concerned the advancement of his sect. We have seen our prisons gorged with poor, mistaken wretches, whom he has exhorted without ceasing, consoled or confirmed by letters; nor were messengers wanting, to whom the doors were open, notwithstanding all the diligence exercised by the gaolers. Such were the proceedings by which he commenced, and by which he gained, step by step, a part of our France." … These days of Gospel seed-sowing were perhaps the quietest of Calvin's life. Avoiding disputations with the Sorbonne doctors, and quietly going with "the Book" from door to door, he won many a soul from the kingdom of darkness to the realm of light and truth.'[15]

WITNESSING WIVES

Thus two Christian men, Moody and Calvin, from different ages and countries and with very different backgrounds, gifts, and theological emphases, were united in seeking urgently to make the truth of God's gospel known publicly. They lived out in their own lives the responsibility to do it *personally*. Their examples should embolden us to preach Christ in our daily personal lives, too. But what of today's jet and space age? And what about the part women can play as well as men? The old saying that 'Behind every good man is a good woman' is very often true in evangelism. Behind many evangelistic husbands are godly women who also have a heart for souls. In fact any man who wants his life to be used in this highest calling, of seeking souls for Christ, should consider the missionary heartbeat of his spouse as an absolute necessity. I love the account given in a prayer letter of Roger Carswell, whose consistent public and personal proclamation of Christ is such an inspirational example to many. Once on a flight, his wife, Dot, and he had to sit in separate rows, one behind the other. The prayer letter records: 'On an internal flight in the USA I got into spiritual conversation with a Swedish girl who was a Buddhist. After quite some time of conversation, the man in the row in front of me turned to the lady sitting next to him, and said, "I'm glad I'm not sitting next to that man!", to which she replied, "Well actually he is my husband!" They too began talking about the Lord.'[16] (Was God's hand on the fact that adjacent seats had not been available on that flight for Roger and Dot? Sometimes we grumble when that happens!) Thank God for wives with right priorities, a sense of humour and the gracious boldness to share their Saviour with anyone they meet!

SOME MISSED OUT

I said that it was realistic of Paul to record that 'most' of his Christian brothers were affected. He says 'most', not 'all'. There are always some who seem to lack the willingness or faith that bring others into blessedness, discipleship and usefulness. Established Christians should never ignore them or give them up as a bad job, but keep on praying for and encouraging those whose Christian lives do not have the evidence of growth and vitality in His service. It is so easy to write them off, but many of us have been there. Perhaps some of us are still there. We need to be careful. Consider this NASB quotation from Jesus: 'whoever says to his brother "You good-for-nothing," shall be guilty before the supreme court'.[17] We should seek to be gracious examples of Christ's disciples and turn the searchlight within to ask ourselves if we are responding to the stirring examples of others whose boldness for Christ should shame us into action. Praise God for the storehouse of excellent biographies we have of recorded examples of sacrifice and witness of faithful and zealous followers of Christ. How often God seems to touch our hearts and change our lives through biographies of those whose bold example calls us to an altogether different lifestyle. When we read them we should pray for grace to live like that.

CONFIDENCE BY CHAINS: BUT HOW?

You might think that if the respected leader had been put in chains, others would shrink from engaging in the same activities. But that is not so when God is at work. It seems that God uses the persecution, suffering and even martyrdom of those who love Christ to *encourage* truly born-again Christians rather than *discourage* them. 'The blood of the martyrs is the seed of the church' is often quoted and is true. A surge of missionary interest encountered my generation after the martyrdom of the five young American 'Mid-Century Martyrs'. Their lives were snuffed out by the lances of the Auca Indians, those feared Ecuadorian head-hunters, whom they had tried to reach with the gospel.[18] Jim Elliot's famous saying 'He is no fool who gives what he cannot keep to gain what he cannot lose' became a clarion call for sacrificial missionary service and many young folks responded to serve Christ overseas. The more recent martyrdom in the Philippines of New Tribes Missionary, Martin Burnham, and the traumatic ordeal suffered with him by his wife, Gracia, has already challenged many. Doubtless, it will galvanise more Christians to become missionaries. Here we see Paul in chains. But he openly rejoices for the God-given opportunity to proclaim Jesus and to live his life, with the Spirit's help, under the close scrutiny of those he so dearly wants to see saved. No wonder he says in verse 12, 'I want you to know, brethren'. He is keen to get across to the Philippian Christians that he has 'been there' (and still is), faced it (and still does), and that it is worth it all if he can further the gospel. Picture a batter in cricket who is nervous about facing the very fast opposing bowler. He then sees his fellow team member, of a similar standard to him, go to bat before him and hit the ball out of the ground! His nerves are calmed. 'If he can do it, so can I,' he says to himself. So it is with Paul's brothers at Philippi: they have seen what Paul has been enabled by God to do in the worst of circumstances. That nerves them and inspires them for the battle. If Paul can witness effectively and rejoice in the 'lion's den', they certainly can do so at what is, by comparison, merely the 'zoo'! Thus Paul gratefully says that they have 'become confident by my chains'.

THE RESULT—BOLD WITNESS AND NO FEAR

Let's be honest: we do get scared sometimes. We know that 'perfect love casts out fear'[19] but we often fail to 'connect' with that love. If only we could keep Calvary as a reality in the forefront of our minds and experience the outpouring of God's love into our hearts more often, we would fear less. But we fail often and as a result do not show that holy boldness to witness which we read about in the Acts of the Apostles and note in church history. Yet sometimes, when we see others exalting their Saviour, no matter what the world may think, we find our love and faith rising, our fear receding, and self-indulgent flabbiness giving way to spiritual muscle. Only God can give us His love and boldness that we so much need, but He often gives it after we have seen the example of others. So it is here with Paul and the Philippians. The confidence given them by his chains has, in turn, resulted in a boldness and a love which respectively ignore and cast out fear. We hear much about the influence of the Holy Spirit in the lives of the early Christians. No doubt some have misinterpreted this and have promoted their own emphasis and followed their own agenda, not always in accordance with the context of Scripture. But surely all must agree that the huge distinguishing mark of early church Christians, taken over by the Holy Spirit and taken up with our Lord's gospel, is their *boldness* in preaching and witnessing. The words 'bold', 'boldly', and 'boldness' feature nine times in the Acts of the Apostles[20] and the quality of boldness is demonstrated throughout. If someone is truly filled with the Spirit, he will be bold about his Master's gospel business and confident in his Father's love.

'THE WORD'

The activity of an emboldened, inspired, committed, evangelising

Christian is, according to Paul, straightforward. He will 'speak the word'. Whatever value we may put on what currently passes for Christian service, one thing is sure, God's method of winning a lost world is for His people to 'speak the word'. The undiluted message of the Bible focuses on Christ crucified and risen again[21] and insists on personal repentance from sins and personal faith in Christ alone,[22] as the *only* means of salvation.[23] This is so, whether we consider witness in private or in public, in the pew or from the pulpit, in the main street or at the special guest dinner, in the prison or in the palace, on the factory floor or in the university senior common room, on the doorstep or in the aeroplane, as a lone witness or with others, in English or in other languages, to western atheists or followers of eastern or mid-eastern religions, to scientists or to artists, to poor or to rich. In fact in all circumstances with all types of people everywhere, we must 'speak the word'. Charles Haddon Spurgeon was said to have answered a man who asked him how he intended to defend the Bible by saying that he would sooner defend a lion than the Bible. All he had to do was let it off its chain and it would more than adequately defend itself! 'Speak the word!'

1:15 Why preach?

[15] Some indeed preach Christ even from envy and strife, and some also
   from good will;

FIRST, WHAT IS THE MESSAGE?

There is only one message to present to sinful men and women: 'Preach Christ'! Paul simply assumes that this is the sole message to present when he says that 'Some indeed preach Christ'. Remember that to the Corinthians he declared that 'Jesus Christ and Him crucified' was his exclusive theme,[24] and that his preaching was around the twin foundation of the cross and the resurrection of the Lord Jesus Christ.[25] Philip, in the desert with the Ethiopian eunuch, hears him reading from Isaiah chapter 53, which prophesies the death of the Man of Sorrows,[26] and instantly 'opened his mouth, and beginning at this Scripture, preached Jesus to him'.[27]

The Philippians themselves had been clearly pointed to Jesus. Lydia had heeded 'the things spoken by Paul'[28] which, as we know from his 'mission statement',[29] was centred on Christ, His death and His resurrection. The possessed slave girl was liberated by the apostle's command 'in the name of Jesus Christ',[30] and Paul told the jailer to 'Believe on the Lord Jesus Christ and you shall be saved'.[31] Sadly today even the evangelical church often puts other emphases before lost souls. We *must* 'preach Christ'. I was once asked how today's man could still hold to something as old fashioned as the Christian message. Having pointed out that 'old fashioned' did not mean 'out of date'—consider breathing, food and drink, for example—I replied that modern man is still a dying sinner and that a dying sinner needs a living Saviour. Jesus is the living Saviour. What other answer could there be? No wonder we count it a privilege to 'preach Christ'. But what does it mean to 'preach Christ'? We must show forth who Jesus is and what He has done to save us, and how we can appropriate that greatest of blessings by faith in Him. We make it clear that Jesus is not merely a name, or else He would not be distinguished from the mutilated theology or philosophy of those who interpret Him into their own non-biblical teachings, such as liberal theologians, Jehovah's Witnesses, Mormons, Roman Catholics, New Age devotees or followers of Islam, to name a few. Those using His name are often not talking about the same Person, who is the only Saviour of sinners. As a minimum we must present the Lord Jesus Christ as the eternal and infallible Son of God, as God the Son,[32] and as the only fully sinless and completely righteous Man.[33] We must show that His death on the cross in our place was to take the eternal wrath from God that we sinners deserve as punishment in hell.[34] We must insist that God the Father, by raising Him bodily from the dead, declared that His Son would judge unrepentant sinners on Judgement Day[35] and accepted His Son's sacrifice on behalf of all who trust in Him.[36] We must urge sinners to confess their sins, with repentant shame, and cast themselves on God's mercy and grace in Christ, in calling upon Him and receiving Him as Saviour and Lord.[37] Such saving faith heralds an amazing change within the sinner who comes to Christ, which Jesus called being 'born again'. That is the new birth which is the experience of every Christian by the immediate indwelling of Christ, though God the Holy Spirit.[38] To 'preach Christ' involves all that.

TWO MOTIVES FOR PREACHING: THE RIGHT ONE

Paul makes it clear that there are two motives for preaching. We look first at the right motive for preaching Christ: 'from good will'. This preaching 'from good will' is set against other preaching 'from envy and strife', which is dealt with shortly. The good will of some shines out in sharp contrast to that pernicious background of other people sharing God's good news for bad reasons. Those who love Paul find their loyalty to him is heightened by his imprisonment. They want to stand with him, encourage him and fill his absent place in the ranks, rather than try to usurp his place as a new apostle, leader or preacher. They are like the corporal who takes over in the trenches from his fallen sergeant. He does not do this to gain authority and position, but because the battle demands it and it is what the dead sergeant would have wanted. They know that their preaching of the gospel not only glorifies God and offers an eternal lifeline to lost sinners, but it also will greatly encourage their imprisoned gospel-hearted father in the faith. There is also a general sense in which they preached through 'good will'. Each true disciple of Christ at Philippi is so captivated by 'The Son of God, who loved me and gave Himself for me'[39] that his ongoing spirit of prayer will surely be:

Oh make me understand it,
Help me to take it in:
What it meant to Thee, the Holy One,
To bear away my sin.[40]

Any Christian who focuses, like that, on what Jesus has done for him will not be able to preach His gospel with other than 'good will'. He will be compelled by the thought that Christ's blood was shed for him, and find in his heart the same grateful determination of the hymn writer who penned those stirring words:

E'er since by faith I saw the stream
Thy flowing wounds supply
Redeeming love has been my theme
And shall be till I die.[41]

TWO MOTIVES FOR PREACHING: THE WRONG ONE—THE COCKTAIL OF ENVY AND STRIFE

The anti-Paul faction in the Christian church at Philippi preaches the gospel through completely wrong motives—'envy and strife.' But how can 'envy and strife' ever motivate saved sinners to preach the gospel of reconciliation and peace? It seems incredible. Jesus died to deal with both the results and the root of our selfishness and pride. He was punished to appease the holy wrath of God against sins, including envy and strife. James tells us 'where envy and self-seeking exist, confusion and every evil deed will be there'.[42] Envy, in verse 15, is inevitably followed by self-seeking in the next verse, parading itself as 'selfish ambition'. James' 'every evil deed' includes the 'strife' here engendered by that envy. 'Confusion' speaks for itself: how very confusing, both to the church and to the outside world, that Christians who attempt to present the Saviour from sin should be marked by so much sin that He came to prevent! Jeremiah's plea to Baruch, although in a different context of Israel's judgement for its sins, is a continual searching reminder to us all. He said, 'And do you seek great things for yourself? Do not seek them'.[43]

'TIME OUT'

In commenting on the wrong motives of some in Philippi, we should take some time out to consider our own motives in serving Christ. We need to be careful lest we criticise in others what is present in our own hearts. Strife will always follow envy and can surface in many different ways. How many preachers can honestly say that they never battle with envy? Jealousy of the gifts, opportunities and acclaim accorded to others is not unknown. It is possible to deny opportunities to others to preach, simply to protect one's own ministry. Maintaining the continuity of the ministry is not always the reason, though it is sometimes the quoted justification. Few preachers are so indispensable that they cannot make way for others from time to time. And how about 'roast preacher' for Sunday lunch, especially if God has used him to put His finger on a sore spot in our own lives? Criticism is not always constructive, or for the best of motives. Our condemning others can be a form of commending or excusing ourselves. It says that we are competent judges of excellence, and so puts us on a higher level than the object of our destructive criticism. We can pull others down, either by our faint praise or our unfair criticism. If all else fails, we find it easy to focus on another person's blind spot, such as a perceived doctrinal weaknesses, however marginal. We, of course, have perfect understanding! It would surprise congregations to know what battles preachers can have. We all hate ourselves for it. But the same sins can easily occur at all levels of service and relationships. This self-seeking and harmful critical spirit differs from necessary constructive discernment, in motive, goal and manner. Such discernment arises from love, is gracious, and aims at God-honouring improvement. It is based on biblical principle and bathed in prayer. It is important to keep short accounts with God and to guard against envy by a close walk with God. Should the searching insight of A. W. Tozer not underline this truth, not only to leaders and preachers, but to all who lead by example? He says: 'Today Christianity in the Western world is what its leaders were in the recent past and is becoming what its present leaders are'.[44] May God grant us honesty and repentance.

1:16 Ambition bringing Affliction

16 The former preach Christ from selfish ambition, not sincerely, supposing to add affliction to my chains;

RIGHT MESSAGE, WRONG MOTIVE

There is no criticism here of the content of the message. These self-seeking preachers make it their practice to 'preach Christ'. A preacher must preach the right content, but it is a mistake to think that someone presenting biblical truth is necessarily walking with Christ. Neither is someone in a right relationship with God just because his message was effective in touching someone's life. We have all heard of those who preach publicly but whose lives, in moral terms, are in a mess. Good results do not necessarily mean that biblical principles or holiness have been honoured. Some, but happily not all, televangelists bring the gospel into disrepute by their inconsistent lifestyles, yet they are often people who present aspects of the gospel, and sometimes with genuine spiritual results. Sadly there are pastors living immoral lives whilst carrying on preaching biblical truth. God is gracious and sometimes brings people to

Himself through a backslidden or self-seeking Christian. A converted ex-prisoner I know well saw his partner turn to Christ through his explanation of the gospel long before he became a Christian and despite the fact he did not want her to be saved! He knew he could not handle the repercussions! Roger Carswell tells about someone who was converted in one of his missions. The man was under conviction because a pub comedian blasphemously paraded a Bible text as a joke! It is the 'gospel of Christ' that is 'the power of God to salvation for everyone who believes'.[45] It is the *message* that saves. Jesus taught that the seed that was sown is God's Word.[46] God's Word *can* produce fruit, whoever sows it. We need to remember that, in the parable of the sower, it was the *seed* that produced the crop, not the sower.[47] Although we must insist on doctrinal correctness and pray for blessing, we should never assume that these things imply a holy life is being lived. Pastor-search committees would do well to remember that and probe more diligently the personal lives and daily spiritual devotions of those whose ministry, gifts and experience they usually scrutinise with such great care.

SINCERITY AND SELFISH AMBITION

We have already seen that envy was the root problem of the inconsistent preachers at Philippi. Some are happy that Paul is in prison because they can both question his apostolic authority and seek to lift their profile as preachers whilst (they think!) he is inactive in the gospel. Their selfish ambition engenders a desire to be more popular than the much-respected Paul. They see Paul not as an apostle or co-labourer, but as a competitor. For them preaching is like a beauty contest, and their concern is only to win the applause of men. Clearly in that situation there can be no sincere passion or concern to see God glorified, souls saved, or disciples established. Writing of 'A number of factors [that] contribute to bad spiritual leadership', Tozer has said this of 'ambition': 'When Christ is not all in all to the minister he is tempted to seek place for himself, and pleasing the crowds is a time-proved way to get on in church circles. Instead of leading his people where they ought to go, he skilfully leads them where he knows they *want* to go. In this way he gives the appearance of being a bold leader of men, but avoids offending anyone, and thus assures ecclesiastical preferment when the big church or the high office is open'.[48] In preaching truth that his hearers want to hear, it may be that what he leaves out is even more important than what he puts in.

BEWARE! NOT ONLY PREACHERS GO WRONG!

Some Christians and even some congregations can treat preachers as if they are competitors. Instead of letting the preached Word of God sink into their lives to bless and change them spiritually, their main concern seems to be to compare one speaker against another, or to approve those who are most comfortable to hear. The continuum of attitudes towards preachers can range from near idolatry to harsh and unfair criticism. This can be a particular temptation when a church has lost its pastor and, whilst seeking the successor, is listening to those from whom they may find his potential successor. But it is not only the 'between pastors' situation which focuses the wrong sort of attention on the preacher. The question often asked is, 'How did the preacher get on?' when it should be, 'How did God speak to you through his preaching?' It is not a new problem as Paul, Apollos and the Corinthian church knew full well.[49]

THE PURPOSE—TO ADD TO PAUL'S AFFLICTION

These insincere approval-seekers, Paul knows, are 'supposing to add affliction' to his chains. They will answer to God one day for that attitude, but that word 'supposing' shows just how much Paul is experiencing God's help and peace. It implies that their efforts are by no means successful. When God's grace is upon His faithful servant, he is not defeated by the malice or selfishness of others. Paul has God's grace, peace and presence with him in that prison. Yet they know that Paul is vulnerable here; they know his heart for both the gospel and the church. If they can make him anxious, worried, distressed and sad at their sinful behaviour, this could afflict him more than his prison beatings or hostile handling by an angry mob. Their selfish ambition, envy and strife could be like a malicious three-corded scourge which lashes the affectionate and caring heart of the one who admits that what 'comes upon [him] daily' is '[his] deep concern for all the churches.'[50] Can you believe that Christian preachers plan to preach the gospel deliberately *intending* to add to all the sufferings of Paul, to whom the church owes so much? How great is God's consolation and help to His dependent servant that the harm they 'supposed' to do to him did not materialise.

1:17 Set to defend

[17] but the latter out of love, knowing that I am appointed for the defence of the gospel.

THE CONTRAST OF GRACE

What a refreshing comfort to the Lord's imprisoned servant to know that there were others preaching Christ 'out of love.' We have already seen that the immediate context is their loyal and supportive love for Paul. But they cannot preach the gospel 'out of love' without first having a love for their God and Saviour. No doubt that love also produced a compassionate love for the lost. It is so encouraging to hear of Christians who are sincerely doing their best, for Christ's sake, to preach the right message with the right attitude. Some prayer letters I get cause my heart to rejoice for that very reason. Paul rejoices in the contrast that God's grace effects in the hearts, lives and ministry of those motivated by love.

AN IMPORTANT APPOINTMENT

'I am appointed' is a military term. In the AV, the translation is 'I am set'. Here is no self-pitying prisoner, licking his wounds, but a Christian soldier on duty where his Commanding Officer has posted him. What a difference this knowledge makes to Paul's attitude, and will make to ours, too, if we remember that we are always on duty for our King. He sees his prison as the nerve centre of his evangelistic prayers and direction of the work, and as a springboard for service! He is on duty!

JOHN HUSS

One person who lived out that reality of always being on duty for his King, and was indeed 'appointed for the defence of the gospel', was the brave reformer, John Huss. He was burned at the stake in 1414 at Constance, in Germany, for his faith in Christ and insistence on biblical truth. Cheated by the Pope, after he had relied upon the safe conduct which the Emperor had issued to come and answer the charges of heresy against him, he was then heavily fettered in a filthy prison. He was subjected to many 'examinations' by bishops and lords, and put under the pressure to escape martyrdom if he would but recant and renounce his evangelical faith. *Foxe's Book of Martyrs* records: 'But he called God to witness, with tears in his eyes, that he was not conscious of having preached or written anything against the truth of God, or the faith of his orthodox church'.[51] So 'set' was he in God's grace and Word, even in his great vulnerability, for 'the defence of the gospel' that Foxe adds, 'As soon as the faggots were lighted, the martyr sung a hymn, with so cheerful a voice, that he was heard above the cracklings of the fire and the noise of the multitude. At length his voice was interrupted by the flames, which soon put an end to his existence.'[52] It goes without saying that flames did not put an end to his eternal bliss, but ushered it in! Neither did they extinguish his witness: many have become 'on fire for God' through those cruel flames that destroyed his body. That phrase 'On Fire for God' is the title of an excellent book by the late Victor Budgen.[53]

THE DEFENCE OF THE GOSPEL

The previous comments on verse 7 have already covered this ground. Suffice it to add that the preciousness of the gospel and maintaining its safety, as truth to be held and preached, was high on Paul's priority list, and should be on ours. The 'defence of the gospel' is made up of just two basic elements— proclaim truth and refute error. There is nothing else involved! Wherever the place, whoever the opposition, whenever the occasion arises, and whatever the personal cost, may we remember our appointment for 'the defence of the gospel'. Surely the God who enabled and strengthened John Huss to face martyrdom for the faith can uphold us in our 'defence of the gospel' as he also did for Paul in those early days of the Christian church.

CONFIDENCE IN PAUL

Those who preach with correct content and motive know that they can count on Paul, and know that he is set to defend the gospel. May those readers who are older Christians, or in prominent leadership, be diligent to keep closer still to God in advancing years. There are many younger Christians who are looking to you. May your life be such that you can transparently hold it up as a pattern to others, just as Paul can in this letter.[54] Some men err with old age and I, too, pray for myself the words of the *The Christian Life Hymnal* version of the beautiful hymn, 'O sacred head sore wounded' (and note the emphasis of the last two lines):

O make me Thine for ever!
And should I fainting be,
Lord let me never, never
Outlive my love for Thee.[55]

1:18 Determination to rejoice

[18] What then? Only that in every way, whether in pretence or in truth, Christ is preached; and in this I rejoice, yes, and will rejoice.

'WHAT THEN?'

This is a direct question! It is good sometimes to stop and ask that question. We should sometimes stop to ask where we are with God, and what our true spiritual condition is. When we are more willing to challenge and question ourselves we are more open with God and our fellow Christians, and more effective in commending Christ to the outsider. Here Paul asks what results from the opposition of those who preach Christ to hurt him and how it relates to his grateful joy that some preach Christ from the motive of love and from good will.

'I REJOICE, YES, AND WILL REJOICE'

Can you believe that imprisoned Paul really rejoices that his insincere critics are preaching the gospel, when they are so unloving towards him? It is easy to understand his joy over those who are 'real' in presenting the message of the cross. They not only preach the revealed truth of God, but have God's truth as the foundational garment for their Christian armour.[56] But to rejoice at those self-styled competitors of his! That takes grace and an overwhelming desire to see the gospel shared. It seems as if Paul already understands ahead that his supporters then, and we today, find this hard to grasp. He realises that others could react very differently in the same circumstances. So he adds one little word to underline his resolve to rejoice. 'Yes!' Have you struggled, in frustration, with a non-compliant computer for a long time? Suddenly, when all seems hopeless, you find the solution! I have a good friend like that, and just one triumphant word leaves his lips: 'Yes!' Oh, and do not forget that smile of satisfaction and relief also! The gospel-centred apostle is rejoicing that the claims of Jesus are being made known, and plans to do so in the future. This attitude will keep him from bitterness and self-pity.

EVERY WAY COUNTS

Do you hear, in the words 'Only that in every way … Christ is preached, I rejoice', another echo of 1 Corinthians 9:22—'I have become all things to all men, that by all means I might save some'? Paul's deep trust in God's sovereignty certainly does not take away his enthusiastic evangelistic and missionary zeal, even if he may not be the channel God is using at the moment. Neither does it diminish his rejoicing, that lost and condemned sinners are having the gospel preached to them. Heaven knows about this rejoicing[57] and we should share in it too, with Paul and with the angels! In Oswald J. Smith's book *Passion for Souls*, he asks a searching question as a chapter title: 'What is the supreme task of the church?' He responds to his own question as follows: 'Down through the years my life has been tremendously motivated by great missionary mottoes. May I give you one now that perhaps has meant more to me than any other. It is this, "The supreme task of the Church is the evangelisation of the world." I believe that with all my heart. The most important work of the church of Jesus Christ is world evangelisation.'[58] Is my imagination running wild, or do I hear a loud 'Amen' to that timeless priority from a certain prisoner in a Roman jail?

Notes

1   Romans 8:28.
2   **Warren W. Wiersbe,** *On being a Servant of God* (Nelson), page 102.
3   Hebrews 13:5, citing Deuteronomy 31:6.
4   Proverbs 16:33.
5   **F.W. Bourne,** *The King's Son or A Memoir of Billy Bray* (Henry Hooks/Simpkin, Marshall, Hamilton, Kent and Co.), pages 145 and 146.
6   **Moody Adams,** *The Titanic's Last Hero* (Ambassador), pages 14 and 15.

7 Charles Wesley, 'Jesus! the name high over all', *The Christian Life Hymnal* (National Young Life Campaign), number 221.

8 1 Corinthians 9:22.

9 2 Corinthians 5:11.

10 2 Corinthians 3:17.

11 Mark 16:15 (TAB).

12 2 Corinthians 12:9,10.

13 Corrie ten Boom, *Each New Day with Corrie ten Boom* (Kingsway Publications and Christian Literature Crusade), see entry for 26 May.

14 John Pollock, *Moody Without Sankey* (Hodder and Stoughton, page 259.

15 William Wileman, *John Calvin. His Life, his teaching, and his influence* (Robert Banks and Son), pages 33–35.

16 Past prayer letter of Roger Carswell, International Evangelist. (Exact reference lost.)

17 Matthew 5:22 (NASB).

18 Elisabeth Elliot, *Through gates of Splendour* (OM Publishing); **Russell T. Hitt,** *Jungle Pilot* (Hodder and Stoughton).

19 1 John 4:18.

20 Acts 13:46; 9:27; 9:29; 14:3; 18:26; 19:8; 4:13; 4:29; 4:31.

21 1 Corinthians 15:3,4; 1 Corinthians 2:2.

22 Mark1:15; Acts 2:38, 3:19, 8:22, 17:30, 26:20.

23 John 14:6, Acts 4:12.

24 1 Corinthians 2:2.

25 1 Corinthians 15:3,4.

26 Isaiah 53:3–9 especially, but the whole chapter is on this point.

27 Acts 8:35.

28 Acts 16:14.

29 1 Corinthians 15:3,4; 1 Corinthians 2:2.

30 Acts 16:18.

31 Acts 16:31.

32 Luke 1:35; Acts 9:20; Romans 8:3.

33 Hebrews 9:14; 1 Peter 1:19.

34 Isaiah 53:4; Acts 8:32–35; 1 Peter 2:24; 1 Peter 3:18; Hebrews 9:26; Romans 1:18; John 3:36; Revelation 20:11–15.

35 Acts 17:31.

36 Acts 2:29–32; Romans 1:4; 1 Peter 1:3.

37 Acts 2:40; 1 Corinthians 9:22; 2 Corinthians 5:11.

38 John 3:3 and 7; 1 Peter 1:23; Ephesians 3:17; John 14:17.

39 Galatians 2:20.

40 Katherine A.M. Kelly, 'O Make Me Understand It', *The Christian Life Hymnal* (National Young Life Campaign), number 231.

41 W. Cowper, 'There is a fountain filled with a blood', *The Christian Life Hymnal* (National Young Life Campaign), number 239.

42 James 3:16.

43 Jeremiah 45:5.

44 Warren W. Wiersbe (compiler), *The Best of A.W. Tozer* (Kingsway Publications), page 75

45 Romans 1:16.

46 Matthew 13:19.

47 Matthew 13:23.

48 Warren W. Wiersbe (compiler), *The Best of A.W. Tozer* (Kingsway Publications), page 76.

49 1 Corinthians 1:11–13.

50 2 Corinthians 11:28.

51 Marie Gentert King (editor), *Foxe's Book of Martyrs* (Spire Books), page 101.

52 Marie Gentert King (editor), *Foxe's Book of Martyrs* (Spire Books), page 102.

53 Victor Budgen, *On Fire for God* (Evangelical Press).

54 Philippians 3:17.

55 Paul Gerhardt, 'O Sacred Head, Sore Wounded', *The Christian Life Hymnal* (National Young Life Campaign), number 254. Note that this version varies from some others in that the last two lines challenge us to live completely for the Lord by saying 'Lord let me never, never Outlive my love to Thee' rather than 'Lord let me never, never Abuse my love to Thee', which is also true but not as deeply probing as the version I quote.

56 Ephesians 6:10–19.

57 Luke 15:7; 15:10.

58 Oswald J. Smith, *The Passion for Souls* (Marshall Morgan and Scott), page 25.

Mini-overview: 1:19 to 1:26

It is so hard to decide which is best: the blessing of heaven for me or the blessing of helping you? The dilemma of choosing between death, with its immediate personal gain, or remaining alive, with the opportunity that gives to serve God and bless others?

1:19 Two reasons why I will be delivered

19 For I know that this will turn out for my salvation through your prayer and the supply of the Spirit of Jesus Christ,

'MY SALVATION'

What is meant by 'I know that this will turn out for my salvation'? By a process of deduction we can arrive at the answer. Paul *cannot* mean salvation in the sense of escaping God's punishment on his sins and receiving eternal life in Christ. Clearly that rejoicing that 'Christ is preached' (verse 18) does not save anyone eternally. Also, Paul already knew Christ as his Saviour long before he said that. His confidence is bright and certain because he can say, 'I know whom I have believed and am persuaded that He is able to keep what I have committed to Him until that Day'.[1] It *cannot* mean that Paul will necessarily escape the death sentence or martyrdom, since the whole discussion that follows lays open clearly the possibility that he might die for his faith. There is no doubt that God 'has delivered', 'does deliver' and 'will still deliver' Paul and his co-labourers from death if it is His will.[2] However there is no hint or clue in this letter that Paul expects God to save his life, even though he knows full well that He can do so if that is the best thing for the cause of the gospel. Thus it seems that the only 'salvation' left for Paul, in this passage, is that of living the victorious life in, through, and for Christ in the most difficult of adverse circumstances. But for God's help, he would be overcome by all those pressures and problems surrounding and oppressing him. In that respect, the wrongly imprisoned apostle will be saved from self-pity and depression by his positive, Christ-centred, spiritual attitude which allows him to value the greatest priority, namely the preaching of the gospel. His salvation from all the pressures to pull him down is greatly fortified by his determination to rejoice that 'Christ is preached', even if he is not valued by some of the preachers. He will not indulge in self-pity: he will concentrate on seeking first the kingdom of God as Jesus had bidden.[3] That will give him daily salvation.

THE TWO-FOLD SOURCE OF THAT DAILY SALVATION

But this is not a mere stoicism coming from a man with a strong resolution and an iron will! Paul knows that he urgently and specifically needs help from outside his own feeble human resources to win through. But that help is on hand. God-given as it is, it nevertheless has a human aspect as well as a divine one. This help brings certainty: he asserts, 'I know' that salvation will come. He tells the Philippians that the two-fold source is 'through your prayer' on the one hand and 'through … the supply of the Spirit of Jesus Christ' on the other hand. This dual source is often very closely interlinked! As God's people pray for their beloved leader in prison, God answers their prayers by so blessing and upholding Paul, by His Spirit, that his servant will come through his trials trusting in his Saviour and rejoicing in His gospel. We need to keep this in mind for others and for ourselves. We should pray for Christians in the firing line, and in prison. We should specifically ask God so to supply them with grace by His Spirit that they will persevere and triumph in Christ. We also have a great need for others to pray for us and we should trust that, in any situation God calls us to face, He will enable us to conquer through the Holy Spirit who dwells within. It certainly 'works' for Paul—see chapter 4:13—and by God's grace it will also be effective for others and for us.

THE CHURCH TODAY

The church today is so often more impressed with money, manpower, buildings, new equipment and possessions than with true spirituality. It is common to have a greater emphasis on worldly or irrelevant activity than on simple praying together. For example what spiritual and evangelistic emphasis, or what ongoing evangelistic priority, do we see in many of our youth fellowships? How many young men and women are in an evangelical social club rather than fighting in the spiritual 'trenches'? And how many middle-aged Christians, having achieved career success or respected status in life, have 'shouldered arms' in the battle for souls? But perhaps the truest thermometer of our churches' spiritual temperatures is the prayer meeting. How often is the prayer meeting really promoted and supported as the most vital meeting of the church? If measured by regular attendance, is it really the most important meeting of the week, or is it the Cinderella of the church calendar? Why do some numerically large churches have such relatively small prayer meetings?

THE 'MOST DEADLY SYMPTOM'

In applying the lessons Paul brings to the Philippians, in verse 19, we would do well to listen to E.M. Bounds: 'The most deadly symptom which can be seen in a church is the transferring of its strength from spiritual to material forces, from the Holy Spirit to the world. The power of God in the Church is the measure of its strength. This is the quality God looks for in a church. The power of the Holy Spirit gives the Church the ability to accomplish the purposes for which it was designed. On the contrary, show us a church that is poor, illiterate, obscure, and unknown, but composed of praying people. They may not be men of power, wealth, or influence. Their families may not know one week where they are to get their bread for the next. But with them is "the hiding of God's power"[4], and their influence will be felt for eternity. Wherever they go there is a fountain of light, and Christ in them is glorified and His Kingdom advanced. They are His chosen vessels of salvation who reflect His light.'[5] I find E.M. Bounds' linkage between the Holy Spirit and the prayers of God's people very much in line with verse 19, and a challenge to me. How much of my life has the Holy Spirit taken over? Am I willing to search my heart before God, as did one Puritan: 'I bewail my coldness, poverty, emptiness, imperfect vision, languid service, *prayerless prayers, praiseless praises*.'[6] Do I *really* pray as a *priority* practice in my own life? Do I pray, *really pray*, for others?

1:20 The magnifying glass: clear and clean

[20] according to my earnest expectation and hope that in nothing I shall

be ashamed, but with all boldness, as always so now also Christ will be magnified in my body, whether by life or by death.

THE KEY THOUGHT—CHRIST MUST BE MAGNIFIED

Paul's expression of the overriding priority of magnifying the Lord is not new. Mary's rejoicing that 'My soul magnifies the Lord, and my spirit has rejoiced in God my Saviour'[7] is itself an echo of the Psalmist's contagious invitation 'Oh, magnify the LORD with me, And let us exalt His name together'.[8] But how blasphemous would be the apostle's goal and motivation that 'Christ will be magnified' if the Saviour of Calvary was not also 'the Lord of glory!'[9] In effect, the psalmist, Mary and Paul were all asking to be made into magnifying glasses. The very title of J. B. Phillips' book challenges us that *Your God is Too Small*,[10] and so He is in the minds of millions who have never been made to consider what a great and wonderful God He is. It takes a magnifying glass to bring Him to the size in people's thinking where they will begin to appreciate His splendour. The effects of sin and the fall have left man self-centred, blind and dead to the living God. He needs his soul and conscience stirred spiritually before he will admit that not only is there a God, but that He is a great God to whom account for sins must be given, and from whom alone forgiveness and eternal life may be received. An effective magnifying glass must be clear, clean and without distorting faults. So Paul shares his transparent motive that 'whether by life or death' Christ should be magnified through him. If the event that makes men consider the greatness of Christ is to be his martyrdom, then so be it. If not he wants to live such a life of transparent trust and obedience that sinners and saints will see his Saviour clearly. He asks to be God's magnifying glass. We should desire that, too.

THE BATTLE: BOLDNESS VERSUS SHAME

We now see what could enhance or obscure the clarity of the magnification of Christ through the life or death of His servant. Paul's 'earnest expectation and hope' is to magnify Christ through his life, or death, and proclamation of Him. He realises that, on the one hand, it is important that 'in nothing [he] shall be ashamed', and on the other hand that to magnify Christ he must do so 'with all boldness'. The possibility of shame is not here connected with secret sins, the 'hidden things of darkness',[11] or the more obvious sins known to many. It is in the context of falling to the temptation, probably borne of opposition or of fatigue or of both, to fail to make Christ known. The tenor of the message of 2 Timothy echoes this as Paul cautions Timothy of this danger. It is the echo taken up in the book of Romans, where Paul courageously states from his evangelistic heart, 'I am not ashamed of the gospel of Christ, for it is the power of God to salvation for everyone who believes, for the Jew first and also for the Greek'.[12] When we realise the awesome power of the gospel we will be no more ashamed of it than the designer of *Concorde* when it first crossed the Atlantic in supersonic flight. So often shame in spreading the gospel coincides with our failure to trust and obey Christ, which effectively blocks the power supply to our spiritual lives. Paul has no such blockage. He experiences God's power in his own life through 'the supply of the Spirit of Jesus Christ' and in the lives of others through the gospel. Thus he has his 'earnest expectation' (based on deductive logic) and 'hope' (based on the partially experienced but as yet not completely fulfilled promises of God) that there is no way he is going to be ashamed of that unique good news of Jesus Christ, but he will boldly proclaim it. Like Queen Esther, he can say, in effect, 'If I perish, I perish!'[13], but his commitment to the gospel and confidence in it is non-negotiable! Here is a searching question: is there any sin in my life that makes me 'ashamed' of Jesus and of witnessing for him whatever the cost?

Jesus, and shall it ever be,
A mortal man ashamed of Thee,
Ashamed of Thee, Whom angels praise,
Whose glories shine through endless days?

Ashamed of Jesus!—Sooner far
Let evening blush to own a star;
He sheds the beams of light divine
O'er this benighted soul of mine.

Ashamed of Jesus! Just as soon
Let midnight be ashamed of noon;

'Tis midnight with my soul till He,
Bright Morning Star, bid darkness flee.

Ashamed of Jesus, that dear Friend
On Whom my hopes of heaven depend!
No! When I blush, be this my shame,
That I no more revere His name.

Ashamed of Jesus!—Yes, I may
When I've no guilt to wash away,
No tears to wipe, no good to crave,
No fears to quell, no soul to save.

Till then—nor is my boasting vain—
Till then I boast a Saviour slain;
And O may this my glory be,
That Christ is not ashamed of me![14]

'AS ALWAYS, SO NOW ALSO'

There have been occasions when our emotions were so stirred that we felt we could and would yield all to Christ and His service. Perhaps those moments were when powerful preaching laid us open before the Word of God, or in a missionary meeting where we have been challenged by those who have surrendered to Jesus and His work. Or maybe we have read a particularly moving biography. Perhaps, on occasions our morning quiet times really *felt* like meeting with God. Then the emotion of the moment passed and everyday life resumed. In the light of day, our resolve receded. But Paul's resolve here is not caused by a mere emotional response. He can say, 'as always, so now also' his desire is to magnify Christ. What he seeks now, he always has sought. Whether on his own or with others, whether fettered or free, whether struggling or successful, he wants the Lord Jesus Christ to be magnified. I do not suppose he always *felt* like that, but I believe he constantly *prayed and lived* like that. Here is a godly example for us all. Give God our will and our willingness first. Sometimes our emotions will lag behind, and sometimes they will rush in front. The important thing is not how we feel, but how we follow. We need to establish a lifestyle of putting Him first in all circumstances.

MAGNIFIED BY DEATH

If Christ is 'made big' to others through a Christian's life, He will be made 'bigger still' through his death. Those who die early deaths because they have been spent in gospel service, or are murdered as missionaries or executed for being Christians will make their Saviour 'even bigger still' in the eyes of those who look on. Only those who live to magnify Christ will magnify him by their death. Death to them is just the final tape to break in the race they have run, by God's grace, for God. Martyrs were not made overnight. They were living a 'death to self' life already, before they breathed their last breath. Could I face death for Christ? Not without His help, grace and presence. But with His enabling, even the weakest of us 'can do all things through Christ who strengthens [us]'.[15] We have no room for presumption, but we can rely on God to do for us what we can never do for ourselves. And how encouraging and motivating when we read of others who ran that race. 'Looking unto Jesus, the author and finisher of our faith'.[16]

'AFRAID? OF WHAT?'

Such people were John and Betty Stam. I am not a particularly emotional person—average, I would say—but I could not fight back the tears as *I read the Triumph of John and Betty Stam*[17] on a train journey. Those brave and compassionate China Inland Missionaries[18] were led out to be beheaded on a hillside by Japanese soldiers invading China. As they walked out, they were trusting that the Lord would protect and deliver their darling baby girl whom they had hidden from sight. (God *did* answer their prayers in His own marvellous way after their death.) Their sacrificial testimony made the Saviour seem so big to me, as I read the book. Here were a man and his wife, in whom Christ had been magnified in their bodies, by life *and* by death. Betty had written a poem years before. It showed the basis for their powerful resolve:

Afraid? Of What?
To feel the spirit's glad release?

To pass from pain to perfect peace,
The strife and strain of life to cease?
Afraid—of that?

Afraid? Of What?
Afraid to see the Saviour's face,
To hear His welcome, and to trace
The glory gleam from wounds of grace?
Afraid—of that?

Afraid? Of What?
A flash, a crash, a piercèd heart;
Darkness, light, O heaven's art!
A wound of His a counterpart!
Afraid—of that?

Afraid? Of What?
To do by death what life could not—
Baptise with blood a stony plot,
'Till souls shall blossom from the spot?
Afraid—of that?[19]

Paul's words echo through that young mother's poem: 'as always so now also Christ will be magnified in my body, whether by life or by death'. What an objective to have! See how it leads naturally on to the next verse.

1:21 I cannot lose!
[21] For to me, to live is Christ, and to die is gain.

IS THIS THE REAL KEY TO THE CHRISTIAN LIFE?
It is dangerous and highly subjective to declare any one truth, or verse, to be 'the key' to the Christian life. The fact is that God's revelation, the Bible, is a huge bunch of keys and a different key may open up a fresh area of truth for a particular person at a specific time. Yet some truths undergird all the others, especially the death and resurrection of God the Son. Here, in verse

21, is a truth about the attitude of the Christian that can be the building block of all the other blessings that come to him in Christ. The point made in the second half of the verse is a huge one: 'to die is gain'. If I know Christ as my Saviour, when I die it is 'gain'. It is 'far better' (verse 23). It is being 'present with the Lord'.[20] This confidence in the fact that 'our names are written in heaven' is something that Jesus taught was to be the bedrock of our rejoicing: this is far greater than the most fruitful and successful service, because it cannot change.[21] Thus if the 'worst comes to the worst', for Paul it is the very best! The same is true for the weakest and the youngest person who trusts in Christ. We can all confidently rejoice in Job's amazing prophetic statement, with much more evidence for it than Job had, about our resurrected Saviour: 'I know that my Redeemer lives ... in my flesh I shall see God, Whom I shall see for myself'![22] Once we have that settled, we are founded on the Rock of Ages and able to reach out to others with a confidence that we are saved, safe and secure. Could this be said to be the real key to Christian life and service? There is a 'mirror image' truth surrounding this whole situation: we will not really live for Christ unless we are prepared, by God's grace, to die for Him; we will never be ready to die for Christ unless and until we are determined to live for Him.

CHRIST ENCOMPASSES ALL THAT IS GOOD FOR ME

If 'to live is Christ', then all my Christian life must centre on Christ. He must be its centre, its foundation, its purpose, its help, its power, its satisfaction, its reward: in fact, He must be my everything. My worship must be centred on 'Christ', not methods. My evangelism must be proclaiming 'Christ', not just His benefits to those who trust Him. My walk should depend on Him, not on the means of grace—the Bible, church, fellowship, prayer, the Lord's Day, the Lord's table, baptism, service—but on the gracious Provider of those means. Those means are essential and helpful, but must all be used to increase our trust in, and gratitude to, our Saviour. He must be my Master and my Friend, my Critic and my Comforter, my Goal and my Guide. Only when Jesus begins to mean this to me can I be open-minded about whether I 'gain' by death or have the privilege of living for and with Him down here. Paul's mind is made up. He has no doubts: 'For to me, to live is Christ'.

'FOR TO ME'

Paul is not implying by 'For to me' that he is expressing merely his opinion, his preference or even his conviction. This is his *mission statement*. When Total Quality Management (TQM) broke on the management scene in the 1990s, many corporations and organisations embraced TQM and adopted their individual 'mission statements'. Many people and organisations had adopted such statements, or mottoes, long before TQM became the fashion. I know a family who adopted a Latin one, *Facta non verba* (meaning 'deeds not words'). In each Crown Court and Magistrate's Court in Britain is the French phrase *Honi soit qui mal y pense*, meaning 'Evil be to those who think evil'. One regiment declares, 'Who dares wins.' A removals firm in York boasted, 'Across the street, or across the world.' (That would be a good evangelistic mission statement for every church and Christian!) Those mission statements all say: 'This *is* who we are!' or 'Here is *why* we really are here!' When Paul says 'For to me to live is Christ', he is saying, 'This *is* me!' Think of Paul, and think of this—'Christ'. Jesus Christ is his heartbeat and passion, his hope and his preoccupation, his happiness and peace. 'I am here to live Christ, preach Christ, honour Christ, trust in Christ, and know Christ far better,' he effectively says. 'This is *why* I am here!' How will you complete the sentence that begins with 'For to me'?

GEORGE WHITEFIELD

It has been said that England might have suffered a revolution as violent as in France but for the spiritual awakening which God gave largely through George Whitefield, John Wesley and their associates. A working out of Whitefield's mission statement is found in his *Journals*. It seems he shared that of Paul! On Sunday 3 June 1739, he wrote: 'I now go … knowing not what will befall me, save that the Holy Ghost witnesseth in every place, that labours, afflictions, and trials of all kinds abide me. O my dear friends, pray that none of these things may move me, and that I may not count even my life dear unto myself, so that I may finish my course with joy, and the ministry which I have received of the Lord Jesus. Into His hands I commend my whole spirit, soul and body; His will be done in me, by me, and upon me, for time, and for eternity. Let me do or suffer just as seemeth good in

His sight. Only do Thou, O Lord, give me that wisdom which dwelleth with prudence, that I may never suffer for my own misconduct, but only for righteousness' sake.'[23] Is the reason why God could so easily and effectively use this faithful and prolific preacher of the gospel in Britain and America because his motivation in his life was summarised by Paul's saying: 'For to me, to live is Christ, and to die is gain'? If so, could that be a reason why we are not used far more than we have been so far?

1:22 Fruitfulness comes from labour

22 But if I live on in the flesh, this will mean fruit from my labour; yet what I shall choose I cannot tell.

WHAT LIFE MEANS TO PAUL

He spells it out simply and plainly. For Paul the desire to magnify Christ by living on 'in the flesh' will be fruitful. His life and work will not only make His Saviour bigger to those who see him, but it will thereby produce fruit. I like the phrase 'in the flesh' because it presupposes that Paul will 'live on' anyhow, and he has to distinguish between living on here on earth, or 'in the flesh', and living on with his Lord in heaven. He knows he will live on: it's just a question of where and when. He really seems to have 'eternity' always in his thinking, so that everything he sees is viewed with that in mind. But his ongoing life will mean productive work for Christ, which is what the word 'labour' means. He perseveres; he works long and hard; he keeps on keeping on even in the face of opposition and persecution; he faces exhaustion; he knows great pain—pain physically through his lashings and stonings, and pain mentally through seeing loved Christian friends forsake him and abandon their walk with Christ. But through it all, Christ is honoured and fruit is produced.

FRUIT—PAUL'S AND OURS

Successful labour produces good results. Paul expects 'fruit from [my] labour'. Fruit does not come overnight. Patience is required to see it come into being. Paul knows that his faithful God will grant fruit, and that he must patiently endure and look to his Lord for that fruitful outcome in His time plan. Could it be that the church of Christ today would see more fruit, all by God's grace and goodness, if it laboured more intensively? Am I dedicated to personal labour in prayer, in concern, in care, in effort, in making the gospel known, and in seeking to help those who are new in the faith? Am I concerned to see fruit for His glory? We are not told in this passage exactly what Paul expects as the 'fruit from my labour'. It would be surprising if it did not include the blessing of both Christians and non-Christians! As one commentator put it: 'Paul knew the only reason to remain in this world was to bring souls to Christ and build up believers to do the same.' Paul will be seeking the fruit of a glorifying church and obedient Christians. He will also look for gospel fruit from his, and their, witness. He will see some from 'Caesar's household' as we will see in the last chapter. Do I look for fruit from both Christians and non-Christians I meet? Am I faithfully sowing God's Word to both? I need to remember what Paul said in another context: 'He who sows sparingly will also reap sparingly, and he who sows bountifully will also reap bountifully'.[24]

HEAVEN MUST BE GREAT AND THE WORK MUST BE VERY IMPORTANT

'What I shall choose I cannot tell,' Paul admits. It is a good thing that the real choice was God's, and not his! God always knows what is best. Think how highly Paul prizes the priorities of getting the gospel out, building the church and living a life to magnify Christ. Heaven must be overwhelmingly wonderful if he can consider giving up these priorities earlier than absolutely necessary in order to go to be with his Lord. Similarly, the need to preach Christ, establish the church, and glorify his Saviour by his life must carry an immense weight of desire and motivation in his life if he can even think about pursuing them a moment longer, rather than immediately fulfil his 'desire to depart and be with Christ, which is far better' (verse 23 below). The three lessons we learn are clear: first, Paul wants 'Christ' above everything and everyone else, be he on earth or in heaven; second, heaven *is* a wonderful place to go to; and third, Christ's service *is* more important on earth than any other activity we can ever engage in. John MacArthur hits the nail squarely on the head: 'Paul knew that the only reason to remain in this world was to bring souls to Christ and build up believers to do the same.'[25]

1:23 The pressure of blessing!

23 For I am hard-pressed between the two, having a desire to be with
Christ, which is far better.

OUR GENEROUS GOD

We have already considered, from Paul's previous words, the tension
between his two dearest ambitions—namely either to be soon with Jesus in
heaven, or to serve Him wholeheartedly here—and I only intend to make
one further comment on it now. What a generous God we have when the
two biggest blessings known to man after conversion are so wonderful that,
were we to choose which to experience next, it would be a great pressure on
us. Paul says, 'I am hard-pressed'. When an individual walks in close
fellowship with God, whatever choices God sanctions and selects are so
good for that person at that time, that all he is aware of is a changeless God,
who is with him to bless him, and who always will be.

'SOUL-SLEEP' IS OUT

But the 'desire to be with Christ, which is far better' must always be the
joyful background wish of the Christian, as it is for Paul. Very few of us
actually want to go 'at this moment'. However, our natural desire to stay
earthbound can be changed. God can make our minds focus
heavenwards. This can arise if the pain is overwhelming, or if special
grace is given to us to long for Him above the immediate sensations and
considerations of illness or persecution. So it was with those valiant men
who were enabled to rise above the pain and challenge of the fires of
martyrdom of whom we read in *Foxe's Book of Martyrs*.[26] Sometimes the
fatigue of a long and blessed life makes the saint of God similar to the
dying Abraham who was 'in a ripe old age, an old man and satisfied *with
life*'.[27] But although it is the rare exception for the born-again believer
consciously to want to die right *now*, what a comfort and confidence it
gives to know that something not only 'better', but 'far better', than even
the most blessed walk with Christ on earth, awaits him immediately on
release from his body in death. No wonder the Salvation Army talks of
'promotion to glory'! Some people teach that after death, the soul of a
Christian goes into a prolonged state of unconsciousness until the

resurrection body is bestowed upon it. I would ask them to consider how a state of non-consciousness could be better that knowing the Lord Jesus Christ as our Saviour and the assurance of His presence with us even through the 'valley of the shadow of death.' Paul says it is 'far better' (or 'very much better', NASB) to 'be with Christ'. That cannot be nothingness—even temporarily. It has to be better than the joy and blessing of communion with Christ and the privilege of serving and being with which Paul speaks of so enthusiastically. Soul-sleep is definitely not a biblical, logical or acceptable alternative.

'NOT SOMEHOW—BUT TRIUMPHANTLY'

Frank Dane was a dear and faithful Christian man who always stood by others and supported them in their troubles and illnesses. When his leukaemia deteriorated, he was still more concerned about the spiritual welfare of his neighbours than about his own health. The last time I visited him, before he departed to a far more glorious shore, he gave me two things. One was a replica of a card that he had displayed on his mantelpiece: *Not Somehow—But Triumphantly*. That summarised his Christ-centred life. The other was a poem that explained the reason why he triumphed in life. It was because he knew he would triumph in death through his risen Saviour. The title is *What is Dying?* which is repeated below and depicts someone who has come to know Christ passing from this scene of time, like a ship.

'What is Dying?'

A ship sails and I stand
Watching till she fades
On the horizon, and someone
At my side says: 'She's gone.'
Gone where? Gone from my sight,
That is all; she is just as large
As when I saw her.
The diminished size and
Total loss of sight is in me,
Not in her, and just at the moment

When someone at my side says:
'She's gone', there are others who
Are watching her coming,
And other voices
Take up a glad shout,
'Here she comes!'
And that is dying.

1:24 'Others'

24 Nevertheless to remain in the flesh is more needful for you.

'NEVERTHELESS'

Paul now widens his view from his personal preference to be either rejoicing in heaven for ever, or rejoicing in the work of the gospel on earth. He looks at what is 'more needful for you'. He evaluates the choice solely from the view of the Christian church at Philippi, and concludes that, notwithstanding it being 'far better' to be with Christ, the Philippians need him. It is a comment on his love for the church and his value to it. Matthew Henry's brief comment on this verse is worth quoting here: 'Paul's strait was not between living in this world and living in heaven; between these two there is no comparison: but his strait was between serving Christ in this world and enjoying Him in another. To advance the interest of Christ and His church, he chose rather to tarry here, where he met with oppositions and difficulties, and to deny himself for a while the satisfaction of his reward.'[28]

RARE TO LIVE FOR 'OTHERS'

It is said that the last word that passed the lips of godly General Booth of the Salvation Army was 'Others!' To find someone who is genuinely taken up with the needs of others, at personal cost, is rare. I myself came back to Christ as a half-hearted backslider because one man and his wife gave me their time and their personal involvement, often well after normal folks' bedtime. (I was a student at the time!) Whilst he dealt with my 'clever' arguments against a Bible, whose standards I preferred not to follow (which was my real problem, as he knew full well), she kept the supply line of coffee and biscuits coming. When I came back to the Lord, what a role model for service I had received from them both. 'Others' seemed to motivate them too. How often do *we* alter our cherished plans in order that the needs of others may be dealt with, thereby making sure that God is glorified? We need a 'nevertheless' to punctuate the grammar and vocabulary of our lives every now and then. Paul lived out this lifestyle wherever he went so that he could say to some, who did not appreciate him as they should have done, 'I will very gladly spend and be spent for your souls, though the more abundantly I love you, the less I am loved'.[29]

1:25 The link between progress and joy

25 And being confident of this, I know that I shall remain and continue with you all for your progress and joy of faith,

PAUL'S 'NEW' CONFIDENCE

One of the unanswered, and perhaps unanswerable, questions of Scripture is how and why Paul expresses his confidence that he 'shall remain and continue with you' when only a short while before he seems to have regarded death at least as a strong possibility? One commentator[30] has remarked, 'The atmosphere of verses 20, 23 was heavy with the thought of imminent martyrdom, and it seemed that death was just around the corner'. Views differ and we cannot be dogmatic about any. John MacArthur says it is simply 'Paul's conviction—not a supernatural revelation—that their need would determine that he stay on earth longer'.[31] Others could speculate whether it was a 'word of knowledge',[32] that many agree, from both charismatic and traditional evangelical viewpoints, was a gift of the Spirit then available to the apostle, even if it is true that that gift is no longer available to us now that the canon of Scripture is complete. Or is it a prophetic illumination? Or is it simply a conclusion he has reached based on his belief that God wants to bless this church at Philippi and that is why he is there? Or does he hear some good news indicating that the judge will reach a decision that means life rather than death? Or is it a mixture of two or more of these elements? Perhaps Matthew Henry's comment is an apt summary: 'What a great confidence Paul had in the divine Providence, that it would order all for the best to him. Whatsoever is the best for the church, we may be sure that God will do.'[33]

HIS JOB IF HE DOES REMAIN ALIVE

Paul has only one aim for the Philippian church if his life is spared. It is to 'continue with you all for the progress and joy of faith'. 'Continue' implies that, as we know already, he has already started a work that blesses them. But he wants to 'continue with you all'—again the all-embracing vision of this great-hearted, but cool-headed apostle is emphasised here. He does not just want to see a few 'spiritual stars' in the church. Christ died for them all. His resurrection gives them all great confidence and new life. They all must live for God in an alien and hostile world and so Paul's offer of help is for them all. He, Paul, wants to continue with them all. His target is that each shall glorify his, or her, personal Lord and Saviour in following Him faithfully.

NO JOY SITTING IN A PUDDLE!

To this end Paul wants to see their faith producing two vitally interconnected things in their lives: 'progress' and 'joy'. After many years of driving a car or walking, a huge hint was given to me one Christmas when my wife bought me a mountain bike! I have been reminded that the only 'joy' in riding a bike is to make 'progress'. From experience I can say that neither landing in the hedge, nor looking up from sitting in a muddy puddle, promotes 'joy'—at least not in me! But when you can remember how to stay upright and get a little fitter, so that you can mount the challenging inclines, the sense of achievement in your progress does bring joy! Progress and joy are inevitably linked. That first welcome experience of joy, bubbling up in many new converts, needs to be deepened and confirmed by going on with Christ in His Word and in His paths of biblical discipleship. Consider, in Acts 2,[34] the continuing progress of the early church 'in the apostles' doctrine and fellowship, in the breaking of bread, and in prayers' that caused the fear of God to come on 'every soul' and was accompanied by the 'many wonders and signs' that 'were done through the apostles'. The key word seems to be 'continue'. We read 'they continued steadfastly' in those vital means of grace and that they were 'continuing daily' in the temple (where no doubt they witnessed to others) and in 'breaking bread from house to house'. But what was their outward mark of discipleship as the onlookers saw them? It was their expression of joy! Even as they were at the meal table 'they ate their food with gladness and simplicity of heart, praising God'! No wonder they were 'having favour with all the people' and that 'the Lord added to the church daily those who were being saved'! Their progress in their faith, aided by scriptural truth, attendance at the Lord's table, fellowship and witness, produced praise and gladness that reminds us that, as Nehemiah found, 'the joy of the LORD is your strength'.[35] That joy can be ours today if we are determined, God helping, to persevere in our walk with God. But, like a river bed deprived of a continual source of running water, the life of any Christian can become dry, arid, and lifeless if he, or she, does not continue with the Lord, using His means of grace. Paul knows this principle very well and intends to see it applied to their blessing if God gives him life and time.

1:26 Rejoicing for others

[26] that your rejoicing for me may be more abundant in Jesus Christ by my coming to you again.

ABUNDANT REJOICING ONLY 'IN JESUS CHRIST'

Here is an obvious, though very important, point. The only real rejoicing, as opposed to temporary 'hype', is 'in Jesus Christ'. It is in Him alone that we have salvation.[36] He is our wisdom, righteousness, sanctification and redemption.[37] He is our power and strength to enable us to do 'all things' which He asks of us.[38] He alone has prepared a home in heaven for us, and He will rule at the end of time[39] and throughout all eternity.[40] Any rejoicing will be temporary unless it is based on who He is, and what He has done. He is the ultimate Cause behind everything and the ultimate Goal of the Christian. 'Rejoice in the Lord always. Again I will say, rejoice!'[41]

YET SOME THINGS MAKE US REJOICE EVEN MORE!

But even though our rejoicing is 'in Jesus Christ' there are circumstances and events that can make it even 'more abundant' in Him. There are times when He so arranges and does things for us that our sense of joyful dependence on His faithfulness and power makes us rejoice even more. It is not that we rejoice in 'happenings' but that we see His hand in all that happens and rejoice in Him more because of it. So Paul acknowledges that there is an event here that will make their 'rejoicing for me ... more abundant in Jesus Christ'.

'FOR ME'—TRULY SELFLESS REJOICING

The rejoicing Paul speaks of is amazing because it is not rejoicing that is primarily caused because they have benefited. It is not rejoicing on their own account! He says 'that your rejoicing *for me* may be more abundant in Jesus Christ'. Without doubt, the spiritual radiance and love from Paul to the Philippians would be the ideal environment to promote and encourage their truly selfless rejoicing. As Sidlow Baxter remarks: 'It follows that if Christ is our life, suffusing the heart and revealing Himself through the whole of our activity, this will greatly affect *the attitude of others towards us*: for the kind of life we live inevitably determines the reaction of those around us ...'[42] This must be true, but it is even harder to rejoice for others than for yourself. Test yourself. Do you find it harder to pray for blessing on others' work with the same fervency that you have when you pray for your own work? Is it not hard to desire the same results from others' labours and plans which you long to see from your own, even when you are impressed, and even blessed, by their quality of spiritual life? Are you happy when someone else understands a difficult passage of the Bible with which you have struggled? Are you glad when your friend has wonderful quiet times each day whilst you battle with staleness and find it hard to pray? If you ever preach or speak at meetings are you grateful for others who do it so much better than you do? If you are finding it hard at work and hear of another Christian who has landed the 'plum job', do you rejoice for him or her? It is not always easy, is it? How come that, in theory, we can rejoice for the good that our brothers and sisters in Christ enjoy and yet, in practice, find it so hard in a particular circumstance really to rejoice for that person? Here Paul has such confidence in the selflessness of the Philippian Christians that he knows their 'more abundant' rejoicing will be for him! May we so be helped by God to seek first His righteousness and His kingdom, and have a practical love for our fellow Christians. Then we can experience God's grace and love encouraging us to rejoice for their blessings when, humanly speaking, we would be grudging or green with envy! Is this not in the spirit of Paul's encouragement to the Corinthians: 'Let no one seek his own, but each one the other's well-being'.43

THE OTHER SECOND COMING

Without doubt the subject of the glorious second coming of the Lord Jesus Christ is one that captivates our minds and souls. But here we read of a far less important 'second coming' that nevertheless will produce rejoicing in Christ by the Philippians on behalf of Paul. It is a commentary on the fellowship and love between the church and the apostle! Paul knows that his hoped-for return to the church will make him so happy and content that the Christians will rejoice for him! Do you have that loving enthusiasm to meet with your brothers and sisters in Christ at your place of worship? Are you such a blessing to them that they see you that way too? God can help us to know that oneness in Him that makes it a joy to meet together and together rejoice in the One who has called us into one body. How often do we attain that? Is there cause here for some prayerful examination of our relationship with Him and with His children, our brothers and sisters in Christ?

Notes

1 2 Timothy 1:18.

2 2 Corinthians 1:10.

3 Matthew 6:33.

4 Habakkuk 3:4.

5 **E.M. Bounds,** *Winning the Invisible War* (Whitaker House), page 42.

6 **Arthur Bennett** (editor), *The Valley of Vision* (The Banner of Truth), page 50.

7 Luke 1:46.

8 Psalm 34:3.

9 1 Corinthians 2:8.

10 **J.B. Phillips,** *Your God is Too Small* (Nelson).

11 1 Corinthians 4:5.

12 Romans 1:16.

13 Esther 4:16.

14 Joseph Grigg, 'Jesus, and it shall it ever be, A mortal man ashamed of Thee', altered by **Benjamin Francis,** *Hymns of Faith,* number 521.

15 Philippians 4:13.

16 Hebrews 12:2.

17 Mrs Howard Taylor, *The Triumph of John and Betty Stam* (China Inland Missionary/Overseas Missionary Fellowship).

18 The China Inland Mission (CIM) is now the Overseas Missionary Fellowship (OMF).

19 Mrs Howard Taylor, *The Triumph of John and Betty Stam* (China Inland Missionary/Overseas Missionary Fellowship), page 105.

20 2 Corinthians 5:8.

21 Luke 10:20.

22 Job 19:25–27.

23 *George Whitefield's Journals* (The Banner of Truth), page 278.

24 2 Corinthians 9:6.

25 John MacArthur (author of commentary/notes and general editor), *The MacArthur Study Bible, NKJV* (Word Bibles), note on Philippians 1:22, page 1821.

26 Marie Gentert King (editor), *Foxe's Book of Martyrs* (Spire Books).

27 Genesis 25:8 (NASB).

28 Rev. Leslie Church (editor), *Matthew Henry's Commentary on the Whole Bible in One Volume* (Marshall, Morgan and Scott), page 660.

29 1 Corinthians 12:15.

30 Rev. Ralph P. Martin, *Tyndale New Testament Commentaries: The Epistle of Paul to the Philippians* (Tyndale Press), page 80.

31 John MacArthur (author of commentary/notes and general editor), *The MacArthur Study Bible, NKJV* (Word Bibles), note on Philippians 1:25, page 1821 and 1822.

32 1 Corinthians 12:8.

33 Rev. Leslie Church (editor), *Matthew Henry's Commentary on the Whole Bible in One Volume* (Marshall, Morgan and Scott), page 660.

34 Acts 2:42–47.

35 Nehemiah 8:10.

36 John 14:6; Acts 4:12.

37 1 Corinthians 1:30.

38 Philippians 4:13.

39 Hebrews 1:9,10.

40 Revelation 1:11,17,18.

41 Philippians 4:4.

42 J. Sidlow Baxter, *Explore the Book, In One Volume* (Zondervan), page 188

43 1 Corinthians 10:24.

Mini-overview: 1:27 to 1:30:

Being 'worthy of the gospel of Christ'—
United together, scorning fear, and suffering for His sake.

1:27 How to stand fast

27 Only let your conduct be worthy of the gospel of Christ, so that whether I come and see you or am absent, I may hear of your affairs, that you stand fast in one spirit, with one mind striving together for the faith of the gospel,

'ONLY'

The first word, 'Only', can easily be missed. '*Only* is placed first and is emphatic. The meaning is, then, "above all, at all costs"'.[1] It means 'of first importance' and gives emphasis to what follows. With that reminder we see what is expected of those in the church at Philippi, and anywhere else, who claim to belong to Jesus. Do you recall the earlier quote from George Whitefield? Here is part of it again, in which he too uses an 'Only' (and with my emphasis made on the text): 'His will be done in me, by me, and upon me, for time, and for eternity. Let me do or suffer just as seemeth good in His sight. *Only do Thou, O Lord, give me that wisdom which dwelleth with prudence, that I may never suffer for my own misconduct, but only for righteousness' sake.*'[2] Here was a great public figure who realised the important truth that mastery of his personal righteousness was even more vital than maintaining his public witness. That desire for personal godliness was reflected in his amazing preaching which helped to make a nation aware of the saving power of Christ.

GOSPEL CONDUCT

Paul could rightly have said, 'Only let your conduct be worthy of *Christ*'. But he does not say that here. That would have meant the exacting task of checking how Jesus would react, inwardly and outwardly, to the things that I would have to face each day. But Paul goes a step further and says that the requirement is the harder one to 'be worthy of the *gospel* of Christ'. Why is that harder? Because it goes further. First, it is true that I cannot behave in a way that is 'worthy of the gospel of Christ' without first of all knowing Him and behaving in a way that is worthy of Him. We should live worthily of Christ irrespective of whether that gives an opportunity to witness. We should never shrink from honouring Him and helping others just because we do not get an immediate opportunity to verbalise our faith in Christ. We should honour and please *Him*. But here Paul tells the Christians to behave in a way which is worthy of *His gospel*. That adds another dimension. They are surrounded by lost sinners for whom Christ died. They will look at their lives to see if their gospel is real. It is one thing for the world to criticise elements of the Christians' walks, but if they see that their *gospel* 'does not work' in practice, then their blood will be on those saints' hands. I have met people who were helped towards the gospel because they had seen a consistent Christian testimony lived before them. They told me of the Christians who had so impressed them. Their conduct was 'worthy of the gospel' and showed their friends that the gospel of redeeming and life-changing love was real and relevant to them. The challenge is that sometimes non-Christian people seem to be more consistent, caring, and reliable than those of us who say we follow Christ. 'What do you do more than others?' is a question that we should apply to our lives far above the immediate context in which Jesus asked it.[3] I also know people who were completely put off the good news of Christ because of the inconsistent lifestyle of Christians they knew. In one instance, the man preached the gospel well, but his lack of purity in (and out) of the workplace made the gospel a laughing stock. Paul is, of course, very mindful of those who 'preach Christ even from envy and strife' (see verse 15, before) and although he rejoices that the gospel is preached, he grieves at the poor example that must have been given to the hearers. I recall, in my early years as a Christian, recounting to an older Christian friend a dispute I had had with another motorist and boasting about how I had handled it. He listened and then quietly and graciously asked me: 'Gerard, did you leave him with a gospel leaflet?' I was immediately cut down to size and learned an important lesson that made a big difference, despite still failing more often than I would care to admit. My conduct had not commended Christ and was not 'worthy of the gospel of Christ'. There was no way I could have commended Christ to that man, or shared the gospel with him, after my poor example. It is important sometimes to win the person, even if sometimes we lose the argument.

'BIG BROTHER' IS *NOT* WATCHING YOU! YOU SHOULD BE CONSISTENT ANYHOW.

Paul continues that this gospel-worthy lifestyle must not be lived just to please him. He is not George Orwell's *1984* 'Big Brother' who is 'watching you'. (We have a Heavenly Father doing that, both as a comfort and as a challenge!4) He reminds the Philippian Christians that he wants to hear of their united stand for Christ whether he is there or not. He is only a man, and they should do the right things, regardless of whether he is there. On the other hand, they should not avoid holy and righteous living simply because he is absent. Irrespective of Paul's absence or presence they should live worthily of the gospel of the One who said, 'I will never leave you nor forsake you'.5 It is so easy to do things to be seen, is it not? Paul's basic message is 'Do it for Him who is unseen but who is there always.'

WHAT PAUL REALLY WANTS TO HEAR

Paul tells them that, whether present or absent, he wants 'to hear of [their] affairs' that they are standing together and striving together, that they have one spirit and one mind, and that the object of their single-minded stand and striving in unity of spirit is the 'faith of the gospel'. If he returns to be among them, he wants to hear that they are disciplined soldiers of the cross, fighting together as a unit under the banner of saving grace.

'STAND FAST IN ONE SPIRIT'

'Stand fast' is a military term and pictures the brave discipline of those who refuse to give ground against the might of the opposition. So it is for the Christian garrison at Philippi, and so it should be for all Christians everywhere. But without oneness of spirit that is impossible. God blesses and helps the Christian by taking over his, or her, spirit by His Holy Spirit, who enters at conversion6 and wishes to be filling and controlling the Christian's life continually.7 When He directs us through His Word, we sense our oneness in Christ and our common cause, His gospel. By His enabling and strengthening us we can stand fast both individually and together against Satan's forces.8 Paul's injunction to his friends in Philippi is for us too: 'stand fast in one spirit'. They must not only be united in their understanding of God's truth, salvation and gospel: they must stand together to defend and propagate it to the outside world.

'WITH ONE MIND STRIVING TOGETHER FOR THE FAITH OF THE GOSPEL'
The unity of the spirit in Christ must come first. There has to be that bonding of forgiven and redeemed hearts that, energised by the Holy Spirit, provides the motivation to let the Bible be paramount in all our thinking and living. When that work of salvation is done, and as the work of sanctification continues, Christians must be increasingly Spirit-led through God's Word. That will produce single-mindedness on the essentials of the Christian faith. The word translated 'mind' here takes in the meaning of 'soul' or 'heart' as well as 'mind'. It is easier to understand than to explain! But in a 'one-souled', 'whole-hearted', 'unanimous' way Christians are to energetically and purposefully engage together to maintain and share the faith of the gospel. The phrase 'strive together' implies team effort in battling and struggling side by side together against the opposition.

1:28 The proof of perdition and salvation
28 and not in any way terrified by your adversaries, which is to them a proof of perdition, but to you of salvation, and that from God.

'... FACING DANGER AND POSSIBLE DEATH ALMOST EVERY DAY'[9]
Just in case we regard physical danger and the possibility of being killed for Christ as too academic, let me set the scene for my comments on verse 28 by referring you to John G. Paton, missionary to the New Hebrides from 1858, as recorded in *King of the Cannibals* by Jim Cromarty. As we consider his experience, let us bear in mind that today thousands of Christians are suffering for their faith in Christ and many are being persecuted cruelly. One acknowledges the valuable contribution that Christian Solidarity International has made in keeping Christians informed about persecution of the church worldwide.[10] It could happen to us in the West, too, perhaps sooner than we imagine. More than once, Paton was surrounded by warriors who intended to kill him. Some chiefs met and decided to put him

to death because they did not like his message. An attack with an axe was avoided by intervention from a nearby sympathetic chief. 'The following day a chief with a loaded gun followed John about for hours, threatening to shoot him. All the time John quietly went about his work as if the man were not there, praying silently to the Lord for His protection as he did so.'[11] After that, he survived an armed attempt to break into his house, God using his little dog to frighten off the attackers! In his book, the author makes the following summary: 'John did not find it easy facing danger and possible death almost every day, but he knew that God had a work for him to do and would preserve him until that work was done. He carried on with his daily life and work, trusting the Lord to take care of him. In fact he found that his experiences of danger and God's deliverance from them strengthened his faith. He was never as conscious of the Lord's presence with him, protecting him and giving him strength he needed to go on, as he was in those days when he faced the danger of death almost every hour. He found great comfort in the promise of Christ: "Lo, I am with you always, even unto the end of the world." He was so conscious of the Lord's power supporting him that he was able to say with Paul, "I can do all things through Christ who strengthens me."'[12] That quotation takes us back to the church at Philippi—a church under attack from different quarters. As we look at them, let us ask ourselves how we respond to those who oppose us.

NO TERROR

You may think that the opposition of all the forces against the witnessing church in Philippi is a terrifying prospect. What a combination of apostasy, ignorant prejudice, legalistic Jews, self-seeking competitors, and uninformed authorities are arrayed against them, consciously or unconsciously manipulated by Satan. Yet Paul records that they are 'not in any way terrified by [their] adversaries'! So real and personal is their Lord and Saviour to them that they know no terror from their opponents. Why, do you suppose, is this so? There seem to be three main reasons. First, the Christians are encouraged by standing firm and striving together as a Spirit-controlled team. Second, as we shall see more fully in the next verse, suffering for Christ is a gift from God and not an intrusive imposition.

More will be said of that soon. Third, their already remarkable degree of God-given love that, in verse 9, Paul prays will 'abound still more and more in knowledge and all discernment' has a considerable effect on them and their attitude to opposition. It is true that the context of the passage deals with their united stand, but that would mean nothing were they not bolstered and strengthened, individually and communally, by God's love. The Bible says, 'Perfect love casts out fear'[13] and we see how Paul prays for the experience of and undergirding by God's love in another persecuted church situation at Ephesus: he prays 'that Christ may dwell in your hearts through faith; that you, being rooted and grounded in love, may be able to comprehend with all the saints what *is* the width and length and depth and height—to know the love of Christ which passes knowledge; that you may be filled with all the fullness of God.'[14] Paul's persuasion expressed to the Christians at Rome is, no doubt, in his heart for the Philippians, too. He says to them that he is 'persuaded that neither death nor life, nor angels nor principalities nor powers, nor things present nor things to come, nor height nor depth, nor any other created thing, shall be able to separate us from the love of God which is in Christ Jesus our Lord.'[15] He wants these Philippian Christians to grasp that and thus be filled with the love of God and with the God of love. Fear must then continue to flee. This is something that only God can do for His trusting people who cast themselves upon Him. It is as if their fear is darkness and God's love is light. As Christians grasp, believe and rely on the amazing love of God for them, the light is switched on and the darkness flees. When we are conscious that we are in the arms of the God of love, our fear of man diminishes. When we encourage each other in that shared love, as fellow team members, we can resist without fear.

THE LOVE THAT INDICATES OUR DESTINATION
Their refusal to be terrorised testifies to the nearness of their loving Saviour and to their consciousness of that nearness. That is why Paul comments that this lack of terror is to them 'a proof … of salvation'. Without the saving grace of God, the saving death of Christ, and the saving faith of these Christians, there would be nothing for the despisers of the gospel to oppose! In that sense, those in the Philippian church have proved that they

are on God's side, because there is a battle against the enemy. But it goes deeper than that. In this battle, their wonder at God's love in sending His completely willing Son, to die on the cross for their sins, drives out the fear of men. So all-pervasive is their gratitude and reverent joy that Jesus should so love them, that they are nerved spiritually in the battle against all odds, and overwhelmed by the *appreciation* of His love for them. Not only is that their reasoned position, but as the Holy Spirit sheds abroad God's love in their hearts, they are warmed within and wonderfully strengthened by their *experience* of His love. One is objective evaluation and appreciation; the other is subjective experience and adoration. Both aspects of God's love in Christ for them, through the Holy Spirit, cause them to be 'more than conquerors through Him who loved [them]'.[16] That wonderful love whispers in each of their souls, and perhaps shouts that truth to others who observe their changed demeanour: 'You really are saved by the Son of God who loved you and gave Himself for you.' That 'inner witness',[17] that becomes an outer testimony under pressure, confirms in their experience what they already know from the Word of God, that they have eternal salvation 'and that from God.' Diamonds occur in mines where the pressure has been greatest. No doubt that all-supporting witness of God's love, in the pressure of opposition, produces the diamond of peace and tranquillity where otherwise there would have been terror.

THE OTHER SIDE: GOSPEL REALITY REMINDS THE LOST THAT THEY ARE LOST

It is against this comforting and encouraging experience and realisation of the love of God that we can see it is also a signpost to the hell-bound sinners who are their adversaries. They have no Saviour who can give them this peace and serenity in the midst of opposition. They know no gospel that so transcends their petty human thoughts and prejudices. They have no worthy cause to fight for without worldly weapons. They only know hate for those who are against them; the whole idea of following Jesus' words to His disciples to 'love your enemies, bless those who curse you, do good to those who hate you, and pray for those who spitefully use you and persecute you'[18] is a foreign spiritual language to them. They cannot understand how it can work. Thus the Philippians' love for God, which takes away the terror of their enemies and enables them to love the very ones so opposed to them, paradoxically confirms to their adversaries that they are now outside the saving relationship with Christ which produces this spiritual 'love-life'. Part of the witness given to the unconverted arises from within themselves. They *know* that they are wrong, even without being told. They *know* they are lost. Their own actions and attitudes confirm it to themselves in their honest moments, and the Spirit-aided preaching of the gospel confirms their lostness to them, and their need of Christ as Saviour. If they die in that state, they will be lost for ever from the warmth of God's love and light which would change them now, were they to turn in repentance to Him. Thus that love in the lives of those they oppose has become to them 'a proof of their perdition'. Think of it! The same love which confirms the Christian in his eternal salvation through his faith in Christ warns the observant non-Christian that he is lost for ever. The same sun that hardens the concrete melts the butter. That same love of Christ, overcoming the great fear and terror of opposition, is like a signpost at the end of a one-way street indicating that the only choice is salvation or perdition. If only the unsaved would see that signpost and turn to the Friend of Sinners for forgiveness and new direction! Which is it for you? The thought of God's grace speaking one way to a person who knows Christ and His salvation, and another way to someone on the 'broad ... way that leads to destruction'[19] is seen again in Paul's second letter to the Corinthians. There we read of the Corinthian Christians, with whom Paul includes himself, saying: 'For we are to God the fragrance of Christ among those who are being saved and among those who are perishing. To the one we are the aroma of death to death, and to the other the aroma of life to life'.[20] Have you noticed that many precious things which non-Christians ridicule, despise and reject make the heart of Christians leap for joy and are precious to His followers? In the case of the Philippian Christians, that fragrance of God's love, overcoming all fear, indicated heaven to the saved and hell to the lost.

1:29 The gift of suffering
29 For to you it has been granted on behalf of Christ, not only to believe in Him, but also to suffer for His sake,

SALVATION INVOLVES SUFFERING

The Philippian church gets the message 'straight from the shoulder'. Paul says, in effect, 'You will suffer.' The link between salvation and suffering may not be popularly received today, but it is quite clearly biblical: those who are saved are not exempt from suffering, of any kind, and in fact suffering may increase because of opposition and persecution. The 'healthy, wealthy and successful' emphasis of recent years—implying that only disobedience robs a believer of the very best in life down here—is completely without scriptural warrant. The theme of 'the fellowship of His sufferings' will be looked at in chapter 3:10. But those who are ill, or lose their jobs, or have financial problems not of their making, or are opposed by others must not think that they are, thereby, 'second class citizens' in the kingdom of God. That is just not true. In fact we often are *really free* to experience spiritual good health, Christ's riches for us, and a measure of success in following Him when the props are knocked away and we are cast upon Him. Over the years I have preached on the prayer of Jabez[21] on a number of occasions. I was in the CNN studio audience in Atlanta, Georgia, when the author of a small best-selling book about that prayer was being interviewed in an hour-long programme. It concerned me to see that both Christians and non-Christians in that audience who had read that book seemed to treat the prayer as a mantra: just repeat it and all will be well. Perhaps that is why the book is a best-seller! I was even more concerned that the author failed even to try to present the gospel in a programme that went out (I was told) to over sixty million people. I shared my sadness at this with him afterwards. I believed it must have 'caused pain'[22] to the Lord of Calvary. It certainly did to me. I wonder how many people would have bought a book on remaining faithful to the Lord and His gospel in suffering. Afterwards I attended a large Christian book fair for the publishers of this book where, again, the book on the prayer of Jabez was achieving a very high profile. Have we reached the stage where the majority of Christians now want their ears tickled, rather than their hearts and lives blessed in faithful service to Christ?

GRANTED = FREELY GIVEN

Just as faith in Christ is a gift of God, so is suffering. 'For you it has been granted on behalf of Christ not only to believe in Him, but also to suffer for His sake'. It cannot be clearer. The Philippian Christians and we ourselves are granted faith to believe on Christ. Similarly, suffering has been granted. The Greek word for 'granted' is elsewhere translated 'given' or 'freely given', and shows that suffering 'for His sake' is a gift that God gives us, even if we do not want it! This gift is comparable with the gift of a good education which sometimes makes great demands on on us and is not always easy, but produces a good result if we persevere. The word translated 'granted' is from the noun meaning 'grace.' Thus the Christian's suffering is a gift of God's grace. In the same way as 'the fellowship of His sufferings' cannot be siphoned off from knowing 'Him and the power of His resurrection,'[23] so we cannot claim the benefits of salvation by faith as a gift from God without also accepting suffering 'for His sake' equally from His loving hand. Matthew Henry rightly remarks: 'Faith is God's gift on the behalf of Christ. To suffer for the sake of Christ is a valuable gift too. If we suffer reproach and loss for Christ, we are to reckon it a great gift, always provided we behave under our sufferings with the genuine temper of martyrs.'[24]

'FOR HIS SAKE'

Note the three words at the end of the verse. Paul makes it clear to his friends at Philippi what the reason for the suffering has to be. A general comment on 'for His sake' is in order. It is no good getting into a position where we are opposed or rejected because of our own stupidity, selfishness or lack of wise consideration for others and then claim we suffer 'for His sake'. That is hypocritical nonsense. But, equally, some suffering 'for His sake' will be encountered as a result of a holy life amongst ungodly standards, or a clear and uncompromising evangelistic life among those who still regard Jesus as 'despised and rejected'.[25] Many Christians do suffer at home or at work, in being snubbed or criticised or passed over for promotion, because they do stand for Christ's holy and sensible standards in a world where almost anything goes. Also those who use God's grace to witness boldly to the saving power of their Saviour, publicly or personally, or both, may well be vilified and find themselves the object of scorn and unkind 'humour'. That certainly is part of suffering 'for His sake'. The root cause of Christians suffering 'for His sake' is because they prize who Jesus is and what He has done for them. They are determined to love Him and stay faithful to Him and His commands, as expressed in the Bible. That marks them out from a careless and rebellious world, from systems of government that oppose the Bible, and from systems of religion which wrongly teach that we can *do* something or *be* something to gain our salvation. They are marked people.

THE IMMEDIATE CONTEXT

The immediate context for the church that Paul addresses is that they will suffer for knowing, loving, following and serving Christ. They will be persecuted for the sake of the gospel. Some will be killed. Others will be marginalised or ostracised. Others will be ridiculed and not make progress with their peer group or in society at large. Perhaps the question is fairly put to us all: do we shrink from following Him when popularity, comfort or safety is threatened? Are we frightened at the thought of standing for Jesus in a hostile environment? If so, let us take courage from the fact that thousands upon thousands of Christians have found that the God who gives 'living grace' to live with, will also give us 'persecuted grace' to face opposition and persecution, and 'dying grace' to die with, if needs be. We cannot. He can! He will! The example under persecution and martyrdom of God's children should be the regular subject of our reading, and we should ask for grace to follow faithfully in their footsteps if and when we are called to suffer similarly. *Foxe's Book of Martyrs*,[26] Merle d'Aubigné's two volumes on *The Reformation in England*,[27] Leonard Verduin's *The Reformers and their Stepchildren*,[28] and Don Cormack's *Killing Fields, Living Fields*[29] all challenge us to turn from our indifference and ease to take our Lord seriously. In fact, very few good biographies or autobiographies of men and women God has used greatly fail to record considerable sufferings of one kind or another in following Christ. And do not forget the gallery of faith in Hebrews chapter 11.

A WIDER APPLICATIONS—GODLY EXAMPLES.

But there is also a wider application of the principle. A Christian's positive faith and confidence in God and dedication to the ongoing tasks of reaching a lost world for Jesus Christ and of doing people good, can make that suffering 'for His sake'. I think of Roy Castle's lovely testimony in his battle with cancer. Whilst working to alleviate the physical suffering of lung cancer victims, his joyful witness for his Saviour gave Christians the opportunity to explain to their friends why he was like that. Professor Verna Wright, the co-founder of United Beach Missions, was asked in a public meeting if, in view of the spreading cancer in his body, he would now take it easy. His reply was: 'Oh no! When you see the tape, you run harder!' And he did—witnessing to all by life and by word in the hospice that was his last residence before he met the Saviour he so dearly loved and faithfully served. Or consider the radiant witness of the dear woman of God, Joni Erickson Tada, who has used her major disability, since breaking her neck as a teenager in a diving accident, as a sounding board for proclaiming the gospel to the lost, encouraging Christians, and offering hope to many others whose injuries and illnesses would leave them depressed and in despair. I have heard some suggest that if only she had faith she could be healed. That thought is as unbiblical as it is cruel. It seems to me that God has given this gracious lady the gift of suffering because He knew she would share its benefits with everyone in such a helpful way. These three examples, like many others who could be quoted, by God's grace have converted their sufferings into opportunities to glorify God and proclaim Christ. They have sanctified their sufferings 'for His sake'. Would we not grumble and complain less, and fall less often into the sin of self-pity, if we looked at unwelcome events and circumstances as suffering 'for His sake'? Let Joni speak for herself!

JONI

Consider what she so rightly says in one of her encouraging books: 'The pages of Scripture teem with good things that can come from suffering. Pain and discomfort get our minds off the temporary things of this world and force us to think about God. They drive us to pull His Word off the shelf far more than usual and to pay more attention when we do. Trials knock us off our proud pedestals and get us relying on God (2 Corinthians 1:9). Then we learn to know God better, for when we have to depend on someone to get us through each hour, we really get to know them. Problems give us the chance to praise God even when its hard. This pleases Him and proves to the spirit world how great He is to inspire such loyalty. And it proves something to us—it gives us a gauge to measure the depth or shallowness of our own commitment to Him.'[30] Have you been diagnosed as having a serious, even terminal, illness? Thank Him that the future prospect is unqualifiedly bright, and ask Him to use you to surprise people you meet with your confidence in Jesus.

1:30 We have the same conflict

[30] having the same conflict which you saw in me and now hear in me.

WITNESSES OF THE CONFLICT

Paul knows that, although miles separate the church in Philippi from his life in a Roman prison, the same conflict which he has encountered and still has to face is also suffered by them. They are well aware of what he had suffered in Philippi because they 'saw' his conflict. He had been dragged away, with Silas, into the marketplace because he had been used to set free a possessed girl, unjustly hauled in front of the magistrates, unlawfully stripped and 'beaten with rods' having received 'many stripes', thrown into prison, and committed to the well-briefed jailer who incarcerated them in the inner prison and put them in stocks there.[31] The Philippian Christians, by this letter, 'now hear' that he is in prison again and they know of the imminent possibility of Paul's execution, and the opposition to him outside prison both from false teachers and from those who regard him as a competitor. So from what the Philippians have already seen, and what they learn now, they know his 'conflict' very well. They are also aware of the 'blessed conflict' he has explained: namely, whether to die and be with Christ, in heaven, or whether to stay alive to serve Christ and be a blessing to others. But this verse concentrates further on Paul's conflict within.

'IN ME'

In this verse Paul notes that the 'same conflict' was 'in me' and is 'in me'. Although the Philippian church is well aware of the range of conflicts they have seen and now hear about, they must also be aware of the consequent tensions within that Paul experiences, and that he knows they have too. It is not outside circumstances that defeat us: it is our response to them. In fact we need challenges to help us build spiritual muscle and Holy Spirit perseverance. I once had an American boss who always reminded me of John Wayne. He told me that he loved stress, and if there was no stress to contend with, he got stressed! (Work that one out, if you can!) In his most helpful book, which is still as relevant today as when it was first published in 1958, *Problems of Christian Discipleship*, J. Oswald Sanders states: 'The word "tension" is defined as "the state of being strained to stiffness; hence mental strain, intensity of striving, nervous anxiety with attending muscular tenseness." It is not suggested that all nervous tension is harmful. The string of a violin fulfils its function only as it attains the tension necessary to produce the correct musical note. It is the same with the human life. Its highest achievement is reached only when every power is harnessed to the fulfilment of a worthy life purpose, and this involves a certain degree of tension. The words of our Lord in Luke 12:50 may be rendered "What tension I suffer until it is all over." The fulfilment of the will of God involved Him in tension.'[32] So Paul is not saying that the consequent inner conflict, or stress—or 'tension' as J. Oswald Sanders puts it—is wrong. He is simply saying that he has it and he knows they have it too. It is how you tackle that conflict, thankfully with the help and wisdom of our all-powerful Lord available to us, that makes the difference between a beautiful God-honouring melody and the screechy discords of self-centredness and self-pity. In the final analysis, all conflict ends up as internal, since that covers our inward and personal response to all outward circumstances and stimuli, good and bad. Even pain from outside injury is felt inwardly in the anxiety and responses it causes. So are hunger, loneliness and coldness. The real battle concerns the Christian's response to those things. Paul and the Philippian church know, as we do today, that our Saviour God is at work 'in us'.[33]

SHARERS IN THAT CONFLICT

So the apostle identifies with the church. He says they have 'the same conflict' as he had and has. He knows that they too are in the King's service in enemy territory. In principle, that which he faces, they face. In practice, the details may differ from circumstance to circumstance and from place to place, but their 'gift' of suffering, like his, includes opposition from those outside Christ, who neither understand nor want his gospel, and from those who confess to be Christians, who sinfully have an agenda other than glorifying God and seeing lost souls saved. This makes worse the existing inner conflicts that Satan would seek to use to wreck God's peace within. If such suffering is 'granted to' the Christians, in that Roman colony, and to Paul, in that Roman prison, why should we be surprised if we are opposed from without, and assailed from within, for the privilege of believing in Christ in this third millennium? And should we not expect that those pressures will get stronger, and the opposition worse, as more and more standards of biblical righteousness are abandoned, even legally, by our lost and dark society in which we are to shine as 'lights in the world'?[34] Praise God that the conflicts we face enable us to prove His abundant grace in our lives. We have the absolute certainty of heaven to come, the knowledge of the Comforter's presence now, the solid rock of the Bible on which to build our lives, and the priceless privilege of witnessing for our dear Saviour until He promotes us to glory! With every challenge, external and internal, is comfort from God, and with every task, however hard, is His help and presence! The Philippians, seeing and hearing how God helps and blesses Paul, will feel equal to the task by divine assistance. May we have a similarly encouraging and positive effect on others as we wait upon the Lord!

Notes

1 **Rev. Ralph P. Martin,** *Tyndale New Testament Commentaries: The Epistle of Paul to the Philippians* (Tyndale Press), page 82.

2 *George Whitefield's Journals* (Banner of Truth), page 278.

3 Matthew 5:47.

4 Proverbs 15:3.

5 Hebrews 13:5.

6 John 7:39; 1 Corinthians 3:16.

7 Ephesians 5:18.

8 Ephesians 6:13,14.

9 Jim Cromarty, *King of the Cannibals* (Evangelical Press), pages 107–109.

10 Details from Christian Solidarity Worldwide, PO Box 99, New Malden, Surrey, KT3 3YF, England. Telephone 020 8942 8810. E-mail: csw@csw.org.uk.

11 Jim Cromarty, *King of the Cannibals* (Evangelical Press), page 109.

12 Philippians 4:13.

13 1 John 4:18.

14 Ephesians 3:17–19.

15 Romans 8:38,39.

16 Romans 8:37.

17 1 John 5:10.

18 Matthew 6:44.

19 Matthew 7:13.

20 2 Corinthians 2:15,16.

21 1 Chronicles 4:9,10.

22 'Jabez' literally means 'He gives pain'—per **H.L. Ellison,** *The New Bible Commentary: 1 Chronicles* (Inter-Varsity Press), page 342. See also the use of the word 'pain' in verse 10.

23 Philippians 3:10.

24 Rev. Leslie Church (editor), *Matthew Henry's Commentary on the Whole Bible in One Volume* (Marshall, Morgan and Scott), page 661.

25 Isaiah 53:3.

26 Marie Gentert King (editor), *Foxe's Book of Martyrs* (Spire Books).

27 J.H. Merle d'Aubigné, *The Reformation in England* (two volumes) (Banner of Truth).

28 Leonard Verduin, *The Reformers and their Stepchildren* (Paternoster).

29 Don Cormack, *Killing Fields, Living Fields* (OMF International/MARC Crowborough).

30 Joni Eareckson Tada with Steve Estes, *A Step Further* (Pickering Paperbacks), page 160 and 161.

31 Acts 16: 19–24.

32 J. Oswald Sanders, *Problems of Christian Discipline* (Overseas Missionary Fellowship), pages 11 and 12.

33 Ephesians 3:20.

34 Philippians 2:15.

The letter opened (continued)

Philippians Chapter 2

[1] Therefore if there is any consolation in Christ, if any comfort of love, if any fellowship of the Spirit, if any affection and mercy, [2] fulfill my joy by being like-minded, having the same love, being of one accord, of one mind. [3] Let nothing be done through selfish ambition or conceit, but in lowliness of mind let each esteem others better than himself. [4] Let each of you look out not only for his own interests, but also for the interests of others.

[5] Let this mind be in you which was also in Christ Jesus, [6] who, being in the form of God, did not consider it robbery to be equal with God, [7] but made Himself of no reputation, taking the form of a bondservant, and coming in the likeness of men. [8] And being found in appearance as a man, He humbled Himself and became obedient to the point of death, even the death of the cross. [9] Therefore God also has highly exalted Him and given Him a name which is above every name; [10] that at the name of Jesus every knee should bow, of those in heaven, and of those on earth, and of those under the earth, [11] and that every tongue should confess that Jesus Christ is Lord, to the glory of God the Father.

[12] Therefore, my beloved, as you have always obeyed, not in my presence only, but now much more in my absence, work out your own salvation with fear and trembling, [13] for it is God who works in you both to will and to do for His good pleasure.

[14] Do all things without complaining and disputing, [15] that you may become blameless and harmless, children of God without fault in the midst of a crooked and perverse generation, among whom you shine as lights in the world, [16] holding fast the word of life, so that I may rejoice in the day of Christ that I have not run in vain or laboured in vain. [17] Yes, and if I am being poured out as a drink offering on the sacrifice and service of your faith, I am glad and rejoice with you all. [18] For the same reason you also be glad and rejoice with me.

19 But I trust in the Lord Jesus to send Timothy to you shortly, that I also may be encouraged when I know your state. 20 For I have no-one like-minded, who will sincerely care for your state. 21 For all seek their own, not the things which are of Christ Jesus. 22 But you know his proven character, that as a son with his father he served with me in the gospel. 23 Therefore I hope to send him at once, as soon as I see how it goes with me. 24 But I trust in the Lord that I myself shall also come shortly. 25 Yet I considered it necessary to send to you Epaphroditus, my brother, fellow worker, and fellow soldier, but your messenger and the one who ministered to my need; 26 since he was longing for you all, and was distressed because you had heard that he was sick. 27 For indeed he was sick almost unto death; but God had mercy on him, and not only on him but on me also, lest I should have sorrow upon sorrow. 28 Therefore I sent him the more eagerly, that when you see him again you may rejoice, and I may be less sorrowful. 29 Receive him therefore in the Lord with all gladness, and hold such men in esteem; 30 because for the work of Christ he came close to death, not regarding his life, to supply what was lacking in your service toward me.

Chapter 2

'Lowly-minded—highly exalted'

Mini-overview: 2:1 to 2:4

Mind your mind and pull together!

Paul urges that the practical outworking of the believer's spiritual benefits must be seen in a selfless and sincere mindset and love for each other.

2:1 What blessings we have in Christ!

1 Therefore if there is any consolation in Christ, if any comfort of love, if any fellowship of the Spirit, if any affection and mercy,

'IFFY' VERSES AND A 'THEREFORE'

Someone may suggest that this is an 'iffy' verse! There are four 'if's in it following a 'Therefore'. First, however, let us look at the 'Therefore'. I well remember being told: 'When you see a 'therefore' in the verse, look and see what it is there for!' My Bible study has benefited from that ever since. Here the link is between the one-minded mutual support and fellowship, urged in chapter 2, and the preceding theme, that the Philippian Christians should 'suffer for His sake' in a united way and share in 'the same conflict' of soul as Paul through opposition from the outside world. It is 'a bridge between the apostle's call for the unity of the church in the face of hostility and a continuation of that summons for such concord and harmonious churchmanship as will gladden his heart'.[1] God's spiritual provisions more than compensate for that suffering and those conflicts, and lay a foundation for even deeper shared heartfelt bonds of love in Christ. God provides 'consolation', 'comfort', 'fellowship', 'affection and mercy'. All of them are preceded by an 'if there is any', and lead to immediate practical applications (in verses 2, 3, 4 and 5.)

THE 'IF' OF CERTAINTY, NOT THE 'IF' OF DOUBT!

When Paul says 'if', he is not suggesting that there is any doubt whether God provides consolation, comfort, fellowship, affection and mercy! Each 'if', on the contrary, emphasises that His provision of those blessings will enable them to love, help and support one another. It is the certain 'if' of logical argument, not the hesitant 'if' of doubt, that we see repeated here four times. You could just as easily substitute for the phrases 'if there is any' and 'if any' the words 'given that there is' or 'since there is'. The Amplified Bible gives us each phrase prefixed by 'by whatever' instead of 'if there is any',[2] and this gives us the positive principle behind the argument Paul puts. As we see so often in the Bible, the mainspring for our actions is everything that God is, and all He has done for us. Before He asks us to do anything, God makes it possible for us to do whatever He asks. Unlike Pharaoh's draconian demands of the Israelites,[3] He never asks us to 'make bricks' without providing us with both the clay and the straw we need—and then He comes alongside to show us how to do and to help us to do it! 'Given that' He consoles us in our conflicts 'in Christ'—or 'by whatever' consolation we have 'in Christ'—we can behave towards each other in loving consideration. 'Since there is' sharing together in Holy Spirit fellowship—or 'by whatever' fellowship the Holy Spirit gives us—we can pull together. 'Given that' God moves our heart to have affection for each other—or 'by whatever' affection God gives us for each other—we can look out for each other's best interests. 'Since there is' mercy from our God of mercy when we fail—or 'by whatever' mercy God shows to us in our failures—we can show and be shown mercy to and from each other when we let each other down.

WHAT BLESSINGS!

What blessings are ours! What 'consolation in Christ'! That is a very valuable blessing from the impeccable Source! Christ encourages believers in Him by coming alongside them to confirm His love and benefits. Think of just three of them: never to be judged for sins;[4] never to be forsaken by God;[5] and no temptations beyond His help and care.[6] What 'comfort of love'! Their guilty conscience is put at peace[7] and they need have no fear of death.[8] The Comforter Himself lives within,[9] and knits their hearts together with other

Christians.[10] What 'fellowship of the Spirit'! The Holy Spirit shares His very presence with them,[11] and gives them a new desire to share themselves, with God and with others who know Christ, and help one another on in the Christian life.[12] What joy and comfort so to pool their blessings, thanksgiving, problems, challenges, opportunities and failures. What 'affection and mercy'! They are given a new love for God and His people, born out of God's loving mercy for them, producing mutual affection for others in the same family of God.[13] But, like us, they all know that they fail God and one another, and need His mercy continually. This feeds their willingness to forgive one another, and fulfils the prayer that Jesus taught.[14] 'Given that' all these blessings belong to them, what should they then do? 'By whatever' benefits He has blessed them, how should they live to show their gratitude to Him and be a blessing to others? And remember that 'we' can be substituted for 'they', 'our' for 'their', and 'us' for 'them'!

2:2 True Christian unity

2 fulfill my joy by being like-minded, having the same love, being of one accord, of one mind.

PAUL'S JOY

Someone has called this letter 'the epistle of joy' and George Duncan wrote a short devotional about it called *The Life of Continual Rejoicing*.[15] Paul introduced us to 'joy' as early as verse 4, and that word, or 'rejoice' or 'rejoicing', occurs thirteen times in this short letter. And always it is in the present tense. His joy is *now*—even if the main reason is the great and certain hope of future everlasting blessing in Christ. Our joy and rejoicing should always be present tense. If we concentrate only on past joys, we can become wistful and over-nostalgic and get morose. We can get like the man who complained that 'even nostalgia isn't what it used to be!' But if we *only anticipate* our future joy, failing to rejoice *now* in our salvation, people will ask where is the 'joy of the Lord' which ' *is* your strength'[16] (my emphasis on 'is'). Even though Jesus told His disciples not to rejoice merely that the spirits were subject to them but that their names were written in heaven,[17] He nevertheless urged on them a current joy about their wonderful future certainty. Yes! Rejoice now! Enjoy the journey!

JOY CAN NEVERTHELESS BE VALIDLY 'TOPPED-UP' BY OTHERS' SPIRITUAL PROGRESS!

But, even so, Paul admits his joy can be 'topped-up', or fulfilled ('made complete') by witnessing the life change that God is bringing about in his beloved Christian friends at Philippi. This new life produces like-mindedness, love and oneness, and puts into practice the consolation, comfort, fellowship, affection and mercy seen in verse 1. Like his fellow apostle, John, He will have 'no greater joy', after his salvation in Christ, 'than to know that my children walk in truth'.[18] Every loving Christian parent and concerned Christian leader will echo these sentiments about their respective physical and spiritual children. One organisation distributes a most encouraging booklet, called *No Greater Joy*, which is filled with the testimonies of those who have found Christ through summer evangelism and who walk with Him.[19] . It encourages all those investing time, effort, and money in the gospel to see it translated into new keen disciples of Christ. No wonder Paul says his joy will be fulfilled if the Philippian Christians honour God in oneness of fellowship, despite the pressures upon them.

WHAT PRODUCES THAT JOY?

Four sets of two words in this verse show what really makes Paul rejoice on behalf of the young church in that Roman colony. The words are: 'like-minded', 'same love', 'one accord', and 'one mind'. The Philippians are urged to *be* three of these requirements and to *have* the other one, namely the 'same love'. There are clear distinctions between some of these characteristics but they merge in some areas. The original Greek for 'like-minded' implies 'thinking the same way'. By 'same love' the Christians are urged not to make distinctions between the way they treat some, to whom they may be more naturally drawn, and others. They are to love one another equally. 'United in spirit' or 'one-souled' or 'together in soul' are alternative translations of 'one accord.' It describes the harmonious togetherness of those with similar motivations, longings, ambitions and aspirations and implies a real spiritual unity with other believers. 'Focused on one purpose' coveys the meaning of being of *'one mind.'*[20] We should apply those criteria to our lives and churches. They do not drive us to unthinking unanimity, but encourage us to look at things biblically and spiritually, and then reach our conclusions with

God's grace. We should honour and love all Christians in our fellowships. This should cause us to put ourselves out, in practical terms, to seek the best for those who may seem the least lovely to us.[21] But do we? We are all part of the body of Christ,[22] and should reflect it in our desire to promote oneness in holy and loving relationships with one another. Others should see us 'endeavouring to keep the unity of the Spirit in the bond of peace'.[23] Practically anything we can do to promote the spiritual welfare of one another helps all this to become a reality. For example, fellowship is always helped by those who quietly pray for and share their daily quiet time thoughts with others, thus encouraging them to do the same. That spontaneous fellowship sets the climate for being 'one-souled' with others. To be of 'one mind', or 'intent on one purpose', encourages us individually and collectively to seek God's glory above all else. Together we can thirst for His blessings on us and others and give ourselves to His service in making the gospel known to those who do not know Christ, both at home and abroad. Our singleness of purpose can then be expressed in the following way:

There is only one thing matters in this passing world of sin:
That our lives should tell for Jesus, be of some account for Him.
Let us then be up and doing—strong in faith and scorning fear—
Trusting Him to keep us faithful in His service here.[24]

2:3 The battle for a lowly mind

3 Let nothing be done through selfish ambition or conceit, but in lowliness of mind let each esteem others better than himself.

TRUE SELF-ESTEEM

Paul now urges on the Philippian church the need to have a lowly mind, to esteem others properly, and to avoid acting through selfish ambition or conceit. This teaching comes with the knowledge that those evil attitudes can carry Christians away captive. We have seen, in chapter 1, that Paul's competitors seek to do him harm by preaching the gospel insincerely from envy, strife and selfish ambition. There have, therefore, already been victims in Philippi. Paul wants his beloved Christian friends to be free from these influences in all areas—not just in preaching—and counsels 'lowliness of mind' as the means of combat and liberty. That will also encourage other Christians who will be esteemed and loved by their brothers and sisters in Christ. There is a battle in all children of God to bring our thinking into line with God's Word, and to achieve a truly lowly mind. Those claiming to possess lowliness of mind have just lost it! The Trojan horse of worldly values and psychology has entered into Christian churches. Now much so-called Christian teaching merely reflects that and adds a Bible verse or two. Particularly we hear, *ad nauseam*, that we must be concerned about and nurture our *self-esteem*. It seems that if we can tell ourselves often enough how good we are, we can do whatever we set our minds to do. In this way we will pull ourselves up by our bootlaces and feel good about it, into the bargain. But surely I am only free to be myself when I have gone down, not up. I should face up to what I really am, not thinking of myself fancifully as something else. I then find liberty in confessing my sinfulness to God and asking Him to cleanse me, change me and fill my life. In gratitude for His unconditional love and kindness to me, in Christ, I can then without unreal pressures realise that, although I can be and do nothing of myself, I am a new person in Christ and can do all things that please God by the strength He gives.[25] David's prayer should be mine—often! 'Create in me a clean heart, O God, and renew a steadfast spirit within me.'[26]

RATING OTHERS MORE HIGHLY

It is only when we see ourselves as we are—'poor, wretched, blind' spiritually[27]—that we can look at others we would criticise and see that we are *not* better than they are. If our source of self-evaluation is found in the mud of secular psychology, it is hardly surprising that the water of our thinking is polluted! Paul saw himself as the 'chief' amongst 'sinners',[28] the 'least of the apostles',[29] and as 'less than the least of all the saints'.[30] There is not much talk about 'self-esteem' here! The man who really walks humbly with God can easily esteem others as 'better than himself' because he really believes it! And that is what God wants: the reversal of the arrogant boasting of proud people in a world where the motto seems to be, 'If you don't blow your own trumpet, no one will blow it for you.' But this verse has as its aim that we should 'each *esteem* others better' than ourselves. The word 'esteem' has as its primary meeting 'to have great respect or high regard for'.[31] We are not to overlook others' weaknesses. In fact there are times when we should humbly and prayerfully confront the failures of others, for their good and blessing. However, we are to have 'great respect' for our brothers and sisters in Christ and genuinely have a 'high regard for' them. How can that be? Simply look at their good points, which can teach us so much. Or consider the battles they face in their lives. Admit that we might have run away or capitulated under similar stresses and strains: we can so easily and wrongly see as stains what really are scars received in battles from which we would have fled in fear. Or we can look at their forward progress, compared with our static spirituality. Or consider their honesty, in admitting their sins and failures, which challenges our willingness to be open. Soon we may see that the weakest of Christians has qualities or achievements that we lack. Instead of looking down from the 'high ground', we should praise God for His continuing work in them and ask if we are open to change for Him.

THE TWO FOES AGAINST A LOWLY MIND

Paul warns the Philippian believers that here are two spiritual 'thugs' who will seek to rob them of that lowly mind that esteems others better than themselves. They both have long and nasty criminal records and have stolen from multitudes of other Christians so many valuable possessions that God has given them. Their many spoils—taken from churches and individuals around the world and from different time spans—include graciousness, concern for others, generosity, effective service and unity. These regular offenders need no identification parade! They are well known! They are 'selfish ambition' and 'conceit'. How many of God's servants and God's works have been harmed by their violent assaults? How much blessing has been lost through their wicked behaviour when they disguised themselves as 'resolute determination' and 'boldness' rather than 'selfish ambition' and 'conceit'? Ambition itself is right, not wrong. But what kind of ambition? Not 'selfish' ambition—but the ambition to crown Christ as king in our lives and in the hearts of others. The ambition we should seek should be that of John the Baptist: 'He must increase, but I must decrease'.[32] Paul's desire to major on Christ and minor on Paul should be our ambition and goal, too.[33] *Those* ambitions can help us to cultivate a lowly mind and a higher view of others than ourselves, by God's grace. But where we seek our own gain, preferences, way or agenda, true spirituality evaporates and we are so taken with self that others take a back seat. The cross needs to be applied to the sinner as well as to his sins. We need to regard our own ambitions, as opposed to God-given ones, as crucified too. That crucifixion will precede the resurrection of God's will in our priorities and in our life. The same is true of conceit, a 'high, often exaggerated, opinion of oneself or one's accomplishments, vanity'.[34] When my ambition is selfish, then conceit is my own empty applause at what I perceive myself to *have become* or to *have accomplished*. It goes hand in hand with the 'self-made man' who, so obviously, worships his creator—himself. It has absolutely no place in the life of one who understands that he can only stand before God because of God's great mercy and grace, and that any real and lasting accomplishments are only because of God's enabling, gifts, and grace. No man can ever take any credit for that, whoever he is. Like the Philippians, we face these two potential destroyers, selfish ambition and conceit. Paul tells the Philippian church and us: 'Let nothing be done' through them. Where we have tolerated or encouraged either or both of these wicked influences, we must repent of and forsake them. This requires a willingness to die to self and let Christ live His life in us on a daily basis. As a much-used book over the years, *Calvary Road*, puts it: 'This simply means that the hard, unyielding self, which justifies itself, wants its own way, stands up for its rights, and seeks its own glory, at last bows its head to God's will, admits its wrong, gives up its own way to Jesus, surrenders its rights, and discards its own glory—that the Lord Jesus might have all and be all. In other words, it is dying to self and self-attitudes.'[35] Those violent thugs of selfish ambition and conceit need to be apprehended and dealt with on a daily basis for us today, just as is the case at Philippi.

2:4 The practical outworking—others' interests

4 Let each of you look out not only for his own interests, but also for the
  interests of others.

THE BALANCE

Looking out for one another is to be the norm, Paul tells his brothers and sisters. Each has to look after his, or her, own matters of course. Being concerned for others does *not* mean that they ignore the things they have to do for themselves. God knows that they also have lives to live. Paul makes this very clear to the Philippians. He says, 'Let each of you look out *not only* for his own interests'. Clearly, God knows that we, too, have our own 'vineyard' to keep, spiritually (our own devotional life) and physically (our own everyday life). Jesus endorsed, as the second greatest commandment, that you should love 'your neighbour *as yourself*.'[36] It is quite right for the Philippians to give some attention and concern to themselves, otherwise 'as yourself' would be a meaningless addition to 'love your neighbour.' So looking after others' interests, important as it is, is no reason for allowing metaphorical weeds to grow in the gardens of our own lives. We should be well organised and efficient in our use of time.

BUT DO NOT FORGET THE INTERESTS OF OTHERS

But it does not stop there. Other people are important too, and they, and we, *do* have to love our neighbours. This simple command of the apostle, to the Philippian Christians and to us, to look out for the interests of others, should cause us to search our hearts in the twenty-first century. Whilst it true that we must not ignore our own interests, we must bring them under His control and leadership and put God first. After all, the first commandment is to 'love the LORD your God with all your heart, with all your soul, with all your strength, and with all your mind.'[37] When that is applied, we will love our neighbours better. The mark of the God-honouring Christian is his selflessness that involves him in the lives of other people, Christian and non-Christian. He really must 'look out … for the interests of others'. It is of little value coming through the spiritual battle with selfish ambition and conceit, and cultivating the qualities of like-mindedness, mutual love, unity in the spirit by being 'one-souled', and singular purposefulness, if we then do nothing! We are to be concerned about our brothers in Christ, and seek to help and support them, and about lost sinners, and seek to win them for Christ. I know a very busy and effective pastor who will always seem to drop what he is doing for himself to help others. He is so respected and valued as he thereby adorns the gospel of God. No wonder people listen to him when he needs to bring a rebuke or give unpopular counsel, and it is little surprise that his influence for the gospel has spread far more widely than the town where he exercises his ministry. He is a blessing to Christians on other continents too. *He always has time for others.* I think also of the man who counselled me when I was a backslider and helped me back to Christ, teaching me my formative lessons in Christian service and evangelism. He operated very successfully at the top of his professional tree, had a large family, chaired the elders of an evangelical church, headed up two vibrant Bible-believing interdenominational evangelistic works, was an author in his profession and of Christian books, contributed regularly to a Christian periodical, preached every Sunday and during the week nights too, conducted open-air meetings in his lunch times, *but he always had time for individuals and for their concerns.* Different missionaries have told me that he was quietly faithful in writing to them regularly—a thing no one else knew. Many men and women are in influential roles for Christ throughout the world today, because he nurtured individuals and always was available to advise and to help at any time of the day or night. And his wife supported him in it. He made time to look out for the interests of others, and his influence was great because of it. True, we must look on our own interests, but let us never forget the interests of others. That is close to the heart of God.

Notes

1 **Rev. Ralph P. Martin,** *Tyndale New Testament Commentaries: The Epistle of Paul to the Philippians* (Tyndale Press), page 90.

2 TAB, Philippians 2:1.

3 Exodus 5:7.

4 Romans 8:1.

5 Hebrews 13:5.

6 1 Corinthians 10:13.

7 2 Thessalonians 3:16.

8 1 Corinthians 15:53.

9 John 14:16.

10 1 John 3:14.

11 1 Corinthians 3:16.

12 Hebrews 10:24,25.

13 1 John 5:2.

14 Matthew 6:12.

15 Rev. George B. Duncan, *The Life of Continual Rejoicing* (New Mildmay Press).

16 Nehemiah 8:10.

17 Luke 10:20.

18 3 John 4.

19 *No Greater Joy,* written and published by United Beach Missions, free of charge from UBM, Spring Cottage, Spring Road, Leeds, LS6 1AD: Tel: 0113 230 4362.

20 John MacArthur (author of commentary/notes and general editor), *The MacArthur Study Bible, NKJV,* (Word Bibles), note on Philippians 2:2, page 1822.

21 Acts 10:34 (AV).

22 1 Corinthians 12:27.

23 Ephesians 4:3.

24 *Sing—Young Life Choruses* (National Young Life Campaign), number 206.

25 Romans 12:3; 2 Corinthians 5:17; Philippians 4:13.

26 Psalm 51:10.

27 From **C. Elliott,** 'Just As I Am', *Christian Life Hymnal* (National Young Life Campaign), number 202.

28 1 Timothy 1:15.

29 1 Corinthians 15:9.

30 Ephesians 3:8.

31 *Collins English Dictionary, Third Edition* (HarperCollins Publishers), page 532.

32 John 3:30.

33 2 Corinthians 4:5.

34 *Collins English Dictionary, Third Edition* (HarperCollins Publishers), page 332.

35 Roy Hession, *The Calvary Road* (Christian Literature Crusade), page 15.

36 Matthew 19:19.

37 Matthew 22:36–38.

Mini-overview 2:5 to 2:11

Christ, our Example.

The humble mind of God our Saviour is shown in His incarnation and crucifixion.

His sevenfold Self-humbling is met by the greatest ever step of exaltation, through resurrection to ascension to heaven!

2:5 Christ's example to be applied, not just appreciated

5 Let this mind be in you which was also in Christ Jesus,

THE LINK

We have heard Paul exhorting the Philippian church concerning the need to be like-minded. They must strive together 'with one mind', 'for the faith of the gospel', fulfil his joy by being 'of one mind', and exercise 'lowliness of mind' towards one another. They have received admonitions about how to live the Christian life in the context of suffering, opposition and conflict. They have been reminded of the great resource blessings available 'in Christ'. Paul now turns to *how* this can be accomplished. The apostle turns to the One with the solution for this and every question and problem. He talks about the 'mind ... which was also in Christ Jesus' before making practical applications for them.

HOLY GROUND

We are about to tread on truly sacred ground. Paul, under the inspiration of the Holy Spirit, continues to pen not only his own thoughts but also the very Word of God. He is about to reveal something of the mind of the Lord Jesus Christ, shown in what He did and why. This passage so clearly and simply puts the staggering facts of what Wesley called 'God contracted to a span: incomprehensibly made Man'. No words can do justice to this glorious and gracious theme. Here is a 'purple patch' of Scripture. All God's Word is equally *inspired* and infallible, but some parts are more *inspiring* than others. (Who would not prefer the Emmaus Road account[1] to a genealogy in 1 Chronicles? Yet the genealogies, too, show the factuality and dependability of the Bible and to ignore them is to ignore the footings and foundations of a building.[2]) This is one of the most inspiring passages of the Bible, to put alongside Isaiah chapter 53 or the gospel accounts of Gethsemane, the crucifixion and resurrection of the 'Friend of sinners'.

THE ANTIQUE MIRROR

Imagine a valuable antique mirror in a high-class shop. The pundits and experts gather round to examine it and appreciate its beauty and worth. That is good. But it is not why the mirror was originally made. The first owner might have been an elegant lady who brushed her hair in front of it. She would have used the mirror to see how she looked and to improve her appearance. So often we Christians rightly admire the Bible as God's inspired, infallible and revealed truth—especially a passage like the one which we now consider. *But that is not enough!* God gave us the mirror of His Word to *use*, not merely to appreciate and admire. It is true that this passage succinctly and beautifully emphasises Christ's deity, humility, incarnation, manhood, filial obedience, sacrificial death, resurrection, ascension, glorification and victorious second coming—all in seven verses!—but the passage is there *primarily for a practical reason*. What reason? To make the Philippians, and Christians throughout history, imitate Christ. That can be done by God's grace and enabling alone. The very passage starts with the injunction 'Let this mind be in you which was also in Christ Jesus'. For them, it is only by having the Saviour's indwelling mind that they can strive together 'with one mind' 'for the faith of the gospel', fulfil his joy by being 'of one mind', and exercise 'lowliness of mind' towards each other. Those things cannot be achieved by human effort alone. They need the Spirit's aid through the Saviour's mind. Christ has to be our Saviour from sin before His mind can dwell in us and enable us to follow in His steps. Christ's example cannot save us, since we are saved by grace through faith and not by trying to imitate Him. But when we know and surrender our mind to Him as our Saviour and Lord, He is not only our Redeemer, Saviour, Substitute, Advocate, and Lord—He is also our Example to follow. As He indwells us and we abide in Him, we need to heed that 'He who says he abides in Him ought himself also to walk just as He walked'.[3] We must continually ask God to replace our mind and its selfish thoughts, which produce not only selfish ambition and conceit but also a host of other ugly sins, with the mind and thoughts of Jesus. That is especially so to know His genuine humility and to esteem others better than ourselves. It will produce that concern for others that we can never engender ourselves. That mind was also clean, pure and holy. When we surrender to Christ's mind in humility, we will also experience His desire for purity and holiness, which are dealt with later in this letter. But *how* can we let His mind be in us?

Here are some steps to knowing His mind.

1. Make sure you are converted. Christ must be in your heart before His thoughts can dominate you mind.

2. Equally be sure that your desire is to crown Him as your Lord in every area of your life. This may mean specific repentance on specific points and a turning to God for His cleansing and to ask Him to lovingly control you. Keep short accounts with God, confessing and forsaking sin as it arises, and thus avoid the build up of un-confessed sin which would become like sea-weed around the propeller of your Christian life. Especially confess failures to engage the mind of Christ as soon as you realise, and believe you are forgiven and cleansed. Admit to others that you are wrong when you know you are. Ask God to fill you with His Spirit constantly.

3. Get to know His mind every day from His Word. Read the Bible much. Study it carefully, both on your own and in the fellowship of others. Let the principles of God's Word be your highway.

4. Exclude all the voluntary inputs that you allow into your life that feed sewage into the clean water system of your soul. Do not watch videos or TV programmes where language is bad or blasphemous, where wrong is portrayed as normal, or where there is sexual immodesty or perversion. Similarly, do not feast your eyes or mind on literature which will take the edge off any holiness you seek. Refuse to seek your pleasures where the temptation to dishonour Christ is strong or where peer pressure is overwhelming to conform. If you drink from polluted sources, it will affect your health and degrade your mind. That is not the mind 'which was also in Christ Jesus'. The immediate context of Philippians chapter 2 is the

humility and like-mindedness of the mind of Christ. But if Satan can enter your mind through dirt and immorality of thought, he has a bridgehead from which to attack all aspects of the mind of Christ within you.

5. Cultivate the habit of immediate obedient trust—and pray each day for grace to do that, because it never comes easily.

6. Ask yourselves what Jesus would do in any given situation and then ask God's grace to help you do the same. Especially ask if His humility is reflected in your attitude and action.

7. Each day, seek to do what the commands and principles of God's Word demand. But do not wait until you *feel* you can do that. By faith trust Him and you will find He will enable you as you obey Him;

8. Cultivate a good and open relationship with a spiritual minded Christian of the same sex who will tell you what you ought to hear and not what you want to hear. Be open with him or her, in confidence, and pray with him or her.

9. Avoid giving and receiving flattery. It produces the wrong mindset.

10. Read good Christian books and listen to good Christian sermons and Bible studies. Their tapes or CDs will be of more benefit to you more than any secular radio station!

Howard Guiness' book *Sacrifice* has been the instrument of bringing many into the blessing of a surrendered life. In a paragraph on *The Mind and Its Thoughts* he says: 'Our thoughts are moulded largely by those things which enter our minds. It is, therefore, of vital importance to see that our mental food is chosen as carefully as our physical food. To assimilate mental poison is far more dangerous than to take physical poison because its presence is not so easily detected or eliminated, and its effects are more insidiously harmful and often less obnoxious. How important it is to choose correctly and adamantly refuse anything less than the best!' He then asks some questions which are pertinent for us also as we consider letting the mind of Christ be in us. Here are some: 'What sort of books do we read?'; 'Are we guided in what we read?'; 'Do wandering thoughts and daydreams fritter away our time?'; 'Are we doing a *real* day's work?'; 'Are we disciplined in our reading of the Bible?'; 'Have you ever tried memorising an important chapter or Epistle?'; 'What sort of pictures do we look at?' (Note—when Guiness wrote this, televisions and videos were not available to watch—I wonder what he would have said about them today?) He then states that 'All deliberate sin starts in the mind' (my emphasis) and concludes by quoting Philippians 4:8 (see chapter 4 of this section) and 2 Corinthians 10:5 which, in the NKJV, is rendered 'bringing every thought into captivity to the obedience of Christ'.4

THE APPLICATION AND THE MOTIVATION

The immediate Philippian application of having the mind of Christ within is, as we have seen, not relating to the mind's purity but to that humility that esteems others and does them good. But the wider principle of the use of our mind should be faced also, as Howard Guiness faced it. Without His mind, your Christian life will always tend to run into the gutter of your own sinfulness. Above all, the motivation and result of all that you do should be actively to encourage letting *His* mind be in you. You may not always instinctively know what His mind is, but more often than not you will know full well what it is *not* if you are honest with yourself and God. Humble willingness is the key.

2:6 Christ—Genuinely God

6 who, being in the form of God, did not consider it robbery to be equal with God,

'BEING IN THE FORM OF GOD'

The Christians at Philippi are going to be taught about what 'the mind which was also in Christ Jesus' implies. Paul starts by reminding them that Christ's mind is the mind of God and so any humility they need to be like-minded and lowly minded is nothing compared to the humility He possessed. As we shall see, the letter to the Philippians and the Bible as a whole teach clearly that the Lord Jesus Christ is both fully God and fully Man at the same time. A reading of Hebrews chapter 1 and John chapter 1 specifically, and the gospels generally, shows that He is the second Person in the Trinity, He is the pre-existent Son of God, He claimed and exercised the attributes of Godhead, and He accepted worship as God. Jesus is God. He is also Man. He is at the same time fully God and fully Man. Verses 6, 7 and 8 refer to Christ Jesus 'being in the form of God', being 'equal with God', 'taking the form of a bondservant' and 'coming in the likeness of men'. Consider first Paul's phrase 'Being in the form of God' and especially what some commentators say about the words 'being' and 'form'. Martin says '*Being in the form of God* looks back to our Lord's pre-temporal existence as the second Person of the Trinity. His being is eternal.' He then goes on to say that '*The form of God* may be taken in two ways' and explains them as God defined by His attributes, and Christ's Godhead shown by His pre-existence and His position in glory.[5] Davidson also focuses on the words 'being' (which refers to His essential eternal essence) and 'form' and concludes, 'Essence, existence or being, is fundamental and must exist in some form and when once adopted always keeps to the same form. Form is the permanent expression of existence. Thus we have the form of God, the form of an angel, the form of man, and the form of a beast; all of which are immovable manifestations of being or existence'. He then goes on to compare that with the word 'fashion' in the AV, (translated 'appearance' in the NKJV text), in verse 8, which is a temporary state (as fashions are today!).[6] MacArthur states: 'Paul affirms that Jesus eternally has been God. The usual Greek word for "being" is not used here. Instead Paul chose another term that stresses the essence of a person's nature—his continuous state or condition. Paul also could have chosen one of two Greek words for "form", but he chose the one that specifically denotes the essential unchanging character of something—what it is in and of itself. The fundamental doctrine of Christ's deity has always encompassed these crucial characteristics.'[7] The insights of these well-read men of God confirm what is obvious to every honest reader of the Bible. Not only is the Lord Jesus Christ God, but by Scripture and logic He always was God and He always will be God. He is God because of His inherent divine nature as God the Son. He is God because of His eternal nature as the pre-existent Son of God. Yet He became fully Man whilst remaining fully God. These conclusions reflect the teaching of Scripture as a whole. In discussing the effect of the resurrection of Jesus on Christian teaching, in my earlier book *The Resurrection: the unopened gift*, I tried to make it clear from the Bible that Jesus Himself showed His claims to deity in that 'He confidently applied to Himself the Old Testament title of Jehovah God', 'He claimed that seeing Him was seeing God', 'He accepted worship' and 'He did what God would do.'[8] As you would expect, the apostle's teaching here is perfectly in accord with that of his Master.

EQUALITY WITH GOD

It is therefore no surprise to us that Paul tells the Philippians that Jesus Christ did not consider Himself as illegally or dishonestly appropriating the claim to be God: He 'did not consider it robbery to be equal with God'. The Greek word rendered 'equal' describes things identical in size, quality, amount, type, and number. Jesus is always equal to God and never suggested otherwise in His life on earth. If He had been less than God, Jesus would have been guilty of both attempted robbery and cynical blasphemy. Other translations or paraphrases of 'did not consider it robbery to equal with God' are: 'did not count equality with God a thing to be grasped' (RSV); 'did not cling to His prerogatives as God's equal' (Phillips); 'counted it not a prize to be on an equality with God' (RV); 'did not think that equality with God was a thing to be eagerly grasped or retained' (AB); 'did not regard equality with God something to be grasped' (NIV); and 'did not regard equality with God a thing to be grasped' (or 'utilized' or 'asserted', as per the margin) (NASB). All the versions have two crucial truths in common: first, Jesus Christ was and is God; second, although He was (and is) fully possessed of all God's essence, attributes, characteristics, powers, gifts, prerogatives and authority, in becoming Man, He was willing to release His grip on the earthly *exercise* of some aspects of His Godhead. In His equality with the Father He accepted human limitations, without ever resigning His essential being and form of God. This He did to come to earth to die to accomplish the salvation of sinners. Regarding His willingness to 'step down', the verses which immediately follow will demonstrate the truth of the great Christmas carol, *Hark, the herald angels sing*, when it states (and note the wording of the first line):

Mild, He lays His glory by:
Born that man no more may die.
Born to raise the sons of earth.
Born to give them second birth.

For example, as the 'Man, Christ Jesus', He willingly and lovingly laid aside on earth His continuous experience of His dazzling heavenly glory, which was pre-existent and is eternally lasting, even though His glory was evident in His every act and thought as He 'dwelt among us'.[9] That He willingly curtailed His exercise of His omnipresence, when in a human body, is obvious. He voluntarily restricted His knowledge so that He chose not to know the exact timing of His second coming.[10] But He never laid aside His deity. He did not seek to 'rob' to gain it, and He never insisted on His rights regarding it when He came as Man to be rejected and to die. It was in this sense alone that Jesus could say that 'My Father is greater than I' (literally, 'more exalted than I'), without contradicting the fact that He 'did not consider it robbery to be equal with God'. The very fact that the incarnate Son of God found it necessary to say those words is itself evidence of His deity. How many people throughout history needed to assure the public that they were not greater than God the Father? No one, but the Lord Jesus Christ! Jesus made it clear that, before returning to His place of co-equality with the Father in heaven, His self-humbling on earth (see verse 8, below) meant that His Father was temporarily greater in the exercise of some of the prerogatives of Godhead. In His rescue mission to lost men and women, the Lord Jesus temporarily suspended His exercise of some of those, but never suspended His deity. As has been well observed, 'Though Christ had all the rights, privileges, and honours of deity … which he was worthy of and could not be disqualified from … His attitude was not to cling to those things or His position but to be willing to give them up for a season.'[11]

2:7 What Jesus did to Himself
7 but made Himself of no reputation, taking the form of a bondservant, and coming in the likeness of men.

REPUTATION
No one with a good reputation likes to lose it. 'It takes a very short time to lose a good reputation but a long, long time to get another one.'[12] It is, accordingly, completely against human nature and self-interest deliberately to *lose* a good one. Jesus had the best of reputations, as God, in the best of places, in heaven! He was, as we have seen, God in essence and

form. He was the Lord of glory, the one who could say, 'Before Abraham was, I AM'.[13] He was the Creator and Sustainer of the universe. The brash boast of Cassius Clay, alias Mohammed Ali, was 'I am the greatest!' The Beatles said they were more important than Jesus Christ. These claims are seen as empty by comparison with Jesus who is 'the Alpha and the Omega, the First and the Last'.[14] He was known as that in heaven as the eternal God long before He took on flesh. His reputation (quite literally!) could not have been higher. He could easily have maintained it, without any effort, throughout eternity—if His love for us had not motivated Him to come to earth to die for us. As part of that process and sacrifice He *made Himself of no reputation*. No one else could take His true reputation from Him—He alone could have 'made Himself' like that. The verse continues by saying, 'taking the form of a bondservant'. That means 'slave'. Before ever Jesus *did* anything to demonstrate it, He had already resolved that His reputation must go and He must become a human slave. I imagine that the angels must have been amazed when they heard that the One whom they reverently worshipped would go to earth to die for sinners and that, to do this, He had already 'made Himself of no reputation'.

JESUS 'EMPTIED HIMSELF'

My Interlinear Greek New Testament puts the actual Greek word order of this verse (which obviously had to be reorganised to be fully understood in English) as follows: 'Christ Jesus, who in [the] form of God subsisting, not robbery deemed [it] *the* to be equal *things* with God, *but himself emptied* [the form] of a slave taking, in likeness of men.' (My emphasis on 'but Himself emptied'.) 'Made Himself of no reputation' means that He temporarily 'emptied Himself' at His incarnation, not of His nature as God, but of some of the rights and benefits accruing to Him because of His deity. This self-emptying is known as *kenosis*. We have already noted that these included His glory in heaven and some of His prerogatives of Deity. His self-emptying also included His unique and intrinsic authority in heaven, His eternal riches, and His unbroken fellowship with His Father. His Father, inseparable from His Son from eternity past, would have to punish His Son with His eternal judgement on sin, because Jesus would bear our sins in His body on the cross. Regarding His prerogatives and authority, He nevertheless reclaimed some of these when it would glorify His Father and bless others. As He was (and is) nothing less than the eternal God, He resumed all His prerogatives at His triumphant return to glory as the crucified, resurrected, ascended Victor. But before that could happen, His self-emptying was essential, even though the 'self-life' of Jesus was never tainted with even a hint of sin. Frank Houghton's hymn so well expresses the redeeming love of Christ which surrendered the perfect riches of heaven when, for us, He poured out Himself in poverty on earth, to become our Emmanuel:

Thou Who wast rich, beyond all splendour,
All for love's sake becamest poor:
Thrones for a manger didst surrender,
Sapphire-paved courts for stable floor.
Thou Who wast rich beyond all splendour,
All for love's sake becamest poor.[15]

Against the resolute determination of the Saviour to do that, the Philippian saints will see what is involved in applying this same mind of their Saviour to their own attitude, situation, relationships and service. Self-image and pettiness must evaporate before the burning heat of such love. We also should ask if our reputation and 'self-image' are too important to us. Are we prepared to be so identified with the Lord Jesus Christ in our life and witness that, above everything else, we want to be known as lovers and followers of Him? Are we prepared to descend the ladder of our own pride and consider others in the way the Philippians are told to? If the eternal and glorious Son of God emptied Himself of some of His privileges of His perfection, then why are we so slow to allow God to empty us of our sin and selfish aspirations and preferences? Let us turn the statement of C. T. Studd, who declined a fortune to serve God in sacrificial missionary service, into a question: 'If Jesus Christ is God and died for me, then what sacrifice can be too great for me to make for Him?'

NO REPUTATION—STAGE ONE
It seems that up to half the population of the Roman colony at Philippi are

bondservants (or 'slaves'). When Paul uses the image of a bondservant to explain how Jesus came to earth, thus demonstrating 'the mind that is in Christ Jesus', the church members will immediately be on his wavelength. The abandoning of self-reputation and determination to empty Himself meant, for Jesus, 'taking the form of a bondservant'. 'A bondservant'! The Creator of the universe, the Lord of glory, the King of kings and Lord of lords—a 'bondservant'? When Christ came to the earth it was to serve. Not for Him to stand on His rights or seek earth's best comforts. No! 'A bondservant'! A slave! Slaves had no rights. Most slaves were not slaves by their own choice. They had been born into slavery, or had it imposed upon them. Just occasionally a particular slave would so love his master that he might choose to continue as his slave[16]—but that was not how he had first come into that bondage. Most of the slaves at Philippi cannot wait to be set free. Some of them are, no doubt, in the church hearing Paul's letter from prison read to them. But Jesus chose slavery for Himself. He made Himself a slave. Perhaps that is why Paul and Timothy were able so gratefully and enthusiastically to make that same choice, to be the 'bondservants of Jesus Christ' as we saw in 1:1. So here we see the One with all power and authority putting Himself in the position where His personal rights are suspended, and where He binds Himself to serve unconditionally the rebel sinners whom He has come to save. Rightly did He say: 'For who is the greater, he who sits at the table or he who serves? Is it not he who sits at the table? Yet I am among you as the One Who serves.'[17] Down through the years, some Christians have answered the challenge of that truth by putting life and health at risk to serve Him and reach the lost. Some have gone to areas of great disease and risk for their Saviour, and have suffered and died as a result. Some missionaries in the Philippines went to live on Smokey Mountain, a huge burning refuse dump, to reach its residents. Average life expectancy on that tip is only thirty-five years. Others have lived in a better climate and area, but have so pushed themselves to 'spend and be spent' for others that their health has suffered. Self-imposed slavery leading to His death was in the mind of the Master who told His disciples: 'He who is the greatest among you, let him be as the younger, and he who governs as he who serves.'[18] This was not mere self-denial: It was denial of self. 'Denial of self is not the same as self-denial. The latter means forgoing certain foods, pleasures, or possessions. But denial of self means such complete submission to the lordship of Christ that self has no rights or authority at all.'[19]

NO REPUTATION—STAGE TWO

We now consider the Lord Jesus 'coming in the likeness of men' as a slave to earth. Perhaps Jesus could have accomplished a mighty step down from His position of full deity and come as a super-angel, and still have been a comparative slave. That would have given Him positional equality with Satan, a fallen angel.[20] But that would not have allowed Jesus to come 'in the likeness of sinful flesh'[21] as man's representative, the second Adam,[22] so that God was able to condemn our sin 'in the flesh'.[23] He could not have 'borne our sins in His own body on the tree'[24] as the truly sinless and perfect human being. Never could He, as the great High Priest, have sympathised with the human temptations and weaknesses of either the Christians in Philippi or with us, as the Bible states He did.[25] Also His bodily resurrection from the dead would have meant nothing if that body had not been a human body. It was in that sinless and morally spotless body of the 'one Mediator', 'the Man, Christ Jesus'[26] that Jesus was both punished for our sins and raised again as proof that His total sacrifice was accepted by God the Father as a substitute for us. Thus it was important that, when Jesus 'made Himself of no reputation' and took upon Himself 'the form of a bondservant', the bondservant was not of angelic nature, or divine nature only, but that He was a man. Thus, as a bondservant, Jesus came 'in the likeness of men'. Jesus was fully God and fully Man at the same time, when He came to earth. As God, it meant that the efficacy of His sacrifice was infinite in worth and eternal in nature. As Man it meant that sin was borne and punished in the flesh of His complete humanity when God the Father 'made Him who knew no sin to be sin for us, that we might become the righteousness of God in Him'.[27] But what a humbling step to take on Himself the very flesh of those who had caused the great problem by rebelling in sin against God's will. To go on a rescue mission as the Supreme Being would have been amazing. For God actually to visit the earth in Person would surely have been infinitesimally more remarkable and staggering than man going to the moon. But the personal coming of that Supreme Being to earth, *as a man*, blows the mind. I recall hearing one preacher describing how he once inadvertently trod on an anthill and crushed some of the ants. He painted the picture of dead and injured ants lying on the ground and how sorry he felt for them. (I would have found it hard to be as emotional!) He went on to ask how he could possibly relay his sadness and concern to those ants: he could not talk to them for he was a man and they were insects. The only way it could have been possible would have been if he could have become an ant himself and crawl among them and communicate with them and try to help them. But he could not do that, because humanity cannot become an ant. He then powerfully and quietly explained that we were like those ants, crushed and maimed by sin (not by the foot of the Creator, of course—here the illustration came short.) We were lost and doomed and helpless. What could God do? *He became a man—the 'Man, Christ Jesus'.*[28] As perfect Man He dwelt among us and showed His love and care for us. He had to take flesh upon Himself to do that. And then, in that flesh, His supreme and ultimate act of help was to go to the cross to die for our sins. He could only do that because He came 'in the likeness of men' to give us 'the right to become children of God' and to 'believe in His name'.[29]

2:8 THE CROSS

8 And being found in appearance as a man, He humbled Himself and became obedient to the point of death, even the death of the cross.

EXAMPLE NOT ENOUGH

There are some misguided preachers and teachers who assert that the blood of Christ was of more value when circulating through his veins as our perfect example, than when it flowed from His body on the cross as our sin-bearer and substitute. Any such assertion is not true. The example of the God-man's self-humbling, His self-imposed slavery and self-emptying and His taking upon Himself the flesh of humanity could never bring a sinner a decimal fraction of a millimetre nearer to God. This is despite the fact that in that flesh Jesus never sinned but lived a perfect and righteous life. Everything about Jesus—His person and His work—emphasise the great gulf between His perfection and our sinful pride and failure. He was the one great Person who was born to die, and whose biggest accomplishment could never be realised without His shed blood. He came to go to 'the death of the cross'. He could not have done that unless He first was 'found in appearance as a man' (or, AV, 'found in fashion as a man'). His journey down to death followed further self-humbling after He appeared on earth 'as a man'. Emmanuel, 'God with us'[30] was clothed in true humanity, but He still had further to go. It was vital that He should do that in order to 'became obedient *to the point* of death'. (The words 'to the point of' are italicised in the Bible to indicate that they are not there in the original but are added to help to give the best meaning.) When Jesus 'became obedient' to death, it does not mean that, at any time, He was previously disobedient. For Him, this was simply His first—and only—experience of a situation where He would choose willingly to die.

ONENESS IN THE GODHEAD

This was in accord with will of God, agreed upon between the Persons of the Trinity. The Bible says that 'the Father has *sent* the Son *as* Saviour of the world'.[31] But Jesus, the eternal Son, was a willing party to the agreement that He would come to die. Jesus said: 'My Father loves Me because I lay down My life that I may take it again. No one takes it from Me, but I lay it down of Myself. I have power to lay it down and I have power to take it again'.[32] He then added that it was the Father's command to the Son that He, Jesus, personally had this power to exercise. Again, we know that 'God so loved the world that *He gave* His only begotten Son',[33] and also that 'the Son of God loved me and *gave Himself* for me'.[34] There was perfect oneness in the Godhead—the Father would send the Son, and the Son would willingly come, to die for us. Now consider the part of God, the Holy Spirit, in this. It was by His agency that the baby born at Bethlehem was conceived.[35] Although the deity of Christ is already strongly, clearly and biblically established from what has already been discussed, is it not logical to deduce that the Holy Spirit thereby imparted His own nature to Mary's baby? Is it not true that any offspring takes the nature of his father and his mother? The human nature of Jesus Christ was imparted by His sexually pure virgin mother. The Bible clearly shows that the nature of God, the Holy Spirit, is divine. In any case the very involvement of God, the Holy Spirit, in the virgin conception of the Emmanuel Babe demonstrates powerfully that each of the three Persons of the Trinity was fully involved and agreed in the saving mission of Christ.

THE COST OF THE CROSS

Whole books have been written about the cross of the Lord Jesus Christ—and still the wonder of the cross can never be exhausted. In the context of this verse it is the cross as applied to the Self-humbling of the incarnate Son that is emphasised. His cross provided redemption, substitution, atonement, sacrifice, ransom, pardon, expiation, propitiation, mediation, mercy, and forgiveness. But it is in the amazing context of the willingness of Jesus Christ, the Lord of glory, to go even lower than slavery, than humanity, than self-emptying, and than death itself that we will now consider that cross. We will not ask now how His death could save us from an eternal hell, from the viewpoint of biblical theology, though that is by far the most important aspect of it. Rather, we will briefly look at what it personally cost the sinless Saviour, who deserved the limitless praise and worship of men and of angels, to come to die on the cross for us. Again, we need to hear Paul urging both the Philippians and us to see this as the continuation of the working out of the 'mind that was in Christ Jesus' which have to be applied by them and us in the difficult and demanding circumstances of life.

'THE DEATH OF A COMMON CRIMINAL'

I am a cautious user of paraphrases, rather than translations, of the Bible because they can carry a highly subjective view of any verse into the public gaze. But sometimes they do help. I feel this is the case with J. B. Phillips' italicised rendering of part of this verse, which follows in its entirety.[36] 'And, having become man, he humbled himself by living a life of utter obedience, even to the extent of dying, *and the death he died was the death of a common criminal*'. Phillips immediately makes the mental link between 'the death of the cross' and '*the death of a common criminal*'. He is right. Death by crucifixion was totally unknown when the detailed prophecies of Christ's death were made in Psalm 22 and Isaiah 53 hundreds of years before. But the degrading and painful means of execution by crucifying convicted criminals was in use when Jesus walked on the earth.

(The wonder of the Bible as God's inspired Word is again endorsed by this fact.) That is why Jesus was flanked by two thieves,[37] and substituted for Barabbas.[38] From being the very centre of glory, He sank to the shame and degradation of public execution as a common criminal hanging between two common criminals! But His route to that depth was via a sinless and spotless life, in which He did nothing but good and showed nothing but love and righteousness. What a stoop of grace that was! In its train this meant loneliness, and identification with evil, which we can only just begin to understand.

REMEMBER HIS MIND

What a perfectly humble 'mind … in Christ Jesus' we see, just as the Philippians saw it too.

Remember that the Lord Jesus Christ had the mind of supreme humility that allowed and motivated Him to do this for the glory of His Father and for the blessing of sinners. It is this massive humility of mind that Paul asks his Christian friends to consider both at Philippi then and worldwide now. This is the mind that must be in us! This should drive us back in humility to God for His help and grace.

2:9 The exaltation of Christ

9 Therefore God also has highly exalted Him and given Him a name which is above every name;

THE HUMILITY OF CHRIST

For Jesus, His self-humbling could never include repentance from sin, because He had no sin.[39] But He is our example of true spiritual grace. If He, the Almighty God, would voluntarily deal in such humility, then how much more should pardoned and reprieved rebels approach God and each other in a humble and self-effacing spirit. That is the challenge for those in the church in that Roman colony and in churches everywhere else. Jesus is the role model for us all. No one could show humility as He did. 'But,' you may say, 'I thought this verse dealt with His exaltation and not with His humiliation again.' Yes, but to see how and why He was so elevated, we first need to remind ourselves that His elevation was preceded by the great self-humbling we have considered. And second, we need to realise that the same principle applies to the spiritual life of us all.

THE STEPS HE TOOK DOWN

So let us trace His seven willing and progressive steps down from His position 'in the form of God' and 'equal with God' to His death on Calvary for you and me:

1. He 'made Himself of no reputation'—He 'emptied Himself';
2. He took upon Himself 'the form of a bondservant';
3. He came in 'the likeness of men';
4. As a man, 'He humbled Himself';
5. He 'became obedient';
6. His obedience took Him to 'the point of death';
7. His death was 'even the death of the cross'.

J. Sidlow Baxter comments: 'Marvel again at the wonder of it—God ... Man ... Slave ... Criminal! In time or eternity, on earth or throughout the universe, this is the supreme expression of self-sacrificing *otherism*. Here is the supreme example. "Let *this* mind be in you."'[40] There could never be a series of steps of humility of that magnitude ever again. But observe the principle at work as we see how God the Father responded with the huge step up! I am sure it thrills the Philippians as it should thrill us in a different time and place.

THE HUGE STEP UP!

For the very reason that His beloved Son willingly humbled Himself in the manner and ways we have considered, God the Father worked the biggest miracle of the Bible. Note 'Therefore' again! '*Therefore* God also has highly exalted Him'. From death on the cross, via the miraculous and marvellous resurrection and glorious ascension, He 'highly exalted Him'. See the wonder of the Person of Christ! See the principles of humility before honour, and grace before glory! The despised 'criminal' of Calvary resumes the position which is solely His in glory: through the cross, and through the power of God, He is the everlasting Victor. Heaven itself will take up the refrain:

You are worthy to take the scroll,
And to open its seals;
For You were slain,
And have redeemed us to God by Your blood
Out of every tribe and tongue and people and nation,
And have made us kings and priests to our God;
And we shall reign on the earth.[41]

And again:

Worthy is the Lamb who was slain
To receive power and riches and wisdom,
And strength and honour and glory and blessing.[42]

And again:

Blessing and honour and glory and power
Be to Him who sits on the throne,
And to the Lamb, for ever and ever!
Then the four living creatures said "Amen!"
 And the twenty four elders fell down and worshipped Him who lives for ever and ever.[43]

The deepest descent known to man or to God is met by the highest exaltation that even Almighty God can accomplish. Even He can work no mightier or more important miracle than this. Jesus is LORD—and His Father is overjoyed to demonstrate it to all the principalities and powers, and to have it proclaimed to the rebel sinners who crucified His Son, and to hear it as the theme of worship in heaven!

THAT NAME
Now the despised and rejected Man of Sorrows has received the name, from the Father, 'which is above every name'. That holy name in the Old Testament was written by the Jews without vowels so that it could not be pronounced: YHWH. To enable us to pronounce it we call it 'YAHWEH'

or 'Jehovah'.[44] When the announcement of the birth of Christ was made by the angel Gabriel to Mary,[45] she was told 'you will conceive in your womb and bring forth a Son, and shall call His name JESUS. He will be great and will be called the Son of the Highest'. 'Jesus' literally means 'the LORD is salvation', or more briefly, 'Jehovah saves'. Now consider that the angel said to Joseph that Mary 'will bring forth a Son, and you shall call His name JESUS, for He will save His people from their sins'.[46] Put that back into what Gabriel said to Mary! His name would be 'the LORD is salvation', or 'God saves', *because* Jesus will save people from sins. Who can the Owner of that name be, then, except 'the LORD' or 'God'? That thought is buttressed by the fact that Jesus would also be known as 'Immanuel' which the Bible confirms 'is translated "God with us"'.[47] Now, in His ascension, the highly exalted Son receives back that name which orthodox Jews feared to use, but by which we joyfully identify our once crucified, mightily risen, gloriously ascended Lord Jesus Christ, Who—as we shall see in the next verse—is going to return as King of kings and Lord of lords!

'THE WAY UP IS DOWN'

'The way up is down,' wrote evangelical Methodist, Dr Sangster. It not only embraces key Bible principles for us as Christians, but it reflects the truth of the greatest exaltation in history—that of the Lord Jesus Christ. We have just seen that the great sevenfold humbling to the cross by Jesus was met by the mighty exaltation through His resurrection and ascension to glory. Clearly we will never know Jesus Christ's degrees of humility or exaltation but there is a principle in the Bible that humility precedes exaltation. That principle applies for both the Philippian Christians and for us. We will be lifted spiritually if we humble ourselves by allowing the 'mind of Christ' to dominate our attitudes, thoughts and actions. We will know God's upholding and blessing of us as we humbly cast ourselves upon Him and seek to think His thoughts and put them into practice in our lives. Jesus said, 'whoever exalts himself will be humbled, and he who humbles himself will be exalted.'[48] The apostle Peter encourages his readers to 'humble yourselves under the mighty hand of God, that He might exalt you in due time',[49] because he has already reminded us of the Old Testament truth that 'God resists the proud, but gives grace to the humble.'[50] James reveals that the key to winning battles with Satan is to 'submit to God. Resist the devil and he will flee from you.'[51] Submission to God is clearly humbling ourselves before Him, which is why James also precedes his comments, as Peter did, with 'God resists the proud, but gives grace to the humble.'[52] We are told in the book of Micah what God requires of us (my emphasis follows): 'To do justly, to love mercy, and to *walk humbly with your God.*'[53] In each case, truly 'the way up is down'. The Bible teaches that 'before honour is humility'.[54] May we be encouraged by our risen and ascended Lord to seek to reproduce His mind in us, just as Paul encourages those believers in Philippi.

2:10 No exceptions!

[10] that at the name of Jesus every knee should bow, of those in heaven, and of those on earth, and of those under the earth,

THE POWER OF HIS NAME

There is no 'magic' in the mere repetition of the name 'Jesus'. From time to time exaggerated stories are passed on which suggest that the mere utterance of the name works miracles. That has more to do with superstition than with biblical truth: if it were so then the same should happen when the name 'Joshua' is used because that is the Hebrew form of the Greek word 'Jesus'. The power of the name of Jesus does not consist of a magical combination of syllables, in which it could be used like a New Age mantra to seek to whip up emotion and attain a 'higher consciousness' (or 'unconsciousness', more likely!) but in *Who* the owner of the name is. Even then it must be said that, when Jesus was recognised by His name two thousand years ago, it did not work mystical or magical protection for Him. His name went with Him to the cross where He died a cruel death. But God has His timetable! The day will come when the heralding of His name, and the glorious appearance of Jesus as rightful King of kings and Lord of lords, will have a truly amazing effect on the inhabitants of this world, and others too. Not only on earth, but in heaven, and 'under the earth' every knee will bow to Him on that day! For some it will be in voluntary adoration and praise—those knees will have bowed often before, unless newly converted and thus only recently acquainted with Jesus as their personal Saviour from sin. For others it will be involuntary. Those who despised His name, and rebelled against the claims of His kingdom in their own hearts and lives, will in awesome fear find their knees bent before the heralding of His name. In heaven, the angels will continue to worship Him[55] knowing that only God must be worshipped.[56] The demons in hell—those 'under the earth'—will find they have no power whatsoever to resist His omnipotent majesty and their grudging, though immediate, acknowledging of His supremacy will make them kneel too. 'Jesus Christ—He is Lord of all'![57] On that day, when He returns in glory, every knee will bow to affirm it. *There will be no exceptions!* All will know then, what the committed Christian rejoices in now, that 'to this end Christ died and rose and lived again, that He might be Lord of both the dead and the living'.[58] I like the way John MacArthur summarises this in his *Study Bible*: 'The entire intelligent universe is called to worship Jesus Christ as Lord (*cf.* Psalm.2). This mandate includes the angels in heaven (Revelation 4:2–9), the spirits of the redeemed (Revelation 4:10,11), obedient believers on earth (Romans 10:9), the disobedient rebels on earth (2 Thessalonians 1:7–9), demons and lost humanity in hell (1 Peter 3:18–22).'[59] Naturally, much of the background and considerations applying to the bowing of the universal knee also applies to the confessing by the universal tongue that 'Jesus Christ is Lord, to the glory of God the Father'. We will soon consider that aspect. In Philippi, Paul will rejoice as the Christians there bow the knee and proclaim by tongue, in the gospel and in praise, the name and worth of the Lord Jesus Christ.

A PERSONAL QUESTION

Why wait until then to bow the knee? If you are not yet converted, there is no better time than *now* to come humbly to Him. If you are a straying or rebelling child of God, now is the time to bow the knee before Him again. If you seek to continue walking with your precious Lord and Saviour, now is *always* the time to kneel before Him again in consecration and praise.

2:11 Still no exceptions!

11 and that every tongue should confess that Jesus Christ is Lord, to the glory of God the Father.

WHEN EVERYONE WILL SAY THE SAME THING!

Just as every knee will bow before the Lord Jesus Christ at His glorious second coming, so every tongue will confess His Lordship too. And that will be 'to the glory of God the Father'. Imagine the scene. It is vividly painted in 1 Thessalonians 4:13 to 5:11, in 2 Thessalonians 1:7 to 2:12, in Matthew 24:27–31, in Mark 13:24–27, and in Luke 21:25–28. Christ will come again in glory! He will have the last word in history. He will come with the redeemed souls of the 'dead in Christ' and their resurrection bodies will rise to be united with their souls and their Saviour in the air. Then Christians alive on the earth will be instantly transformed and taken up in their resurrection bodies. Then judgement will be pronounced upon those who did not bow the knee to Christ in their lifetime. But all will be agreed upon one thing, and everyone's tongue will proclaim it: 'Jesus Christ is Lord'. Some will gladly and joyfully affirm at His coming what they had been seeking to testify to in His absence. For them, it will be thrilling to see their faith and witness vindicated. I can imagine others saying in amazement: 'Jesus Christ [really] *is* Lord.' Their arrogant pride and Babel-type thinking had hardened their hearts and blinded their minds—until now. Now they know—and it is too late for them, sadly. Others will say it in fear, as they now realise that judgement is to come from the Judge of the earth. Others will admit it in the same way as a humiliated opponent now knows he has met his master. For others it will be involuntary, but they will know it is the truth: 'Jesus Christ is Lord'. Demons, who we know 'believe and tremble',[60] may now scream that eternal reality in abject horror. Angels will say it in confident and worshipful assurance. It will be repeated in all the languages of the world, where the gospel has been preached and souls have come to know, well before this great day, that 'Jesus Christ is Lord'. The martyrs will say it. The youngest child with faith in Christ will say it. The backslidden Christian will say it with a strange blend of regret and joy. The preachers will say it. The congregations will say it. It will come from the palaces and from the prisons, from the hospitals and from the hotels. From black, white, yellow, and brown-skinned people of all shapes and sizes—from clever and dull, from rich and poor, from strong and weak, from healthy and (previously!) sick, from women and men, from people in Philippi and those in every other place—in fact from everyone! *Jesus Christ is Lord!* And, still, *no exceptions.* And this will not only glorify the Lord Jesus Christ. It will be 'to the glory of God the Father' who loves and admires the eternal Son of His love even more than we do, or even will be able to do on that day.

Notes

1 Luke 24:13–35.

2 For example, look at the prayer of Jabez in 1 Chronicles 4:10.

3 1 John 2:6.

4 **Howard Guinness,** 'Sacrifice' (Young Life), pages 38–40.

5 **Rev. Ralph P. Martin,** *Tyndale New Testament Commentaries: The Epistle of Paul to the Philippians* (Tyndale Press), page 96.

6 **Prof. Francis Davidson,** *The New Bible Commentary: The Epistle to the Philippians* (Inter–Varsity Press), page 1037.

7 John 1:1,3–4,14; 8:58; Colossians 1:15–17; Hebrews 1:3—these are MacArthur's quoted references. **John MacArthur** (author of commentary/notes and general editor), *The MacArthur Study Bible,* NKJV (Word Bibles), note on Philippians 2:6, page 1822.

8 **Gerard A. Chrispin,** *The Resurrection: the unopened gift* (Day One), pages 52–54.

9 John 17:5; John 1:14.

10 Mark 13:32.

11 **John MacArthur** (author of commentary/notes and general editor), *The MacArthur Study Bible, NKJV* (Word Bibles), note on Philippians 2:6, page 1823.

12 *Muncie Evening Press,* quoted in **Lloyd Cory,** *Quotable Quotes* (Victor Books).

13 John 8:58.

14 Revelation 1:11.

15 **Frank Houghton,** 'Thou Who wast rich beyond all splendour' in *Hymns of Faith* (Scripture Union), number 142.

16 Exodus 21:5 and 6.

17 Luke 22:27.

18 Luke 22.26.

19 **William Macdonald,** *True Discipleship* (S.T.L. Books), page 10.

20 Luke 10:18.

21 Romans 8:3.

22 1 Corinthians 15:45.

23 Romans 8:3.

24 1 Peter 2:24.

25 Hebrews 4:15.

26 1 Timothy 2:5.

27 2 Corinthians 5:21.

28 1 Timothy 2:5.

29 John 1:12.

30 Matthew 1:23.

31 1 John 4:14.

32 John 10:17,18.

33 John 3:16.

34 Galatians 2:20.

35 Matthew 1:18–25; Luke 1:26–38; Isaiah 7:14.

36 Philippians 2:8 (Phillips).

37 Matthew 27:38.

38 Matthew 27:26.

39 2 Corinthians 5:21.

40 J. Sidlow Baxter, *Explore the Book*, in one volume (Zondervan), page 189.

41 Revelation 5:9,10.

42 Revelation 5:12.

43 Revelation 5:13,14.

44 J.D. Douglas (originating editor), *The New Bible Dictionary* (Inter Varsity Press); see under 'God, Names of'—pages 477–480, especially 478.

45 Luke 1:31,32.

46 Matthew 1:20,21.

47 Matthew 1:22,23.

48 Matthew 23:12.

49 1 Peter 5:6.

50 1 Peter 5:5.

51 James 4:7.

52 James 4:6.

53 Micah 6:8.

54 Proverbs 15:33; Proverbs 18:12.

55 Hebrews 1:9.

56 Luke 4:8.

57 Acts 10:36.

58 Romans 14:9.

59 John MacArthur (author of commentary/notes and general editor, *The MacArthur Study Bible, NKJV* (Word Bibles), note on Philippians 2:10,11 page 1823.

60 James 2:19.

Mini-overview 2:12 and 2:13

How conversion works—

The inward and outward signs of conversion.

2:12 The Christian 'work-out'

12 Therefore, my beloved, as you have always obeyed, not in my presence only, but now much more in my absence, work out your own salvation with fear and trembling,

WHEN THE TEACHER IS OUT OF THE ROOM ...

One of my schoolboy memories was to be found fighting in the unattended classroom on the last day of a school term by a strongly disciplinarian headmaster. He made a chance visit. He had corrected me on the appropriate 'seat of learning' once before, and I was scared when his piercing eyes bored right through me! I often managed to obey when supervised by a strong-minded teacher, but found it far harder when he was out of the room! In this letter, Paul commends the Philippian Christians in that their obedience to God, and His Word, never abated in Paul's absence. Whether the schoolmaster was in the room or not, they behaved in a God-honouring way. How easy it is for us today to do the right 'spiritual' things when others are watching. How differently we can behave when left on our own or when a strong Christian leadership is absent. I know of one Christian man, much respected in his church, who stayed up late on a pretext but did so to watch pornography clandestinely on TV . Perhaps that was an extreme case, but the principle is there for all of us. Alone with God, are we the people we pretend to be in the company of others or when speaking to those we wish to impress? And how about the church or fellowship we attend? When others visit they may see only sweetness and light, but is there infighting, gossip and 'politics' under the surface? I wonder what newcomers make of some churches' members' meetings or leadership committees. Thankfully this is not a problem for Paul's Philippian brothers and sisters. They are consistent, irrespective of the apostle's absence or presence. Perhaps they already know something of the 'mind of Christ' and realise that God is always there.

SALVATION WORKED *OUT*, NOT WORKED *FOR*

The Philippians' actions will follow their thinking, which will be determined by the indwelling 'mind of Christ'. That mind is worked *in* at salvation and is to be strengthened through daily sanctification before being worked *out* in service and saintliness. That is why the Philippian Christians are encouraged by Paul to 'work out [their] own salvation'. Some have read into that phrase a false meaning, of salvation by works. But that receives no support from the immediate context of verse 13, from the context of Paul's letter, or from the context of the Bible as a whole. The Bible is very clear that we cannot be saved by our works.[1] Our sin has separated us from God, and we need a Saviour from sin. Nothing and no one can save us except the Lord Jesus Christ.[2] And we can only approach Him by faith,[3] with repentance for sin.[4] So we cannot successfully work *for* our salvation—the only work that can produce that for us is the finished work of Christ on our behalf, as our Substitute, on the cross.[5] But at the moment when a repentant sinner puts his saving faith in Jesus, and receives the Lord into his heart as his Saviour, God's saving work within that new believer begins to be experienced as the Spirit of Christ enters.[6] In fact, God will have been at work before. He will already have convicted that sinner of his deliberate sin, and of his hopeless lack of personal righteousness,[7] compared with God's required perfect standard of holiness and righteousness shown in His Word and manifested in His Son. God, the Holy Spirit, will also have convinced him of the divine judgement to come against his sin.[8] He will have made the wonder and reality of Christ, and His redeeming death, personal to that sinner. The response of faith to such a divine 'wake up call' is to cry out for mercy and forgiveness, and receive the risen Christ as Saviour and Master. And still today, as in Paul's day, God uses both the sharing of the gospel and the sinner's conscious need for forgiveness, as the raw materials of salvation upon which the Spirit works. Today the communication of God's salvation is still by sounding forth the gospel. Preaching is always God's primary means, be it one man preaching to others or one-to-one witness. But God also uses different forms of evangelism to introduce the preached word, and also saves people by their reading the Bible or Christian literature, or hearing His truths clearly put to music. The avenues of conveying the good news include not only services and meetings, but also radio, TV, compact discs, videos, tapes, internet presentations or films. So often, personal testimony acts as the catalyst in this. This causes interest in the gospel and often gives a Christian an opportunity to bring others along to hear the gospel preached. But God prepares and ploughs the needy heart of the sinner well before he is convicted of his sin and puts his trust in Jesus Christ. Clearly, therefore, we cannot do anything to work *for* our salvation. We can only work it *out* after God has worked it in. But work it out, we will—*if* we have truly turned to Christ and been 'born again' by the Spirit's entrance into our lives. James says that 'faith without works is dead'.[9] Jesus taught the clear principle that 'You will know them by their fruits'[10] in the immediate context of false teachers. But it has a wider application in principle. Although works can never save us, if a whole new life does not evidence the works 'that accompany salvation'[11] then there is no salvation at all. If no 'fruits' of new life in Christ appear, then I have not been 'planted' into Him, and I lack His life within me that alone can produce those fruits. Works, therefore, are an inevitable *result* but never an indispensable *cause* of our salvation. Let me use an analogy. A man can arrange for a dilapidated old house to be repaired, modernised, cleaned, painted, furnished and equipped. But, unless he buys it and lives in it, the house does not become a residence that he owns. No amount of our working on the house of our life, spoiled as it is by sin and selfishness, can make us become Christians. Jesus has to purchase and indwell us if we are really to be His. By his death on the cross He paid the price with His blood to buy us for Himself. It is only when we as individuals turn our back on our sins and call on Him to have mercy on us that Jesus Christ enters our lives as our Saviour. We then become truly His by purchase and possession. The Bible says: 'Do you not know that your body is the temple of the Holy Spirit who is in you, whom you have from God, and you are not your own? For you were bought at a price; therefore glorify God in your body and in your spirit which are God's'.[12] When someone has bought an old house with the intent of living in it, changes are expected. The works undertaken demonstrate the change of ownership and possession. So it is with the Christian: once Christ has taken over and entered a person's life, things will change: works will be produced, some radical and some less obvious.

But they underline a change of ownership and possession that has already taken place; they do not constitute that change themselves. So what we work out in our lives demonstrates the change of ownership: now we belong to Jesus. Unlike an inanimate and unfeeling object like a house, we will want to be put right, be clean, be useful, be welcoming, and pleasing to our new Owner. As we get to love Him more, those desires will be translated into how we spend our time, what we do with our money, our attitude to other Christians as part of the same family, our concern for non-Christians as people needing His salvation, our worship of Him and time spent with Him each day in personal devotions. We will refuse to do, or spend time and money on, the things that make the house of our new life look shabby. Above all, we shall want to *obey* Him if we really have come to love Him, for Jesus said, 'If you love Me, keep my commandments'.[13] R.A. Torrey remarks, with great insight, that our experience tells us is the truth: 'Nothing clears the mind like obedience: nothing darkens the mind like disobedience. To obey a truth you see prepares you to see other truths. To disobey a truth you see darkens your mind to all truths.'[14] There can be no working out *by* us of what God has worked *in* us unless we obey His Word. That is true love for the Saviour.

WHY 'WITH FEAR AND TREMBLING'?
Why does Paul tell the Philippian saints to work out what He works in 'with fear and trembling?' Clearly he is not looking for them to manifest the 'fear of man' which 'brings a snare.'[15] The whole tenor of the letter repudiates that possibility. There are two 'candidates' to consider as the reason why 'fear and trembling' should accompany their outworking of the salvation and mind that is 'in Christ'. Those candidates are not mutually exclusive: in fact they canvass together for our allegiance. Briefly put, they are the avoidance of presumptuous complacency, on the one hand, and the practice of reverential fear of God, on the other. Thus equipped, we (and the Philippians) will be well pleasing to God, as we shall see from the next verse. This is His purpose in saving sinners.

PRESUMPTION IS NOT THE SAME AS ASSURANCE
Paul's assurance of his own salvation shines throughout the letter, and is

the birthright of every child of God. To have confidence in God's salvation and His promise is not presumption. Paul makes it clear to the Ephesians that his desire for them is 'that you may know what is the hope of His calling, what are the riches of the glory of His inheritance in the saints'[16] and this finds resonance with the words of his fellow apostle, John. He declared, 'These things I have written to you who believe in the name of the Son of God, that you may know that you have eternal life, and that you may continue to believe in the name of the Son of God.'[17] Clearly, it is God's intention that when sinners are truly saved by Christ, be it in Ephesus or in Philippi or elsewhere, that they should *know* that they *are* saved. But that is not the same as a complacent presumption that someone has passed from death to life, where there is no evidence of the outworking of the new birth, and no practical demonstration of the mind of Christ. Such presumption can pave the road to hell. Neither the church adherents in that Roman colony, nor we today, should imagine personal salvation if the testimony of lives lived out denies the claims made in words. If life and lip are united in pointing to a new life in Christ, however imperfect, every Christian can and should rejoice in that assurance.

'THE FEAR OF THE LORD'

If the mind of Christ has been received by the Philippians by conversion, they will also be concerned for God's holiness and good name in a world that has little time for Him. They will have a natural and proper godly fear of letting Him down. That is wise humility. It is 'The fear of the LORD' which 'is the beginning of wisdom'[18] and 'of knowledge.'[19] God looks for the same reverential fear in us. Such a godly fear for my heavenly Father will characterise our lives and our works for Him. Such reverence will exclude and expel the pride of self-effort and replace it with gratitude that we have been spared the wrath our sin deserves. It will promote a godliness that yearns to see our holy Saviour honoured. God will honour that and increasingly become the strength and joy of His people. As we shall see in the next verse, a Christian's sanctification is serious business, and God's name in the world can be magnified or minimised in the eyes of onlookers, dependent upon how believers co-operate with God's loving grace in and through them. In working out our salvation 'with fear and trembling' the overwhelming concern will be to glorify God. There will be no flippancy, indifference or trivial thinking about Who He is. Christians will do well to note the truth of Wiersbe's comment that: 'Since God is the highest being in the universe, he is worthy of our worship and praise. In fact, the highest privilege we have as His children is to worship and serve Him and do everything for His glory alone. God created the universe to glorify Him (Numbers 14:21; Psalm 19:1) so when we glorify the Lord, we co-operate with his creation and it co-operates with us. The great plan of salvation has as its goal "the praise of His glory" (Ephesians 1:16,12,14), not just the rescuing of sinners from hell.'[20]

2:13 God at work

[13] for it is God who works in you both to will and to do for His good
   pleasure.

THE PURPOSE—HIS PLEASURE

We will start at the end: God's work in us has as its goal that which pleases *Him*. It is 'for *His* good pleasure'. Like the Philippians, we need to remember that. Our trust in Christ heralds the start of God's ongoing work of sanctification in our lives and produces glorious bi-products. These include 'the peace of God that surpasses all understanding',[21] 'joy inexpressible and full of glory',[22] and the many-flavoured experience of the the fruit of the Spirit.[23] This fruit in the life of the believer is characterised by 'love, joy, peace, longsuffering, kindness, goodness, faithfulness, gentleness and self-control'. It should be ripening as we daily get closer to Christ. But God does not work in us *primarily* for our own enjoyment: that is an added bonus of His grace. Oswald Chambers hits straight from the shoulder when he says: 'God is not an eternal blessing-machine for men; He did not come to save men out of pity: He came to save men because He had created them to be holy.'[24] To make us holy, He works in us 'for His good pleasure' and we should follow our Saviour Who could say of His desire to please His Father, 'I always do those things that please Him.'[25]. God is generous. When He sees in us a desire to please Him, He responds by blessing us with the highest possible level of personal fulfilment and blessing. As Jesus promised, it truly 'is more blessed to give than receive'[26] and if we seek to give Him first place in our lives, He will certainly give us first place in His blessings. If we obey Christ's encouraging command to 'seek first the kingdom of God and His righteousness' we will find that, as He promised, 'all these things shall be added to you'.[27] That will be especially true of our spiritual blessings in Christ.

HOW GOD WORKS IN US

But note that Christians cannot please Him by works originating in themselves, be they first century Christians at Philippi or modern believers today. It is our response to *His* overtures of love and grace that pleases God. 'It is God who works in you both to will and to do for His good pleasure'. We considered under the preceding verse how God stirs the heart of a sinful person to bring him to Himself. Now we will consider how He works in us to make us willing to please God and then to do it. His work in our lives will be carried on by the Lord right until the day when we enjoy Him in heaven. Remember what we considered in Philippians 1:6: 'He who has begun a good work in you will complete it until the day of Jesus Christ'. We sometimes tire of an ongoing job of work. God never tires of encouraging our hearts to 'grow in the grace and knowledge of our Lord and Saviour Jesus Christ'.[28] So He works by persevering with us: even when we feel we have failed and wonder how we can carry on, He knows that He is going to carry on with us. That is the reason why we will persevere too! This is often known as the 'perseverance of the saints'. I prefer to regard it as 'the perseverance of the Saviour with the saints'. Whichever phrase you prefer, we are unable to continue in the Christian walk without His motivational love and enabling strength. The clear comment of Jesus on the subject was: 'Without Me you can do nothing'.[29] How grateful and glad we are that He is constantly with us! God's working is not only continual, it is also spiritual. We may be growing old or suffering from a terminal disease, but 'we do not lose heart. Even though our outward man is perishing, yet the inward man is being renewed day by day'[30] because God works by His Spirit in our spirit. And because it is a spiritual work, He uses spiritual means. His work is not helped in our lives by our emphasis on worldly entertainment and ambition,[31] or on a love of ease or shirking of spiritual duties,[32] or on 'fleshly lusts which war against the soul'.[33] Just as 'salvation is of the

LORD'[34] but calls for a response of repentance and trust from the sinner for it to be experienced, so similarly sanctification is also God's work[35] which calls for a response from the Christian for it to be furthered.[36] That is why the Philippians must *'Let'* (my emphasis) the mind of Christ be in them. His working in us will lead to our doing 'His good pleasure' in direct proportion to our attitude towards Him and His Word and our willingness to let Him and His Word have first place in our lives. His Word, the Bible, must continually be open. We should read it, study it, learn it, trust it and apply it every day personally. It is our map, our sword, our food, our marching orders, our handbook, our love letter, our light, and our seed from which spiritual growth comes. But we must also have open wills to do what He says. If we read the Bible often, without being willing to put into action what we read, we are only hearers and not doers. That is in direct rebellion to God's Word, and causes us to deceive even ourselves.[37] Our quiet times should include a time when we pray in the lessons gleaned from our reading: we should humbly ask God's forgiveness for not having applied His Word as we should have done, and seek His help to put that right on a daily basis. God continues to work within us according to His will and in response to our earnest prayers. The same is true when we hear the Word of God preached on the Lord's Day and at other times and when we attend our church Bible study. It is not enough to be there. Neither is hearing and agreeing sufficient. We must ask God to make real in our experience that which we heard preached or taught. We should cultivate the godly habit, also, of turning helpful Christian literature, and challenging Christian fellowship, into prayers to make us more like the Lord Jesus. Godliness should be our goal. As we say 'no' to things that would drag us down—whatever others may think or do—and 'yes' to God through the means that He has provided so that we can know Him better, He works within us. He even works to show us our non-compliance with His will and to convict us of our need to repent and seek His face and help. He continues to work within us when circumstances arise in our lives which we do not like, or even may fear. Sometimes He has to reduce us to the real truth that we are nothing and can do nothing without Him, before He makes serious progress in His work in us. That requires honest co-operation on our part. Oswald Sanders asks: 'Am I willing to reduce myself simply to "me", determinedly to strip myself of all my friends think of me, of all I think of myself, and to hand the simple naked self over to God? Immediately I am, He will sanctify me wholly, and my life will begin to be free from earnestness in connection with everything but God.'[38] This is challenging, and we need to remember that such an attitude of self-humbling and commitment needs to be repeated again and again. It is not 'once for all'. With such a response to the Spirit's promptings, under His supervision and strength, my God-centred Christian life will continue to grow and strengthen. The weightlifter gains muscle and strength by pushing a little harder each day against constantly increasing loads. So it is with our growth spiritually: God may well increase the burdens we have to bear so that we learn how to pray and trust Him. In that, He is at work in us. Be encouraged: He knows just how much to give you to bear, 'For we do not have a High Priest who cannot sympathise with our weaknesses, but was in all points tempted as we are, yet without sin. Let us therefore come boldly to the throne of grace, that we may obtain mercy and find grace to help in time of need.'[39] He *is* working within you even now—if you know Christ.

WILLING AND DOING

Between God's working in the Philippian Christians and God's 'good pleasure' are two things: their willingness and their doing. His working in them produces their willingness and their doing. What is true for them is true for us. God is eminently reasonable! He does not expect us to be able to do things He knows we cannot do without His help. The comfort in that thought is that He will never give us anything to do which we cannot accomplish in and through Him. Thus when the Bible makes demands of us, or we are convinced that the obedient application of a certain principle must lead us to a difficult decision or course of action, we can be confident that God will enable us to do the right thing. He is at work in us and His Word is His enabling. The corollary of that thought is that God accepts our willingness totally. 'If there is first a willing mind, it is accepted according to what one has, and not according to what he does not have.'[40] It is clear from Scripture that a one hundred per cent willingness to obey, whatever the cost, is the only path to full Christian blessing and usefulness. William MacDonald writes: 'All who come into contact with the Saviour of the world must learn sooner or later that in Christianity, it must be everything or nothing. Our Lord can never be satisfied with only part of the human life. There can be no half-hearted allegiance, no divided loyalty. He is worthy either of all, or of nothing'.[41] A willingness thus to make Him Lord, which we must humbly admit is *His* work in us, is essential to walking with Him in discipleship. But willingness is the beginning and not the end. It is tested by what we *do*. We cannot claim to be willing to put Him first if we do not do it. Willingness without doing is not really willingness. And the 'doing' is not by self-effort. Like Paul we have to say, 'I know that in me (that is, in my flesh) nothing good dwells; for to will is present with me, but how to perform what is good I do not find.'[42] And yet, if our very helplessness and inability to please God is repentantly turned into a prayer of submission to Him, asking for His enabling, we can find that 'when [we are] weak then [we are] strong'.[43] We can be confident because God is working in us to make us willing. When our God-given willingness is thus linked with *His* strength, we can do what He asks of us. Have you said that you will never do a certain thing again? Well then, take that promise to God as a prayer and proceed to do what you promised, in His strength. Did you say you would start each day with the Bible and prayer? Then tell God you have promised—and just do it! Have you lamented your lack of personal witness, but recently told God that you will speak to people each day about Christ? Renew your promise to Him now, therefore, and start looking for opportunities today or (if it is too late in the evening when you read this) tomorrow. Be careful and sensitive, prayerful and natural—but ask God for opportunities and then *take them!* To show you mean it, put some good gospel literature in your pocket, case, handbag, wallet, purse, house, car or desk as appropriate. And in all the things concerning which you have expressed a willingness to God to go His way, start organising your life as if you meant it. Get a page-a-day diary to note your quiet time thoughts. Produce your personal daily prayer list. Make a note of names of those you will pray for every day—family, neighbours, work mates or fellow students, non-Christians you have witnessed to, and Christians who need your prayers in your church and on the mission field. Do not just be willing. Do it! As God works in your heart, and as you become willing to crown Him as your daily Lord, do the things that you know He wants you to do, and cut out the things that He frowns upon. You will find you are beginning to live 'for His good pleasure'.

Notes

1 Ephesians 2:8,9.

2 John 14:6; Acts 4:12.

3 Acts 16:31.

4 Acts 3:19.

5 1 Peter 2:24.

6 Romans 8:15,16.

7 John 16:7–11.

8 John 16:7–11.

9 James 2:20.

10 Matthew 7:16.

11 Hebrews 8:9.

12 1 Corinthians 6:19,20.

13 John 14:15.

14 **R.A. Torrey,** *How to Succeed in the Christian Life* (Whittaker), pages 57 and 58.

15 Proverbs 29:25.

16 Ephesians 1:18.

17 1 John 5:13.

18 Psalm 111:10.

19 Proverbs 1:7.

20 **Warren W. and David W. Wiersbe,** *10 Power Principles for Christian Service* (Baker Book House Co.), page 72.

21 Philippians 4:7.

22 1 Peter 1:8.

23 Galatians 5:22,23.

24 **Oswald Chambers,** *My Utmost For His Highest* (Oswald Chambers Publications Associations Limited), page 251.

25 John 8:29.

26 Acts 20:35.

27 Matthew 6:33.

28 2 Peter 3:18.

29 John 15:5.

30 2 Corinthians 4:16.

31 James 4:4.

32 Matthew 26:41.

33 1 Peter 2:11.

34 Jonah 2:9.

35 2 Thessalonians 2:13.

36 Romans 12:1,2.

37 James 1:22.

38 Oswald Chambers, *My Utmost For His Highest* (Oswald Chambers Publications Association Limited), page 210.

39 Hebrews 4:15,16.

40 2 Corinthians 8:12.

41 William MacDonald, *True Discipleship* (S.T.L. Books), page 72.

42 Romans 7:18.

43 2 Corinthians 12:10.

Mini-overview 2:14 to 18

Shining and being poured out—
The relationship between a radiant Christian life and
sacrificial service.

2:14 Be positive about the negatives

14 Do all things without complaining and disputing,

A BLEMISH

It is a pity, and a slight blemish on the Philippian church, that so much of
their good witness appears to be spoiled by lapses that we too can make
every day. As Matthew Henry quaintly puts it: 'The light of truth and the
life of religion are often lost in the heats and mists of disputation'.[1] We have
already had a pen-sketch of Euodia and Syntyche, and we shall meet them
again in chapter 4:2. But the fact that the apostle, who has more cause than
they have to grumble and complain from his involuntary residence, must
caution them so directly shows that even Christians who get so much else
right can get this wrong. Chuck Swindoll's remarks confirm that the
problem is with us still today: 'One of the marks of maturity is the ability to
disagree without becoming disagreeable. It takes grace. In fact, handling
disagreements with tact is one of the crowning achievements of grace.
Unfortunately, the older we get, the more brittle we become in our
reactions, the more tedious and stubborn and fragile. For some strange
reason, this is especially true among evangelical Christians. You would
think that the church would be one place where we could find tolerance,
tact, plenty of room for disagreement, and open discussion. Not so! It is a
rare delight to come across those in the family of God who have grown old
in grace as well as in knowledge'.[2] Wow! And the text does not say, 'do the
hard things without complaining and disputing'. Its all-inclusive charge is
to 'Do all things' without letting God down or spoiling the fellowship in
those ways. This includes the routine as well as the exceptionally
demanding, and things to be done with and for those they are not drawn to
naturally, as well as for their 'closest buddies'. Things of a spiritual
nature—preaching, teaching, praying, and pastoring—are no more

important to be done with the right attitude than cleaning the home, driving through rush hour, or helping someone with a task beyond him or her that is tiresome in itself to the helper. We may wonder how the Philippians, on one hand, can face opposition with grace and fortitude, and yet, on the other hand, need this reminder from Paul not to grumble, murmur or dispute. But let us stop and look within, in case we are being hypocrites. Come on, admit it! You have a precious hour to yourself. You planned to do something you needed to do, or wanted to do. You are in the middle of it and the phone rings. Worse still, it is Mrs Fussypot on the other end, *again*! You can tell her what she needs to know in ten seconds, but you have to listen to the whole story. By the time you are through with that, your hour is down to half an hour and it's hardly worth starting! But you decide you will salvage that half hour, and then there is a knock on the door. '*Oh, NO!*' You really do *not* want to discuss, right now, whether you have any things to give to the next-door neighbour for her son's scouts' jumble sale. Fifteen minutes later you are frustrated and a little hot and bothered. The phone rings again and, feeling frustrated and irritated, you have to measure your speech carefully. The young man at the other end of the phone surprises and shames you. He warmly says 'thank you' for the care you took over talking to his mother about the Lord last Sunday, and pays you the compliment that your witness, of always having time for people, is such a blessing to him! You feel about two millimetres high and like crawling through the nearest hole! 'Oh, Lord! I am sorry: please forgive me and give me your grace.' Does it ring any bells—perhaps in different circumstances, but with similar pressures? If we are following Him, we should believe that, in His sovereignty, He knows what is best. We should not grumble about our lot—after all we are on the way to heaven! Neither should we dispute with others. Take Mary as our example.[3] When Martha complained about her observation of Mary's comparatively low work rate, Mary did not bite back but made it her spiritual priority to be at the Lord's feet. Jesus said, 'one thing is needed, and Mary has chosen that good part that will not be taken away from her'. To murmur or complain about other Christians, or to enter into dispute with the Lord's servants, is fruitless and mars our fellowship with them and with Him. We should bring them to Him in prayer before ever we consider giving a reprimand or entering into any dispute. But first, we should bring ourselves to Him to ask Him to 'renew a steadfast spirit within' us.[4] Like King David, the man who prayed that first, we need to start by asking for His cleansing: 'Create in me a clean heart, O God.'[5] Let us avoid these blemishes of complaining and disputing. Complaining is a selfish way of calling God a flop. Disputing is a more open way of also calling His servants a flop. Let us avoid both of these ugly blemishes like the plague, in case they turn into one! Let the Master deal with them—and with us—in these things, and let us give a positive witness, as we shall see in the next verses. This is certainly the aspiration that the apostle Paul has, from prison, for the young church in Philippi.

2:15 You are different, so be different

[15] that you may become blameless and harmless, children of God without fault in the midst of a crooked and perverse generation, among whom you shine as lights in the world,

THE AWFUL BACKGROUND DARKNESS OF SIN

The Philippians are told to shine 'as lights in the world'. We will look soon at how they are to become those lights, but we start by considering the dark world around them against which they are to shine in contrast. They live 'in the midst of a crooked and perverse generation' in that Roman colony. The word translated 'crooked' can be applied to a spinal column which has ceased to be straight but has curved, causing pain, discomfort and a degree of disability. 'Perverse' implies a far distant straying from the path. Both words apply to the Roman colony of Philippi—with its pride in Rome, its degenerate moral standards, its ignorance of God and His law, and its affluent materialism. They are twisted in sin, in pain of guilt, without comfort, and morally deformed. They have strayed a long way from God. The words also describe our twenty-first century world, where the same tokens of rebellion against God and moral degradation abound. It is this shining, against the shameful dark background of godlessness, that works out the salvation that God has worked in them and in us. The mind of Christ, that governs Christians' internal relationships and humble disposition, will seem like a huge lighthouse against the benighted thinking of pagan and immorally idolatrous fellow residents of Philippi and our fellow citizens today. Psalm 1 warns us against walking 'in the counsel of the ungodly', standing 'in the path of sinners', and sitting 'in the seat of the scornful'—that downward regression of walking, standing and sitting with those who do not love the Lord.[6] The spirit of worldliness resides amongst and is promoted by worldly people, namely those who do not welcome the lordship of Christ in their lives. But that same group of people are the 'world' in the other sense of being the people whom 'God so loved ... that He gave His only begotten Son, that whoever believes in Him should not perish but have everlasting life'.[7] It is that group of people for whom 'God did not send His Son into the world to condemn the world, but that the world through Him might be saved'.[8] Thus, to attempt to live blameless, harmless and faultless lives for, and by, God is not only something that will glorify Him, and encourage other Christians, but it is a means of witness to a lost world. The philosopher, Kant, is reported to have said, 'No straight thing was ever made from the crooked timber of humanity.' That 'perverse generation' is '*crooked*' because of sin within. Only Jesus can change that in the lives of morally and spiritually crippled mankind. The 'crooked' generation is 'perverse', or 'foolish', because 'All we like sheep have gone astray; we have turned, every one, to his own way'.[9] But that outward waywardness mirrors the inward waywardness and is the reason why, as the verse goes on to say, 'the LORD [God the Father] has laid on Him [Jesus, God the Son] the iniquity of us all'. God's love for a lost world was such that the Lord Jesus Christ went to the cross to take the punishment for the 'iniquity of us all' in His own body. If God loved lost sinners like that, then we should love them too. And we should shine as lights to shed light on their darkness and point them away from their sins and to the Lord Jesus Christ. Hendriksen pinpoints it this way: 'the objective in the Christian life is to populate heaven and depopulate hell'.[10] I think he means 'to populate heaven and decrease the flow of people to hell', since sadly we cannot now take from that place, of eternal and conscious punishment for sin, those who have already died and failed to turn to Christ during their lifetime.

'BLAMELESS AND HARMLESS'

Christians, Philippian or in the twenty-first century, have already become 'children of God' having received Christ.[11] Now that must be demonstrated in the outworking of salvation by being 'blameless and harmless, children of God, without fault in the midst of a crooked and perverse generation'. Sanctification is an argument: 'be what you are.' Sanctification and witness are inseparably linked, for if God is working within us, we shall be so different from the world around that our light really will beam out the fact that Christ is our Lord. The path we shall tread will then be so straight that it will be easily and readily distinguished from the way that carries a 'crooked' generation. God's wisdom—which will 'place on your head an ornament of grace' and deliver to you, spiritually, 'a crown of beauty'—[12] will, at once, distinguish our appearance from that of the 'perverse', and sometimes 'perverted', generation to which we seek to recommend our Saviour. Christians are not only to be different in that we do not complain, murmur, or dispute: the standard is that we are to be 'blameless', 'harmless' and 'without fault'—and this is in front of a critical 'generation' which is wayward, twisted, and foolish. Our manner of life is to be entirely different. God does not expect us to be *sinless*, because He knows we have inherently sinful natures and that only One Person, His Son, is without sin. But we are to be 'blameless', meaning we must be 'free from responsibility for something that is wrong or deserving censure'.[13] It implies behaviour which avoids wrong, or anything appearing wrong, for which accusation could be made and blame attached. We must avoid acting in such a way that we deserve a bad reputation in the outside world for our wrong acts or omissions. We are also to be 'harmless'. 'Harmless' is to do with the way others are treated, and means right behaviour to others who might wrong me. The Philippians are to let their lights shine in working out God's salvation in such a way that no wrong accusations will attach to them and neither will anyone be able to say that the believers have harmed others, even though they have been harmed themselves. They follow their Saviour,[14] who was 'led as a lamb to the slaughter',[15] and who prophetically said, through the Psalmist, 'I am a worm and no man'.[16] No one has ever been mauled by a lamb, or bitten by a worm. These are animals which portray the harmlessness of the gracious Saviour whom we are to follow. We, too, are not to harm anyone—physically, verbally, emotionally, or spiritually. Our standard is also to be 'without fault'. We will be constantly coming to the Lord, in the light of Scripture, to ask Him to deal with our faults and make us more like Christ. That is how Paul asks the Philippian believers to live. This is what God expects of us, too. It is how we should be living through and for Christ today. They and we are so to demonstrate all that God has done and is doing by His grace in believers that it becomes obvious to all that here are 'children of God without fault' in the watching and wicked world. And this is to be done 'in the midst of' that crooked and wayward world: the Christian cannot retreat to the nearest monastery garden.

SHINING AS LIGHTS

The Christians at Philippi are told that they already 'shine as lights in the world'. This reminds us that Jesus stated 'I am the light of the world',[17] and also said to His disciples 'You are the light of the world'.[18] They were to give light to the world as He did. Like it or not, followers of Christ *are* lights already: how and where they shine may vary, but each Christian is already clearly noticed in the surrounding and dark world of sin and compromise. A light is noticed, especially on a very dark night. It enables others to see what otherwise they would not see. It can also act as warning where there are hazards. The lights that the Philippians use are most likely burning torches. Now our lights come from many more sophisticated sources. We could not conceive of houses, streets, cars, buses, trains or aeroplanes without lights. Before technology advanced to its current position, once lighthouses proliferated in Great Britain and majestically marked the coastline like sentries, Christians are still lighthouses to men and women today. They are there to be seen by all, to warn others not to shipwreck their lives on the rocks of sin, to guide those in the choppy sea of life, and to shed light in darkness. I think it particularly appropriate that the *Association of Evangelists*, comprising a number of burdened and gifted British evangelists, has adopted the lighthouse as its symbol. Those lighthouses kept their reflecting surfaces clean continually and each day ensured that the most powerful beams of light possible would flash their whereabouts to keep shipping safe. If those lighthouses had failed to function, there could have been tragedies involving much loss of life. So it is for Christians: we are lighthouses—but we need daily and constantly to be kept under the cleansing of the blood of Christ and to be energised by the Holy Spirit in bright lives and shining witness for Him. We can be powerful lights, to His glory and to the saving of others, or we can give a poor sickly flicker to a lost world. As we shall see in the next verse, for the Philippians and for us, that shining for Christ is inexorably linked with 'holding fast the word of life.'

2:16 Encouraging the encourager

[16] holding fast the word of life, so that I may rejoice in the day of Christ that I have not run in vain or laboured in vain.

THE FLOW

We now see the continuing flow in Paul's Spirit-led instruction to the Philippian Christians. He has reminded them that God is working His salvation within them. They must work it out to please God. This means the absence of complaining and disputing. On the contrary they are to shine as lights, being blameless and harmless, in the middle of a crooked and wayward world. That shining will not only involve who they *are*— 'blameless and harmless'—but also what they *do*. They will be 'holding fast the word of life' in and to that dark world in which they shine. This will cause Paul to rejoice and will give eternal evidence that his work was not 'in vain'. What is true for them is, as always, true for us in our context and world.

NOT IN VAIN

We have all seen someone's 'folly'. It is a wall, or a tower, or a building which was started but never finished—usually through lack of resources. Imagine what it must mean to start the project with high hopes, and to see the bricks mounting and the building taking place—and then stop! The work had been in vain. One thing would convince Paul that his life's work, since turning to Christ, was not in vain. It is seeing them involved in 'holding fast the word of life'. The NASB translates this 'holding forth' in the margin. Nestles renders it 'holding up'[19] and The *Tyndale Commentary* on Philippians remarks, 'The Philippian Christians are to remain firm in their adherence to the truth of the gospel, to hold it fast as a torch-bearer would grasp securely the light he carries, and to let no opposition daunt their spirits'.[20] 'Holding out' and 'offering to' provide the same sense in The Amplified Bible. No doubt, you cannot hold forth to others, in that sense, what you do not hold fast yourself. You have to hold the torch securely for it to give light to others. Paul will be encouraged to see his young friends in the faith shining as lights, both by the quality of their different lives and also by making efforts to hold firm to the gospel and preach it to the lost. The same thing gladdens the heart of every committed Christian leader and pastor today. There is no greater joy than to see young Christians earnestly following the Lord and witnessing for Him. The corollary is also, sadly, very true. Well has Warren Wiersbe said, 'You have probably learned from painful experience that the mountaintops of ministry are often accompanied by deep valleys of disappointment. What hurts leaders the most are the failures of the people we're trying to help, people who really have every reason to succeed.'[21] Note what they are to hold out. It is the 'word of life'. No compromise here! No question of 'being more like them to win them by worldliness', but rather 'be more like Christ to win them by witness'. When Paul sees them doing that, he already knows now and will also rejoice 'in the day of Christ' that he has not worked in vain. God has honoured his work, and it will count for eternity.

WHAT MEASURE?

What measure does Paul use to determine how the Philippian Christians shine as lights? How do we determine the effectiveness of a church or group, today? Large numbers? Lively music? Relaxed atmosphere? Money in the collection? Paul's measure of progress is none of those. He evaluates their attitudes and activities against what they did with the 'word of life'. This phrase can mean either the message that promises life or 'the life-giving word'. What did they do with the Word of God and with the gospel? The right response to the 'word of life' would help Paul see his converts going on in discipleship, evidenced by a holy life and a strong emphasis on simple evangelism, centred on making God's Word known. This emphasis is often missing in our churches. Why is it easier to pack a church with Christians wanting to listen to a Christian group playing contemporary music than to get one per cent of that number doing door to door visitation? Why will older Christians flock to hear Handel's *Messiah* yet never consider having a meeting in the precinct to tell the lost world of the Saviour? If we use Paul's yardstick for encouragement, how encouraged will we really be about our work? Are we producing evangelising disciples, irrespective of their age? Are we even seeking to, and giving the lead by our own example? Sidney Barnes, a former Australian cricketer and team captain, made famous a position on the cricket field, now known as 'silly mid on'. For the uninitiated in this fine sport, it meant that he stood within pick-pocketing distance of the batsman, and risked serious injury if the batsman took a huge and hard swing at the very hard ball with his very hard bat. And this was in the days before fielders wore protective helmets! Why did Barnes do that? For two reasons: first, he hoped to make a catch if the batsman mishit the ball; second, as captain his philosophy was never to ask a member of his team to do what he would not do himself. Hardly surprising, the Australian team spirit was high and their fielding brilliant. Could it be that today's lack of holy discipleship and sacrificial evangelism simply reflects the weak personal example of today's Christian leadership? How inspirational, sacrificial and evangelistic are we as role models? If Christian leaders truly have the gospel as a priority, then surely others will be motivated. We need to take heed what the Puritan, Richard Baxter, said: 'The work of conversion is the first and great thing we must drive at; after this we must labour with all our might. Alas! The misery of the unconverted is so great, that it calleth loudest to us for compassion.'[22] Having taken heed to that, we need to live it out in our daily lives and witness. We will then be, without trying, good examples to others. Paul's gospel-centred example has obviously impressed and encouraged the Christians in Philippi and now they reciprocate! He is impressed and encouraged. We should pray that we see the same thing happening in many of our churches! May we all hold fast and hold forth the 'word of life'!

HOW PAUL SEES HIS SERVICE FOR JESUS

Paul speaks of his rejoicing, after this life, about the fact that his service was not 'in vain'.

He uses two verbs to portray that fact. He says he will rejoice both that he has not '*run* in vain' and that he has not '*laboured* in vain'. He includes those same images in a number of pictures of Christian discipleship. In 2 Timothy 2, he likens a Christian disciple to a soldier, an athlete, a farmer, a worker, a vessel, and a servant. The athlete and the farmer have this as common ground, that they both work hard at their activity, and that neither will succeed without persevering until the end. They both need self-discipline. As Howard Guiness wrote: 'The effective Christian is disciplined in every part of his personality and being—mind, heart, will, body and spirit'.[23] The athlete aims for the prize, and the farmer for the bringing in of the crops. It will be worth it for both of them when they see their desires achieved: their hard work, perseverance and discipline will seem as nothing to them then. Why is it that at the famous annual boat race on London's River Thames, between Oxford and Cambridge Universities, members of the winning team always looks less tired than the losers? Presumably no less effort has been spent in winning than in losing! It is to do with satisfaction in achieving. For Paul, he will rejoice in what God's grace has allowed him to achieve—he will have laboured well and run well. May we have those same goals, the same application to hard work and persevering, and that same rejoicing! And may we see others in heaven who have been similarly blessed because God has graciously used even us! At the end of a match the victorious players consider their hard work was all worth it. Does not the new mother concentrate on the joy of having produced her baby, after its birth, more than how hard it was before? Are not tired and jaded students, who have had little sleep and too much work prior to their final examinations, transformed into different beings when they find out their results are good? And, with the added dimension of eternal life and God's felt nearness, will not the Christian rejoice greatly, when his earthly life is over, that God has saved him, kept him, blessed him, used him to bless others, and made him thereby please his Saviour? Paul considers his loyal Philippian Christian friends and says to himself, in prison, 'Not in vain!'

2:17 Gladness and rejoicing in sacrifice and service

17 Yes, and if I am being poured out as a drink offering on the sacrifice and service of your faith, I am glad and rejoice with you all.

POURED OUT

First, what does the phrase 'poured out' mean? The Nestle Interlinear Greek New Testament renders the original of verse 17 as: 'But if I indeed I am poured out on the sacrifice and service of the faith of you …'[24] Paul regards his life as a drink offering which is poured out near to, or on, an animal when it is being sacrificed. The altar on which this happens is the Philippians' service and sacrifice, which gives evidence of their faith in Christ and faithfulness to Him. It is their sacrifice and service for God which motivate them to pray for, give to and support the imprisoned apostle, who is forgotten, abandoned or opposed by others. Some commentators see this as a reference to the possibility of Paul's impending martyrdom[25] and no doubt Paul is ready for this too, if the Lord so chooses. But others see in the phrase 'I am being poured out' the thought of being offered *right now* as a libation or drink offering as he suffers in prison for the gospel and gives himself wholeheartedly to them. He is one with them in their sacrifice of faith, even as he writes.[26] MacArthur points out that the present tense of the verb links better to his existing self-giving work with the Philippian church. Doubtless, his current sacrificial service includes a readiness, and possibly an expectation, that he will die for his faith. But Paul is being poured out for them right now, by his selfless efforts in the gospel on their behalf, as well as being willing to be literally poured out for them in death, if needs be. The Corinthian church saw his same willingness to live a life of self-crucifixion to be a blessing to them, when Paul said, 'I will very gladly spend and be spent for your souls, though the more abundantly I love you, the less I am loved'.[27] A drink offering accompanied animal sacrifice among pagans, as well as being legitimate worship of God in the Pentateuch. The outpoured drink on the animal sacrifice would rise as vapour, which pictured the lifting up of the thing offered to either the deity (for pagans) or to the LORD (for Israel).[28] That is how Paul saw his poured-out life for the Philippian church. What does his example mean to us practically today? Perhaps the challenge is too much for us to face. Here is a great apostle, gifted preacher and teacher, uniquely Spirit-led writer, and master missionary tactician living at such a level of disregard for his own preferences and comforts that he is 'poured out' for others. He is prepared to 'be spent for' them. What personal commitment do we really have to other Christians? Are we prepared to sacrifice time, money, and our own agenda personally to see others blessed? Do we actually do it? How easy it is for us, as age and time build up some kind of 'reputation', to be more concerned with that reputation—perhaps as a preacher, leader or teacher—than to have such a heart for people that we will sacrifice for them. Are we ready to be poured out for them? The following excerpt from a Japanese pastor's talk, recorded in Helen Roseveare's book, *Living Stones*, repays careful self-examination and remedial action. 'At a recent meeting in Japan ... the missionaries spoke of the kind of gifts that new workers should have, whereas we Japanese spoke of the kind of person we need ... We need missionaries who can show us what we must do and then lead us to do that work ... It is therefore reasonable that the worker ... needs a heart to nurture and train others. It is important to have a parent heart rather than a teacher heart, a heart that loves God's children, that desires their growth and that counts it a joy to make whatever sacrifice is necessary for that growth'.[29] That is another way of saying that, whatever a leader's gifts, he himself will never be a producer of disciples unless he lives a 'poured out' life. But those of us who are not leaders cannot duck the challenge because we do not have leading positions. Our example is, in itself, leadership to all with whom we come in contact. If our attitude is to be poured out for others, combining our sacrifice with theirs, we will influence preachers and pastors by our example even more than they will influence us by their preaching and teaching.

THE ALTAR

It is 'on the service and sacrifice of your faith' that Paul declares himself to be the poured out drink offering. We have already considered the question of service, and the need to live sacrificially in order to serve Him who gave all for us. But the reason for this 'altar' of service and sacrifice, where Paul is willing to give himself, is 'your faith'. Their faith, like ours today, has two dimensions. First, there is that revealed body of faith that defines Christian teaching as found in God's Word, the Bible, and nowhere else. Paul labours to instruct them in that aspect of their faith: he wants to be sure they know the basic and fundamental teachings of the gospel and what pleases God in their Christian lives. He will give himself to make sure that they know God's truth. We too should be much concerned that all the teaching we accept as 'Christian' is truly found in the Bible, in context. We must know *what* we believe as well as *Whom* we believe. We must also be occupied in passing that on to others as God's Word, and to contend for its truth. Then, second, their faith means that trust in God which they themselves have personally. It was first exercised when they trusted Christ as their own Saviour and Lord: it continues day by day as they 'walk by faith'.[30] Paul will work his fingers to the bone, and face the executioner if necessary, in order that 'ordinary' Christians, like you and like me, come to know Christ and get to know Him better. I remember meeting a Yorkshire miner who went to see his newly-converted friend every day for years to show him how to study and understand his Bible. No wonder that his friend also stood in the challenging rigours of the Yorkshire coalface! The faith of the new convert was so important to the Christian I met, that his daily programme was arranged around the needs of his friend to go on with the Lord. Sadly, I have forgotten the dear man's name—but certainly not his 'poured out' example. I went to teach the Bible at his chapel, and came away blessed and realising who the *real* teacher was. Altars were messy places. There were no cushions there either! So it is today if we are really given to advancing the faith of others—both what they know of the faith, and their personal growth in the faith—we must expect our comforts and our preferences to be part of our pouring out of ourselves.

NOT STOICISM—BUT HAPPINESS!

Paul's selfless attitude towards and actions for the Philippians were not manifested through gritted teeth and with stoical endurance. He actually says he is glad! He rejoices 'with you all'. Note the word 'all' again! It is not so much, on reflection, that Paul has *no* favourites. He has *nothing but* favourites! He loves them *all*. Perhaps that is one reason why he is glad to be of service to them when it hurts him. Maybe the reason he rejoices with them in giving himself for them, and even in the prospect of laying down his life in serving them, is because he loves them so much that it just seems perfectly natural to him to do so. Whatever the reason, there is a lightness in his liberated heart as he bears his cross each day in his cell. God has so cleansed, overcome and filled his selfish, darkened and sinful heart with

His Spirit, mercy, love and truth, that he longs to give himself for others—in life and in death. That is a far cry from grumbling because someone chooses the wrong hymn tune, or getting upset because something thoughtless and uncomplimentary is said, or being overly critical of the faults of another person with a heart as sinful as our own. This rejoicing, coming from an outpoured life, is infectious.

2:18 Mutual gladness and rejoicing

^{18} For the same reason you also be glad and rejoice with me.

THE SAME REASON

Paul tells the Philippians that they must be as glad as he is, and rejoice with him just as he rejoices with them. In short, he says, in effect, 'Do not be sad that my service has led me into prison and do not despair if my life is taken.' He tells them that their gladness and rejoicing is to be 'for the same reason' as his. We need to remember this generally, quite apart from any consideration of persecution or martyrdom, when a loved one dies as a Christian. Although bereavement and natural sorrow over loss is right and biblical, we need to have 'eternity' impressed in our minds. We should see things from heaven's perspective. When a Christian loved one dies, earth says, 'He's gone,' but heaven says, 'He's come'. The rejoicing of our loved ones in heaven knows no limits at all. So we need to 'also be glad and rejoice with' them, whilst mourning their loss to us below at the same time. We do not 'sorrow as others who have no hope'.[31] But what is true generally of the imminent departure of a Christian, is equally true of his impending 'promotion to glory' through martyrdom. Paul tells the Philippians to be glad and to rejoice because his life is being poured out for them, knowing that one day it may lead to an earlier entrance to glory than otherwise would be the case. He wants them to know he is happy with the situation, and he wants them to be, too. Even his joy and rejoicing is not selfish! He wants to share it with others. No recriminations. No 'If only …' mentality. No 'Has God made a mistake?' doubting. Only 'you also be glad and rejoice with me.' After all, that is what they will do in eternity, is it not? And Paul has eternity very much in mind!

Notes

1 **Rev. Leslie Church** (editor), Matthew Henry's Commentary on the Whole Bible in One Volume Editor (Marshall, Morgan and Scott), page 662.

2 **Charles R. Swindoll,** *The Grace Awakening* (Word Books), page 173.

3 Luke 10:38–42.

4 Psalm 51:10.

5 Psalm 51:10.

6 Psalm 1:1.

7 John 3:16.

8 John 3:17.

9 Isaiah 53:6.

10 **Walter A. Henrichsen,** *Disciples Are Made Not Born* (Victor Books), page 52.

11 John 1:12.

12 Proverbs 4:9.

13 *Collins English Dictionary, Third Edition* (HarperCollins Publishers), page 164: this definition was reached by putting together Collins' comments on both 'blameless' and 'blame' to amplify the former.

14 Hebrews 7:26.

15 Isaiah 53:7.

16 Psalm 22:6.

17 John 8:12.

18 Matthew 5:14.

19 **Nestle and Marshall,** *The Interlinear Greek—English New Testament* (Samuel Bagster and Sons Ltd.), page 782.

20 **Rev. Ralph P. Martin,** *Tyndale New Testament Commentaries: The Epistle of Paul to the Philippians* (Tyndale Press), page 117.

21 **Warren W. Wiersbe,** On Being a Servant of God (Nelson), page 120.

22 **Richard Baxter,** *The Reformed Pastor* (SCM Press Ltd.), page 51.

23 **Howard Guinness,** *Sacrifice* (Young Life), pages 38–40.

24 **Nestle and Marshall,** *The Interlinear Greek-English New Testament* (Samuel Bagster and Sons Ltd.), page 782.

25 **Rev. Ralph P. Martin,** *Tyndale New Testament Commentaries: The Epistle of Paul to the Philippians* (Tyndale Press), page 120. **R.C. Sproul** (general editor), *The Reformation Study Bible, NKJV* (Nelson), notes on Philippians 3:4–6, page 1878.

26 **John MacArthur** (author of commentary/notes and general editor), *The MacArthur Study Bible, NKJV* (Word Bibles), note on Philippians 2:17, page 1824. *The NIV Study Bible* (Zondervan Publishing House), note on Philippians 2:17, page 1808.

27 2 Corinthians 12:15

28 Exodus.29:38:41; 2 Kings.16:13; Jeremiah 7:18; Hosea 9:4. **John MacArthur** (author of commentary/notes and general editor), *The MacArthur Study Bible, NKJV* (Word Bibles), note on Philippians 2:17, page 1824.

29 **Helen Roseveare,** *Living Stones* (Hodder and Stoughton), pages 205 and 206, where she quotes a Japanese Pastor, Ruichi Nakazawa.

30 2 Corinthians 5:7.

31 1 Thessalonians 4:13.

Mini-overview 2:19 to 30

The examples of men Paul can trust: Timothy and Epaphroditus—
The like-minded son and the selfless sufferer.

2:19 The Apostle's apostle

19 But I trust in the Lord Jesus to send Timothy to you shortly, that I also may be encouraged when I know your state.

TWO OTHER 'POURED OUT' PEOPLE WHO ARE PRESSING ON!

The last twelve verses of the chapter centre on two of Paul's loyal Christian companions and co-labourers in the gospel who exemplify both the poured out life and the mentality of pressing on for God. They also display the like-mindedness that is a recurring theme of Paul's letter. In verses 19 to 24, Paul concentrates on Timothy. In verses 25 to 30 he majors on Epaphroditus. They are both clear and eloquent letters 'known and read by all men.'[1] God's saving grace and sanctifying Spirit is clearly seen written throughout their lives and service for Him and their loving support of Paul and the Philippian Christians.

TIMOTHY TRUSTED TO REPRESENT PAUL

Timothy is an exceptional servant of God and loyal supporter of his father in Christ, Paul. Whilst some read into Paul's two letters to Timothy that the younger man displays some weaknesses and failures that need buttressing by Paul's guidance and exhortation, it can also be argued that this is simply a father-son intimacy and a sharing of Paul's heart and experience. Be that as it may, it seems that Timothy readily takes on board, in his ministry, what Paul urges on him in those letters, and applies it to the blessing of others and to the glory of God. In that, he is a great example to all of us, and especially to those who play 'second fiddle' to someone else. He serves the Lord before he serves Paul, and thus honours God in his support of the apostle, too. The Philippians are told of Paul's high, even unique, respect for him. I have called him the 'Apostle's apostle' and used a capital 'A' and a small 'a' to make the distinction. By that, I mean that Paul had a special historic place as a foundational Apostle, through whom God's inspired revelation would be given by the Holy Spirit as part of the New Testament, and that Timothy was his apostle, in the sense that he was the one 'sent' by Paul to represent him. 'Apostle' literally means 'sent from' and is the Greek-derived word meaning 'missionary'. So Timothy is the greatest missionary's missionary! What a responsibility to be trusted by Paul to represent him at Philippi in order to encourage, rebuke, instruct and put in order the matters that Paul would have dealt with, were he not imprisoned. He refers to Timothy 'as a son' in verse 22, and there is no doubt that divine grace has helped his protégé to learn the 'family business' very well, to be so trusted. It raises the question whether we, who have been blessed through some Christian as a spiritual role model in the Lord's work, are willing and trying to continue the work which was such a blessing to us through that person. Do we prolong and promote the blessing by being to someone else what a believer has been to us? This seems to be the other side of the coin, where Paul urges Timothy to 'command and teach' the things he passes on to him, and to '*be an example* to the believers in word, in conduct, in love, in spirit, in faith, in purity'.[2]

TRUSTING JESUS FOR SERVICE AS WELL AS FOR SALVATION
Paul does not assume that, because he thinks it is a good idea to send Timothy to the Philippian Christians, the required visit is bound to happen. He is aware that the Lord is in control of all circumstances and that he must trust Him, even for Timothy's intended visit. So he says: 'But I trust in the Lord Jesus to send Timothy to you shortly'. It is a good thing to pray for God's enabling and timing on all our plans, and never to assume that it is right because we think it is right. If and when Timothy does visit them, his time with them will be more closely covered in prayer because Paul starts his plans with the Lord and trusts His overruling hand to make it possible. As the hymn, *What a friend we have in Jesus* urges, we also need to bring 'everything to God in prayer'. Paul knows that if the visit does not materialise, it will be because God thinks otherwise, since he has laid the whole situation before Him first. Paul told the Romans that his plans to come and see them were hindered.[3] Making that admission did not detract from his spirituality, leadership credentials or apostolic authority. The idea

that all our plans have to click together on schedule and without any hitch never constituted a sign to the great apostle that God was at work or that an absence of smooth execution of his plans meant that God disapproved. It is also interesting to consider the 'But' in this verse. Despite the gladness and rejoicing involved in sacrificial service for God, and the willingness to be 'poured out' in martyrdom if needs be, Paul will still be encouraged to have a progress report from Timothy. He fully trusts God, but he does all he can as a prudent human being to find out the latest news about them. This balance of God's overruling power, and man's participation in His will, runs throughout the Bible and touches a number of subjects on the way through. It is true of salvation, of service, of guidance and of protection. Let us never be so 'spiritual' that we neglect the good and obvious duties that God has enabled us to perform.

ENCOURAGED BY THEIR STATE

No doubt 'your state', that Paul wants to know about, refers to the Philippians' spiritual and physical condition. He will be most encouraged if he hears they are walking close with God, witnessing boldly, and being like-minded. Paul shares the apostle John's joy over spiritual children walking in the truth of God. In 2 John 4, his fellow apostle rejoices in another's children's spiritual progress, and in 3 John 4 he gratefully admits that he has 'no greater joy than to hear that [his] children walk in truth.' To hear they walk in God's truth, in his absence, underlines the deep work of God that is being done in their hearts to give them the desire and determination so to walk. Likewise, Paul will be relieved, and grateful, as a loving father figure, to hear that his Philippian family in Christ are safe and well. In this is an example to us all: do we earnestly seek and pray for the spiritual help of those Christians we have come to know? Do we have young, or needy, Christians under our wing? Do we show an interest in their physical welfare as well as their spiritual health? Every older Christian needs at least one younger one to look after. He will also find that often the younger will bless the older—quite apart from the hoped-for help that the older can give the younger! Undoubtedly the encouragement and help was mutually given and mutually enjoyed by Paul and by Timothy.

2:20 Only one option!
20 For I have no-one like-minded, who will sincerely care for your state.

CARING FOR OTHERS

There are two reasons why Paul hopes to send Timothy, in his place, to the Philippian Christians. The first is that he implicitly trusts his son in the faith. That is a wonderful reason for sending him. The second reason is that there is no one else he can send. That is a very sad reason for sending Timothy. If it were simply a question that Timothy had the unique gifts and ideal experience for the job, and thus was the only obvious choice for it, then no blame would attach to others. But verse 21 tells us that it was the self-centredness of other men, who otherwise would have been available, that limits Paul's choice to Timothy. Timothy is the only one who will 'sincerely care for your state'. 'Sincerely' is translated 'naturally' in the AV and 'genuinely' in the NASB: the overtones are that this is a genuine and natural sincerity which causes Timothy to do something that he does not have to be told to do. His natural response, as a committed Christian seeking to please his Lord, is to care for others, and especially the man to whom he owes so much spiritually and personally. Timothy was a rarity among the potential Christian servants then. The premium on genuinely, naturally caring Christians is just as high today.

THE LACK OF LIKE-MINDED MEN

Paul is one such carer, and that is why he refers to Timothy as being uniquely 'like-minded' with him. NASB uses 'of kindred spirit' to convey like-mindedness. Literally, the Greek means 'same-souled'. To be a close fellow-worker in the gospel with someone, not only do we need to be enthusiastically united on the basic Christian doctrines of the gospel, of sanctification and of biblical inerrancy, but we also need to have that oneness of soul, that 'kindred spirit' and to be 'like-minded'. It is a great treasure to work with those who, though not necessarily unanimous on all details, are wholeheartedly agreed on the basic essentials of the faith and whose heart and spirit is one hundred per cent in the work and eager to apply the principles of God's Word as an absolute priority. I am encouraged by an American pastor friend in Arkansas like that. He and I disagree about a number of relatively peripheral points—and sometimes have very interesting and detailed discussions on them—but we work together in the gospel hand in glove. One of the blessings of involvement with United Beach Missions, itself inter-denominational and thoroughly Bible-believing, is to see amongst its leadership the rock solid oneness concerning the place of the Bible, the importance of discipleship, and the most urgent need to evangelise. This overcomes any relatively smaller points of divergence. The fellowship is strengthened, not weakened, by sharing different perspectives from that basis. Like-mindedness is a gift of God, when centred on the Bible, and should be valued as such. Very often, Christians with a heart for holiness and for soul winning feel alone in pursuing these goals in their fellowships and churches, which may have a lesser agenda. They should take heart that even Paul has to say that he has only Timothy who is really like-minded. All of us should search our souls to see if we share the same concerns and priorities as Paul and Timothy. If so, we should seek to encourage others in those directions too. Like-minded men who know and follow Christ will seek to embrace Paul's personal mission statement of 2 Corinthians 4:5, where he declares: 'we do not preach ourselves, but Christ Jesus the Lord, and ourselves your bondservants for Jesus' sake.'

2:21 The common failure

21 For all seek their own, not the things which are of Christ Jesus.

SELF-SEEKING

The word 'seek' repays personal study in the Bible. 'Seek and you shall find'[4] and 'Seek the LORD while He may be found'[5] have encouraged many to set their hearts seriously to seek God, and, in repenting from sins and turning to Christ, they have found Him. 'He who seeks, finds'[6] provided the seeking is whole-hearted.[7] But there is valuable counsel from the Bible about how to seek *after* we have come to Christ. We must 'seek first the kingdom of God and His righteousness'.[8] In the context of relationships, we must 'seek peace, and pursue it'.[9] 'Let no one seek his own, but each one the other's well being'[10] is a New Testament progression on the Old Testament's rhetorical question, 'Do you seek great things for yourself? Do not seek them.'[11] If we are single-minded, and have our hearts set on seeking first the things that please God and then on seeking the things that will bless others, we will be 'of kindred spirit' with Timothy and Paul. But Paul tells the Christians at Philippi that there is no one with him, obviously apart from Timothy, who is doing this! What an amazing admission, so soon in the era of the New Testament church. No matter how gifted people may have been, it is not a lack of gifts, but a lack of willingness to put first things first, that is the problem, here. Why is there no one else to send to minister, in Paul's place, to the Philippians? Because 'all seek their own, not the things which are of Jesus Christ'. Let us bring it up to date. Why does a certain weekly open-air meeting grind to a halt if two people are away, even though others could easily be there? It was once very well attended every Saturday morning and schooled a number of folks in how to preach the gospel and contact people wisely for the Lord. Could it be that it does not have the glamour of other counter attractions, or the easy comfort of a lazier Saturday morning? Why do so many churches find it hard to attract people, young or older, to the prayer meeting? Why is it that a 'Christian band' will bring young Christians out in numbers but they never seem to consider regular support as a praying member of the wider church family? Why do some richer middle-aged Christians give themselves vigorously to marketing their companies' products but leave the door-to-door visitation to older and less energetic saints who can feel so lonely in that work? Why is a missionary meeting like Cinderella in comparison with lighter evening pursuits? Why can a saved person spend hours on the Internet and yet rarely spend an hour in writing to missionaries? Why is it so prevalent to regard the easy things to do as our duty, but imagine that visiting hospitals, old folks' homes, and prisoners is for people with a 'special calling'? Why do many Christians discuss Saturday's big soccer match enthusiastically with each other at church on Sunday, but rarely share any thoughts from their quiet time—if they have one? Why are some pastors and missionaries expected to live near the breadline whilst some members of their churches or fellowships do not think twice before getting a new car, or a better computer, or the latest fitted kitchen, or a replacement carpet or suite? How sacrificially do we live when we make those demands on others? Is not all of this similar to Paul's problem here? 'For all seek their own, not the things which are of Jesus Christ.' How sad that the great apostle had to admit he only had one option—Timothy. In your church, are you an option, or are you not available because you 'seek [your] own'?

2:22 What makes a man dependable?

22 But you know his proven character, that as a son with his father he served with me in the gospel.

PROVEN CHARACTER

The contrast between dependable Timothy and the self-seeking Christians, upon whom Paul could never depend, is now in focus. It is not just a case of Paul being able to express an opinion and a preference: he can say to the Philippians: 'But *you know* his *proven* character'. Timothy does not serve God to impress others, but his single-mindedness in the gospel has impressed the onlookers anyhow. His character is 'proven'. Paul reminds his Christian friends in Philippi that '*you know*.' They had seen him at work since the first visit with Paul, detailed in Acts chapter 16. They had experienced his applied spirituality and faithfulness, as well as his gifts, at first hand. Having been proved as God's servant is an essential point in considering anyone for spiritual responsibility. It is for this reason, for example, that 1 Timothy reveals that an elder of a church must have a good and wholesome reputation from those outside the church.[12] The same thinking excludes an inexperienced man from that responsibility, for the preceding verse says he must not be 'a novice, lest being puffed up with pride he fall into the same condemnation as the devil'. This is an apt reminder to us today, when a pop or film star, or a sporting hero, or a well-known politician can be popularly regarded as an authority on spiritual matters so soon after profession of conversion. He, or she, should learn in humility from those in spiritual leadership: perhaps some celebrity converts should accept, as part of their cross, that the God-directed change in their lifestyle might remove them from their place of public focus. For example, would it not be a great testimony to the Lord, His Word, and His special first day of the week, if a converted sportsman took his stand on not playing (in his case, also working) on the Lord's Day—even if it meant the end of his sporting career? When

Michael Jones, the formidable All Blacks' loose forward, refused to play in the New Zealand *versus* Wales semi-final in a Rugby Union World Cup, because it was on the Lord's Day, it had such a helpful influence on young Christians—and older ones too. How inspirational to know that Eric Liddell, the 'flying Scotsman', who became a household name by the (not entirely factual) film *Chariots of Fire*, refused to run in the Paris Olympics on a Sunday, choosing to rather keep the Lord's Day. For Jones and for Liddell, God's command and God's blessing meant more to them than their sporting careers or winning their expected medals. The point is that they were both men of proven spiritual character. Today the tendency seems to be to capitalise on the media interest—which may be excellent of itself if a true conversion can thus be shown to the world. Sadly, some then erroneously argue that it is more important that the young convert stays in the public spotlight and under the public gaze, pursuing a career in which worldly standards and compromised testimony will damage his spiritual life, rather than to walk in holiness and in obedience to the teaching of Scripture. How many young Christians have carried on with pop music, or an active interest in the theatre or films, because some new celebrity convert has stayed there since conversion? When they later hear their new role models swear and blaspheme, and see them involved in compromising situations, they think that there is nothing wrong in watching and listening to such ungodly influences for pleasure. They can be tempted so easily to do the same. The next step is to regard the newly converted celebrities on the same level as spiritual men who have invested their lives in the Word of God and in serving Christ in holiness and discipleship. I have heard such godly and proven servants of Christ referred to derogatorily as 'spiritual dinosaurs'! Although God has blessed and used them, and still does, they now become regarded as dowdy and irrelevant! Why? Because a new standard of worldliness has become the norm. The Bible's standards and principles become 'old hat' for many as they seek to be as like the world as they can be, without verbally denying Christ or the Bible. One Northern Irish church elder said, on the witness stand in court, that he would not be surprised to hear that his church members watched pornographic videos! It is high time that the church faces these issues and returns to biblical and spiritual standards. However old, gifted, popular, intelligent or well known, Christian novices should not be regarded as Christian leaders or teachers, but should submit to the teaching of the Bible from godly leaders. In this respect, perhaps it should be noted that it was an exceptional providence that C. H. Spurgeon was a pastor at a very young age. It is never a principle that the end justifies the means, even when the person in consideration is regarded with much respect and affection and when God has blessed. God's Word should be applied even-handedly to all. Timothy certainly passed the test of proven character: under God's guidance and enabling, and encouraged by his apostle father/friend, he concentrated on things that enabled him to 'seek first the kingdom of God and His righteousness'.[13] In the same way, every young convert should be advised and encouraged to sow spiritual seed in order to reap a spiritual harvest,[14] by those with a burden to see dependable disciples made and true Christian leaders raised.

SERVICE, APPRENTICESHIP AND TEAMWORK IN THE GOSPEL

What important principles of training young men into Christian leadership are included in the last phrase of the verse: 'he served with me in the gospel'. Timothy learned to serve, not to be 'catered for', though in that service he could have no better spiritual care than to be yoked with Paul. A Wycliffe Bible Translators' magazine compared the life of a recently-martyred missionary with the kind of activities that young Christians were being encouraged to undertake in many churches. In the analysis it referred to the activities of many young people's fellowships as 'the club-like activities of churchianity'. How that phrase hit home. I know, on the other hand, of many young and inexperienced Christians, whose lives went through a significant turning point when they set themselves *to serve* rather than *to be served*. How often have service organisations, such as Operation Mobilisation, Open Air Mission, Home Evangelism or United Beach Missions, been a catalyst in this regard. How useful have churches and fellowships been which have encouraged a regular 'non-glamorous' outreach, such as door-to-door visitation, street contact work, questionnaire work, or open airs in the city centre. When faced with those challenges and opportunities, all are forced to seek the Lord's strength and enabling and to ask Him for the willingness to work for Him. No wonder young Christians grow in that kind of environment, based on a balanced spiritual diet of a personal quiet time, attendance at a church where the Word of God is preached and Jesus is honoured, sharing in the weekly prayer meeting and Bible study, actively keeping Sunday as the Lord's Day, engaging in reading good Christian books, and seeking close friends and confidants who love the Lord. There follows below a translation of an article called *The Christian Commitment*, which I heard read by Val English, the pastor of a Baptist Church in Northern Ireland, when he spoke at a conference there. He told me that its author was an unnamed young Russian Christian in his twenties who was killed by communists six months after this was written:

I am part of the fellowship of the unashamed.
I have the Holy Spirit's power within me.
The dye has been cast; I have stepped over the line.
The decision has been made—I'm a disciple of JESUS.

I won't look back, I won't let up, slow down,
back away or be still.
My past is redeemed, my present makes sense.
My future is secure.

I'm finished and done with low living, sight-walking,
small planning, smooth knees, colourless dreams,
tamed visions, worldly talking, cheap giving and dwarfed goals.

I no longer need pre-eminence, prosperity, position,
promotion, applauding or popularity.
I don't have to be right, first, tops, recognised, praised
regarded or rewarded.

I now live by faith, lean on His presence, walk by patience;
I am uplifted by prayer and labour by power—
The power of Almighty God.

My face is set, my gaze is fast,
My goal is heaven, my road is narrow.
My way is rough, my companions few,
My guide reliable, my mission clear.

I cannot be bought, compromised, detoured, lured away,
turned back, deluded or delayed.

I will not flinch in the face of sacrifice,
Hesitate in the presence of adversity,
Negotiate at the table of the enemy,
Ponder at the pool of popularity or
Meander in the maze of mediocrity.
I won't GIVE up, SHUT up, LET up, until I've
STAYED up, STORED up, PRAYED up, PAID up and
PREACHED up for the cause of Christ.

I am a disciple of Jesus.

I must go till He comes, give till I drop,
Preach till all know, and work till He stops me.
And when He comes for His own
He'll have no trouble recognising me in a crowd
Because MY COLOURS ARE CLEAR!

Here was someone whose commitment proved his character. May we follow in his steps!

APPRENTICED TO THE APOSTLE

In Timothy's case, his spiritual development was helped because he worked as a team member with others, especially Paul. In the context of that teamwork, he was 'apprenticed' to the apostle. This underlines the dual benefit of working closely with others in the gospel and of humbly learning on the job from mature Christians whose maturity is no more important than their zeal. They are a rare breed. When a young Christian sees someone like that, he ought to spend as much time learning from and working with that person as possible. I recall the immense privilege of working with and learning from a dedicated older Christian in my early days after I had committed myself to Christ and his work. Especially did I learn some valuable 'down to earth' theology, as I heard that godly man answer testing questions in a deep, but simple, way in the Tuesday city centre weekly open air meeting, and in the even less rarified atmosphere of the Saturday nights in the city centre. But his knowledge and technique was not what really won me over to following the Lord: it was his enthusiastic resolution to crown Christ as Lord in every department of his life. His oft-quoted couplet—'If He's not Lord of all, He's not Lord at all'—was real to me because I saw it lived out. What a privilege to be in a team of keen Christians and being 'apprenticed' to a man like that.

FATHER AND SON

What comes across so warmly is that there is a loving family relationship between the 'master' and his apprentice. If Timothy's discipleship and leadership were the only products of his fellowship in the gospel with Paul, that would have been wonderful enough! But the *way* he serves says a lot about the attitudes and affections of both men. Both the Philippians and Paul know that Timothy's track record of serving with him has been 'as a son with his father'. Timothy is not simply a 'product of training' but rather a son who is cared for. And Paul is not merely the professor, or the sergeant major, or the chief executive: he is a spiritual father to the younger man. Think what relationships like these can teach us! If only we will take down some of the organisational fences we erect in our churches to keep the age levels apart, and encourage fellowship across the spectrum of ages, perhaps all will benefit. I am not advocating that, for example, young people should not meet together as young people regularly, or that the women's fellowship should cease. I am rather suggesting that *additionally* there is great profit in people of different ages learning from each other and getting to know each other on a spiritual basis and in sharing the gospel together. Why do the different age groups not pray regularly together, for example? Certainly when youth, young adults, middle-aged folks, and senior citizens meet together with a desire to seek God through His Word, and with the determination to pray together, all are on common level ground. It may well be that the older ones may have to speak or pray a little less, and the younger ones a little more, in their time together. But to try to blend all God's family together is a blessing in itself. Young folks realise that they can both learn from the older ones and encourage them by sharing what they are doing for Christ. Older members can begin to see that they have a great contribution to make in the spiritual lives of the younger folks, and thus in the life of the body as a whole. Perhaps some will recall and recapture some of the zeal they had when younger. Additionally the father/son relationship, exemplified by Paul and Timothy, has a lot to demonstrate about loving concern, spiritual oversight of another, careful discipline, openness in sharing, mutual confidence, teaching by example, and—the rarest of commodities today—real loyalty. And it underlines that we are interested in people, and not just in workers. No wonder that Timothy's character was 'proven': Paul knew all about him, helped him, fellowshipped with him, and loved him as a father loves his son. No doubt the 'first commandment with a promise', namely 'Honour your father and mother'[15] is graciously applied by Timothy to his spiritual father, just as much as he applied it physically to his godly mother, Eunice.[16] Too few older Christians take a personal, direct and loving interest in young people in our churches. Younger Christians should respect and honour some who may have forgotten far more than their younger brothers and sisters have yet learned about knowing and serving God. Let us all pray for that mind 'which was also in Christ Jesus'[17] in these matters.

2:23 The place of prudent planning

23 Therefore I hope to send him at once, as soon as I see how it goes with me.

URGENCY

Because Timothy is faithful and reliable, and because Paul so much wants to know the 'state' of the Philippian church, Paul hopes to send him 'at once'. His desire is urgent to despatch his younger colleague to

Philippi for the good of the Christians there. We should never allow our trust in God, and our belief in His overruling, to take away our sense of urgency to do things that need immediate action. Much that is wrongly taken as a peaceful spirit and serene trust can, in reality, be lethargic indifference or just laziness. It is true that 'Laziness grows on people; it begins in cobwebs and ends in iron chains'[18] and that 'the lazier a man is the more he plans to do tomorrow'.[19] I heard *Mañana* once described as indicating a 'sense of urgency' for one man I knew! There is a time to wait, to consider carefully, to discuss in detail, and to pray persistently. But there is also a time to act, and still to pray. Paul decides this is the time to send Timothy. How many times have we missed opportunities to be a blessing to others, and to be blessed ourselves, by delaying? Some will spend eternity separate from God, because their hearts were hardened by initially refusing to turn to God at a specific point in time, preferring to delay unnecessarily.[20] Some lost men and women never heard the gospel because Christians kept putting off the need to tell them. The questions, 'And how shall they believe in Him of whom they have not heard? And how shall they hear without a preacher?'[21] may pursue us until the day when 'we shall all stand before the judgement seat of Christ',[22] and let us remember that delayed obedience is disobedience.

CAUTION

The Greek means 'I hope to send him the very moment' that Paul sees how it goes with him. Clearly, Paul has an urgency about wanting to send Timothy. But he displays a healthy caution, too. Unlike some today, it is not for him to presume to know the details of God's will in advance. If ever anyone had the gifts of the Spirit, this unique apostle had. Yet he does not claim a 'word of knowledge' or the ability to foresee the future, even when he is directly concerned with the Lord's work. The gospel singer who made an impact in the 1950s and beyond, George Beverly Shea, made the lines of the solo famous: 'I don't know what the future holds, but I know Who holds the future.' So it is here that Paul's caution is shown in two ways. First, he says '*I hope* to send him at once'; second, he adds, '*as soon as I see how it goes* with me'. It is not wrong to have our personal hopes, but it is prudent to see how things work out, and how God moves the circumstances. James tells us that we should not say: 'Today or tomorrow we will go to such and such a city, spend a year there, buy and sell, and make a profit' but tells us: 'Instead you ought to say, "If the Lord wills, we shall live and do this or that."'[23] That is not as a 'fail-safe' in case God does not do what we have asked Him to do, but just as a reminder that our lives are very short and uncertain, that He is in control, that our wills are to be obedient to His, and that our trust is not to be in circumstances but in Him alone. So Paul's caution is both practical and spiritual, and an example to us. We should live with Jesus' words in our minds, 'without Me you can do nothing'.[24] To face the facts, in deciding what plan of action to take, is not unspiritual or lacking in faith: it is sanctified common sense that pleases God. May Paul's blend of eager urgency for the task, and sensible trusting caution, be ours too!

2:24 The personal note
[24] But I trust in the Lord that I myself shall also come shortly.

TRUSTING
After the urgency and the caution comes the personal note. Paul is trusting in the Lord to let him go shortly to see them. He is not rashly going to make that decision himself, even if he is given freedom, but trusting in the Lord to get him there, if indeed that is what God wants for him. This verse links with the previous one in the Greek to give the following sense: 'On the one hand, as soon as I know what is happening I will send Timothy to you. But on the other hand, I trust in the Lord that I myself will come soon.' Paul's hope is that Timothy will come to care for the church soon, but that he will follow close behind. As soon as he sees how the land lies he will despatch Timothy, and he trusts God that as soon as he is released (if he is released) he will go too. Paul rightly has his plans in mind. Yet his 'I trust in the Lord that' reminds the Philippians and us of one of the key principles in guidance, namely that we can only trust in the Lord for any future event or happening. Our plans are good, but He is in control. We should take Proverbs to heart: 'Trust in the LORD with all your heart, and lean not on your own understanding; in all your ways

acknowledge Him, and He shall direct your paths.'[25] We need to be reminded often that the secret of guidance is to stay close to the guide and trust Him for the future. It is easy to do that when your guide is completely trustworthy and wants to help you. Our guide does! His name is Jesus.

WANTING

But through all the spiritual trust, practical obedience, and biblically-based common sense, we can almost hear Paul's heart beating for them. He wants to 'also come shortly'. He has great confidence in Timothy, and that he will perform his delegated tasks to God's glory, but Paul also wants to go there and see them himself! Here is yet another expression of his love for them. It makes us ask if we love our church members, or members of other churches and fellowships where we have got to know God's people, with anything approaching this kind of love. What a blessing to have Christian family all round the world! It is worth investing time, love and prayer in such a uniquely God-given relationship. Surely loving the brethren is a most important outworking of Christian teaching and is a true test of real discipleship. The logic of George Verwer, of Operation Mobilisation, is thoroughly biblical and practical when he says: '"Oh," someone says, "there is a good, evangelical Christian … he has good sound doctrine. He does not have much love for others and he is not very humble, but he's very sound in doctrine." He is *not* sound in doctrine if he does not love the brethren. What do we read in 1 John 4:8? "He that loveth not knoweth not God." There is no sounder doctrine than love, and apart from love there is no sound doctrine. This is the basis of all Bible doctrine. You take the base out and everything you build will eventually collapse.'[26] Paul's love for them means he will send his most trusted co-worker and spiritual son and then get there himself if God so enables him!

2:25 The all-rounder

25 Yet I considered it necessary to send to you Epaphroditus, my brother, fellow worker and fellow soldier, but your messenger and the one who ministered to my need,

A NECESSARY CONSIDERATION

Paul's sending of Epaphroditus back to his own church community in Philippi is both considered and necessary. Paul has put a lot of thought and no doubt much prayer into that decision. His paramount concern is the good of the church. That is why, until it is clear that Timothy and possibly he himself will be able to go to Philippi, he considers it very important to send Epaphroditus. It is good to consider things carefully and to deal with others' necessities before our preferences. Paul exemplifies this, yet again.

A SELFLESS MAN

All we know about Epaphroditus is found in this chapter and in chapter 4:18. His name means 'loving' or 'charming' and he certainly lives out God's love in the charming way that, like Paul, he puts others before himself. He has been sent with a financial gift for Paul, and stays to be a great blessing to him. And yet the selfless apostle sends this selfless man back to the church, not concentrating on his own needs or preferences. It is rare and challenging to find someone who will put the needs and good of others before his own real and legitimate needs, especially in prison! Paul follows the principle of Christ's teaching that 'He who has two tunics, let him give to him who has none; and he who has food, let him do likewise.'[27] He has two loyal working companions and he gives them both to the Philippian church. Epaphroditus is dispatched to them first, with the promise of Timothy soon after, and then Paul himself, if the Lord so allows. Epaphroditus is, first of all, Paul's Christian brother. He shares a common Heavenly Father, having been brought into the family of God by grace. But he both works and battles for the gospel with the senior apostle: he is a 'fellow worker and fellow soldier'. He can also be trusted to carry both news and money with integrity and honesty as the 'messenger' of the Philippians. And he is a servant-hearted saint, conscious of Paul's needs. He is a true 'all-rounder' for God. Just the kind of man you would like to visit you in prison! But there is more!

2:26 The non-hypochondriac!

[26] since he was longing for you all, and was distressed because you had heard that he was sick

DISTRESS OF A DIFFERENT KIND

'Jennifer (not her real name) does not enjoy good health,' was my comment to the chairman of the committee from which she was absent. 'No, brother,' he replied, 'but she enjoys bad health a lot more!' Perhaps a little unloving, he had noted that her main topic of conversation was how ill she felt, even though she was in pretty good health generally. Not so, Epaphroditus! His concern is not that he has been very ill, but that the church at Philippi will worry about him. In fact, the thought distresses him. Imagine a sick man becoming distressed not because he is weak, or feeling terrible physically, or unable to go where he wants or do what he likes, but because others have heard about his sickness! The AV translates the word rendered 'distressed' and the NKJV as 'full of heaviness.' It is the same word 'used to describe the Lord's agony in Gethsemane, and denotes great mental and spiritual perturbation.'[28] Imagine a sick man being so overwhelmed in case the news of his sickness should worry a church for which he longed. Such is his love for his fellow saints in that Roman colony. He is not the kind of man who would miss the prayer meeting because he felt tired, or shun the open-air witness because of a cold! How does he compare with self-pampering twenty-first century western Christians who neglect Christian fellowship and service on only the slightest excuse of being slightly off-colour or feeling a little weary?

LONGING

It seems that his genuine love and compassion for others so fills his mind that he does not take too much notice of 'little things', such as if he will live or die. Furthermore he is 'longing' for *all* of the Christians. Fellowship with others means so much to him that he needs no reason to go and accepts no excuse to stay away. This is the same word that already has described Paul's longing for all the Philippian Christians 'with the affection of Jesus Christ.'[29] When we are away from our home church or Christian group, on business, holiday, other duties or through sickness, do we have such a strong desire and pull to get back into fellowship with our Christian family? Is it just a meeting to go to, or a family to greet, help and support? When tempted to be too easy on ourselves, may we remember how Epaphroditus poured himself out for them?

2:27 Two-sided mercy

27 For indeed he was sick almost unto death; but God had mercy on him, and not only on him but on me also, lest I should have sorrow upon sorrow.

MERCY ON THE EDGE OF DEATH

Paul tells the Philippians something about Epaphroditus that Epaphroditus would never tell them himself: he really had been at death's door. His sickness had been very serious and his life had hung in the balance. Whilst it is sometimes appropriate to share details of one's physical illnesses with others who need to know or who will pray for the sick person, we see here that there was no automatic calling for healing. The fact that the church did not hear from Epaphroditus himself about his near-terminal illness shows that a Christian soldier can demonstrate his faith in God sometimes by *not* sharing his needs as well as by sharing them for prayer at other times. There is no fixed way to deal with our illnesses. God is sovereign and can be trusted to do what is right in each case. To heal is not a problem for an omnipotent God, but it is not always his will to heal. Here, God had mercy on Epaphroditus and restored him. We are not told whether that was in answer to the prayer of the sick man, concerned individual Christians, or the church that heard he was sick. But we know it was God who healed him, in His own way and in His own time. God's mercy does not consist only of forgiveness of sins through repentant faith in Christ. It includes God's compassionate treatment of His people in each and every circumstance of life, even on the very edge of life itself. The word 'mercy', or a derivative of it, occurs 339 times in the Bible! Paul, Epaphroditus, the Philippian Christians, and those knowing Christ today all have benefited, do benefit and will benefit from the mercy and mercies of our most merciful God.

WHY WAS EPAPHRODITUS SO ILL?

We will see in verse 20 that this dedicated man had worked so hard and persistently for the Kingdom of God, and for Paul's support, that he had driven himself into the ground. Whether his sickness was caused by disease, lack of good food, driving himself too hard or physical persecution and hardship, we do not know. We do know that, near to breathing his last, God saved him from death and he is now duly available to work for God again, as verses 25 and 28 show us. Like him, we will not receive our home call, through whatever means, until the Lord has decided we have finished the agenda and the work He has for us on earth. Like Paul, we should be eagerly anticipating our 'promotion to glory' whilst gratefully knowing the blessing of working for Christ in such a needy and lost world. Also like him, we know that our sovereign God will fulfil His timetable for each one of us personally as well as for the world globally and His creation universally! The challenging question to us, posed by men like Paul, Timothy and Epaphroditus, is how much will the work of God and the people of God miss us when we go? I recall a business associate who said that his manager tried to fill in for him when he was away on vacation, but could not. The reason given was that his boss could not find out what work, if any, my friend was supposed to be doing! Would we really be missed? Will the Kingdom of God lose a significant quality and quantity of prayer, giving, service, care, missionary interest, witness and encouragement to others when we die? It is not too late to make the response to that question 'Yes!' by God's grace, and our rededication to Him and His work, even as we read this now.

MERCY FOR PAUL TOO

Paul not only rejoices that his brother is well again. He sees it as a mercy to him, too. His Lord knows full well how much the suffering apostle can bear. He will never permit one of His children to carry a load which he cannot take. For Paul, the loss of his dear brother would have given him 'sorrow upon sorrow'. Grieving over the death of a loved one or a dear friend is natural and right. In fact, there would be something seriously wrong if we did not miss someone who had been precious to us. The Christian is not told not to sorrow over the death of his Christian brothers and sisters. He is told not to 'sorrow as others who have no hope.'[30] Our sorrow, in that case, is because we miss someone we love. It is not because it is worse for the person who has gone on to 'be with Christ which is far better'![31] Our sorrow is not like that of an unbeliever. And we know that God is in control and that His will and timing is perfect, even if we do not understand that timing. But, even with this knowledge and all the means of grace at Paul's disposal, as well as the very presence of the Holy Spirit, Paul could have been facing one sorrow too many. For this reason, God limits the temptation to despair and give up that Epaphroditus' sad death might have provoked. God will always give the Christian the wonderful mercy of being able to overcome any temptation faced in the line of duty, both by His help in the temptation and in His limiting of it. God's Spirit guides Paul's pen as he writes to the Corinthians: 'No temptation has overtaken you except such as is common to man; but God is faithful, who will not allow you to be tempted beyond what you are able, but with the temptation will also make the way of escape, that you may be able to bear it.'[32] Here the 'way of escape', which so encouraged the isolated servant of God in prison, is that God saves Epaphroditus from death. Paul's grateful acknowledgement of that reveals that Epaphroditus' home call then could have been the straw that broke the camel's back. He had taken as much sorrow as he felt he could. God knew exactly what the weight should be on His child, before He lifted the burden from him. He still acts towards us in that same grace today. He is a loving Heavenly Father, not a malicious torturer. The mercy we obtain from God from His throne of grace *always* enables us to 'find grace to help in time of need.'[33] It may take us time to realise that in practice, but it is *always* so.

2:28 Back in service

²⁸ Therefore I sent him the more eagerly, that when you see him again you may rejoice, and I may be less sorrowful.

EAGERNESS

Much as Paul has a Christian love and affection for Epaphroditus, he does not however take his recovery from illness selfishly. Much as he would love to spend more time with him in fellowship in that lonely prison cell, he recognises that God has raised up the sick servant to glorify Him and to bless others, notably the Philippians. We should not monopolise the time and attention of servants of Christ, but release them to do the work they are called to. The need of others is to be a more important priority to us than our own liking to spend too much time with a man who has a more vital job to do. That does not mean that we do not have some precious times of fellowship with men and women of God, but just that we keep our priorities right. Here we see Paul's *eagerness* to send Epaphroditus to them to serve Christ. This is what both men live for and no doubt one was as eager to go as the other was to send him. Restored health should always be invested in new opportunities for service, whilst it lasts. One day our health will fail. It will become insufficient to do such work, either through illness or home call, and we must work whilst it is still day. In this, like Paul and Epaphroditus, we must follow our Master's example.[34]

REJOICING

Paul knows that such eagerness to send the restored missionary to Philippi will cause the church to rejoice. It is worth contemplating why that should be, and testing our own motivations in the light of our findings. First, they would see for themselves that the man they were worried about was fully fit again. Second, as presumably they had prayed for his recovery they would rejoice in answered prayer. Third, they could anticipate benefiting from his ministry and working with him in the gospel. Fourth, they knew what his recovery would mean to Paul, with whom they had a close and loving relationship. Fifth, there are some who feel that Epaphroditus' return to his native Philippi, at a time when their beloved apostle was lonely in prison, may indicate that Paul had found some fault in him and was sending back a failure. So Paul tells them that his return is a cause for rejoicing, not for reproach or regret.[35] For example, Ralph Martin comments that 'The unexpected return may have caused great disappointment in the church, and have led some to conclude that his mission had failed, and that Paul had been bereft of sympathetic human friendship at an hour when he needed it most. Paul would answer that criticism in advance by a glowing appraisal of the worth of their leader, and a record of circumstances which led to his departure homewards. Not only should they forbear from fault-finding, they should *rejoice* that he had been restored to health and is to be with them once again.' John MacArthur comments more succinctly: 'Paul's sending him back to the church with this letter needed an explanation, lest they think that Epaphroditus had not served Paul well.' In telling the Philippians to rejoice, Paul sets a good example of doing all he can to maintain the reputation and character of God's servant. We should do the same, as we shall see emphasised in the next verse. A final reason for rejoicing would be that, rather than criticise Epaphroditus, the Philippian Christians would long to see the man who was 'longing' to see them so that they could spoil him a little! All this would add up to receiving the much-esteemed Epaphroditus 'with all gladness' as verse 29 shows is the expectation and recommendation of Paul. This rejoicing of the church will find its echo in the prison cell! Paul will be 'less sorrowful' at both missing Epahroditus and not yet being able to visit the Philippian Christians himself. He knows that at least one of the dedicated trio can go immediately to be a blessing to a church he loves. And Paul has cultivated the godly habit of rejoicing with those who rejoice, which itself will heighten his selfless rejoicing for them that we have already seen in verse 17 of this chapter. Again the recurrent theme of rejoicing lightens that darkened cell.

2:29 Gladness and esteem

29 Receive him therefore in the Lord with all gladness, and hold such men in esteem;

HOW TO RECEIVE A SERVANT OF GOD

Paul encourages his friends in Philippi to receive Epaphroditus. He also tells them *how* they should welcome this servant of God, whom they know already as a fellow Philippian. His advice to them holds good for us today. Here are important principles about how Christians should receive those dedicated disciples who come to serve the Lord amongst them. First, there is a 'therefore.' It is because of all that they have just had put to them about Epaphroditus that they should receive him. He is a faithful, dedicated, selfless, caring, servant of God and supporter of God's people. That is enough reason for any Christian or church to receive someone coming to them. Though not esteemed by the God-hating world around, and maybe not catching the imagination of a worldly and compromised church which prefers gimmicks and entertainment to true spirituality, the fact that a person is a dedicated disciple of Jesus Christ is always a reason to receive him, or her. When that person has hazarded his life to be a blessing to them, there is an even stronger reason to receive him. Then Epaphroditus is to be received by them 'in the Lord.' The most important thing about any fellow Christian is that he, or she, is 'in the Lord'. The Holy Spirit has 'baptised' or 'placed' us all into the body of Christ at conversion so we are jointly found in Him. We are told that 'by one Spirit we were all baptised into one body ... whether Jews or Greeks, whether slaves or free ... and have all been made to drink into one Spirit.'[36] That is why, with all other true Christians, we see our rock-solid confidence for our common salvation—'in the Lord'. Here is the basis for our fellowship together, therefore. Here we see our true family ties. Here is our joint source of power through prayer. Here we see what our home in heaven is based on. There is never anything more basic that we will have in common with anyone on earth or in heaven than that we, with them, are 'in the Lord'. All else may de different: age, colour, race, gender, experience of life, geographical location, material background, intellectual abilities, natural gifts, physical appearance, preferred tastes and pursuits, artistic or sporting aptitudes—all of these are so variable and so passing in our brief existence on this side of eternity. But to be 'in the Lord' gives us a deep spiritual, personal and eternal oneness with others 'in the Lord' that the world cannot replicate or take away. A Christian is someone whose confidence is 'in the Lord' and who is accepted in heaven because of that saving position 'in the Lord'. It is not because the Philippians and Epaphroditus are all from Philippi that they are dear to each other. It is because, by God's mercy and grace in the gospel of the Lord Jesus Christ, they are all found anchored 'in the Lord.' All else is secondary by comparison. And, as we have already seen from the continual reminders from Paul about joy and rejoicing, this godly missionary from Paul is to be received 'with all gladness'. The angels in heaven rejoice when sinners are saved[37] and we should rejoice when we can share some of that salvation blessing and fellowship with them down here. What a joy it is to be welcomed by wholehearted Christians whether you meet them for the first time and know little about them, or whether they form part of your regular Christian supporting family at home. When we lack that gladness to meet with others 'in the Lord', something has to be wrong in us or in them or in us all. We should be happier to be with fellow committed Christians than any party goer is at his party, or opera fan is at his opera, or theatre goer or cinema goer is at his place of entertainment, or football supporter is at his home game. When our fellowship with each other 'in the Lord' is less socially superficial and more spiritually searching we will rejoice more in the company of others as we seek to encourage each other on to 'love and good works'.[38]

HOW TO REGARD GOD'S SERVANTS

Paul tells the Philippians not only to esteem Epaphroditus, but also to do so for similar followers of Christ. He says 'hold such men in esteem.' The world at large, at best, only gives lip service to true men of God. More often than not they will be vilified, criticised and ridiculed. The world is no more worthy of them than in the suffering heros in the gallery of faith of Hebrews chapter 11.[39] The world thrusts its cheap and worthless plastic accolades at the passing and falling stars of stage, screen, sport, wealth and politics. The Christian should rather esteem the faithful Christian servant: he is better for the world than any actor, footballer, millionaire or prime minister. His work is eternal in value, lasting in quality, and meets real human need at its deepest point. He should be supported in every way by those who know Christ. That is why Paul tells the Philippians not only to receive this man gladly, but to esteem all like him. There are not too many of them around!

BUT DO WE FALL INTO THE WORLD'S TRAP, TOO?

So often, Christians have to take a middle path of sanity between too silly extremes. It is the same with how ministers of the gospel are to be esteemed. On the one hand, we see the excesses of adulation and film star status given to certain televangelists, or we hear of ministers who seem to be more like a king or chief executive of a company than a servant of One who washed the disciples' feet.[40] Whilst our church leaders, including full-time paid ministers of the gospel, should be treated with friendly respect, they should not think more highly of themselves than they ought.[41] The trend to imitate those in authority or high positions in the world is to be deplored: Christian ministers are to be servant-hearted examples to the Christian church, not overlords.[42] But, at the same time, men who give themselves to the Lord and His work—especially to do with teaching the Word of God—must be treated with high esteem by those they serve in the church. Those in leadership, referred to in the New Testament as 'elders' or 'bishops',[43] are to be honoured and those who 'rule well' in that role are 'to be counted worthy of double honour, especially those who labour in the word and doctrine.'[44] Why, then, are some churches so often prepared to be mean in their remuneration of such men and pay them a salary that clearly indicates their work is not esteemed highly, and which those paying him would never accept for themselves? Why are they expected by some to do all the menial tasks that others could easily do and that can detract from the main point of their calling? Why is the willingness of many ministers to sacrifice sometimes traded on, and used as an excuse for treating them in a way that they do not deserve? Should not the principle be that 'the labourer is worthy of his wages'[45] and should he not be so paid, even if through love for Christ he is willing to live below the bread line? But how do we esteem our ministers and spiritual leaders in other ways? Do we *really* pray for them each day and at our church prayer meetings? Are we concerned about their physical health, as the Philippians were about Epaphroditus and Paul? Do we submit to their spiritual leadership insofar as they are faithful to the Bible? Do we seek to encourage them as spiritual elders, and when we feel we have to criticise them, is it done humbly and lovingly to their faces, after prayer and careful thought, and as respectfully as a child should approach his father?[46] Do we ever offer to help them, in whatever way they would like, as far as we are able? Do we regard it as our duty, as well as our privilege, to support their ministry by being there whenever we can and by seeking to encourage and take others to be there too? Do we support them by being willing to be an extra pair of eyes, ears and hands for them, without being seen to push ourselves for the sake of being recognised ourselves? Are we considerate and kind to their loved ones too? So often the pastor's wife or children can be hurt because they are regarded as part of his furniture. They are people who also need friends and supportive fellowship. Should there be dissension in the church, do we support them to the very limit possible whilst remaining true to biblical principle and godly practice? If they do fall, do we approach them in the same way as we would like others to approach us in those circumstances? Do we lovingly exhort them, rather than slyly snipe at them? Do we ever thank them for what they do? There is so much more that could be said, but are we falling into the world's trap of over-exalting them on the one hand, or treating them in mean contempt on the other? Do we esteem them highly as beloved brothers in Christ who seek to further the work of their, and our, Saviour and Lord?

2:30 He gave what you could not

30 because for the work of Christ he came close to death, not regarding his life, to supply what was lacking in your service toward me.

THE WORK OF CHRIST

The 'work of Christ' is a key part in the life of Epaphroditus. The phrase has three meanings, only one of which applies here. Without the 'work of Christ' in the other two senses, however, it could not have its third meaning. There is 'the work of Christ' already achieved. His finished work on Calvary, where he bore our sins and the punishment for them when bearing the wrath of God in His body in our place, is the *finished* 'work of Christ.' His resurrection and ascension underline the once and for all nature of that substitutionary death.[47] There is the ongoing 'work of Christ' in the hearts and minds of believers.[48] Christ is at work, through the Spirit, to conform us to His image. But 'the work of Christ', referred to here, is the Saviour's commission to go and preach the gospel and to make disciples.[49] Epaphroditus thus shares the concern of his imprisoned senior colleague. He wants to make Christ known and to see disciples coming from his work, emanating in churches being formed from the 'living stones'[50] of converted lives. In this case, 'the work of Christ' means his close and costly association with his own home church in Philippi, and his unreserved support for Paul.

Some people give their lives in attempting to conquer Everest or outer space, or for political aims. Some work themselves into ill health to increase their financial prosperity. But these goals are temporary and of no significance in eternity. Epaphroditus had his eyes fixed firmly on 'the work of Christ'. If he was going to die, he would do so for something that would outlast this passing world. In heaven, he would rejoice with those who had been won, partly or wholly, through God's having used him in the gospel. Christ's work is worth living for and dying for. So his life was of secondary importance to him. More important was how he would spend it, and for Whom would he live it.

A LIFE INVESTMENT

The fact that this Philippian Christian leader 'came close to death' was not a surprise to him. He chose to live 'not regarding his life' in his supportive service for Paul. I suspect it was not a surprise to Paul either, as is shown by his words to the Corinthians that he 'will very gladly spend and be spent for your souls; though the more abundantly I love you, the less I am loved.'[51] Paul's whole life shows that faithfulness to God and His gospel mean more to him than survival. Consider his account of his 'normal' Christian life when, defending his apostleship, he recalls: 'in labours more abundant, in stripes above measure, in prisons more frequently, in deaths often. From the Jews five times I received forty stripes minus one. Three times I was beaten with rods; once I was stoned; three times I was shipwrecked; a night and a day I have been in the deep; in journeys often, in perils of waters, in perils of robbers, in perils of my own countrymen, in perils of the Gentiles, in perils in the city, in perils in the wilderness, in perils in the sea, in perils among false brethren; in weariness and toil, in sleeplessness often, in hunger and thirst, in fastings often, in cold and nakedness … besides the other things, what comes upon me daily: my deep concern for all the churches.'[52] Epaphroditus will, no doubt, accept all that as normal also, in following and making Christ known in a hostile world. How that shames much of our spineless discipleship today. These men can accept a measured disregarding of their lives and come 'close to death' because it really is true, as Paul put it, that 'for me, to live is Christ'.[53] Each has a life fully invested *in and for* Christ. Can we say the same?

FILLING THE GAP

Epaphroditus had to work so much harder to make up for the lack of help from the Philippian church. Paul's commendation of their care for him, in chapter 4:14–20, conclusively demonstrates that this failure to help was caused by circumstances outside their control, rather than wilful neglect. They did the best that they could, but it was just not enough. It is as if someone has given sacrificially a huge financial gift to help to meet an ever-bigger need. He has done what he can, but still more is needed. That is why in the next chapter Paul gratefully acknowledges their resumption of support by saying: 'I rejoiced in the Lord greatly that now at last your care for me has flourished again; though you surely did care, but you lacked opportunity.'[54] Geography was perhaps the Philippians' biggest problem, in the same way as a Christian in the West cannot physically be with his needy brothers in Christ in China or Pakistan. In those days there were no telegraphic transfers, on-line banking, or DHL courier! Jet travel and car hire did not feature then! But Epaphroditus spent himself and his health to fill the gap which his Christian brothers would have liked to fill themselves. It remains a fact that, whatever the reason, when Christians do not support the work of Christ, others have to work harder to do so. When that is beyond our control, God understands. When it is because we do not care enough, that is very sad. One day the Lord of the harvest will ask us why. They had the willingness but not the opportunity. We have many opportunities to help and support other needy Christians. Do we have the willingness? Do we do it?

Notes

1 2 Corinthians 3:2.
2 1 Timothy 4:11,12.
3 Romans 15:22.
4 Matthew 7:7.
5 Isaiah 55:6.
6 Luke 11:10.
7 Jeremiah 29:13.
8 Matthew 6:33.
9 Psalm 34:14.
10 1 Corinthians 10:24.
11 Jeremiah 45:5.
12 1 Timothy 3:7.
13 Matthew 6:33.
14 Galatians 6:7,8.
15 Ephesians 6:2.
16 2 Timothy 1:5.
17 Philippians 2:5.
18 **M. Hale** quoted in **Lloyd Cory** (compiler), *Quotable Quotations* (Victor Books), page 209.

19 As quoted in **Lloyd Cory** (compiler), *Quotable Quotations* (Victor Books), page 210.

20 Hebrews 4:7–15.

21 Romans 10:14.

22 Romans 14:10.

23 James 4:13,15.

24 John 15:5.

25 Proverbs 3:5,6.

26 George Verwer, *A Revolution of Love and Balance* (STL Productions), page 12

27 Luke 3:11.

28 Rev. Ralph P. Martin, *Tyndale New Testament Commentaries: The Epistle of Paul to the Philippians* (Tyndale Press), page 130.

29 Philippians 1:8.

30 1 Thessalonians 4:13.

31 Philippians 1:23.

32 1 Corinthians 10:13.

33 Hebrews 4:16.

34 John 9:4.

35 Rev. Ralph P. Martin, *Tyndale New Testament Commentaries: The Epistle of Paul to the Philippians* (Tyndale Press), page 132. **John MacArthur** (author of commentary/notes and general editor), *The MacArthur Study Bible, NKJV* (Word Bibles), note on Philippians 2:25, page 1824

36 1 Corinthians 12:13

37 Luke 15:10.

38 Hebrews 10:24.

39 Hebrews 11:38.

40 John 13:5–14.

41 Romans 12:3.

42 1 Peter 5:3.

43 See, for example, Philippians 1:1; 1 Timothy 3:1,2; Titus 1:7; Titus 1:5; 1 Peter5:1.

44 1 Timothy 5:17.

45 1 Timothy 5:18.

46 1 Timothy 5:1.

47 John 19:30; Hebrews 1:3; 1 Peter 2:24; 1 Peter 3:18; Hebrews 10:10; Acts 2:24; Acts 3:36; Romans 4:25; Ephesians 1:20.

48 Romans 8:9–11; Galatians 4:19; Ephesians 3:17.

49 Mark 16:15; Matthew 28:19.
50 1 Peter 2:5.
51 2 Corinthians 12:15.
52 2 Corinthians 11:23–28.
53 Philippians 1:21.
54 Philippians 4:10.

The letter opened (continued)

Philippians Chapter 3

[1] Finally, my brethren, rejoice in the Lord. For me to write the same things to you is not tedious, but for you it is safe.

[2] Beware of dogs, beware of evil workers, beware of the mutilation! [3] For we are the circumcision, who worship God in the Spirit, rejoice in Christ Jesus, and have no confidence in the flesh, [4] though I also might have confidence in the flesh. If anyone else thinks he may have confidence in the flesh, I more so: [5] circumcised the eighth day, of the stock of Israel, of the tribe of Benjamin, a Hebrew of the Hebrews; concerning the law, a Pharisee; [6] concerning zeal, persecuting the church; concerning the righteousness which is in the law, blameless. [7] But what things were gain to me, these I have counted loss for Christ. [8] Yet indeed I also count all things loss for the excellence of the knowledge of Christ Jesus my Lord, for whom I have suffered the loss of all things, and count them as rubbish, that I may gain Christ [9] and be found in Him, not having my own righteousness, which is from the law, but that which is through faith in Christ, the righteousness which is from God by faith; [10] that I may know Him and the power of His resurrection, and the fellowship of His sufferings, being conformed to His death, [11] if, by any means, I may attain to the resurrection from the dead. [12] Not that I have already attained, or am already perfected; but I press on, that I may lay hold of that for which Christ Jesus has also laid hold of me. [13] Brethren, I do not count myself to have apprehended; but one thing I do, forgetting those things which are behind and reaching forward to those things which are ahead, [14] I press toward the goal for the prize of the upward call of God in Christ Jesus. [15] Therefore let us, as many as are mature, have this mind; and if in anything you think otherwise, God will reveal even this to you. [16] Nevertheless, to the degree that we have already attained, let us walk by the same rule, let us be of the same mind.

[17] Brethren, join in following my example, and note those who so walk, as you have us for a pattern. [18] For many walk, of whom I have told you often, and now tell you even weeping, that they are the enemies of the cross of Christ: [19] whose end is destruction, whose god is their belly, and whose glory is in their shame—who set their mind on earthly things. [20] For our citizenship is in heaven, from which we also eagerly wait for the Saviour, the Lord Jesus Christ, [21] who will transform our lowly body that it may be conformed to His glorious body, according to the working by which He is able even to subdue all things to Himself.

Four threes from Philippians 3
Mini-overview 3:1 to 3:6

First set of threes—description of a Christian.
In warning the church about a wrong emphasis on mere externals (here circumcision), Paul majors on three characteristics that describe a real Christian.

3:1 Better safe than sorry!
1 Finally, my brethren, rejoice in the Lord. For me to write the same things to you is not tedious, but for you it is safe.

'FINALLY'

'Finally' is the word that links chapter 2 to chapter 3. Paul has just extolled the faithfulness of Epaphroditus, whom Paul sends to the Philippians. He believes that seeing this dear brother will make them 'rejoice' in receiving him with 'all gladness.' Paul also knows that he will be 'less sorrowful' in the knowledge that such a good servant of Christ will be in fellowship with such a beloved group of Christians. Their rejoicing, however, is not to be only on the level of Epaphroditus' restored health and coming visit. Rejoicing in the preaching of the true gospel (chapter 1), in realising that he has been enabled to do effective work for the Lord and that his sacrificial outpouring of himself helps the Philippians service for God (chapter 2) are good and right. But, like the rejoicing over Epaphroditus, they are to rejoice on a far deeper and permanent basis, as we shall now see.

SOURCE OF REJOICING

The pleasing taste of rejoicing has already flavoured this 'letter of rejoicing'. Here we have the real source of rejoicing stated again. On six occasions the word 'rejoice' is used previously in this letter to his beloved Philippian friends, and Paul repeats it twice in this chapter and will repeat it twice in the final chapter, as we shall see later. However, this is the first time that the apostle commands the church in Philippi, and us today, to 'rejoice *in the Lord*'. Only Christ can give us His joy and peace, and only He can give us a place in heaven, where rejoicing will not be limited or spoiled by our sin. Paul goes on in these first six verses to show what it means to be 'in the Lord', for only then can the Philippians, or we, rejoice 'in the Lord', especially when the going gets hard. As Alexander MacLaren put it so well: 'A very slight glance over the Epistle will show how continually the note of gladness is struck in it. Whatever in Paul's circumstances was "at enmity with joy" could not darken his sunny outlook. This bird could sing in a darkened cage. If we brought together the expressions of joy in this letter, they would yield us some precious lessons as to what were the sources of his, and what may be the sources of ours.'[1] Jesus gave important teaching on rejoicing, and we must take His commentary on it to understand better what it means to rejoice 'in the Lord'. After His disciples had come back 'buzzing' because of their God-given success in casting out demons, He set the priorities for rejoicing when He told them: 'do not rejoice in this, that the spirits are subject to you, but rather rejoice because your names are written in heaven.'[2] In other words, their assurance of salvation and security in heaven was to trigger their rejoicing more than any temporary success, however marvellous, miraculous and spiritual that might be. Tomorrow they could fail, but their names would still be written in heaven by indelible grace and underlined by the Saviour's coming sacrifice. So, for the Philippians, rejoicing 'in the Lord' means entering into the joy of His salvation, which He alone has accomplished by Himself for us. That is why David's repentant prayer, in Psalm 51:6, is 'Restore to me the joy of *Your* salvation'. David's experience of his salvation would go up and down. He needed to rely on the constancy of God's unchanging salvation. He knew, as Jonah did, that 'Salvation is of the LORD'[3] and God who provided it was faithful. So Paul underlines that any rejoicing that really lasts can only be 'in the Lord'. That is why, later in this chapter, he will express that his ambition and goal is, before everything else, 'to know *Him*'.

REJOICING IS FOR FAMILY ONLY!

Two words can easily be missed, but they are important. The Philippians can only 'Rejoice in the Lord' because Paul knows they are 'my brethren'.

In other words, they are all in the family of God through having received the new birth. Jesus told Nicodemus, the Jewish teacher, that the new birth was essential before anyone could either 'see' or 'enter' the kingdom of God.4 Under Paul's preaching the gospel and teaching God's Word, the Christians in Philippi know well that, as another apostle put it, they have 'been born again, not of corruptible seed but incorruptible, through the word of God which lives and abides forever.'5 Those trusting in Christ now share that knowledge with Paul, the Philippians and all who have been thus 'born again' and become brothers and sisters in the blood-bought family of God. To 'rejoice in the Lord' is for those who know Him as family members!

NOT TEDIOUS REPETITION BUT WISE COUNSEL!
A simple thought emerges. At the risk of being thought 'tedious' or boring, Paul is a faithful minister of God who will remind his hearers about certain dangers as many times as he needs to. A young mother tells her children more than once how to cross the road, if she really cares for them and is wise. Safety in spiritual things is very important, especially when some proclaim a so-called 'gospel' which not only cannot save, but also confirms lost souls in errors that will lead them to hell. Faithful pastors will therefore risk the criticism of being 'tedious' rather than fail to repeat warnings that can save their flock from spiritual danger. I like the story about the preacher who was being considered as the new minister of a church. He went three times and preached the same sermon on each occasion. After the first sermon, the people were euphoric. When he repeated it on his return, they graciously thought he had simply forgotten he had preached it. When he delivered the same message yet again, the church leaders expressed concern and asked him why. He replied: 'I am still waiting for you to act on the first message, so I told you again.' Instead of criticising the preacher for repeating important biblical injunctions, we should make sure we are obeying God concerning those things. Paul's words in verse 1 prepare the Philippian saints for the red alert signalled by verse 2 and the rest of this chapter. In stark contrast to looking at Epaphroditus and Timothy and being told to 'hold such men in esteem', Paul will now warn against 'dogs', 'evil workers' and 'the mutilation'. In today's churches we need to

distinguish between teachers who are faithful to God, and those who would bring havoc by adding to, or talking away from, the Word of God.

3:2 Beware—false teachers at work!

² Beware of dogs, beware of evil workers, beware of the mutilation.

DOGS = EVIL WORKERS = THE MUTILATION

'Beware of the dog' is a sign we see often! Paul is concerned that the pure doctrine of the gospel is not infected with rabies by being bitten by poisonous teaching on circumcision. In Acts 15:1 we read that such false teachers had previously visited Antioch 'from Judea and taught the brethren, "Unless you are circumcised according to the custom of Moses, you cannot be saved."' Their unsettling and erroneous teaching had been resisted by the apostles, church elders and believers, as the rest of that chapter demonstrates. Circumcision was an Old Testament Jewish rite which meant that the cutting away of the foreskin of a Jewish male baby, eight days after birth, (see Luke 2:22, for example), and it marked him as a member of God's Old Testament covenant people. 'Circumcision' thus became a synonym for being Jewish.⁶ But it could never put away sin, and was a sign of a better covenant to come, that which would involve the putting away of sin from the sinful human heart, through faith in Christ crucified.⁷ In fact, that God-given rite for His earthly covenant people of Israel is now nothing more than a *mutilation* of the flesh, if those who practise circumcision apply it as as a means of *salvation*. That is why Paul derisively calls them 'the mutilation'. Paul normally refers to circumcision with due respect, but when it comes to someone teaching that it can make a sinner acceptable to God, he exposes it for what it is—mere cutting away of flesh, or 'mutilation.' Cutting away flesh cannot cut away sin. Paul also calls these people 'dogs'. The dogs around Philippi were filthy scavengers, and some Jews insultingly referred to Christians as 'dogs'. Here Paul implies the insult is rightly true of those who insist on circumcision for salvation—they prey on others and keep them in a state which is dirtied by sin. Theirs is an evil work that mutilates the flesh but does nothing to cleanse a sinful heart or save a lost soul. As Ralph Martin (quoting Strack-Billerbeck) puts it, 'The charge levelled against the Judaizers whose activities were an imminent danger to the community at Philippi is expressed in fierce terms. *Dogs* were regarded by the Jews as "the most despised, insolent and miserable" of creatures and as unclean. It was a derogatory title used by orthodox Jews for the Gentile nations who were treated as Israel's enemies and therefore God's. In the present verse the application is reversed; and the enemies of God are now those Jewish Christians who misrepresent the gospel and thereby put themselves under the ban of God.'[8] But these false teachers in Philippi are not only dangerous 'dogs' which still live in the dirt of unforgiven sin. Neither are they mere mutilators who have no solution to spiritual problems in their emphasis on the flesh. They are 'evil workers' also. Anything that takes away from the truths of the gospel is evil. Paradoxically, gospel truth can be taken away by *adding* requirements that God has never stipulated and will not accept. Such contamination of God's only message of forgiveness that can turn a sinner from hell to heaven is so evil that the incensed Paul pronounces a curse on those who thus are peddling a gospel substitute in Galatia. He then repeats the curse in the very next verse.[9] In effect these people, by preaching a message of Christ crucified *plus* circumcision, have demolished God's only offer of mercy and grace. That is why, in the next verse, Paul gives his classic threefold description of what Christians really are, being referred to there as 'the circumcision'. That term does not refer to Jewish baby boys who were circumcised eight days after birth, or to any Gentile who went through the rite of circumcison later, but to those who have been 'circumcised with the circumcision made without hands, by putting off the body of the sins of the flesh, by the circumcision of Christ'.[10] They are sinners who have been born again, as is every true Christian today. How we need to watch out for, avoid, resist and warn against the modern counterparts of those who would add *anything* to the simple gospel of repentance and faith in Christ crucified and risen again! Beware of today's 'evil workers' who insist on baptism—with more or with less water—as a means of salvation, or as one of the conditions for it. Resist such teaching wherever you find it. The doctrine of Roman Catholicism (sadly accepted in some Anglican churches also) is as erroneous, in this respect, as that of Mormons, Jehovah's Witnesses, Seventh Day Adventists and others. But the principle goes further. Any Christian who seeks to insist on post-conversion experiences to make you into the 'complete Christian' is mutilating the gospel of Christ and our completeness in Him. Remember that, as Paul assures the Colossians, in the context of circumcision of the heart: 'you are *complete in Him*, who is the head of all principality and power.' He has just told them that 'in Him dwells all the fullness of the Godhead bodily.'[11] Anyone is evil who seeks to add to, or subtract from, the all sufficiency of Christ's Person and work, in His substitutionary death and resurrection for us. So is the teacher, however religious or 'spiritual' his teaching may sound, who questions the completeness in Christ of even the vilest sinner who believes in the Saviour. That in no way denies that every Christian has a lot more to learn and to experience in his, or her, relationship with Christ. But that is not the same as propagating the false doctrine of *'Christ plus'*—rather, it is seeking to follow the biblical injunction to get to know Him better!

PROBLEM! WHY WAS TIMOTHY CIRCUMCISED?

Teaching circumcision, or any religious ceremony or human effort as a means of salvation, is heresy. In Acts chapter 16, Paul has Timothy circumcised. Why then was Timothy circumcised, as a believer? His father was Greek and his mother was Jewish. The reason was not to confer salvation upon him, as Timothy was already saved! Rather, it was to help the Jews to accept a man who was determined to be as like them as he legitimately could in order to win them. Paul's 'mission statement' for evangelising Jews was simple: 'to the Jews I became as a Jew, that I might win Jews; to those who are under the law, as under the law, that I might win those who are under the law; to those who are without law, as without law (not being without law toward God, but under law toward Christ), that I might win those who are without law.'[12] That is why he has semi-gentile Timothy circumcised. Paul was a Jew, as verses 5 and 6 of this chapter 3 show clearly. Because of Timothy's circumcision, Timothy would be able to join Paul in reaching the Jews with the gospel, without having his non-Jewishness paraded as a stumbling block to that priority gospel work. There is no record of Paul's having any other co-labourer circumcised. Timothy's circumcision was just a means he used, with his younger co-labourer's willing consent, to reach the Jews whom they both longed to win for Christ. In so doing, they contravened no command of God or biblical principle. Hudson Taylor, the pioneer missionary to China, followed the same principle against the Victorian culture of his day when he, an Englishman, dressed like a Chinaman and even wore a pigtail in order to get alongside Chinese people whom he so longed to see saved. Paul, Timothy and Hudson Taylor are examples for us all! Like them, we should sacrifice our preferences, but not biblical principles, in order to put ourselves in a better position to win lost souls for our Saviour. Without sinning or participating in anything that would mar our testimony to Christ or jeopardise our holy walk with Him, are we prepared to identify with lost people as far as we can, even if it costs us our reputation or preferences?

3:3 A three-fold description of a Christian

3 For we are the circumcision, who worship God in the Spirit, rejoice in Christ Jesus, and have no confidence in the flesh,

'THE CIRCUMCISION' RATHER THAN 'THE MUTILATION'

It was necessary for us to see what circumcision meant in order to appreciate, in verse 2, what Paul means by 'dogs', 'evil workers', and 'the mutilation'. We have seen that to be circumcised originally had great covenant significance and validity for Old Testament Jews. But to be circumcised now as a means of salvation or to teach that circumcision is needed in addition to faith in Christ is merely mutilating the flesh. So the false teachers are called 'the mutilation', so identified are they with cutting off flesh that never can rid a soul of the guilt of sin. In the same way, Paul now calls his Gentile believing brothers at Philippi 'the circumcision'. He is saying that they are Christians, they are saved, they are cleansed from sin and forgiven for it, and they are in God's born-again family by His covenant sealed with the blood of Christ. He says this to non-Jews to emphasise that circumcision is now a question of the heart being purified, not the foreskin being detached. He then goes on to explain how someone can say that he, or she, is one of 'the circumcision' brought about by the gospel of the Lord Jesus Christ. These truths apply to Christians today as much as to them. If we are in Christ, we are 'the circumcision' of God, be we Jew or Gentile.

FIRST SET OF THREES!

Verse 3 of Philippians 3 is one of the best and most succinct descriptions of what it means to be a Christian. It contains three elements that give a person the assurance that he is part of 'the circumcision'. It is a verse that gives both comfort and a cause for self-examination. If a Philippian then, or anyone now, claims to be a Christian, the evidence of conversion must include the first set of three statements that we consider in this chapter. Those three reasons for comfort, or tests of conversion, are to do with worship in the Spirit, rejoicing in Christ Jesus, and having no confidence in any self-effort. We will look at those in reverse order.

'NO CONFIDENCE IN THE FLESH'

In the Bible, the word 'flesh' not only means that which is attached to my physical bones and bounded by skin, but also my sinful nature outside Christ. Paul makes it quite clear to the Philippian church what he means by having 'no confidence in the flesh.' In verses 4 to 6 he details what confidence he could have were he to depend on 'the flesh'. He could try to present his own efforts, pedigree and credentials. He says he would be top candidate to qualify for acceptance by God, if God would perform a value analysis on him. We will examine his credentials in more detail below. A brief summary is that Paul might have thought that he qualified because of his circumcision, true Jewishness, religious knowledge, elevated position, zeal against perceived error, and unimpeachable personal observance of the letter of the law. He now has 'no confidence' in these to save him. His fully justified lack of confidence in anything he is or can do is echoed in his teaching the Ephesians that 'by grace you have been saved through faith, and that not of yourselves; it is the gift of God, *not of works*, lest anyone should boast.'[13] I read somewhere that Spurgeon quoted so often from Toplady's hymn, *Rock of Ages*, the words *'Nothing in my hand I bring, Simply to Thy cross I cling'*, that one of his regular correspondents told him that he was 'by now well acquainted with the vacuity of your hand!' Spurgeon was right to emphasise that: he, too, had 'no confidence in the flesh'. If a man is convicted of a crime he will not avoid sentence because he has done good deeds at other times or because he comes from a good family. Neither can sinners claim good works or personal pedigree as an escape from God's judgement for their sin. 'You would never get a job you applied for if you approached it like that,' said a promoter of self-esteem philosophy to me after I had shared the gospel. My reply was that I was not applying for a job based on merit, but for forgiveness based on mercy. To receive mercy I must admit guilt. Look at a king who did many good works and could boast an impeccable pedigree, David. He asks for *mercy* in Psalm 51 for his sins which included adultery and murder. He offered no well-presented *curriculum vitae*. Rather he cried heartfelt pleas for mercy and restoration. No sinner can trust in anything he does, or can do, or can go through (such as a ceremony) to make him right with God. King David, Paul the imprisoned apostle, the Philippian Christians and all of us are sinners who are guilty before God, deserving His punishment for our sins. We cannot save ourselves. The Puritans understood this well. One prayed, 'I bewail my coldness, poverty, emptiness, imperfect vision, languid service, prayerless prayers, praiseless praises. Suffer me not to grieve or resist Thee.'[14] He too had 'no confidence in the flesh', and neither should we.

REJOICE IN CHRIST JESUS

In verse 1, we considered what it meant to 'rejoice in the Lord'. The theme of rejoicing comes up again as evidence that the Philippians, and any claiming to be Christians, are 'the circumcision'. It also underlines the assurance that we know we are saved and can be called 'the circumcision.' Here Paul says that such rejoicing is '*in Christ Jesus*'. As John says in his first letter,[15] it is Jesus' blood that cleanses us from '*all sin*', whatever that sin includes. No one else's blood could do that. Jesus' blood could not do that for us when flowing through his veins as our perfect example. It could only cleanse us after it was shed at Calvary. Peter tells us that it was there that 'Christ also suffered once for sins, the just for the unjust, that He might bring us to God, being put to death in the flesh but made alive by the Spirit.'[16] Because of the worth and the work of Jesus as our Redeemer, John goes on to say: 'If we confess our sins, He is faithful and just to forgive us our sins and to cleanse us from all unrighteousness.' The three best-known apostles—Paul, Peter and John—make it clear to us through God the Holy Spirit's inspiration that without Christ we would be *nowhere* spiritually. In fact we would be *lost* eternally. If Christ's sole achievement was to cleanse us from sin, that would be abundant reason to 'rejoice in Christ Jesus'. But the immediate context of the passage gives us another insight into salvation through Christ that underlines why the saved person rejoices in Him. We have already seen that our spiritual and moral bankruptcy offers us 'no confidence in the flesh'. Verse 9 will reveal that Paul's confidence in the imputed righteousness of Christ—Christ's invaluable merit poured into the repentant sinner's bankrupt account—is another overwhelming reason to 'rejoice in Christ Jesus'. The lowly mind of the exalted King of kings caused Him to be born, to live, to die, to be resurrected, and to ascend to heaven. This was so that He could cleanse sinners from sins, provide His righteousness for them, and, as Lord and Saviour, take possession of them. No wonder we 'rejoice in Christ Jesus!' And He is coming again! But that is another truth to examine later. A drowning man who has been saved by a lifeguard does not boast about his own ability to swim! Christians do not rejoice in their floundering and useless efforts to save themselves, but in the One who came to save sinners. A real Christian is glad and grateful to 'rejoice in Christ Jesus' who alone is 'the way, the truth and the life'.[17] Are you someone who really has no confidence in yourself to save yourself? If so, have you trusted Jesus Christ so that you find it natural and sincere to rejoice in Him and His death on the cross for you? The true 'circumcision' of saved sinners will 'rejoice in Christ Jesus'. If you have any doubts about your own conversion, why not pray with a Puritan who asked Christ to 'give me the faith to behold my name engraven in Thy hand, my soul and body redeemed by Thy blood, my sinfulness covered by Thy life of pure obedience.'[18]

'WORSHIP GOD IN THE SPIRIT'

Paul's begins his description of each person included in the real 'circumcision' by saying that they are those, as in Philippi, 'who worship God in the Spirit'. He then unpacks that phrase to show that those who 'worship God in the Spirit' put no confidence in who they are or what they have done, but whose rejoicing is 'in Christ Jesus'. To abandon confidence in achieving one's own salvation but to trust and rejoice in the Person, work and power of Christ Jesus leads any sinner to 'worship God in the Spirit'. The work of the Spirit of God is vitally important in all of this. The Holy Spirit's first operation in a sinner is to awaken that person to a hopelessly lost condition spiritually and convict him, or her, of 'sin, righteousness and judgement'. He then reveals the truth of God's Word and points the troubled sinner to Christ spiritually, just as John the Baptist sought to do physically.[19] When someone is brought to repentance and faith in Christ such a person becomes 'born again' by the Holy Spirit. Jesus taught Nicodemus that this was essential for salvation.[20] At conversion every child of God receives the Holy Spirit.[21] He is not the prerogative of some select 'supercharged Christians' with a particular doctrinal emphasis. He is the birthright of everyone who is born again by His action. Putting sins to death, being led by Him, and a growing assurance of having become a child of God are all works that the Holy Spirit begins to introduce in the life of a believer.[22] The Christian is to be continually being filled with the Holy Spirit,[23] and is to avoid grieving Him, as He is a Person and not a thing.[24] As the Holy Spirit increases His daily influence in the life of a Christian, the fruit of the Spirit will increase in that person's life.[25] It is the Holy Spirit who inspired holy men of God to write the Bible, which is therefore God's infallible book.[26] Christians will find that reading and studying the Bible is essential for their worship of God, their walk with God, and their witness for God. The Holy Spirit is involved in every part of the Christian's conversion and sanctification and has made His mind clear in the Bible. Jesus said that God was seeking people to worship Him and that those who worship God must 'worship Him in Spirit and in truth'.[27] Putting this cameo of the person and work of the Holy Spirit together, we can see that the only ultimate revealed written *truth* is the Bible, and the only *Spirit* who is at work in bringing people to know and worship God is the Holy Spirit. So the only way that a person can worship God 'in the Spirit' is to be indwelt and led by the Holy Spirit and to be a serious reader and follower of the Bible. When someone comes to Christ it is hardly surprising that, as the Holy Spirit takes up controlling residence within, that person begins to find the Bible coming to life. He, or she, receives an appetite for it as a newly born Christian, just as a newly born baby receives an appetite for milk. Worshipping God then becomes praising and thanking God, as revealed in the Bible. Any other 'God' is not 'God'. But worship is not mere external appreciation of the Bible, because the Holy Spirit who caused it to be written now lives inside that believer who reads and follows God's Word. The Spirit prompts him, or her, towards God and makes that family relationship both real and personal. That is why the letter to the Galatians states, 'because you are sons, God has sent forth the Spirit of His Son into your hearts, crying out, "Abba, Father!"'[28] 'Abba' means 'Daddy'! We now have, as our father, the God we have begun to get to know and to worship. To 'worship God in Spirit' is nothing to do with the kind of music we use, the atmosphere of a meeting, or praying in a 'holy building'. It is all to do with our knowing Him, trusting and obeying Him, and learning about who He is from the Bible. We worship Him privately on our own. But we also will come together to hear His Word taught and to praise Him with other Christians, especially on the Lord's Day. In our worship, we will express our humble and grateful appreciation of who He is and what He has done. Those who say that we need a further experience of God to worship Him in Spirit have missed the point. To worship Him 'in Spirit and in truth' is to see Him as He is in His Word and respond to that by a devoted life which extols by life and lip our wonderful Saviour. This is both a test and a privilege of being a Christian.

3:4 Self-confident Saul—before he became penitent Paul
4 though I also might have confidence in the flesh. If anyone else thinks
    he may have confidence in the flesh, I more so:

FLESH
Paul develops the theme that if the 'flesh' could save, he would be home and dry. His worldly, religious and personal qualifications would have made impressive reading on a job application! Now he knows that when his *name* was changed from Saul to Paul, at his conversion, so was his nature from fallen and lost to new and saved. How then can he trust in his fallen nature any more? We have already seen that he has 'no confidence in the flesh' and knows that his salvation, like his rejoicing, can only be 'in Christ Jesus'. He has realised that this is *not* a job application. Like David, he needs God's mercy. This has been covered already in the comments on verse 3, but before looking at his credentials which could not save him, we will consider modern man.

MODERN MAN
The trouble is that the modern man and woman are raised with a different

mindset. We are told to promote ourselves to get on, and it is quite a shock for some to hear, for the first time, that the approach to God is downward, not upward. Dr Lloyd-Jones encapsulated this worldly attitude nearly fifty years ago: 'If you want to succeed in a profession, the great thing is to give the impression that you are a success so you suggest that you are more successful than you actually are, and people say "That is the man to go to." That is the whole principle on which life is run at the present time—express yourself, believe in yourself, realise the powers that are innate in yourself and let the whole world see and know them. Self-confidence, assurance, self-reliance.'[29] Things have only changed for the worse since then, with the constant emphasis on self-esteem. Certainly, we do well to remember Paul's realistic assessment of how sinful and weak he was, and how he needed God. But as Christians we also need to be careful not to fall into the same way of thinking. We can easily err into assuming that our Christian achievements, faithful service, acclaim of others, or evangelical 'stable' make us more acceptable to God than those who we may think are 'less spiritual'. Our continuation with God, like our acceptance by Him in the first place, is all through His mercy and grace, and because we have a Saviour who loves us and who continues with us. There is always a need for that lowly mind.

3:5 Details of Saul's previous self-confidence
5 circumcised the eighth day, of the stock of Israel, of the tribe of Benjamin, a Hebrew of the Hebrews; concerning the law, a Pharisee;

PITIFUL PEDIGREE!
Now Paul lists what R.C. Sproul calls his 'sevenfold pedigree under the law'[30] which would have been his only plea, insubstantial as it was, for acceptance by a holy sin-hating God, had he not turned to the Lord Jesus Christ to save him. This list of self-effort has less chance of rescuing hardened Saul of Tarsus from judgement than a series of good school reports would cause a man to avoid conviction for crime when the evidence was strongly and clearly against him. Though it may look impressive when compared with other lost sinners' pedigrees, the former Pharisee could find in it no defence to avoid or avert the wrath of God against his sin.

WHO HE WAS

Paul had been circumcised on the right day prescribed by Old Testament law, the eighth day after birth.[31] He was a direct descendant of Abraham, Isaac and Jacob as one 'of the stock of Israel'. Benjamin, his tribal founder, was one of two of Israel's favourite sons (Joseph being the other) and was regarded, along with the tribe of Judah, with which the tribe of Benjamin was closely allied in the south, as the best of the tribes. The apostle's namesake, Saul, was also from the same tribe and became the first king of Israel.[32] That would only increase Saul of Tarsus' sense of being rather special. Hebrew parentage, Hebrew language, and a deep knowledge of Hebrew traditions made Paul 'a Hebrew of the Hebrews'. On top of all this he went through intense training as a Pharisee, under the renowned teacher, Gamaliel.[33] Whatever the faults of the Pharisees, they knew the law and were very influential. Despite their legalistic hypocrisy, they also performed religious duties in a way that few others would.[34] Paul's pre-conversion religious *curriculum vitae* may be impressive—but completely ineffective to bring him to God.

3:6 Saul's 'blameless' zeal

6 concerning zeal, persecuting the church; concerning the righteousness which is in the law, blameless.

ZEALOUS AND JEALOUS

The New Testament record underlines Saul's misplaced zeal.[35] He was so incensed in his opposition to the church of Christ that he persecuted it, imprisoned believers, and consented to the death of Stephen, its first recorded martyr. Jealous for Judaism and believing that Christianity was a blasphemy against God, he gave himself unstintingly to its annihilation. Indeed, religious zeal can be misplaced, and is by no means a necessary indicator of a real personal relationship with God. His passion was to persecute the church which infuriated him so much. This kind of consuming desire is referred to in the famous quotation of the socialist politician, Barbara Castle, in *The Guardian* of 14 January 1996: 'I will fight for what I believe in until I drop dead. And that's what keeps you alive.' The future apostle's misplaced zeal kept him alive: it was his *raison d'être*, until he came to know Christ. The fact that such a hostile antagonist to the gospel should get converted is an evidence of God's 'amazing Grace'. It also encourages the Philippians, who know the gospel works! It also encourages us today. Christians should be praying that those who cruelly persecute the church would also come to know the peace and love of Christ. This should be as true of Islamic and Hindu extremists who shed the blood of Christ's servants, as it was once of Eastern block communists. We should remember also to pray for the persecuted church worldwide and ask if we are willing to seal our testimony in our blood, God enabling us, if the need arises. Paul's example from prison surely will encourage the Philippians to be ready for that.

LEGALISTIC BLAMELESSNESS

Saul was meticulous in keeping the detail of the Old Testament law, without ever having his heart changed. He did not join the ranks of Old Testament *believers*. He was an Old Testament legal *observer*, which is very different. Similarly today, a religious 'observer' can go through detailed ordinances to the letter, no matter what religion is involved, but still stand in need of God's forgiveness and a God-given change of the sinful heart within. As a Pharisee, he would also have kept the minutiae of Pharisaic rules which were placed around the Old Testament law and which obscured the spirit of the law. He would have gone through all their ceremony and eye-catching arrogance of self-important men trying to be impressive by religious duty and position. He was proud of his performance and lost in his legalism. How many are there today who seek to build their eternal future on the shifting sands of religious observance? Some of them may even think they are Christians. Christians need to obey God's changeless moral law, encapsulated in the Ten Commandments, as a sign of love for Christ[36] but never as a means of salvation.[37]

Notes

1 **Alexander MacLaren, Expositions of Holy Scripture,** Volume XIV (Eerdmans), page 313.
2 Luke 10:20.
3 Jonah 2:9.
4 John 3:3–5.
5 1 Peter 1:23.

6 Acts 10:45.

7 Romans 2:28,29.

8 Rev. Ralph P. Martin, *Tyndale New Testament Commentaries: The Epistle of Paul to the Philippians* (Tyndale Press), pages 136,137.

9 Galatians 1:8,9.

10 Colossians 2:11.

11 Colossians 2:9,10.

12 1 Corinthians 9:20,21.

13 Ephesians 2:8,9.

14 Arthur Bennett (editor), *The Valley of Vision* (Banner of Truth), page 28.

15 1 John 1:8,9.

16 1 Peter 3:18.

17 John 14:6.

18 Arthur Bennett (editor), *The Valley of Vision* (Banner of Truth), page 30

19 John 1:29 and 36; John 16:7–15.

20 John 3:1–8.

21 Romans 8:1–11.

22 Romans 8:13–16.

23 Ephesians 5:18.

24 Ephesians 4:30.

25 Galatians 5:22.

26 2 Peter 1:21.

27 John 4:23,24.

28 Galatians 4:6.

29 Dr Martyn Lloyd Jones, *Studies in the Sermon on the Mount,* Volume 1 (IVF), page 45.

30 R.C. Sproul (general editor), *The Reformation Study Bible, NKJV* (Nelson), notes on Philippians 3:4–6, page 1879.

31 Philippians 3:5.

32 1 Samuel 9:21.

33 Acts 22:3.

34 Luke 18:12.

35 Acts 22:3–5; 19,20.

36 John 14:15; 15:10.

37 Galatians 2:16.

Mini-overview 3:7 to 3:11

Second set of threes—what a Christian longs to know.
Paul proceeds to talk about his changed priorities
and his overwhelming three-part ambition as a new
creation in Christ.

3:7 Lost gains

7 But what things were gain to me, these I have counted loss for Christ.

THINGS ARE DIFFERENT NOW!

A well-known chorus expresses the truth of verse 7:

Things are different now. Something happened to me
Since I gave my life to Jesus.
Things are different now. What a change! It must be
Since I gave my life to Him.
Things I loved before have passed away.
Things I love much more are here to stay.
Things are different now. What a change!
It must be since I gave my life to Him.

God's Word puts it in a nutshell: 'if anyone is in Christ, he is a new creation; old things have passed away; behold, all things have become new.'[1] So it is with Paul. He now finds that all his religious qualifications and zeal, formerly counted as big 'plus points', he now regards as loss. As his confidence and trust have been placed on the solid rock of Christ, he has no time any more for those shifting sands of religious background, attainments and activity. He is like a man cured from an addiction who now willingly throws away the substance that once enslaved him, and which he prized so highly. Now that liberty has come, he does not wish to be chained by it any longer. Paul looks at his balance sheet of life. He sees that what he then thought to be gains, on the credit side, were all the time huge losses that would have destroyed his life eternally. The trouble was that his eyes were scaled over, and he could not read the balance sheet correctly. Now he sees with his new eyes of conversion and notes a huge input of credit into his account. It has been deposited there in love, grace and mercy by the Lord Jesus. It is not a loan, which would have been another liability, but a free gift. He can never pay it back and is not asked to do so by his gratuitous and generous Creditor. Now Paul is happy to count his supposed gains as loss, because he sees the real gains in Christ who has become his Saviour. Note that Paul says this computes well. He has '*counted* loss for Christ' those dead religious things that were once seen as gains. There is nothing incorrect or badly calculated about coming to Christ. It makes sense—we can count on it, whatever others may think or say.

3:8 The principle goes further

8 Yet indeed I also count all things loss for the excellence of the knowledge of Christ Jesus my Lord, for whom I have suffered the loss of all things, and count them as rubbish, that I may gain Christ

FROM USELESS RELIGION TO EVERYTHING ELSE

Paul not only realises the poverty of his spiritual position in mistakenly trusting his previous religious background to save him. Having come to Christ he now realises that everything else in his life is worthless in comparison with knowing Christ. He has renounced his rights to everything he is or has to the extent that he says, 'I have suffered the loss of all things' and regards them as 'rubbish' in comparison with the privilege of knowing Christ. Although he knows Christ he wants to gain a greater knowledge of Him, as we shall see in verse 10, below.

BACK TO THAT BALANCE SHEET

We have seen that Paul looks at his balance sheet. What has his Christian faith cost him? His Judaism, his religious respectability, his ready authority in the eyes of the world in which he lived, his freedom and health at times, his comfort, his friends, his religious career path, his security, his settled existence and even his right to live. On the credit side he lists one asset of limitless value. It is a pearl of truly great price.[2] It is the 'excellence of the knowledge of Christ Jesus'. He adds, with a glow of gratitude, '*my* Lord'. He is overwhelmed by the riches of his personal knowledge of the Lord God who has become his Saviour. The value of such an amazing credit causes Paul to throw all his debits, which he regarded before as his credits, in the dustbin! They are 'rubbish' by comparison. The Greek word for 'rubbish' can also be translated 'dung', and is so preferred by some. Imagine that Paul has huge sacks full of gold and sacks also of horse manure. He is going to put the gold in safekeeping and has limited storage space. What will he do with the horse manure? Will he save that too? Of course not! Similarly he throws out everything he once held dear that would rival the Lordship of Christ. He discards it in order to keep the gold of His relationship with Christ. He has no place for rubbish or dung. But contrast his attitude towards Christ. An entrepreneur seeking more gold from his present gold, through investment, is not in the same league as Paul who wants to 'gain Christ.' In fact, although he already knows Christ and regards that privilege as excellent, he wants to get to know his Lord so much better that he refers to his single aim to 'gain Christ'. He wants to get to know Christ better, as we shall see in verse 10. Jim Elliot, the missionary martyred by the Auca Indians in Ecuador, also talked about gain. He said, 'He is no fool who gives what he cannot keep to *gain* what he cannot lose' (my emphasis on 'gain'). Paul knows the truth of that! He appreciates the great value of knowing Christ, but wants to invest more of his time, attention and effort in Christ to increasingly and continually 'gain' His lordship and grace over all areas of his life. He also knows that to know Christ better is the essence of godliness and that 'godliness with contentment is great gain.'[3] As Christians, how do we face up to the opportunity to 'gain Christ' in today's materialistic, rebellious and godless world? Are we markedly different from those who do not know Christ? Do we convert our opportunities to 'gain Christ'? How do we use our time? What benefits do we realise from fellowship with other Christians? How does our time with the Bible compare to our time watching television or pursuing other interests? Do we keep the manure in the store chambers of our hearts and minds and thus displace an increasing knowledge and influence of Christ there? Are material gains and life's comforts more important to us than Jesus? In practice do we seek to count secondary things as 'rubbish' so we 'may gain Christ'? The Philippians can see a man in prison who is rich and with a growing credit balance. Would they think that we, who are free, are poor and getting further into the red? Do we choose the right investments?

3:9 Another's righteousness

9 and be found in Him, not having my own righteousness, which is from the law, but that which is through faith in Christ, the righteousness which is from God by faith;

HALF IN, HALF OUT OR COMPLETELY OUT?

There are two kinds of righteousness. One is the same kind that Paul has renounced, his 'own righteousness, which is from the law.' That is a legalistic observance of the outward requirement of the Old Testament regulations, embellished by some other requirements that the Pharisees had added. It neither forgives our sin, nor gives us the perfect righteousness in which we need to stand to be accepted by God. We have already seen in Paul's 'sevenfold pedigree under the law' what Paul regarded as his own 'righteousness' which could never save him. He now states that he cannot be relying on that 'righteousness' if he is 'found in' Christ. His position in Christ excludes any grounds of forgiveness outside Christ. I am either 'found in Him' and am saved, or I look outside Him and I am lost. I cannot be half in! A friend of mine was fined for parking wrongly. There was half a parking space and he moved into it, but his car was too big for the space. He argued with the traffic officer. He claimed he was 'half in'. The traffic officer said he was 'half out' and that if he was 'half out' it was the same as being completely out! He had to pay the fine. Either I am completely trusting Christ, and thus am 'in Him' positionally or I am completely lost and facing a completely lost eternity. This kind of righteousness is as repulsive and ineffective as the 'filthy rags' to which Isaiah refers.4 The second type of righteousness, which alone is acceptable to God, is 'through faith in Christ, the righteousness which is from God by faith'. When a repentant sinner turns to Christ for forgiveness, he is not only pardoned through the merits of Christ's shed blood and the mercy of God, but the total and complete righteousness of the Lord Jesus is counted as his, or hers. This perfect righteousness is like a huge credit in my formerly bankrupt moral account. I am guilty and poor before a holy God.

I trust Jesus, and all His righteousness floods into my account, and His credit is counted as mine! It becomes mine by faith in Him, not by works of my own. It is not 'my own righteousness' but His own righteousness, becoming mine through the exercise of my own faith in Him. It is not that God waives the requirement of the law and accepts a lower standard of 'easy believism'. Rather it is that *all Christ's righteousness* is appropriated by my faith in Him. To change the illustration, not only am I cleansed within from sin. I am also clothed in a spotless white garment of Christ's righteousness. Spurgeon quotes Sir Richard Baker on this point: 'And such a whiteness it is that God's washing works upon us, makes within us; for no snow is so white in the eyes of men as a soul cleansed from sin is in the sight of God. And yet, a whiter whiteness than this too: for being purged from sin we shall, *induere stolam album*, put on the white robe; and this is a whiteness as much whiter than snow as an angelical whiteness is more than elemental.'[5] What a privilege to be cleansed within and clothed without! All seeking the cleansing within and the clothing outside must come in sorrow for sin to Christ. He will cleanse and clothe at the same time. Everyone who would know the inflow of Christ's riches of righteousness into their accounts, which are in debit through sin, must trust Him and His righteous sacrifice for them. That is as true today for a Jew as for a Gentile, for a Hindu as for a Buddhist, for a Sunni Muslim as for a Shi-ite Muslim, for a Roman Catholic as for a Protestant, and for all the sects such as Mormons, Jehovah's Witnesses, Christadelphians, Seventh Day Adventists, Christian Scientists, or New Age devotees. All are sinners with no acceptable righteousness to offer except that found in Christ. All religious adherents need to abandon not only their sins but also their reliance on any religion to save them. They need to trust in Jesus Christ, His blood and His righteousness. Those without a religion need to come as they are and receive Christ. Well does the hymn express the wonder of the saving righteousness of Christ:

Jesus, Thy robe of righteousness
My beauty is, my glorious dress;
'Midst flaming worlds, in these arrayed,
With joy shall I lift up my head.

Bold shall I stand in that great day,
For who aught to my charge shall lay?
While through Thy blood absolved I am
From sin and fear, from guilt and shame.

When from the dust of death I rise
To claim my mansion in the skies,
E'en then shall this be all my plea,
'Jesus hath lived, and died, for me.'

This spotless robe the same appears
When ruined nature sinks in years;
No age can change its glorious hue,
The robe of Christ is ever new.

O let the dead now hear Thy voice,
Bid, Lord, Thy banished ones rejoice;
Their beauty this, their glorious dress,
Jesus, the Lord our Righteousness!

3:10 Christ, His life, His death—made more real to me

¹⁰ that I may know Him and the power of His resurrection, and the
fellowship of His sufferings, being conformed to His death,

KNOWING THE ONE YOU ALREADY KNOW!

In the Bible the word 'know' sometimes means to know something, and
sometimes it implies more intimate knowledge, or knowing someone. It is
even used in the second sense, on some occasions, of intimate sexual
relationships between man and wife.[6] It reminds us of the difference
between the French words for 'to know *something*' (*savoir*) and 'to know
someone' (*connaître*). Some of the saddest words in the Bible belong to
Jesus. He said: 'I never *knew* you; depart from Me.'[7] Someone who does not
know Christ is lost even though he, or she, knows much about theology, the
church, morality, church history, helping others and even much about Jesus

Himself. Is Paul saying here that he does not *know* Christ, personally? Certainly not! He has already said, in the first chapter, that his personal knowledge of Christ means that 'to live is Christ', and he will go on to say, in the last chapter, that his confidence in the Saviour he knows is such that he 'can do all things through Christ who strengthens' him. Rather, in verse 10, the apostle tells the Philippians that, having been counted as righteous, through trusting Christ, his desire is to 'know' Him, in the sense of getting to know Him very well and very personally. But, suppose they say to him: 'But, Paul, you *already* know Jesus!' I can almost hear Paul's reply in my imagination, now: 'Yes, that is true. But I want to *know* Him more closely and more deeply.' As for any converted person today, so for Paul then: he longs for a better knowledge of his Saviour. Knowing Christ more deeply brings with it all the things we have been considering so far, such as having a lowly mind, trusting in Him, rejoicing, living to preach the gospel and realising that everything else but faith in Jesus is rubbish by comparison. In sound and happy marriages the husband and wife get to know each other more and more as the days go on. That is what is meant by 'growing together'. This is the first part of Paul's threefold ambition: to get to know Christ more closely. Without doubt, he wants that for each Christian at Philippi. We should have that same desire, and that is why we should use all the means that God gives us to enable that to happen. Each day we should spend quality time in reading and studying the Bible and in personal prayer. It is through the Bible that we see everything about Christ that God deems is important enough to record for us. It is by spending time speaking to Him in prayer that our personal knowledge of Him finds its expression to Him. Each Lord's Day we should give God the whole day, and be fervent in our worship, service and use of that day. We get to know someone better by spending time with him or her. That is what the Christian's quiet time each day is really about. Similarly, when our church or fellowship has a time of prayer and Bible study together, we should make it a priority to be there. This helps the whole fellowship to get closer to Him as part of His greater body, the church universal. We should read good Bible-based books. They can help us to see how others deepened their relationship with Christ, and how we can too. All blessing starts with knowing Christ and that is why Paul puts this first of the three goals he states in verse 10, when he says, 'that

I may know Him'. Grudem rightly says that 'If we are to know God, it is necessary that He reveal Himself to us,' and, concerning knowing God as our Saviour through Christ, 'This kind of knowledge of God is not found through human effort or wisdom'.[8] We come to know Christ and His salvation though His revealed Word, the Bible, and His revealing Spirit. To get to know Him more deeply, we need more of His Word and more of His Spirit's deeper working in our hearts.

RESURRECTION POWER

The Greek word translated 'power' means 'ability to do'. It does not mean 'power' in the sense of 'authority'. It is a power that acts. It is only when we know Christ that we can know His power. But that power is truly amazing. It is the same power that raised Jesus from the dead. In verse 10, Paul volunteers that he wants to know 'the power of His resurrection'. He already knows it! But, just as he wants an increasing knowledge of Christ, he wants to know more of His resurrection power each day, too. It is Jesus' risen power that enables Paul to say, honestly and humbly in chapter 4, 'I can do all things through Christ who strengthens me.' The power of Christ's resurrection is available to help the spiritual life of the weakest believer whose faith is in the risen Christ! Applied in our lives by God the Holy Spirit, it is this power that enables us to grow and make progress in a sinful world whose standards and ideals would otherwise drag us down. It enables us to serve Him effectively, when we just could not do it ourselves. It is the power and quality of risen life, and it not only empowers us, but helps us to be different, too. Paradoxically, it only becomes our power when we admit we have no power of our own. Paul illustrates this principle when he tells the church at Corinth that God said to him, 'My grace is sufficient for you, for My strength is made perfect in weakness,' and then adds that 'most gladly I will rather boast in my infirmities, that the power of Christ may rest upon me. Therefore I take pleasure in infirmities, in reproaches, in needs, in persecutions, in distresses, for Christ's sake. For when I am weak, then I am strong.'[9] Like salvation itself, we experience God's enabling strength most fully when we confess our own inadequacy and trust ourselves to the risen Lord. Just think! God's power that raised Jesus from the dead is available to help us live our new life in Him!

THE FORGOTTEN MEMBER OF THE TRIO!

I have heard concerned Christians in prayer meetings rightly pleading for a closer knowledge of Christ and of the power of His resurrection. We should all say a hearty 'Amen!' to those prayers. The third part of Paul's spiritual desire, however, is not so attractive to us. What is it? It is 'that I may know … the fellowship of His sufferings, being conformed to His death'. What does he ask? Does he really ask to know 'the fellowship of His sufferings', even though he is already suffering for Christ in that Roman prison? Is he not already bearing the same kind of physical and mental suffering as His Saviour did? Is he not seen as a criminal, an outcast, a heretic, a religious bigot and extremist? Is he not opposed by the enemies of the cross of Christ and even rejected by some Christians? Yes, indeed! All that, and much more. He is already following in the footsteps of his Lord. Those who can no longer spit on the Master now show hateful contempt for His faithful servant. Yet Paul continues to pray to know increasingly the 'fellowship' of Christ's sufferings. He can never share in that awful substitutionary death on the cross, where wrath and anger were poured out upon the innocent Lamb of God. But he can share in suffering for Christ's sake, as he gets to know Him and His resurrection power better each day. Paul needs God-given grace to die to self, to take up his cross daily, and to reckon himself dead to sin.[10] There is no other way he can joyfully undergo such unjust suffering. He must be 'conformed to His death'. He first came to know the fellowship of Christ's sufferings when he became identified with His crucified Saviour, whose blood was shed to cleanse him from his sins. That knowledge of Christ—with its spiritual peace, joy and assurance—gives him a yearning to know more of that fellowship. He knows now that the cross is not only to deal with the sin, but with the sinner too. 'I am crucified with Christ'[11] shows Paul's personal understanding of the outworking of the death-to-self life, which was triggered at Calvary. He cannot know an ongoing 'resurrection' spiritually without an ongoing Calvary in his heart. Jesus gave Himself completely on the cross. He emptied Himself. He suffered. Paul asks for grace to do the same, out of love for his Lord, with whom he is now identified. Especially for one whose great desire was to preach Christ to others, he knows that the cross of Jesus must be at the heart of the messenger as well as at the heart of the message. Only then can he experience the fellowship of that suffering which John MacArthur calls 'a partnership—a deep communion of suffering that every believer shares with Christ, who is able to comfort suffering Christians because He has already experienced the same suffering, and infinitely more'.[12] Whether western Christians will yet suffer imprisonment for Christ and His gospel is a far more open question than it was a relatively short time ago. Perhaps *our* fellowship of His sufferings might lead to that in the future, as standards decline and hostility to the Bible's message seems to mount each day. But we certainly should be seeking God's grace to live that crucified life that enables us, with joy, to live for Christ amidst the sneers, anger, ridicule, hostility, indifference and scheming opposition from a world which would crucify Christ again, were that possible. That death-to-self fellowship and that resurrection power provide the seed bed from which our daily desire, to know Christ better, flourishes.

3:11 Resurrection follows crucifixion

[11] if, by any means, I may attain to the resurrection from the dead.

BACK TO RESURRECTION POWER

Does verse 11 imply a doubt in the mind of the apostle that he will feature in the future resurrection? Obviously not, as that is contrary to the whole context of confidence displayed in this letter by a saved sinner who is looking forward to being with his Saviour when his service on earth is completed. The NASB translates the verse 'in order that I may attain to the resurrection of the dead'. There is no uncertainty here. Paul refers back to his desire to 'know … the power of His resurrection' in the previous verse. In fact, verse 11 underlines what we saw in verse 10. If Paul is to know that resurrection experience, it has to be through knowing Christ and carrying his daily cross of dying to self. R. C. Sproul's comment on the previous verse is helpful here: 'For Paul, identification with the crucified and risen Christ is fundamental to Christian living.'[13] Paul's determination to apply this principle to his life means he will use 'any means' God gives him to achieve it. Obviously, he can only use the God-given 'means of grace' to know God's grace in this way. But he will use them! That is how serious he is about living for Christ. He knows that without a daily experience of God's resurrection power in his life, he has nothing to offer. He is determined to live a resurrection life. It is a good thing to have ambitions which are spiritual and to turn them into prayer and praise. It is even better to recognise that it is only by God's grace that we can attain (literally 'arrive at') those ambitions. But that does not prevent God-aided and godly effort! As Barnes says, in his *New Testament Notes*, the phrase 'by all means' implies that Paul 'meant to make use of the most strenuous exertions to obtain the object.' That is a good example for us all. We trust the God of all grace and use the means of grace He gives to us. Whilst this verse refers to Paul's experience of Christ's resurrection in his daily living, it also reminds us that all the fellowship of Christ's suffering, dealt with in verse 10, will be totally eclipsed by that resurrection to new life in Christ, yet to come. Just as we saw, in chapter 2, that Jesus was humbled beyond imagination and then exalted above everyone and everything, so the despised and suffering servant of Jesus Christ will be raised to a new realm in his risen Lord.[14]

Notes

1 2 Corinthians 5:17.
2 Matthew 13:45,46.
3 1 Timothy 6:6.
4 Isaiah 64:6.
5 **Charles H. Spurgeon,** *The Treasury of David,* Volume 1, page 410.
6 Genesis 4:1, 1Kings 1:4, Matthew 1:25.
7 Matthew 7:23.
8 **Wayne Grudem,** *Systematic Theology* (IVP), page 149.
9 2Corinthians 12:9,10.
10 Romans 8:11.
11 Galatians 2:20.
12 **John MacArthur** (author of commentary/notes and general editor), *The MacArthur Study Bible, NKJV* (Word Bibles), note on Philippians 3:10, page 1826.
13 **R.C. Sproul** (general editor), *The Reformation Study Bible, NKJV* (Nelson), notes on Philippians 3:10, page 1879.
14 1 Thessalonians 4:16–18.

Mini-overview 3:12 to 3:16

Third set of threes—past, present and future.

Paul's honest assessment of where he is spiritually, and what to do about it.

3:12 Still striving

12 Not that I have already attained, or am already perfected; but I press on, that I may lay hold of that for which Christ Jesus has also laid hold of me.

REALISM AND SPIRITUAL DESIRE

Verse 12 triggers a train of realism that runs through the next eight verses. From verses 12 to 14 he says, in effect, 'I have not arrived, but I am determined to strive to get there.' In verse 15 he urges mature Christians to pursue that attitude, knowing that God will reveal to them, and us, when we fail to do that. In verse 16, he reminds his fellow Christians, nevertheless, to hang on to the good lessons and proven spiritual paths which have so far produced blessing. Then, in verse 17, he wisely tells the Philippians to follow good spiritual role model examples. In the next two verses Paul warns them to mark and avoid the earthy and fleshly lifestyles of those who deny and oppose the message and outliving of the cross of Christ. The fact that the great apostle admits immediately that he has not 'arrived' is both an encouragement and a challenge. His honesty is refreshing. It is sad that, so often, Christians with a high profile seem concerned to parade their achievements, conquests and abilities. The Christian minister should not be like a job applicant, eager to make his *curriculum vitae* the most attractive and possibly the most exaggerated, parading his supposed strong points and achievements. Here, arguably the most influential Christian of all time says, 'Not that I have already attained', for he is not 'already perfected'. He is honest about his failure to be what he could be in Christ and knows he has a long way to go. Sometimes a humble confession of weakness, or even of sin, can be a bigger blessing to us than a catalogue of what God has done through a certain person. 'The best men in the world will readily own their imperfection, in the present state. If Paul had not attained to perfection, much less have we.' So says Matthew Henry.[1] To admit we are not living continually as a 'super-powered' or highly gifted child of God is seen by some today as an admission of being a second class citizen. The challenge is obvious. How honest am I about what I am really like as a Christian? We should reply that we are even worse than that, and that our sufficiency is in Christ alone. The same apostle cries out elsewhere[2] 'Oh wretched man that I am! Who will deliver me from this body of death?' God cannot bless untruthfulness. That is why Paul is so honest before God and before men that he has still a long way to go on the learning curve!

ADMISSION OF DEFEAT IS NOT ACCEPTANCE OF DEFEAT

Does Paul shrug his shoulders, say, 'Well, that's what I'm like. Too bad!' and accept that, because he has not attained so far, he never will? Certainly not! He is trusting and following the One who said, 'Therefore you shall be perfect, just as your Father in heaven is perfect.'[3] Instead, his very lack of achievement drives him to say, 'I press on, that I may lay hold of that for which Christ Jesus has also laid hold of me.' We will consider what it means to 'press on' when we look at verse 14, where the same Greek word is used. But the reason he states for pursuing that positive attitude now is so that he can be what Christ wants him to be, and do what Christ wants him to do. Admitting failure, he is determined, through grace, always to seek to please and follow his Lord. Jesus has saved him for a purpose, and he knows it. He will constantly aim at fulfilling that purpose. God has saved us, too, to glorify Him, to save others, and to be a blessing in His work and to His people. Let no past failure to attain blunt our edge to continue in the future more enthusiastically and earnestly in pursuit of the best for God. May the grindstone of our failure sharpen the blade of our resolve to achieve for Him.

HE HAS HOLD OF ME!

Like a mountain climber, already secured by carefully placed spikes and ropes, or like a deep sea diver with his air line operated from above, Paul knows that the only reason he can climb or work for God in reaches beyond his natural ability and strength is that God has got hold of him. Spikes can become detached and ropes can break. Air supply lines can leak or be severed. But God's grip on his children, whether in Philippi then or on us now, cannot be broken or relaxed. We may loosen our hold on Him, but He always holds on to us. Matthew Henry again put it concisely and correctly: 'It is not our laying hold of Christ first, but His laying hold of us, which is our happiness and our salvation. Not our keeping hold of Christ, but His keeping hold of us, is our safety.'[4] Through the gospel, God takes hold of the sinner by His grace and keeps hold of him for all eternity. Jesus said that no one was able to pluck His sheep from the grip of either the Son or the Father, especially when that grip is a joint and combined one in the oneness of the Deity![5] Our security depends upon His hold on us, but is demonstrated by our determination to 'lay hold' of Him. When I cross a road with my granddaughter I hold her wrist to keep her safe, but she hangs on to my dangling finger as if crossing that road all depended upon her. Her security is in me, but her relationship with me means she lays hold of me!

3:13 Still striving

13 Brethren, I do not count myself to have apprehended; but one thing I do, forgetting those things which are behind and reaching forward to those things which are ahead,

PRIMING US FOR PRESSING ON

Verse 13 primes us for the next verse that tells us that Paul's aim and practice is to 'press toward the goal.' We will consider that a little later, but it is important to look at his launching pad from which he presses on. What is this 'one thing' that he does to guarantee future progress as a Christian?

THE 'ONE THING' THAT IS THREE THINGS!

Paul summarises the truth of the previous verse in underlining to his brothers in Christ at Philippi that (however others may see it) he does not count himself as yet holding a spiritual place of attainment. But that reminder does not mean he has given up the fight! I have a friend who says, 'The past is never the measure of the future—failure is *never final* in the Christian life.' There is 'one thing' Paul does which equips him for that fight. It is 'one thing' consisting of *three* parts! The first two are in this verse and the third is in the next verse. Together, they deal with his life so far, his current situation, and his road ahead. They are summarised by the words 'forgetting', 'reaching forward', and 'press on'. The first two deal with the past and the future. The third, in verse 14, describes his present action and attitude.

'FORGETTING THOSE THINGS WHICH ARE BEHIND'

Paul has already assigned the former qualities, achievements, and qualifications of Saul to the garbage bin. All his religious background and training, as we have seen, is regarded as mere rubbish, compared with knowing Jesus Christ personally. In that forgotten past are all his sins, now forgiven, knowing that God will 'remember them no more.'[6] All his failures lie there, buried by God's grace. All his unrealised aspirations are similarly gone. Apart from his remembering God's help and faithfulness, his successes too are remembered no more as a monument to his ability, industry and success. *All* that is behind him lies forgotten. So should it be for you and me. No pride in our Christless past, no guilt for our many past failures which God has forgiven and chooses never to dig up again, and no 'If onlys' for our past dreams that broke before they could be fulfilled. Our past, whether formerly a matter for boasting or notorious for its blame and shame, is washed clean in 'the blood of Jesus Christ, His Son' which 'cleanses us from all sin',[7] once it has been confessed to God and forsaken. In fact all our sins and failures lie unremembered there as we personally trust Christ as Saviour. In our desire to duplicate in our lives that blessed refusal of God to remember the past, we will be snared neither by Satan's taunts about past failures that would lead to despair, nor by his appealing to our pride over supposed triumphs and accomplishments.

'AND REACHING FORWARD TO THOSE THINGS WHICH ARE AHEAD'

The words 'reaching forward' imply a continuing forward movement. We do not read 'snatching forward' or 'jumping forward' but 'reaching forward'. No matter what a person's background or spiritual maturity, a healthy Christian attitude was then, and still is today, that there is much more to be appropriated and achieved in and through God. A child whose growth remains static causes great concern. But so does a child who does not grow regularly and gradually, but rather with the odd spurt now and then. A student who never proceeds beyond his first year examinations is doomed. But the best students are those who keep on at a steady work rate, rather than labouring intensively after periods of indolence. A plant keeps reaching for the sun, and so it grows. So it is for Paul, and every other Christian, that our progress must be gradual and forwards, though with occasional inputs that specifically help that process. But there is encouragement that there are 'things … ahead' to bless us and challenge us. It is only when we are 'reaching forward' spiritually that we can really advance in our service and endeavours for God. That is why the only survivor of the vicious Simba massacre at Banalia, in Congo, who nevertheless underwent demeaning and trying experiences, went back to serve God not long afterwards. If she had not been 'reaching forward' in her own spiritual life she would not have been able to do that. Margaret Hayes' story is told in *Missing, believed killed* and *A reluctant missionary*.[8]

3.14 PRESSING ON

14 I press toward the goal for the prize of the upward call of God in Christ Jesus.

THE PRESENT ALWAYS CALLS FOR MAXIMUM COMMITMENT

Imagine a player with possession of the ball in soccer, American football, or rugby. He sees a clear opportunity to score in the dying moments of a tied match. With the ball in his control, what does he do? Wait for support? Pass the ball back? Kick the ball dead? No, he heads for the goal or the line at his top speed to use all his efforts to score a goal, touchdown or try, as the case may be. It is with the same sense of urgency, and with time running out on a life which could be soon ended, that Paul explains that he presses toward the goal. His past is covered. His future is secure. Right now he has the truth of the gospel in his possession. The Referee may end the match at any time. There is an important threefold result to achieve. He wants to glorify his Lord, live his closing time as close to Him as he can, and see others coming to salvation and discipleship. So, God enabling him, he is goal orientated. Are we? Am I? Are you? Do we dilly-dally with the ball, or wish someone else would run with it? Or do we take the challenge, and the grace that comes with it, to 'go for goal' whatever anyone else might say or think? We will never make any progress in reaching forward, in the future, unless in our present circumstances we seek to be 'all for Jesus'. Then, and only then, shall we see gradual growth on a daily basis. The question of Jesus, in Matthew chapter 5:47, challenges us: 'what do you more than others?' We can learn from some of the qualities of non-Christian people, even if we can also learn a great deal from their failures! John F. Kennedy, the US President murdered in Dallas, throws out a challenge to all who should be committed to Christ and with an eye on eternity. In his inaugural speech on 20 January 1961 he said: 'All this will not be finished in the first one hundred days. Nor will it be finished in the first thousand days, nor in the life of this Administration, nor even perhaps in our lifetime on this planet. But let us begin.' *Now* is the time to press on. In Kennedy's words, 'Let us begin!'

THE PRIZE

Is Paul pressing on in order to be rewarded by receiving a prize? Or is he pressing on and a prize inevitably awaits him? Or, as he is even now pressing on, is he experiencing the prize in his own life, in terms of the peace and presence of God enjoyed by those who are committed to Christ? Or is it a mixture of two or more of these possibilities? This raises the question of what the prize is. Paul counts everything as loss and rubbish outside Christ, and is amazed by God's mercy, grace and blessing upon him, which he could never merit or deserve. The whole tenor of Paul's life seems to reflect a debt of gratitude to his Saviour.[9] Although, as 1 Corinthians 9:24–27 demonstrates, he will run the race of Christian living and service with a self-imposed discipline and singleness of purpose which would put any professional athlete to shame, he will not do his work for Christ just to get a reward for personal gain. In fact such a selfish attitude would disqualify him from that reward. There is no doubt that God has indicated that, independent of our salvation, there are rewards in heaven,[10] and it seems inconceivable that Paul will not receive his. But to work in order to get a reward is not the motivation of a man who sees himself as nothing, and Christ as everything. It seems more likely that the very 'pressing on' produces its own blessing and spiritual fulfilment, here on earth, albeit partially. In heaven, that blessing will be perfected. Some consider that Christlikeness in heaven is that prize.[11] So Paul presses on to please God and, as always, with our generous God, he will receive benefits thereby both during his life here, and gloriously in heaven. Whatever that prize is, we can be sure that it is the best possible! It is the 'prize of the upward call of God in Christ Jesus'. Any prize which involves the call of God, and being 'in Christ Jesus' has to be perfect and unmerited. My ability to 'perform' is entirely and only possible 'through Christ who strengthens me'.[12] But, like Paul, I should make my spiritual fitness for that race my top priority. Anything that slows me down or makes me less than fully fit to compete should be rejected, whatever the cost. Whatever the 'prize of the upward call of God in Christ Jesus' is, it is infinitely more valuable than any gold medal, trophy or visit to the winner's rostrum. For all who, by God's grace, fight the fight of faith, run the race of faith, and keep the faith that God has given them, there is 'laid up' for them, as with Paul, 'the crown of righteousness, which the Lord, the righteous Judge, will give … on that Day … to all who love His appearing'.[13] As we shall see in the last chapter, there is a similar result produced in the life of the believer by both the personal knowledge of the risen Christ now, and the fact that He will come again soon. These two factors should help us to press on for Him.

3:15 The mature mind and the learning curve

15 Therefore let us, as many as are mature, have this mind; and if in anything you think otherwise, God will reveal even this to you.

TRUE SPIRITUAL MATURITY PRODUCES ZEAL

Middle age spread is bad enough physically and it is worse spiritually. So often the stereotype of a middle aged Christian is someone who is nice, knowledgeable, reasonably generous, rock solid in a crisis, but rather *comfortable* and in no danger of overdoing it in evangelistic zeal or sacrificial living or giving. Without falling into gross sin, most of us who have reached or passed middle age would have to admit to losing our edge. We could all probably look back to past periods and peaks of living and witnessing for Christ that would make us ashamed of how we live and share the gospel now. It ought not to be so. Paul says that the mind he has been describing in the last few verses—the mind that forgets its 'triumphs' and its sins, that reaches forward to glorify Christ and count for Him, and that presses on even now—should belong to those who are 'mature'. Maturity should bring increased, not decreased, resolve to live for Him. After all, we know that we are now nearer the final whistle than many, and certainly nearer to it than we have ever been. Spiritual maturity and zeal should be inseparable: that is why a man should not be an elder unless he is setting the pace in holy living and unstinting service.[14] Warren Wiersbe puts it in a nutshell: 'In the Christian life, we never stand still: we either go forward or gradually slip backward. "Let us go on to maturity!" is the call we must obey (Hebrews 6:1 literal translation). The Christian who is not making spiritual progress is an open target for the enemy to attack and destroy'.[15]

THE ONGOING LEARNING CURVE

Maturity spiritually does not mean 'sinlessly perfect' or imply we have nothing else to learn about God, the Bible, or ourselves. In fact the closer we get to him, the more will we realise just how far away we really are. Only those in the darkness think their hands are clean. Only those living far enough away from Christ to forget who He is and what He is like can imagine they are pleasing to Him. But God has promised that if we do have the mature mind described in this chapter, He will keep pushing us up His learning curve. That is encouraging! If our mind strays away from scriptural principles, spiritual goals, and personal holiness, He 'will reveal even this to you'. It might be during your quiet time. It could be that one speaker after another just 'happens' to lighten our blind spots or scratch where we are secretly itching in our hearts. Or perhaps fellowship with faithful like-minded people will produce someone who loves us enough to challenge us. The principle is clear. Despite our waywardness and proneness to dilute earlier promises made to the Lord (and perhaps to others), if we have asked God to help us to live as Paul obviously does, God will give us no peace until we come back to Him in surrender. If ever we start boasting about what we have, or what we have done, or fail to look ahead with eternity in mind, or take the foot off the pedal of our current commitment, God will work at our consciences by His Holy Spirit. He will show us our sin. When He does that, we will be so grateful that 'the blood of Jesus Christ, God's Son, cleanses us from all sin.'[16] But perhaps a test of our commitment is this: what changes in my lifestyle have been recently prompted by God? If none, is it because I had it right all along, or because I am not close enough to hear what He says? Many people have an annual, or six monthly, appointment with their dentist just to check that there are no holes appearing, no cracks in previous fillings, no warning signs of trouble to come, and nothing needs attention. Such a check-up can guarantee the ongoing dental health of those who follow this as a policy. Christians should have a regular detailed check-up on their lives and service—far more often than every six months!—to ensure that they are spiritually healthy. Of course, the daily quiet time, and self-examination before taking the Lord's Supper,[17] give some opportunity for that. But why not make it a regular habit to review your spiritual life and witness with a view to making corrections and improvements for God's glory? Perhaps it would help to do it reciprocally sometimes with a faithful and loyal like-minded Christian friend? May we all continue to learn and grow in maturity.

3:16 Learning from the past

[16] Nevertheless, to the degree that we have already attained, let us walk by the same rule, let us be of the same mind.

BALANCED COMMON SENSE

Jesus was the Master of balance. He balanced grace and truth, time and eternity, love and justice, humanity and deity, and the miraculous with ordinary daily living. Paul followed his Master's example, by his experience of God's wisdom, in blending biblical principle with sound common sense. So, having talked about the need for mature Philippian Christians to be totally committed, and having shown that God will reveal any strayings from Him, he now effectively says, 'But do benefit from what you have learned: you have learned and experienced a lot that is right and good. Do not throw out the baby with the bathwater! Because you are inconsistent and less than you should be, do not jettison important lessons you have learned over time.' There is a good biblical precedent for this emphasis. We are told that the Old Testament people of God were our examples from which we should learn.[18] I have been told often that a wise man learns from his own mistakes, but a wiser one learns from the mistakes of others! Be that as it may, Paul tells the Philippians, and us, to keep in mind the lessons we have learned. Where God has given success and victory, he implies that

Christians should remember why and apply those truths and principles in the future. When blessing attended God's people, they should look back and ask why the God of all blessing chose to bless in that way at that time. Perhaps they will not know—God does often stagger us all by His grace when there seems to be no reason for it except His grace! But sometimes He has honoured those who have been enabled to honour Him. For example, individuals and fellowships who really pray often see more encouragement than those who do not have a spirit of prayer. And Christians who set their daily stall out to witness for Christ seem to get more 'chance opportunities' to testify than those who do not. Alexander MacLaren says that the 'two convictions, of my own imperfection and the certainty of my reaching the great perfectness beyond, are indispensable to all Christian progress. As soon as a man begins to think that he has realised his ideal, "Goodbye" to all advance.'[19] He must continue with a sense of need and trust.

CONTINUE

The Philippians are told to 'walk by the same rule' as that which has led to progress so far in their spiritual pilgrimage. The literal reading of the verse is: 'Only as far as we have attained, let us walk.'[20] Remember that a walk is a repetition of a step. The more often the step is repeated, the longer the walk. The need to continue is obvious. If one step is missing, the walk ends. So it is with us. When God has shown us His principles, His path to walk, what pleases Him and blesses others, then let us repeat those simple steps of repentant faith, and obedient following, over and over again. Let us continue to walk by that rule, that God, His Word, His Spirit and His faithfulness do not change, and let us continue forgetting the past, reaching forward now and pressing on into the future. 'Continue to walk according to the light you have received' is the gist of the apostle's counsel to the Philippian church and to us. The *Tyndale commentary* on Philippians rightly states: 'The apostle is confident that a desire to know the truth in full measure will be rewarded by God's revelation (verse 15). Meanwhile, he says, until you have fuller light, be content to be open-minded and teachable, and guide your life by the light you have received.'[21] In other words, learn from God's Word and act on it, but meanwhile continue to practise the good principles you already know.

ANOTHER REMINDER OF ONE-MINDEDNESS

Essential to the Philippians' continuing to put good biblical principle into practice, whilst thirsting to get to know God better, is the need to be not only single-minded towards God, but to cultivate one-mindedness towards other Christians. Being of 'the same mind' enables them to continue together with God and also with each other. So Paul goes back to his earlier foundational theme of the need for Christian one-mindedness. As we saw earlier, that can only be by having the same mind as their Saviour. Pressing on for God always involves having a spiritual mindset and seeking the best for other Christians too.

Notes

1 **Rev. Leslie Church** (editor), *Matthew Henry's Commentary on the Whole Bible in One Volume* (Marshall, Morgan and Scott), page 663.

2 Romans 7:24.

3 Matthew 5:48.

4 **Rev. Leslie Church** (editor), *Matthew Henry's Commentary on the Whole Bible in One Volume* (Marshall, Morgan and Scott), page 664.

5 John 10:28–30.

6 Hebrews 8:12; 10:17.

7 1 John 1:7.

8 **Margaret Hayes,** *Missing, believed killed* (Day One), 249 pages; **Margaret Hayes,** *A reluctant missionary* (Day One), 128 pages.

9 Romans 1:14.

10 Matthew 16:27, 1 Corinthians 4:5, 2 Corinthians 5:8–10, Revelation 22:2.

11 For example, **John MacArthur** (author of commentary/notes and general editor), *The MacArthur Study Bible, NKJV* (Word Bibles), note on Philippians 3:14, page 1826.

12 Philippians 4:13.

13 2 Timothy 4:6–8.

14 1 Timothy 3:1–7, Titus 1:5–10.

15 **Warren W. Wiersbe,** *Be Complete* (Victor Books), pages 72,73.

16 1 John 1:7.

17 1 Corinthians 11:28.

18 1 Corinthians 10:11.

19 Alexander MacLaren, *Expositions of Holy Scripture,* Volume XIV (Eerdmans), page 389

20 Rev. Ralph P. Martin, *Tyndale New Testament Commentaries: The Epistle of Paul to the Philippians* (Tyndale Press), page 156.

21 Rev. Ralph P. Martin, *Tyndale New Testament Commentaries: The Epistle of Paul to the Philippians* (Tyndale Press), page 156.

Mini-overview 3:17 to 3:21

Fourth set of threes—living in time with eternity in view.
Examples to follow and to avoid.

3:17 'Follow my pattern'—isn't that arrogant?

17 Brethren, join in following my example, and note those who so walk,
as you have us for a pattern.

IS IT RIGHT FOR A SINNER TO SAY 'FOLLOW ME?'

Is Paul arrogant to tell the Philippian Christians to follow his example?
Surely, you may say, the only human example a Christian must follow is that
of the incarnate Son, our Emmanuel, the Lord Jesus Christ? If they follow the
example of any other sinner, even though he or she may have some great
qualities, will they not fall into party spirit and copy his or her mistakes? In
fact the same apostle does tell the Ephesian Christians to imitate God,[1] but he
also commends the Thessalonian church for imitating the churches of
Judea.[2] They can see God at work in others and learn from their challenging
closeness to Him. But for a man to say, 'Imitate me' rather than 'Imitate them'
may still seem a little egoistic to some. It is not even like 1 Thessalonians 1:6,
where Paul reveals that the same church 'became followers of us and of the
Lord, having received the word in much affliction, with joy of the Holy
Spirit', where he obviously refers to others, of whom he was but one,
reflecting the Lord in their example to the church. So is Paul right to expect his
well loved Philippian church family, or Christians today, to follow *him*?

WHAT EXAMPLE?

Before acting as judge and jury on Paul, let us remind ourselves what his
example was. It was simply the lifestyle we have already considered. As
Trevor Knight noted, Paul simply 'wanted other Christians to have the
same goals as himself'.[3] God had given him those goals. Paul did not esteem
his past, his achievements or himself. We have seen that he was determined,
by God's grace, to forget all that. Now, *that* is a good example to follow!
With a real trust in Christ alone, having admitted he had not yet 'arrived',
he is reaching forward in the future to seek to please Christ. *That too* is a

good example to follow! Conscious that only Christ can enable him and keep him, he seeks to press on now for his Saviour, however imperfectly. *That also* must be a right thing to imitate! With no confidence in the flesh, his rejoicing is in Christ alone. *That* cannot ever be wrong! He worships God, not in his own ability, but only because God's Holy Spirit has been given to him and enables him to do that. Again, this is another example of what he cannot do, but only God can do for him. So Paul is not parading his successes and saying, 'Don't you wish you were like me?' He is saying, on the contrary, 'Be encouraged! God even helps a sinful failure like me to new heights by His grace and by His Spirit.' Whenever you find a Christian with that attitude, imitate him in it, because that is exactly what God requires of us. But never copy his sins and failures, of course. Micah 6:8 reminds us: 'He has shown you, O man, what *is* good; and what does the LORD require of you but to do justly, to love mercy, and to walk humbly with your God?' Paul's self effacing honesty and spiritual aspirations are the very essence of walking 'humbly with your God'. Follow him in that! Here is someone who has not yet attained but who is determined to press on with the support of God's mercy, grace, help, Spirit and people. That is to be the example that both the Philippians and we should follow.

OTHERS DO IT!

To emphasise this point, Paul adds 'and note those who so walk, as you have us for a pattern'. He is saying that other Christians they know, no doubt Timothy and Epaphroditus included, are already walking in this way. Although he is included in the role models, he does not even focus on himself alone as providing this 'pattern' to follow. He includes others, too. In effect he says, 'Look at all those who walk in this way—you know it works! Copy them in their turning from self to sole confidence in the Lord. Their pattern is a good God-given one.'

WE MUST DO IT, TOO!

Just one simple application remains for you and for me. We should live like that too! Those whom we look up to spiritually should be followed not just because we like them, or because we admire some aspect of their lives which is apart from their walk with Christ. We should follow them because they live out Christ in their daily lives and present Him faithfully by life and lip to others. It is so easy to follow a Christian who is a celebrity, when he or she might not be grounded in God's Word and giving a godly example in all things. Our role models should be those who have a proven and faithful walk with God and who esteem and follow the God of the Word, and the Word of God. May we imitate those who imitate Christ to us and whose spiritual lives challenge us to get to know Christ better, rather than give us an excuse for compromise or doing 'our own thing'.

3:18 Weeping over the many enemies of the cross

18 For many walk, of whom I have told you often, and now tell you even weeping, that they are the enemies of the cross of Christ:

REMEMBER THE 'BROAD WAY'

The Philippian church is not to be surprised that those who have salvation in Christ and who believe the Bible to be the Word of God are in the minority and are marginalised. Jesus said that the 'narrow way' that leads to life has 'few' who have found it, but that 'many' are on the 'broad way' leading to 'destruction'.4 Here, Paul tells us that 'many ... are the enemies of the cross of Christ'. Christians today should not be surprised, either, that the media, public opinion, and government legislation are all slanted to standards and principles which do not please God, and which one day He will judge. For example, it seemed incredible that a school in Gateshead, England, should have been so vilified in the British press by some scientists (who are supposed to allow freedom to make experiments and supposed to encourage people to reach their own conclusions) for teaching that the biblical position on creation should be considered as an alternative to the evolutionary model required by the syllabus, which they also teach! It even caused questions to be asked in Parliament and involved the Prime Minister, who very fairly supported the excellent academic record of the school. Those teachers knew they were in a battle! Just like those early Philippian believers, you too are in a battle. Our select band is greatly outnumbered, yet we already have the victory in Christ, and we will spend eternity with the Victor, celebrating His victory.5 Meanwhile, be ready to be counted, and put on the 'whole armour of God'6 to fight and to stand firm.

WHY ARE THEY ENEMIES OF THE ONE THING THAT CAN SAVE THEM?

If ever you need convincing that the natural unregenerate man, even if intelligent or educated, cannot understand the things of God, unless God specifically makes it real to him through His Word and through His Spirit, think about Philippians 3:18. The underlying reason is made very clear in 1 Corinthians 2:14: 'the natural man does not receive the things of the Spirit of God, for they are foolishness to him; nor can he know *them*, because they are spiritually discerned.' Our sinful nature is inherently hostile to the truths of God—especially the redeeming work of the cross of Christ. The only way a guilty sinner can be saved from the eternal punishment he deserves is if a completely sinless and righteous substitute can take his punishment in his place. That substitute's work has to be eternal in nature, because we are considering eternal blessing or eternal condemnation: therefore He has to be God Himself. That is what the cross is all about. God gives that lost and condemned eternal soul a lifeline, if he will repent and turn to Christ. What is the natural response? Unlike a drowning man who urgently grasps for a lifebelt thrown to him, a sinner's spiritual estrangement from and animosity to God makes him hate that very cross which alone offers certain hope and eternal future blessing. We prefer our sin to Christ crucified, as we shall see in the next verse. How sad! That is why any Christian seeking to win someone for Christ must do so with the spiritual weapons of prayer and proclamation of God's Word, rather than with popular worldly means which might attract crowds but cannot be the means of sinners being truly saved. The world will never be saved from the world by worldly means.

TEARS FOR REJECTED TRUTH

Paul is in the front line of those who will contend for the truth of God's Word. He would rather accept the condemnation of those who pervert the cross's unique message of mercy and grace to sinners, than have that only means of salvation obscured by their error.[7] He has such a zeal for the truth of God and the sacredness of the gospel! So we know how deeply the imprisoned servant of God feels, when he admits that he weeps as he reminds his Philippian brothers and sisters that they are being attacked spiritually by 'enemies of the cross of Christ'. Why does Paul weep?

Perhaps because he can see the havoc caused by the unbelief engendered by such doctrinal perversion? Remember how the Saviour wept over the tomb of Lazarus, and over Jerusalem? Jesus knew that people would not trust Him and thus were en route for a lost eternity.[8] Perhaps the apostle's sadness is also because he knows those enemies of Calvary are lost and hell-bound without Christ. Maybe Paul's tears are also because he recalls that those enemies of the cross in Philippi stood where he once did,[9] and the memory of his ignorant rebellion was never far away from his appreciation of God's goodness towards him. Possibly Paul's great love for the Word of God, and the honour of God, is such that to see the gospel opposed makes him feel like an aggrieved child, whose father's efforts and character are being unfairly and falsely criticised and attacked by an ignorant adversary. Certainly the Psalmist felt the same. He said, 'Rivers of water run down from my eyes, because men do not keep Your law.'[10] Whatever the reason, or combination of reasons, Paul now weeps. We rarely see such a concern today. Is that why we do not see God working as we would like Him to? Perhaps He has to melt us first? Perhaps if Christians were motivated by Paul's concern there would be more prayer for the lost. Could a misunderstanding of God's sovereignty combine with a natural inclination *not* to pray for others, and thus stifle prayer and rob people of blessing? In his book, *Nothing But The Truth*, John MacArthur, whose confidence in God's sovereignty is undeniable, discusses why we should pray for the lost under the following sub-titles: *Praying for the Lost Is Morally Right, Praying For The Lost Is Consistent With God's Desire, Praying For The Lost Reflects God's Uniqueness, Praying For The Lost Is Consistent With The Person Of Christ,* and *Praying For The Lost Reflects The Fulness Of The Atonement.* Our concern for God and for the lost should lead us to pray and perhaps to tears also.[11]

REPEATED REPETITION!

We have already seen that Paul was prepared, indeed obliged, to repeat warnings which he knew he must urgently relay to the Philippian Christians. 'I have told you often' does not stop him telling them again, now 'weeping'. If we care for people sufficiently, we will keep calling out, as they get closer towards the cliff top in the dark, until we know they have been turned away to safety. We will not worry if others find such warnings offensive or distasteful. We will have our priorities fixed and will pursue them, regardless of whatever others think.

3:19 Apostles of perdition

19 whose end is destruction, whose god is their belly, and whose glory is in their shame—who set their mind on earthly things.

AGAIN, REMEMBER THE 'BROAD WAY'

In considering verse 18, we saw that the broad way led to 'destruction' for the 'many' on it. The truth that Jesus taught is underlined by the Holy Spirit's teaching through the apostle. So we see that verse 19 endorses Jesus' sombre words in Matthew chapter 7:13. Christ's unrepentant enemies will end up eternally in 'destruction'. Sadly, so will many they influence. How we need to see the gospel shared with 'all men everywhere' so they can be urged to 'repent'.[12] Sproul comments: 'Paul weeps, not because he fears someone can undo what Christ has done, but because of the destruction in store for opponents of the gospel. This destiny completes the destructive process initiated by their own sin (Romans 1:18–32; Galatians 6:7,8).'[13] We, too, should be passionate and compassionate about hell.

THE IDOLATRY OF HUMAN APPETITES

By describing 'their belly' as their 'god', Paul is referring neither to over-indulgence of food, though the principle extends to that, nor to certain dietary restrictions that the Judaizers followed as part of their plan of salvation by works. The belly can refer to what they wrongly believe their 'flesh', in the sense of their old nature, has achieved for them in gaining merit to secure their acceptance with God. It is just as likely that it refers to the indulgence of their physical appetites, which is so much a priority lifestyle to them, that it is an end, and an idol, in itself. The link between doctrinal deviance, an idolatrous spirit, and sexual immorality occurs too often in the Bible, and in history, for it to be a mere coincidence. That provides another reason why they hate the message of the cross. Christ's cross calls and commands them to crucify those sinful passions in repentance, and admit their sins in turning to Christ crucified for forgiveness and restoration. They find that message cuts across their sinful lifestyles and insatiable desires to do what they want to do with their bodies. Today's cries, both of the abortionists and of those advocating sexual immorality, that 'Our bodies are our own' are by no means new or original. There is always a moral element in apostasy. When God's spiritual truth is ignored, man's fleshly lusts take over. This being given over to fleshly appetites, as in Romans chapter 1, precedes being given over to a reprobate mind. Thus the death of moral standards, evidenced by rejection of God's Word and unfettered fleshly indulgence, precedes the death of moral sanity and reason, as rebel sinners literally lose their sound and morally sensitive minds.

SHAMEFUL GLORY AND AN EARTHLY MINDSET

Not only in the twenty-first century's Western 'civilisation' do rebel sinners glory in things that God regards as shameful. It is found here in Philippi's first century church environment. To glory in shame is to elevate those things, repugnant to our Creator, which we as created beings should be ashamed to follow or embrace. These shameful things are then held and elevated, instead of God, by those same rebel sinners. Some of those shameful things would, no doubt, be included in the fleshly passions and false religious pride referred to before. But there seems to be a wider principle of arrogant defiance. The expression of this shameful and arrogant rejection of our holy and sovereign Creator can be as extreme as practicing heterosexual or homosexual immorality, as widely accepted as boasting about how much alcohol a man can drink or how much he can pilfer from the taxman, or as subtle as glorying in religious works or orthodoxy or self-righteousness. The very fact that mean and dirty mankind endeavours to elevate himself in defiance of a holy and omnipotent God, is in itself shameful, especially when God could 'turn him off' at a glance, but has chosen to love him and send His Son to die for him. But then for man to glory in that rebellion, which God allows for His purposes until His timetable comes into effect, is folly in the extreme. Yet, what mankind does generically, many individual men and women glory in individually. Like pigs, with snouts in the filth of this world's sin as they rush toward an acorn dropped in the dirt to encourage them forward, they grunt in self-appreciation as they are led ever closer to the slaughterhouse of eternity which awaits them. Yet forgiveness and cleansing could be theirs if they will but turn and trust. But that is not easy for them. Their minds are not only engaged in such shamefulness, but, like concrete, are completely mixed up and permanently set. Human nature is just so: we choose sinful and fleshly alternatives, and then, instead of repenting and turning to the Christ of the cross for pardon and deliverance, we set our minds upon this filth and shame. No wonder that born-again Christians, who wish to honour their Lord, sometimes find it an uphill struggle! But read on!

3:20 Apostles of perdition

²⁰ For our citizenship is in heaven, from which we also eagerly wait for the Saviour, the Lord Jesus Christ,

THE RESURRECTION LINK WITH THE SECOND COMING OF CHRIST

The themes of resurrection and second coming often intertwine in this letter, and we will see it again in the last chapter. After dealing earlier in this chapter with his aspirations to live the resurrection life of Christ on earth before he benefits from the coming resurrection and his resurrection body, Paul reverts to his eager wait for his 'Saviour, the Lord Jesus Christ' who will come from heaven. As those who have been blessed by Christ's death and resurrection, consistent Christians, in Philippi then and in the world now, live, worship and witness with that same sense of eagerly waiting for our coming King! In this verse, we see how that theme underlines the motivation and reward for pressing on. We are children of the colony of heaven, we shall one day be in heaven, and our Lord will come to and for us from heaven. In pressing on, we should live the life of heaven on earth, a life which is very different from the enemies of Christ's cross. Our life should reflect where we belong—heaven—just as their glorying in shame reflects where they are going to spend their eternity.

WHERE WE ARE REALLY AT HOME

Heaven is where our spiritual and eternal passports were made! It is where we belong, as Christ's people and God's children. Heaven's sun and light, the Lord Jesus, came on heaven's mission to save lost sinners and to make them into heaven's citizens. We now respond to the throne of grace situated there. Our instructions, privileges, and immunities for representing our King down here, come from there through the words that the King has written to us in the Bible. We are as much an ambassador of our Sovereign on this terrestrial globe as any country's ambassador in history has represented his or her monarch in a foreign land. One day, unless He comes to take us there with Him first, the King of Heaven will call us home and await our report of how we represented Him. That is only right, since the very resources of heaven are available to us to enable us to live for Him, and serve Him, here. So neither the Philippians, nor we, should be surprised that our resources, task, lifestyle, and future are so different from those who only know how to live for this sordid, selfish passing world. They get their standing orders from an entirely different source. They will be recompensed differently too, throughout eternity.

WHEN COULD THE KING COME FOR US?

It is from heaven itself that our 'Saviour, the Lord Jesus Christ' will come one day. He will take from this earth all those loyal subjects of His whom He has redeemed by His precious shed blood. He will bring with Him the souls of His subjects, whose bodies have already slept the sleep of death, and re-clothe those souls with the same new resurrection bodies that those who remain on earth shall receive 'in the twinkling of an eye'![14] He will also judge the world that has rejected Him. Those who, by then, have failed to repent and trust Him, will 'be punished with everlasting destruction from the presence of the Lord and from the glory of His power, when He comes, in that Day, to be glorified in His saints and to be admired among all those who believe'.[15] None of us knows when that day will be, but we are to 'eagerly wait' for Christ's second coming. What a combination! 'Eagerly' and 'wait'! Those words imply patience and day-to-day faithfulness, but an enthusiasm about His coming to wind up human history, which is reflected in the penultimate verse of the Bible[16] where the response to the Saviour's last words in Scripture—'Surely I am coming quickly' is met with that eager response 'Amen. Even so, come, Lord Jesus'.

UNTIL THAT DAY

Until that day arrives, we are to keep our feet firmly on the ground, and our heads looking up to heaven, faithfully serving Him as His citizens and ambassadors and following His instructions, whilst longing for the day when His timetable for redemption reaches its ultimate climax. If it is His will that He returns in our lifetimes, and 'no man knows the hour or day of His return',[17] may He find us faithful when he comes. Do you 'eagerly wait for the Saviour'? Grudem's observations are challenging to every Christian: 'Do Christians in fact eagerly long for Christ's return? The more Christians are caught up in enjoying the good things of this life, and the more they neglect genuine Christian fellowship and their personal relationship with Christ, the less they will long for His return. On the other hand, many Christians who are experiencing suffering or persecution, or who are more elderly or infirm, and those whose daily walk with Christ is vital and deep, will have a more intense longing for His return. To some extent, then, the degree to which we actually long for Christ's return is a measure of the spiritual condition of our own lives at the moment.'[18]

3:21 Transformed and conformed!

[21] who will transform our lowly body that it may be conformed to His glorious body, according to the working by which He is able even to subdue all things to Himself.

'HE IS ABLE'!

Consider the privilege of those who are living for the King when He returns. Just as certainly as the decayed and decimated bodies of Christians who have died will be changed into resurrection bodies when the returning Christ brings their souls with Him, so the lowly human bodies of those on the earth will be miraculously changed into the same sort of resurrection bodies. 1 Corinthians 15:42–54 tells us of the corruptible body putting on incorruption, of the dishonourable body becoming glorious, of the body of dust becoming a heavenly body, of the instant change that will take place at Christ's coming, and of mortal physical man putting on the immortality of his resurrection body. 1 Thessalonians chapter 4 goes on from verse 16 to say, in verse 17, that after 'the dead in Christ will rise first' the next thing will be that 'we who are alive *and* remain shall be caught up together with them in the clouds to meet the Lord in the air. And thus we shall always be with the Lord.' So, here the Philippians will share the expectations and hopes of twenty-first century Christians. If they will be on earth when Jesus returns, that is how they will go up! If they die before Christ's return (as in fact is the case) they await coming back with the Lord Jesus, as saved souls, and receiving their new bodies to replace their dead ones. Whichever Christians are alive when Christ returns will rise after them with a wonderfully and instantly changed body! What a prospect! That really is the ultimate and final 'healing'—and a whole lot more! The bodies of those who are trusting Christ will be much more than healthy, for they will be resurrection bodies incapable of deterioration and will reflect God's glory and power! 'Lowly bodies' will be transformed. Bent old people will rejoice in their uprightness, in every sense! Sightless eyes will feast upon Him as they are taken up with Him. Crippled folks will jump for joy, dumb lips praise (in tune!), and the deaf will thrill to hear it all. Those mutilated in persecution, war, or through disease or surgery will be whole. Those wasting away with cancer or AIDS will be made vigorous. Sick children will laugh in full health, and the dying words of those on the edge of the Valley of the Shadow of Death will instantly be changed to praise, as the returning Lord cheats death at the point of its temporary victory! Have I over-indulged my imagination? I do not think so. In fact, the wonder, joy, thrill and splendour of that day will be beyond human anticipation or telling. When the Queen of Sheba saw Solomon's glory, wisdom and especially his ascent into the temple to commune with God,[19] she said, 'the half was not told me'. In that day we will know that the *billionth could never* be told! And remember, as you struggle in daily living for Christ, that He who 'is able' to do all that, is our Saviour who can use that same power to help us to live for Him *right now!*

OUR BODIES TODAY

For most people their most prized treasure is their physical body, which for them includes their mind resident in it. Regularly they rest it, clean it, clothe it, feed it, exercise it, look after it when it hurts, use it for what they want to do, and try to keep it alive as long as possible. Some try to make it look more beautiful than it really is, used to be, or can be! Others seek to make it look very muscular and strong. Most try to help its brain develop by educating it and letting it read or watch things from which it learns. Yet both body and mind get older and the body becomes more wrinkled and creaky as the days go by. Some bodies break down completely, in death, long before their owners thought they would. No body lasts very long. The average is around seventy years, very few get to over a hundred years, and many die very much younger. Others limp along, severely handicapped and sometimes very miserable. No body is ever used to its full potential, because very early on man sinned and has been suffering from death, decay and under-achievement ever since. As a result, only a very small proportion of the brain is fully used. It was built to do far more, before sin came in. No body is without sin, and no body can last for ever by itself. Since sin came in through Adam, owners of bodies misuse and abuse their bodies, in many different ways, in order to do things that God never intended should be done with them. He meant them to glorify Him. One day He will glorify the bodies of those who have trusted Him to save them from sin and its penalty! Those who belong to Christ will receive a glorified body: it will be without defect, weaknesses, blemishes, injuries and illnesses. It will last for ever but never be even partially worn out. It will never sin again. The Christian will receive a new resurrection body by God's transforming the body he, or she, has lived in. That transformation will take place for every Christian when Christ comes again, even if his, or her, body died and decomposed hundreds of years previously! In that glorious, sinless everlasting body he, or she, will enjoy unbroken eternal fellowship with God in His new heavens and earth.

WHAT WILL OUR RESURRECTION BODIES BE LIKE?

Grudem asks that very question and, using the Bible, replies that our Christlike resurrection bodies will be 'imperishable', 'glorious' with a 'bright shining radiance' and that they will be 'raised in power' as a 'spiritual body'. He summarises: 'We will live in bodies that have all the excellent qualities God created us to have, and thereby we will for ever be living proof of the wisdom of God in making a material creation that from the beginning was "very good" (Gen 1:31). We will live as resurrected believers in those new bodies, and they will be suitable for inhabiting the "new heavens and a new earth in which righteousness dwells" (2 Peter 2:13)'[20]

GLORY!

With the King of glory for ever, with a glorious body given to us like His, little wonder that we should look on 'glory' as something to anticipate eagerly. Some people get very excited about achieving their consuming aim, to become very rich on earth. But in a hundred years from now, what good will be their riches to their decayed bodies and lost souls? Who will be the winners then? Who are really rich? Whose joys will not pass away? Who will then have the most important relationship of all—with the King of kings, as their Saviour and Lord? The answer? Unworthy sinners who have received His grace and mercy through repentant trust in Him!

THE KING IS IN COMMAND!

No wonder that Paul concludes this section by saying, 'He is able even to subdue all things to Himself.' The Philippians and perhaps the apostle himself need to be reminded that Jesus is in control. He is co-Creator.[21] He sustains the whole universe right now.[22] He is all-powerful and His power knows no limits.[23] Even death is powerless in His hands.[24] He is sovereign![25] When the time is right, He will come again and resume full command. He who 'is able to subdue all things to Himself' will return in great power and glory to do just that one day. Until then, as we will see in chapter 4, He is with us to help us live for Him and to rejoice in what He does in us, for us, and through us. What a wonderful Lord we have! No wonder that with one mind, forgetting the past and reaching forth to the future, we should 'press toward the prize of the upward call of God in Christ Jesus' and 'press on' through the risen life of the Lord of glory! But that will mean living for Christ in a practical way, as well as thinking of our eternal blessings, and the fourth and last chapter will show us how to live with both the resurrection and the second coming in focus.

Notes

1 Ephesians 5:1.
2 1 Thessalonians 2:14.
3 **Trevor F. Knight,** *God's Wonderful Word,* page 113.
4 Matthew 7:13.

5 Revelation 5.

6 Ephesians 6:11.

7 Galatians 1:8,9.

8 John 11:35 and Matthew 23:37.

9 Acts 26:9.

10 Psalm 119:136.

11 John F. MacArthur, *Nothing But The Truth* (Crossway Books), pages 41–45.

12 Acts 17:30.

13 R.C. Sproul (general editor), *The Reformation Study Bible, NKJV* (Nelson), notes on Philippians 3:18, page 1880.

14 1Thessalonians 4:13–16.

15 2 Thessalonians 1:9,10.

16 Revelation 22:20.

17 Matthew 24:36.

18 Wayne Grudem, *Systematic Theology* (IVP), page 1093.

19 1 Kings 10:7.

20 Wayne Grudem, *Systematic Theology* (IVP), pages 831–835).

21 John 1:3; Hebrews 1:2; Colossians 1:16.

22 Colossians 1:17.

23 Hebrews 7:16.

24 Hebrews 2:14; 1 Corinthians 15:54–57.

25 Acts 10:36; Philippians 2:11.

The letter opened (continued)

Philippians Chapter 4

[1] Therefore, my beloved and longed-for brethren, my joy and crown, so stand fast in the Lord, beloved.

[2] I implore Euodia and I implore Syntyche to be of the same mind in the Lord. [3] And I urge you also, true companion, help these women who laboured with me in the gospel, with Clement also, and the rest of my fellow workers, whose names are in the Book of Life.

[4] Rejoice in the Lord always. Again I will say, rejoice! [5] Let your gentleness be known to all men. The Lord is at hand. [6] Be anxious for nothing, but in everything by prayer and supplication, with thanksgiving, let your requests be made known to God; [7] and the peace of God, which surpasses all understanding, will guard your hearts and minds through Christ Jesus.

[8] Finally, brethren, whatever things are true, whatever things are noble, whatever things are just, whatever things are pure, whatever things are lovely, whatever things are of good report, if there is any virtue and if there is anything praiseworthy, meditate on these things. [9] The things which you learned and received and heard and saw in me, these do, and the God of peace will be with you.

[10] But I rejoiced in the Lord greatly that now at last your care for me has flourished again; though you surely did care, but you lacked opportunity. [11] Not that I speak in regard to need, for I have learned in whatever state I am, to be content: [12] I know how to be abased, and I know how to abound. Everywhere and in all things I have learned both to be full and to be hungry, both to abound and to suffer need. [13] I can do all things through Christ who strengthens me.

[14] Nevertheless you have done well that you shared in my distress. [15]

Now you Philippians know also that in the beginning of the gospel, when I departed from Macedonia, no church shared with me concerning giving and receiving but you only. [16] For even in Thessalonica you sent aid once and again for my necessities. [17] Not that I seek the gift, but I seek the fruit that abounds to your account. [18] Indeed I have all and abound. I am full, having received from Epaphroditus the things sent from you, a sweet-smelling aroma, an acceptable sacrifice, well pleasing to God. [19] And my God shall supply all your need according to His riches in glory by Christ Jesus. [20] Now to our God and Father be glory forever and ever. Amen.

[21] Greet every saint in Christ Jesus. The brethren who are with me greet you. [22] All the saints greet you, but especially those who are of Caesar's household.

[23] The grace of our Lord Jesus Christ be with you all. Amen.

'The nearness of Christ'

Mini-overview 4:1 to 4:9

The challenge and comfort of the nearness of Christ. Realising the deep spiritual and practical effects resulting from the presence and coming return of the Lord Jesus Christ.

4:1 The 'therefore' link

[1] Therefore, my beloved and longed-for brethren, my joy and crown, so stand fast in the Lord, beloved.

'THEREFORE'

Because of what we have just seen, namely the certain fact that God will have the last word in history by the coming of Christ, who will consummate our salvation for us, and 'subdue all things to Himself' the Philippian Christians, and we ourselves, are to 'stand fast'. The 'Therefore' links the need to stand with the sure, but future, certainty of God's final victory. We fight for victory from a victory and to a victory! We stand because God is sovereign and His timetable is certain!

PAUL'S WARMTH TOWARDS CHRISTIANS

Paul demonstrates again his great love for his 'beloved' brethren whom he has 'longed for'. He uses the language of love, calling them 'beloved' twice. This flavour, from a former persecutor of the church and conspirator in the death of hated saints of God, makes the book of Philippians a classic on how to regard other Christians. Paul, behind locked doors, pines for their fellowship and company. Through God's grace in his life, he knows that he has passed from death to life because he really does 'love the brethren'.[1] The Christians at Philippi are a real joy to him, as he sees the work that God has done in them and through them. Just as parents and grandparents are filled with joy as they see a new life come into being and grow through childhood, so the fatherly heart of Paul rejoices over this infant church. He also sees them as his very own crown. Battles and great bravery have been produced by the desire to gain or keep a crown. Paul is bravely involved in the battle for their establishment in Christ. It was for this that he came to preach the gospel to them. This is why he sends Timothy and Epaphroditus to them and why he has laboured to see them established in their walk with God, grounded in His Word. His 'longed-for brethren', his children in the faith, his 'joy and crown' are the recipients and beneficiaries of the heritage of truth he has shared and will yet share in this letter to Philippi.

CROWN

'No pain, no palm; no thorns, no throne; no gall, no glory; *no cross, no crown*,' (my emphasis) said William Penn. Paul's daily cross-bearing for, and through, Jesus Christ brings him the crown he most prizes—that of seeing men and women coming to Christ for forgiveness and going on with Him in trusting obedience. Could it be that one reason why most of us see relatively little blessing of this nature in our lives is because we do not value the result as highly as Paul does? For him, these people are the crowning glory of his work on earth. Nothing means more to him. If we prize our possessions, reputation, comfort, entertainment and well-being more highly, we cannot view the saving of souls and honouring of God in new converts as our 'crown'.

STANDING FAST

Chapter 4:1 links the great confidence, coming from the liberating and awe-inspiring truths of chapter 3, with spiritual and practical daily living detailed in this last chapter. It brings the Philippian Christians, and us, down to earth and reminds us that there is a battle to be fought and that there is a stand for Christ to be made. Paul's biggest concern is that they should now remain stedfast in their faith in Christ. An army that does not stand is destroyed or flees in disarray. All Paul's worthy and right sentiments would be turned to disappointment if his beloved brothers failed to stand. This echoes his admonishing the Ephesian Christians to put on the 'whole armour of God'. Paul then tells them, that 'having done all' they must simply 'stand' and 'stand firm'.[2] Love, concern, joy and God's working in a new convert, and in any Christian church, prepare and require that person or church to stand in and for Christ. Someone who has been changed by faith in Christ, despite his overwhelming sense of personal weakness and inadequacy, cannot but determine to stand by God's enabling for Christ against all that opposes his Lord. This is the spirit of the Reformation, encapsulated in Martin Luther's brief, challenging and historic statement of faith: 'Here I stand. I can do nothing else. God help me. Amen.' Even though the Christians may fall *along* the way at times, Paul's concern is that they will not fall *from* the way. Those who stand in and for Christ are not to be confused with those who never sin or fail again. To stand may well mean coming back with repentance to seek God's pardon and help to get up and fight on. Such people are standing in His grace and mercy and will not give up because of the opposition of the world, the flesh and the devil.

4:2 When instruction turns to imploring

² I implore Euodia and I implore Syntyche to be of the same mind in the Lord.

HARMONY

The NASB translated this verse: 'I urge Euodia and I urge Syntyche to live in harmony in the Lord.' Harmony is most noticeable by its absence, when discordant notes grate in the ear of the listener. That is how God hears the discord which takes place between two people who both claim to perform under His conductor's baton, but who spoil the whole melodious harmony that He intends to produce. It offends and troubles the other players too. The two people out of harmony, and not therefore 'of the same mind', are ladies called Euodia and Syntyche. Sadly many follow them still today. It is interesting that Paul implores, or urges, each of them *individually* to be in harmony, as well as both of them together. Twice he says 'I implore': one for each. If he had merely left his pleadings to the two together, each could have continued to blame the other. But he demands compliance from each individually, in order to have them in harmony together. When you are out of harmony with another Christian, make sure at least that you get back to God's score and melody. If the other person does the same, the harmony is restored. If not, there is only one person left for God to correct in His own way.

WHAT WENT WRONG?

Paul is urgent. As we have seen, He implores Euodia and Syntyche individually to be like-minded in the Lord. In this way he starts the last chapter by repeating his insistence, in chapter 1:27, that the Philippian Christians should be of 'one mind'. He tries to close the circle. But he is not just issuing a command, or merely passing on a recommendation that they be like-minded. Paul urges and appeals to these sisters in Christ to be of the same mind in the Lord. He obviously feels it very strongly indeed. The whole of his earlier thoughts on being 'one-souled' and on having 'the mind of Christ' have led up to this particular situation which must be remedied if God is to be glorified, fellowship is to be restored, and the lost are to sit up and take notice of what Christ can do in producing genuine brotherly love amongst His people. What is the point of the apostle giving his biblical and spiritual grounds for like-mindedness if members in the church do not intend to put it all into practice? They are to remember that this oneness is 'in the Lord'. Disharmony, therefore, can only be when the foundation of fellowship moves from that solid foundational rock to some sands of human weakness and selfishness. But why is this admonition necessary? What has gone wrong? What is the problem? In answering that for the Philippian church then, we may feel there is similar restoration of fellowship to be humbly undertaken in our churches today.

PERSONALITY PROBLEMS

In fact, why the relationship between these Christian workers broke down is neither obvious nor explained. We know that something has arisen to spoil that one-mindedness in the Saviour who died to save them both. God in His wisdom has not revealed what are the particular causes of the disharmony. If He had have done that, perhaps we would have been tempted to think that there is no application to us because we have never fallen out with other Christians for the precise reasons that tripped up Euodia and Syntyche. By keeping the question open, God challenges us to put *all* disputes right in a humble and spiritual manner, and live in one-mindedness in Christ with others who know Him. Was the trigger for the dispute something trivial, with the exact issue perhaps even a little misty now? Sadly, a break in fellowship and friction between blood-bought

Christians may be caused by something trivial or even forgotten. Yet personality conflicts divide more churches than doctrinal differences, and God's holy and loving grief over that must be considerably more intense than any man's grief over these two named Christian sisters. Here is an affront to God, a stumbling block to the church, a terrible example to the outside world, an insult to grace, and a testimony to one or more person's refusal to repent and to let the 'mind which is in Christ Jesus' take over. If we can only enjoy 'fellowship' with those with whom we would be happily associated if we were not Christians, it is not *fellowship* 'in the Lord' at all. True Christian fellowship unites all believers together, reminding us that we are 'all one in Christ Jesus'.[3] When personality problems prevail over the effects of Christ's shed blood, there is serious heart-searching to be done, and much to put right.

THE LINK BETWEEN DEEP DOCTRINE AND SIMPLE OBEDIENCE

We can see why Paul, in this letter to the Philippians, has already laid the foundation of Christian oneness, in view of the great humility in the mind of Christ, which they, and we, are to appropriate and emulate. Chapter 2 develops the need to apply this humility in practice in living for God. Chapter 4 personalises it and, in effect, says to these women: 'Now—here is the real test of your seriousness in walking humbly with your God. If you are serious, put things right between you, and both adopt the mind of Christ in your thinking and in living out that thinking.' Deep biblical doctrine is never far away from practical application. If we believe the truth, we will live it out. Deep doctrine is closely linked to simple obedience. 'As a recipient of God's love … we are morally obligated (*ought*) to love those for whom Christ died, because we have become partakers of the divine life through Christ.'[4] If we obey God and believe His teaching, we have no option but to do what He commands. Not to do so constitutes sinning against Him. That means we are to be reconcilers not dividers.

'JUST DO IT'

We are not told what Euodia and Syntyche have to do to put things right— just that they are implored to do it. When God convicts Christians of sin, they know what they have to do. The Bible is full of it. Confession to our merciful and pardoning God, forsaking of sins, and asking forgiveness from, and giving it to, those with whom open fellowship has been broken or spoiled should be spiritual second nature to a Christian. After all, we are to trust and follow the Lord of grace and humility. But God leaves to the individuals exactly *how* to make that reconciliation. It is said that these Philippian ladies, Euodia and Syntyche, are found in every church under slightly different names of 'Oh dear' and 'Soon touchy'. If they are in your church, or fellowship, and if you recognise yourself as one of them, be implored! Be reconciled! Be of one mind with your brothers and sisters. Whatever you have to do to effect that, do it! And do it now, or as soon as you can. As a well-known advert says, albeit in a different context: 'Just do it!' One-mindedness in Christ demands it.

4:3 Help and heaven

3 And I urge you also, true companion, help these women who laboured with me in the gospel, with Clement also, and the rest of my fellow workers, whose names are in the Book of Life.

URGED TO HELP OTHERS

Paul is an *'urgent'* Christian leader! Here he *urges* someone else in the interests of one-mindedness, Christian fellowship and gospel witness. He does not reveal the identity of the 'true companion' but Paul urges him to help Euodia and Syntyche, who had laboured with Paul in the gospel along with Clement and other companions in the gospel. Paul does not simply leave the two women with an admonition, but asks for help for them. Christians can help each other to deal with their differences and reset their priorities. Inter-personal conflicts and individual sins cannot be resolved without individual humility and repentance, but those close to the 'offenders' can help. Prayer, gracious enquiry, supportive counsel, and instant acceptance when things have been put right can help others back to blessing. When those others are, as with these women, folk who have previously laboured in the gospel, there will be vital spin-off blessings. Lost souls will benefit when a woman with a heart to share the gospel is restored and even more so when two co-labourers for God are restored together and to God! The worship of the church profits by God being glorified and praised from hearts that have been put right. We may never know how our help to other Christians with problems may benefit the kingdom of our Saviour. Imagine the benefit to the individuals, their church, and the work of God generally when true fellowship is restored, so that they can pray with each other and together with others. If what Spurgeon said about the church and its prayer meeting is right—'You can always tell how a church is getting on by the prayer-meetings',[5] it is equally true about Christians who have been close in fellowship and friendliness in the past. Are they spontaneously and willingly praying together? Any Christian who can help those whose estrangement has robbed them each of that privilege, is doing the work of Christ. Here we see Paul the organizer at work. He trusts Divine grace to overrule, but he makes specific plans for a godly 'true companion' to get involved in this divisive situation to help to sort it out.

THE BOOK OF LIFE

We know no details of the rest of Paul's fellow workers, mentioned in this verse. We do know that they are Christians, for their names are in the Book of Life. They will not be blotted out of that book[6] because they have overcome through Christ's cross, resurrection and ascension victories. When working for Christ on earth, it is good to have our minds fixed on heaven! We will get an individual reception there: our names are known. Jesus told some, who rejoiced in the immediacy of wonderful God-given success in His work, that their priority was to rejoice that their 'names are written in heaven'.[7] That will not change, whereas our 'success' can quickly evaporate, be spoiled by pride, or be missing for long periods of time. Our names, however, are written in the glorious Book of Life by the hand of God in the ink of His eternal and indelible grace! Berkhof, writing about the *Perseverance of the Saints*, looks down from God's viewpoint in saying: 'The doctrine of the perseverance of the saints is to the effect that they whom God has regenerated and effectually called to a state of grace, can neither totally nor finally fall away from that state, but shall certainly persevere therein to the end and be eternally saved.'[8] MacArthur looks upward at the same truth through the eyes of a Christian and comments: 'The Trinity secures us for ever so that no Christian who believes in the Lord will ever be lost. Scripture bases the eternal security of the believer on the promise and power of God, the prayers of Christ, and the presence of the Holy Spirit.'9 If God has saved you, you have been saved, are being saved and will be saved. It is wonderful to know, whilst working for Christ, that we are secure for ever in His mighty work of salvation for us, not in our feeble works of service for Him. Euodia, Syntyche, Paul's 'true companion', Clement, the rest of Paul's 'fellow workers' and the apostle himself all know their names are in that Book! All the more reason to live in Christ pleasing oneness of spirit here below!

4:4 Rejoicing

4 Rejoice in the Lord always. Again I will say, rejoice!

REJOICING COMMANDED

If rejoicing is just a by-product of spiritual vibrancy, a mere experience of joy that comes and goes, Paul could not have *commanded* the Philippian Christians to 'rejoice'. Although a modern song urging us to 'Be happy' proved very popular, it is a useless piece of exhortation. If I am sad, or have reason to be troubled, I may feel worse (and cross!) when someone says, 'Be happy!' Why? Because I cannot move myself emotionally to do that. That *is* part of my problem: I am *not* happy! Thus if to rejoice is merely an emotional response, it is pointless of the apostle to command it. But true rejoicing is a matter of *the will* and is based more on logic than on emotion, though it will not be long before biblical rejoicing warms up our emotions too! It asks the Christian to consider all the facts in his favour, especially the fact of His Saviour, and thus to set his mind and will to rejoice when his emotions are on strike. One man whom God used to win many and train them into disciples, half a century ago, enthusiastically laid out some of the reasons why we should rejoice. They were all based on who God is. He explained: 'We joy in God the Father, in His wonderful love, in His almighty power, in His unchanging grace, in His transcendent glory. We joy in God the Son, in His Person, in His redemptive work, in His risen life in the glory, and in the prospect of His return for His children. We joy in God the Holy Ghost, in His indwelling, His illumination, His guidance, His comfort, His abiding presence in our hearts. We joy in the Triune God—Father, Son and Holy Spirit—and so we "rejoice evermore". This is the "joy unspeakable and full of glory."'10 Paradoxically, it is after we have set our minds to rejoice through what Christ has done for us, and who He is, that we see our emotions catch up later and we begin to feel what we already know. Because to rejoice is a command of Scripture, to disobey is a sin, (which is never joyful!). Thus failing to rejoice robs us doubly of blessing: it prevents us experiencing God-centred rejoicing, and adds a further burden of unforgiven sin that we commit in failing or refusing to rejoice. When we repent, trust God, and obey His command to rejoice, we are truly blessed in so doing. Rejoicing is designed to glorify God and bless us.

REJOICING'S SOURCE AND GOAL

But, as we have seen from the last quotation, rejoicing is never in a vacuum. It does not exist in isolation. It has a source and a goal. For the Philippian Christians, that source and goal is one and the same: the Lord Jesus Christ. The command is to rejoice 'in the Lord'. It is because He has taken the curse and punishment for our sins that we can rejoice that our names are written in the 'Book of Life', just mentioned by Paul. It is because He arose, ascended and is present in the life of the saved person, then and now, that we rejoice in His nearness and help. It is because He will come again in great power to wrap up history and usher in His kingdom, in its fullness, that we rejoice in His sovereign and perfect will, which will triumph according to His timetable. Only because we are to 'rejoice in the Lord' can we see the logic of the command to rejoice. He never changes. He is always the same. And so, although our feelings climb and dive with fluctuating uncertainty that surprises us at times, His constancy in His love, mercy, pardon, power, help and grace—all available to us—give us logical and biblical reasons for rejoicing when we just do not feel like it. When our spirits sag, we should keep 'looking unto Jesus' and be ready to 'consider Him'.[11] That will feed our rejoicing and ultimately will bolster our sagging spirits.

WHY SAY IT TWICE?

Without apology, Paul repeats the command to rejoice twice in one short verse and defiantly proclaims 'Again I will say' it! There is one very good reason why. The church members at Philippi do not always find it easy to live like that, and need prodding and reminding that this is the way they must go. Paul knows this is crucial to their walk with God, so he repeats himself. Is that not also true of you and me? If this came naturally or easily, God would have no need to command us to do it! But God will help us to rejoice like this and He will bless us when we do. Remember the earlier story about the visiting preacher who repeated his sermon three times because the congregation failed to respond to the first two! We should be prepared to persevere in our continued exhortations, as Paul is, if needed. We should also respond immediately ourselves to God's commands and promptings, so that others do not have to remind us again of our duty towards God and others. Specifically we must remember to 'rejoice in the Lord.' As we shall be reminded in a key phrase later in this chapter, He is near: His risen presence is with us, and He is coming back soon![12]

4:5a Gentleness
5a Let your gentleness be known to all men.

GENTLE IN A MACHO WORLD?
In this 'macho' age, many men want to appear to be 'tough' and some women seem to want to become more like men. So it is challenging to see that, after urging the saints to rejoice in the Lord, Paul encourages them to practise gentleness. The NASB translates the verse 'Let your gentle spirit be known to all men.' Some see the rare possession of a gentle spirit as weakness. Meekness, which is a close companion of gentleness, is wrongly viewed as weakness. Gentleness is often viewed as a defect, especially in men, rather than as a desirable spiritual quality. Yet the phrase 'gentle giant' implies that a person can be physically big and strong and yet be gentle in attitude and behaviour. In fact, such a person's gentleness underlines his great strength because he does *not need* to parade it unnecessarily. One household brand of tissues declares itself to be 'strong and soft'! Softness can have other implications, but the genuine softness of gentleness is a spiritual quality to be sought and fostered. In fact, it helps us to be strong in Christ. It can only come from Him and can only be given to a person who walks closely with Him. It takes greater strength to exhibit gentleness in a hostile world, especially if you were a stranger to any form of humility before conversion, than to express your self-will and strong emotions audibly and forcibly. In fact, it takes the strength that Christ can give.

'DON'T USE HIS NAME UNLESS YOU LOVE HIM, LAD.'

I met a Christian Regimental Sergeant Major ('RSM') at an army camp where I went to preach the gospel. RSMs are known for their uncompromisingly assertive authority, meticulous attention to detail (especially if you happen to be turned out on parade in anything less than perfect!) and very loud voices that strike terror into the troops being drilled. One of the Christians on the camp related an incident to me about the RSM I met. Hearing a sergeant shouting at a soldier and adding the name of Christ to his torrent of verbal abuse, the RSM quietly walked up behind the sergeant and whispered quietly to him, 'Don't use His name unless you love Him, lad.' Gentle, but by no means weak! A gentle person can take a strong stand for Christ, and strong people need to be gentle. I doubt if the sergeant concerned ever forgot that lesson, whereas no doubt he had been shouted at many times in his career. It is the *difference* of gentleness that makes such an impact.

DEMONSTRATE IT TO ALL

Gentleness is not to be hidden. It is not a thing of which the strongest of men is to be ashamed. Paul tells the Philippians that their gentleness is to be 'known to all men'. In our dark and cruel world, how the light of our Saviour and His gospel shines brightly by gentle words and deeds which come from those who are learning lowliness and meekness from Him who has bidden us to take on His yoke.[13] It will bring derision from some, and thus provide another opportunity to show forth gentleness in gracious responses, by word and deed, that says we are 'under new management'. Gentleness may be the first thing a lost sinner notices about you, long before you have the opportunity to share the gospel verbally with him, or her. Gentleness enables a Christian to relate to children and very old folks, to bereaved and sick sufferers, to those who are depressed and to failures, as well as to those whose life seems 'normal' for the time being. 'Somebody has said that a king may make a nobleman but he cannot make a Gentleman,' Edmund Burke remarked. Yet the gracious King of kings can make a hard and insensitive man into a 'gentle' man by softening his heart by grace and moulding it by His word and Spirit. He can make us all 'gentle' because that is not a natural achievement, but a spiritual gift and fruit.[14] As we concentrate on being deeper spiritual people, so our gentleness will deepen also.

4:5b Jesus is near

5^b The Lord is at hand.

THE HINGE VERSE

Huge doors turn on relatively small, but very strong, hinges. The immediate passage, the whole of chapter 4, and arguably the whole of the letter to the Philippians, turn on the truth of the five words found in the second half of verse 5: 'The Lord is at hand.' This can easily be missed, as it may seem to be a fairly bland adjunct to the first half of the verse. In fact, it pinpoints the nearness of Christ as a motivating, comforting and challenging influence and factor which influences the whole of Christian living and accountability. Whether it is interpreted in the light of the presence of the risen Lord, or with an eager anticipation of His coming again, it is a key that unlocks the deeper significance of everything else in chapter 4.

'THE LORD' WHO IS AT HAND

What did this statement mean to those early Christians in Philippi, and what can it mean to me today? We will look at the two constituent phrases: first, 'The Lord', and then 'is at hand.' 'The Lord' refers to the Lord Jesus Christ, whose deity is well attested in this letter. The name 'Jesus' means 'God saves'. It is, therefore, no surprise to our logic that He 'being in the form of God, did not consider it robbery to be equal with God' as chapter 2:5 reminds us. God the Son is co-equal with God the Father in the Trinity and is introduced to us in chapter 1:2 as the co-equal Son, 'the *Lord* Jesus Christ'. Nor is it surprising that God's Spirit, the third Person of the Trinity, is referred to as 'the Spirit of Jesus Christ' in chapter 1:19. Paul's 'my Lord' of chapter 3:8, is the mighty God whom He notes 'is able even to subdue all things to Himself' in verse 21 of the same chapter. The Lord, who is 'at hand' is, indeed, our 'Emmanuel'—the Lord Jesus Christ who is 'God with us'.[15]

THE LORD WHO IS 'AT HAND'

Do the words 'The Lord is *at hand*' mean that the risen Lord Jesus Christ is near us now? Or do they refer to His glorious second coming that we should eagerly wait for? The phrase 'is at hand' is capable of referring to time *or* to space. If we ignore this verse for a moment, the whole context of the Bible is that Christ can be said to be coming soon—He is 'at hand' in the sense of His impending second coming. He is 'at hand' in these last days of gospel grace in the 'time' sense that He will come again soon in power and great glory. But the Bible also reveals that the Conqueror of the empty tomb will never leave nor forsake us[16] and is also now close by each Christian—literally 'at hand'. One well-known preacher used to remind his hearers that 'The Lord is at your elbow'. In fact, He is even closer than that, because He dwells by faith in the hearts of Christians.[17] Which do you think is the main emphasis here—time or space? Should we apply 'The Lord is at hand' to the present nearness of our risen Lord, or to the certain fact that the King of kings and Lord of lords will come again soon?

DIFFERENT TRANSLATIONS

Some of the different translations and paraphrases of the Bible have rendered the second half of verse 5 as follows:

The Lord is at hand—AV, NASB marginal alternative, NKJV, RSV

The Lord is near—NASB, NEB, Nestles Interlinear NT, NIV, Interlinear Bible

the nearness of the Lord—Phillips

the Lord is coming—Living Bible

The Lord is coming soon—Good News for Modern Man

Perhaps the Amplified Bible's variant reading summarises both views comprehensively:

The Lord is near—He is coming soon—Amplified Bible.

Many commentators suggest that the primary thought is that Christ is near to every believer and fellowship of believers. There is ample justification from this letter so to apply it. The whole letter abounds with the thought of knowing the risen Christ now, and having His mind in us now.[18] But it is also arguable from the clear references to the second coming in the letter that 'The Lord is at hand' could refer to the imminence of His coming, in God's timetable.[19]

GETTING THE JUICE OUT OF EACH ORANGE!

Each portion of Scripture has the one primary meaning intended by the Holy Spirit who inspired it. Sometimes, however, it can be interpreted in more than one way. That is why it is important to look at the context of the Bible as a whole, the part of the Bible where the passage or verse is located, more specifically the book in which it is found, and more specifically still the part of that book and the context of surrounding passages and verses. Then the specific local context can be looked at before applying the truth of the passage to the reader. Only very rarely it is hard to determine what the primary meaning is, and equally rarely, where a passage may allow more than one meaning, it is hard to say for sure what the primary meaning is. In those very rare situations, here is a principle that has served me well in my reading of the Bible. If it seems that there really is more than one genuine, in context, non-contradictory, balanced way of interpreting a part of the Scriptures, why not take each genuine alternative and look at each one as if it is the main application? Why not suck the juice out of all the oranges, rather than argue over which orange you should take? Obviously this should not be extended to out of context, fanciful interpretations intended to bolster up someone's own pet view or experience, when the context of Scripture and of the passage concerned make clear that this is not the primary purpose. In this verse, it does seem that a good argument can be made for applying this to the glorious return of the Lord Jesus Christ, *or* to His nearness to those who know Him as Saviour (whether in Philippi then or elsewhere today), *or* to both! In looking at the nearness of Christ, we must realise that He 'at hand' in both those contexts. In my comments that follow, I will therefore apply both possibilities. Whichever interpretation you prefer from your understanding of the Bible and of the passage, please feel free to suck the juice from that orange—but you are not prohibited from tasting the other!

THE BLESSINGS THAT TURN ON THE HINGES OF CHRIST'S NEARNESS

Thus I am using the key phrase, 'the Lord is at hand', as indicative of both His coming back to earth soon as 'King of kings and Lord of lords'[20] and His presence now with the believer, to see what truths turn on them in chapter 4:

Standing firm for Him in verse 1. We stand fast in the certain knowledge that Christ is sovereign and that He will come again with all power—we really will overcome then! But until then, we have our all-powerful God near us and within us to help us to stand fast.

Same-mindedness in verse 2. Would we want to be found squabbling when the King returns? He whose risen life we all share is next to us. We need to think about that when we are about to fall out with one another. Should we not behave differently in His presence?

Supporting Christ's labourers in verse 3. The time is short before the Lord of the harvest returns, so work whilst you have time. When the divine Foreman returns, would He want to find His workers disputing or slacking? The resurrected Lord, who told us to go and make disciples for Him,[21] stands and works with us.[22] Could we stand and watch Jesus toil when we could work with Him to please Him and help bring in the harvest He longs to see gathered? If I am shovelling or using a sickle, He will know about it if He is at my elbow.

Spirit of rejoicing in verse 4. The coming Lord Jesus will reign and change everything. He will make everything new! Surely we should rejoice in that? He has forgiven our sins, written our names in heaven[23] and now dwells in us and by us through His risen life.[24] Can I fail to rejoice at the thought of being accompanied by the lover of my soul?

Sensitivity towards others in verse 5. It is in the immediate context of gentleness that we read 'The Lord is at hand.' When Jesus gives every Christian a resurrection body at His coming again, both those living on earth and those who have died and whose spirits He will bring with Him,[25] He will treat all His children with the same grace and favour. How can I face Him, and give an account of my life as a Christian,[26] if I fail to treat some Christian brothers and sisters sensitively and gently, possibly just because our 'personal chemistry' differs? Remember that the now risen Lord Jesus said during His earthly ministry 'Take My yoke upon you and learn from Me, for I am gentle and lowly in heart, and you will find rest for your souls.'[27] Remember that 'gentle and lowly' Jesus, who calls me to be gentle, is with me in the yoke and knows if I am gentle in relating to others. He is there when no one else is. Christian sensitivity is needed and He is there to provide it through me to others. That brings us up to where we are at verse

5! We shall see these twin truths applied in the verses of the chapter yet to be examined. See how the nearness of Christ affects us as we look at stress (verse 6 and 7), sanctification in practice (verses 8 and 9), satisfaction (verses 10 to 12), strength (verse 13), sharing (verses 14—20), and even salutations (verses 21 to 23).

4:6 Stress, prayer and peace

6 Be anxious for nothing, but in everything by prayer and supplication, with thanksgiving, let your requests be made known to God;

STRESS

'Stress' must be one word which has grown amazingly in its use over the last decade. Everywhere you go, you hear about stress. A well-known radio station markets its classical music as a stress breaker. People take time off work because of stress. It is a symptom of our modern worried age. The phrase 'stressed-out' is commonplace, and it seems that as long as you use that word, you are permitted to worry, feel sorry for yourself, and be entitled to expect others to feel sorry for you too. No doubt both Paul and the Philippians could claim to be victims of stress: certainly many today would do so if they were in their position. But, on the contrary, Paul tells Christians to refuse to be stressed, not by giving in, but by praying thankfully to God! That sounds old fashioned today, but it is still God's way that His people should handle anxiety and stress.

NOTHING—EVERYTHING

If ever anyone had reasons to be anxious, based on his circumstances and prospects, it has to be Paul awaiting possible execution in that prison. Yet we have seen that God's strength, presence, joy and provision of a few like-minded Christians prevail in his life. He is thus appropriately qualified to tell the Philippians, and us, that anxiety is absolutely wrong and to be resisted. Worry is a sin we choose. Here is a *command* to 'be anxious for nothing' and to break it is to disobey God. That is one reason why worry multiplies itself in our hearts and minds. We add the results of anxious sinning to whatever causes the worry in the first place. And there are no exceptions. In Philippi then and where we live now, we are told to 'be anxious *for nothing*'. That is all inclusive. It is a challenge that is also a comfort. Anxiety is to be rejected and refused as any other sin. It means that there is nothing, large or small, personal or national or international, to do with health or wealth, concerning people or things, in the past or in the present or in the future, concerning which we may, must, or need to worry! God's command is also His enabling, and to underline that He tells how we can act positively to fulfil His command not to 'be anxious'. We are to take *everything*—again no exceptions—to God in prayer. The lovely old hymn, 'What a friend we have in Jesus' encourages us by the following words:

Have we trials and temptations?
Is there trouble anywhere?
We should never be discouraged.
Take it to the Lord in prayer.

The same sentiment is found in the chorus which tells us:

All your anxieties, all your care:
Take to the mercy seat—leave them there.
Never a burden He cannot bear;
Never a Friend like Jesus!

HOW?

The next question is obvious! If I am commanded not to have any anxiety over anything, and if I am told to take everything to God in prayer, then *how can I do it?* The Bible is a wonderful book: it does not just tell you to do something but explains how you can get there! It is a map, as well as a signpost! This verse reveals the open secret.

PRAYER AND SUPPLICATION

Prayer is communing with God spiritually. It has less to do with closed eyes and bent knees than with humble repentant hearts and a reliance on the Person of the Lord Jesus Christ and the promises of God's Word. It can take the form of thanksgiving to God, praising Him for who He is, confession of our sins, intercession for people, supplication for things, or just as a means of sharing with God in prayer. It can be long or short, repeated or uttered only once, silent or aloud, on your own or with others, and can be employed absolutely anywhere and everywhere. It can be a combination of any and all of those things. It depends on God and therefore is dependable! Supplication is that part of prayer that asks for things—either to benefit others or for one's self, or both. By making our requests known to God, in prayer and with supplication, we bring to God the very things that are the source of our problem. Thus our anxieties can be defeated. This is how we 'take it to the Lord in prayer'. We should pour our hearts to Him in detail and let Him know exactly what we are asking, at the same time as asking Him to overrule the outcome to accomplish His will, and our blessing in glorifying Him. We do not get there by an odd panic prayer or time of prayer. It is something we must cultivate, as a godly habit, day by day. But remember that your risen Lord is near—right there with you. Share your heart with Him as your risen Friend. Your best Friend is there to help and is able to do so. He is at your elbow! Confide in Him! Pray! Pray! Pray! And remember too that, in a world of escalating terror and uncertainty, the same Lord is coming back again, when He decides, to take full control and to wrap up history the way He decides. Do not be anxious about that either. Your future in Christ could not be better! Talk to Him about it confidently.

THE PLACE OF GIVING THANKS

The phrase 'with thanksgiving' is important, but easily overlooked. William Shakespeare wrote 'Beggar that I am, I am even poor in thanks.' We are often like that: plentiful in requests and minimal in thanksgiving. What should we thank God for, as we share these burdens that cause us the anxieties we are bidden to reject? Here are a few suggestions of things that we should always be ready to thank God for whether we feel like it or not! Thank God that: He is there with you all the time; you know Him to speak to; He listens to you; your problem is not an eternal one as you have a sure place in heaven; He is powerful enough to solve it when the time is right in the way that is best; your problem is not worse than it is; He will give you grace to cope; you are learning to trust Him more through this; others can pray for you too; He is in control of world affairs; He is infinitely more powerful and wise than any man or group or nation of men; and He will come again in power and great glory! Think thankfully. Be grateful. It will also change your attitude and that will help to lighten your heart, by His grace. And above all, thank Him for His death on the cross for you, for His ongoing presence as your risen Lord, and for the fact that He is returning one day in glory!

THE ONE TO WHOM WE PRAY
Remember the truth about the greatness and authority of our God, expressed in one hymn:

You are coming to a King,
Large petitions with you bring.

The God to whom you come is not only all-powerful and righteous, but He is compassionate. He is your Father. He loves you as His child. He will not deny you what you need. He wants to give you His peace. He does not reject you because of your coldness and inconsistency. One Christian prayed about himself to God as follows: 'Had I been a prince I would long ago have crushed such a rebel; Had I been a father I would long since have rejected my child'[28] and he went on to thank God that He was not like that in His attitude towards him, but that God's grace and mercy were always there for him in Christ.

4:7 Surpassing peace
7 and the peace of God, which surpasses all understanding, will guard your hearts and minds through Christ Jesus.

HIS PEACE IS PROMISED
The result of the Philippians' thankful and prayerful turning from anxious stress to God is that He will give them His peace. This is God's own peace that He will give to His needy subjects. In the midst of turmoil and hurt, in the storms of opposition and misunderstanding, facing persecution and even imprisonment, when racked by pain and sickness, even on the very edge of death itself, the peace of God is promised to praying people who look to their Saviour God, whether in Philippi in the first century, or in your country in the third millennium. Because it is 'the peace of God' it cannot be taken away, imitated, or replaced by a world that rejects our risen Prince

of Peace. When He comes again, and His enemies fall before Him in awe, so much greater will be the peace of God in the hearts and minds of those who trust Him. And this peace is not only an emotional peace of the heart. It is also a rational peace of the mind from someone who can logically work out:

Whatever my lot
You have taught me to know
It is well! It is well with my soul.

Whether that well-being of soul is encouraged by the nearness and presence of our indwelling Saviour, or by the thought of His glorious coming, or both, matters not. The Prince of Peace is here and will be here, and that whispers 'Peace' to my soul!

BEYOND HUMAN UNDERSTANDING BECAUSE IT IS SPIRITUAL
The 'peace of God', that comes to God's people when they pray, 'surpasses all understanding'—even their own! Neither can the brainiest intellectual in the world fathom it! He reasons within himself: 'Why should that person show forth such peace? Everything seems against him, or her, and yet there is a sense of positive tranquillity. Where on earth does that peace come from?' The question gives the game away! 'Where *on earth* does that peace come from?' That is the whole point. It cannot come from '*earth*' and does not! It is a spiritual peace which comes from knowing God who is Spirit, and worshipping Him in Spirit as a result of having no confidence in our flesh, and rejoicing in Christ Jesus! (Remember chapter 3?) That is why we should get to know our ever-present Redeemer better every day by the spiritual means He has given us. That is also why we need a heavenly mindset to look up because our 'redemption draws near'.[29] The second coming of Christ is far more important than any world event, and more relevant than the ranting of any and all nations or groupings of politicians or terrorists. Whilst men still reject Jesus as the 'Man of sorrows', we rejoice in Him and know that He is the coming King. The humblest Christian, in Philippi or near you, knows more than the most influential non-Christian in the world today. And he, or she, knows that the peace the

Saviour gives is because of the spiritual life received and renewed in the hearts and minds of the worst of sinners who turn to Christ.

HEARTS AND MINDS

The body may be afflicted and life may be taken away in martyrdom. Loneliness may be a price to pay for discipleship. But God's living peace will keep the 'hearts and minds' of those who pray because their hearts are open to Christ and their minds are occupied with His mind. Taking 'heart' as the seat of the emotions, the 'real you', and the mind as the centre of our thinking, we can see how important it is to have them kept. In any war the adversary's command and control centre is the first target. In the spiritual warfare that occupies Paul, the Philippians and us, our command and control centre is the combination of our hearts and minds. Motivated by all the teaching that Paul has so far given, and will give, strengthened by the nearness of their Saviour now and the assurance of His coming, and helped by praying with thanksgiving, the Christians at Philippi will find their command and control centres are well protected. They are able to keep up the battle together against the enemy. In the next verse, the apostle will brief them about some specific attacks and how to repel them, but first we note again through whom God's peace will keep their hearts and minds.

WHO ELSE BUT JESUS?

And who will deliver on this promise of protecting peace in the heart and mind that completely baffles the understanding of man? Who else but 'Christ Jesus'? The very One who is at your elbow and who will return as the kings' King and the rulers' Ruler! Those who met Queen Elizabeth II in her Jubilee year tours, during 2002, were thrilled and, no doubt, talked about it for a long time and probably still do. But the Supreme Monarch personally accompanies even the lowliest of His subjects as a Friend! What is more, He has promised to come back in state for him, or her! What peace to know that! What a Saviour!

4:8 Sanctification and the 'off button'

8 Finally, brethren, whatever things are true, whatever things are noble, whatever things are just, whatever things are pure, whatever things

are lovely, whatever things are of good report, if there is any virtue and if there is anything praiseworthy—meditate on these things.

POSITIVE TEACHING TO THE PHILIPPIANS

In developing his battle instructions which complement the Philippians' minds and hearts being kept by the peace of God, Paul goes very positive and stresses the need not only to meditate, but to meditate on good things. The world is always a downward drag for Christians. The flesh is always only too willing to be dragged down. The devil is always keen and active to use the world to drag down the flesh and to seek to achieve his evil ends. Paul's co-apostle, John, summarised an aspect of this battle by saying: 'For all that is in the world—the lust of the flesh, the lust of the eyes, and the pride of life ... is not of the Father but is of the world.'[30] Paul's immediate response is to stress what positively can be done in the battle to thwart and combat the trinity of evil that is too strong for us without Christ. The *only* things which are to receive their attention are to be noble, just, pure, lovely, of good report, virtuous and praiseworthy. Is your reaction to run for cover in self-justification at this point, or are you open to challenge and change to meet the requirements of your ever-present Lord who will come again?

A NEGATIVE VIEW?

Long before today's sex perversion and vile pornography flowed like an open sewer into living rooms and homes through television, the Internet, CDs, DVDs and videos, A.W. Tozer, surely a prophet of his time in renouncing the sins that enslaved millions and turned them into hell, commented on 'The Erotic versus The Spiritual' in his book *Born after Midnight*.[31] Tozer attacked the modern mindset and ideas that caused and allowed these things to happen. But was Tozer too negative? Some thought so, or said so, then, but surely the moral downgrade in our society and in our churches has vindicated this man of God. We are about to consider what Paul instructs the Philippian believers about the positive aspects of holiness which they are to adopt, promote and live out. Again what he says will start with the mind. But to set the background, because the same principles and standards should apply to every Christian today, let us consider some excerpts from Tozer's book, and ask whether it has got any better since, and where does each of us stand personally? How drastic are we prepared to be to avoid the debauchery that many take as the norm? Tozer said: 'Sex love has been elevated into a cult. Eros has more worshipers among civilized men today than any other god. For millions the erotic has completely displaced the spiritual ... the motion picture and television ... enable a whole population to feast their eyes on sensuous women and amorous young men locked in passionate embrace (and this in the living rooms of 'Christian' homes and before the eyes of innocent children) ... degraded columnists ... have consecrated their lives to the task of the publicising of soft, slinky nobodies with the faces of angels and the morals of alley cats; conscienceless novelists who win a doubtful fame and grow rich at the inglorious chore of dredging up literary putridities from the sewers of their souls to provide entertainment for the masses. These tell us something about how Eros has achieved his triumph over the civilised world—the cult of Eros is seriously affecting the Church. The pure religion of Christ that flows like a crystal river from the heart of God is being polluted by the unclean waters that trickle from behind the altars of every abomination that appear on every high hill and under every green tree from New York to Los Angeles. The influence of the erotic spirit is felt almost everywhere in evangelical circles. Much of the singing in certain types of meetings has in it more of romance than it has of the Holy Ghost. Both words and music are designed to rouse the libidinous. Christ is courted with a familiarity that reveals a total ignorance of who He is. It is not the reverent intimacy of the adoring saint but the impudent familiarity of the carnal lover.' And, may I remind you again, that things have deteriorated since the 1970s, when Tozer wrote that, to a degree that would have been incredible to many saints of God, and civilised sinners also, who have passed away since then. So let us consider Paul's urgency about holiness which he presses on his beloved Philippians and, through God's Spirit and Word, on us too.

PLENTY TO GO AT—POSITIVE AS WELL AS NEGATIVE

The nearness of Christ, in both the immediate and the eschatological senses, carries a great challenge as well as a great comfort in this verse. Here, the Philippians are urged to apply their minds positively to meditating on those things which we noted above. The list is worth repeating: things that are true, noble, just, pure, lovely, of good report, virtuous and praiseworthy. A poem entitled 'If Jesus came to your house' challenges the reader about the things done, said and watched in the home, and asks what changes would there be if Jesus turned up as a guest for a day. But He *is* there as the Guest every day! Every day, Emmanuel is with us at home and in the work place. When I speak to others or listen to what they say, He listens, too. He watches with me when I look at the TV. The Philippians did not have televisions, but worldly and sensual distractions have never been absent because of a less developed technology. Problems and temptations in the Christian life are always the same in principle, no matter what part of history we live in. What does Jesus think as he looks over my shoulder at the newspapers I read, even in the hairdresser's shop or in the doctor's waiting room? How true are the things I say, as my Friend listens at my elbow? How noble does my unforsaking Friend judge my attitudes to be when I find I can progress by treading on others' reputations, or when I gossip about others? How just, or righteous, does He regard my conduct when I can gain by bending the rules a little? Would Jesus bend the rules? Would he deal with tax returns and expense sheets the same way that I do? How pure does He see my mind to be as I drink in my entertainment? Would he look at the same things and listen to the same words that I do with approval? How lovely are the lifestyles of those I talk about so much and like to be with? Can I give a good report of where I have accompanied my Companion, and would the venues have changed if I had gone alone or with my usual friends? At the end of the day, will Jesus praise His heavenly Father for the spiritually single-minded and pleasing way I am following Him on the highway of holiness? If Jesus were to return one day, in my lifetime, and find me engaged in those pursuits, attitudes, words, motivations and deeds, would I blush before He changed my 'lowly body' to the holy resurrection body I profess to desire so strongly? Is it not time to consider the 'off button' on some things in my life that have no place in someone claiming to follow Christ? Are there some things, places, pastimes, companions, and intentions that should go—*now*? Is it not time to commit myself, perhaps again, to the things that will feed my spiritual life and please my Lord, who is both with me now, and coming for me on that glorious climactic day in history? A more zealous heart? More holiness? More Bible? More consistent prayer? More God-honouring Sundays? More disciplined reading? Greater effort to attend and participate in the prayer meeting and Bible study? And how about *less*, or *none*, of some of the things that I know deep down do not fit the criteria given here, and that will not help that battle for my heart and mind? Can I change things so that Jesus will be glad to accompany me in my normal pursuits and so that if He were to return in glory, He would be pleased to find me so occupied?

THE LOST ART OF BIBLICAL MEDITATION

The Philippian church members and we Christians today are told to 'meditate on these things' listed twice above. Meditating on God's person and character and on the teaching and themes of Scripture include all those points and can help so much in this battle, especially where meditation is cultivated as a regular godly habit. Biblical meditation has an object: Bible truth. That must form a big plank in the overall scheme of meditation that Paul urges here. Biblical meditation does not consist of 'emptying your mind'—that is the very reverse and can provide a vacuum that the devil will be very happy to fill. Of course, there are other things, besides Bible truths, to consider that are good and wholesome. Concentrating on sunsets, seascapes, mountain ranges, wildlife, flowers, and night skies all are good for us and remind us of a great Creator. And good Christian literature aids our thinking processes too, towards that which is spiritually helpful. But to chew over in our mind the teachings, examples, promises, warnings and questions of Scripture until we are involved in the thinking and implications of those truths is the very best way to meditate. We read and rush off too quickly. We listen to the Bible being expounded and leave too thoughtlessly. We must meditate on these things in order to cultivate that mindset of holiness that we have been considering. To meditate on Bible verses and passages we need to memorise them. A friend of mine says, '*There can be no meditation without memorisation*'. Whilst I would not go quite as far as that, there is no doubt that to memorise Bible verses means I have to meditate on them whilst I am memorising them. Also when I am in a situation where it is impracticable to read, for example when I am driving the car or washing up, I can meditate on what I remembered. The same principle applies to seeking to *remember* points that blessed you from your morning quiet time so that you can recall them during the day.

4:9 What an example!
9 The things which you learned and received and heard and saw in me, these do, and the God of peace will be with you.

LEARNING AND RECEIVING
The Philippians have both learned and received some 'things', and they have also witnessed some 'things' in Paul. They are now told to 'do' them in order to ensure the experience of God's presence with them. Let us consider the things which the Philippians have 'learned and received'. The fact that these two words are used underlines that there is a difference between learning something and receiving it. It is very important that they *learn* God's words and ways, and how to apply them in their corporate and individual lives. But they must also *receive* those things: in other words they must take those lessons to heart, in prayer, trust and obedience. It is not enough simply to know mentally or theoretically what is right. It has to be appropriated personally too. For example, they might have learned about the 'mind that was in Christ Jesus' but they need to 'receive' that truth by asking God for the repentance and grace to change their own hearts and minds to let His mind dwell in them. They cannot 'do' it, in the sense of applying it in practical situations, without first having received it. It is like someone who is ill, whose illness is diagnosed by his doctor before he is told what prescribed medication he needs to obtain, to deal with his illness. If he does not go to the pharmacy to collect the prescription, he has only 'learned', but not 'received' the truth of it. Of course, he still has to 'do it' by taking the medication. We too need to hear, and receive before we can 'do'.

THE LIVING LETTER
Before looking at how the Philippian Christians can 'do' what they should, we need to notice that they must not only 'do' the things heard and received from God's Word but also those things they 'heard and saw in' Paul. To what

things was Paul referring? We could go through the letter so far to answer that question, and list all the specific points where he gives such an excellent example. In each chapter the list would abound. We learn a great principle from this, that those who practise what they preach are far more likely to be a real blessing to others than those who merely relate the truths of God's Word through biblical orthodoxy. Paul showed truth on fire, not on ice. But bearing in mind the immediate context of this chapter, to 'meditate on these things', it seems compelling logic to link them with the 'things' both learned and received and also heard and seen in Paul. So Paul appears to be saying that, by God's grace alone, he has provided an example of how to think on the 'things' that are true, noble, just, pure, lovely, of good report, virtuous and praiseworthy. The Philippian Christians, it seems, would have been unable to point to Paul's inconsistency or hypocrisy in the way he concentrated on things that were positively helpful to his spiritual life and to the spiritual life of other people. By deduction and logic that would mean they never saw or heard him being untruthful or neglecting God's truth, or following a mean or ignoble attitude or course of action, or indulging in impure use of his mouth or eyes or ears, or focusing unnecessarily on nasty or unworthy matters, or giving his time to things that he could not report back to them with a good heart and in good will, or sacrificing Christian virtues for personal entertainment or achievement, or being unable to link the praise of God with any matter he was pursuing or experiencing. What an example indeed! If we really followed those things which the Philippian Christians had observed in Paul, how many of us would never even begin to watch some of the things to which we have allowed ourselves to become accustomed through the media or modern technology? Would we have to change our daily newspaper, regular magazine or reading habits? How would our topics of conversation or range of jokes change? How many times would we look in another direction when lust entered our thinking through our eyes? How many of our preferred music CDs would be confined as trash? Thank God for the small band of faithful Christians who are more in step with God's Word than with the dictates of this passing world. We should note what we see and hear in them, and ask God to challenge and change our own shallowness and unwillingness through the way we see His truths taking on flesh and living differently for Him. Sadly, they too often become the object of ridicule and misplaced humour from those who prefer compromise to obedience. Well has Warren Wiersbe said, whilst commenting on Demetrius in 3 John 11 and 12, 'You and I cannot see God, but we can see God at work in the lives of His children. The godly life and dedicated service of another believer is always an encouragement and a stimulus to me. By our good example, we can "consider one another to provoke unto love and good works". (Hebrews 10:24).'[32] In such a crooked, dirty and dark world how we need to be well fashioned, clean and light letters spelling out God's message of saving and sanctifying grace to those who will read our lives.

'JUST DO IT'

Remember the famous advert 'Just do it'? We get no advantage by merely agreeing that we should learn, receive and long for these truths to be applied things in our lives. We have to 'Just do it'. That one word 'do' from Paul, is worth a thousand books read, or three years at a Bible college or seminary. Jesus said He came 'to do' the will of His Father.[33] James tells those who claim to belong to Christ to be 'doers of the word, and not hearers only'.[34] Well then, Philippian church, do not just sit there—'do' it! Christians today, you 'do' it, too! Reader (and author) go now and 'do' it. He will give enabling grace, wisdom and help. Remember that you can 'do all things through Christ'.[35] Then 'do' it—right now, and keep on doing it!

WHAT IS BETTER THAN THE 'PEACE OF GOD'?

See the amazing result from doing what God commands! We saw, in verse 7, that the 'peace of God' would be present to keep and bless those who knew Christ and replaced anxiety with prayer. But now we see that the 'God of peace' will be with those who go a step further. Those who add holy obedience to prayerful trust will know the personal experience of the 'God of peace!' To have the 'peace of God' is a wonderful privilege. To know the presence of the 'God of peace' is immeasurably better. And God promises that certainty to those who will 'do' the things learned and received, and also heard and seen in His faithful servant. Our 'God of peace', became Man for us, died to give us peace with God,[36] rose again, ascended and will return to establish His reign of peace. And He is with us *now*!

Notes

1 1 John 3:14.

2 Ephesians 6:13,14.

3 Galatians 3:28.

4 "Notes for the Study and Exposition of 1st John" by Eric E. Kress, Kress Christian Publications, page 101.

5 Quoted in **Terence Peter Crosby** (editor, selector and arranger), *365 days with Spurgeon*, Volume 2 (Day One), page 537.

6 Revelation 3:5.

7 Luke 10:20.

8 **L. Berkhof,** *Systematic Theology* (The Banner of Truth), page 545

9 **John MacArthur,** *Saved Without A Doubt* (Chariot Victor Publishing), page 146.

10 **Arthur S. Wood,** *The Greatest Things* (Pickering and Inglis), pages 21, 22.

11 Hebrews 12:1–3.

12 See the comments on Philippians 4:5.

13 Matthew 11:29.

14 Galatians 5:22.

15 Matthew 1:23.

16 Hebrews 13:5.

17 Ephesians 3:17.

18 See, for example, the following verses from Philippians: 1:8; 1:19; 1:21; 1:26; 2:5; 3:3; 3:8–10; 3:12; 3:14; 4:1; 4:6; 4:13; 4:23

19 See, for example, the following verses from Philippians: 2:10,11 which obviously refers to Christ's coming again; 3:20,21 which gives the reason for standing fast that Christ will come again.

20 Revelation 17:14.

21 Matthew 28:19.

22 1 Corinthians 3:9.

23 Luke 10:20.

24 Colossians 1:27.

25 1 Thessalonians 4:14.

26 Romans 14:12.

27 Matthew 11:30.

28 **Arthur Bennett** (editor), *The Valley of Vision* (The Banner of Truth), page 38.

29 Luke 21:28.

30 1 John 2:16.

31 Included in **A.W. Tozer** *The Best of Tozer!* compiled by **Warren W. Wiersbe** (Kingsway Publications), pages 40,41.

32 Warren W. Wiersbe, *Be Alert* (Victor Books), pages 125, 126.

33 John 5:30.

34 James 1:22.

35 Philippians 4:13.

36 Romans 5:1.

Mini-overview 4:10 to 4:13

Satisfaction and strength.
Realising the deep spiritual and practical effects resulting
from the nearness of the Lord Jesus Christ.

4:10 Flourishing care

¹⁰ But I rejoiced in the Lord greatly that now at last your care for me has
    flourished again; though you surely did care, but you lacked
    opportunity.

ONCE AGAIN 'IN THE LORD'

Paul simply cannot keep the Lord from anything in which he is involved,
including his rejoicing, of course! Even now where it is quite clear that his
immediate benefactors are his brothers and sisters in Philippi, his rejoicing is
'in the Lord'. He recognises that this gift is good and perfectly suited for his
needs at just the right time. His personal principle is always to work to support
himself when that is possible and appropriate[1] and that 'the worker is worthy
of his wages'.[2] But he also knows only too well that there are times when he has
survived only because of God's good gifts through others, perfectly provided at
just the right time for him. Like James,[3] he is gratefully aware that 'Every good
gift and every perfect gift is from above, and comes down from the Father of
lights, with whom there is no variation or shadow of turning.' Knowing this his
rejoicing is 'in the Lord'. It is quite amazing how such rejoicing can take place
when all around seems bleak. Habakkuk exemplifies this perfectly: 'Though
the fig tree may not blossom, nor fruit be on the vines; though the labour of the
olive may fail, and the fields yield no food; though the flock may be cut off from
the fold, and there be no herd in the stalls … Yet I will rejoice in the LORD, I will
joy in the God of my salvation. The LORD God is my strength.'[4]

OPPORTUNITY NOT INDIFFERENCE

Even before Epaphroditus took their most recent gift to him, the Philippian
Christians had always wanted to give to Paul. One of the most important
principles in giving, as the same apostle makes clear in Corinthians 8:12, is
that 'if there is first a willing mind, it is accepted according to what a man

has and not according to what he does not have.' The 'it' in this verse refers to the amount given. God grieves over the meanness of Christians who have the funds to give but hold back. But Paul understands and is warmed by the person who has only a little to give, and gives it. In the case of these Philippian Christians, one can never question their intended generosity to Paul, their companion in the gospel, but they were unable to do so until Epaphroditus' recent visit. Now they have some resources and their giving is resumed. The opportunity for generosity being restored, they use it for God's glory and for Paul's encouragement. They were never indifferent to the need, but now they can, and will, do something about it! It could be that they just had insufficient funds before now, after their previous sacrificial gifts and their ongoing urgent needs. Or, they may have not been sure where Paul was geographically. Or, they may have lacked a qualified and experienced courier before Epaphroditus became available to go. (Maybe he was not too well even then?) Or they may have found it hard to get any gift to their man in custody. But now, they have enough to give, they know where Paul is, and, despite his illness and weakness, Epaphroditus is only too happy to take their gift to his beloved senior partner in the gospel. Christ is at their elbow, too, and sees what is going on. He is at our elbow also and feels every movement of the arm as the hand dips into the pocket or handbag, or signs a cheque! With Christ coming back soon, what better posture to be in than to be, as it were, writing Him a cheque or handing money over through love, to encourage and help one of His labourers?

HOW TO MAKE OTHERS REJOICE IN GOD

The very fact that they are so willing to show their love and support for Paul causes him to 'rejoice in the Lord greatly'. It is God who has changed their hearts from 'getters' to 'givers', and this evidence of it causes great joy and rejoicing to Paul. We are not told how much they gave, or promised to give. That does not matter as much as the fact that they want to be involved financially with God, His man, and His gospel. When a Christian supports a faithful Christian worker financially, it encourages and blesses the giver because Jesus taught it was 'more blessed to give than to receive',[5] it encourages the recipient because he is blessed materially and encouraged in fellowship spiritually, and it glorifies and pleases God who 'loves a cheerful giver'.[6] Also, it encourages churches and fellowships. God's full-time labourers have to be supported, running a church has financial implications, and things like Christian literature do not grow on trees. By giving financially to support the expenses incurred in the Lord's work, we encourage others who are involved in that work, and provide a good example to them. Continual and systematic giving can become contagious where folks are urged to put God first. And let us never forget that God gives so much to us. It is right and proper for each of us to give as individual Christians, but there is something even more encouraging when a whole church gets the giving desire and habit. Churches that give generously to missionaries seem to have a dimension that others do not have, however big or gifted they may be.

THE EVIDENCE—'DO IT AGAIN'

The evidence that their realisation of both the nearness and imminent coming of Christ had helped to loosen their purse strings is that they gave *again*. It is sometimes easier to give a large sum away once than to give sacrificial smaller sums regularly and repeatedly. A converted vagrant, whom God had blessed with success so that over the years he prospered and became the owner of a successful chain of shops, told his story to some 'down and outs' at the Christian shelter where he himself had been converted. As soon as he had trusted Christ he gave into the offertory at the shelter all he had, even though it was only two dimes. Previously he had decided to give one dime and keep the other for himself. He told them how he thanked God for having blessed him since. He had learned to tithe directly and immediately to God at least ten per cent of all he received. He stressed it all started when he gave all his money, including that last dime he had, as soon as he was converted. An older lady, who had been one of the Christians who had given him soup before he trusted Jesus, listened very carefully indeed. At the end of his moving testimony, whilst others expressed their wonder and amazement at how God had blessed this former pauper, she simply whispered to him: '*Do it again!*' Are we as generous now that we may have more, as we were when the amount given did not add up to much? Do we need to 'do it again?'

4:11 Satisfaction—grace and the learning curve

11 Not that I speak in regard to need, for I have learned in whatever state I am, to be content:

NOT OBSESSED BY NEED

Although during his life Paul has often been in need, and may be even because of that, he is not obsessed by his sense of need. This must be a lovely state of mind to be in, by God's grace and deep personal faith in a sovereign God. To be humbly pushed back on Christ to supply, but not to let that need become so big that it obscures all else, is a sure fruit of the peace of God which, as we saw in verse 7, 'will guard your hearts and minds through Christ Jesus.' Paul's heart is set and his mind is at peace. He is content whilst myriad reasons for discontentment shout at him though his circumstances. Paul has learned and knows from personal history and from the character of his Saviour that he has no cause to worry just because for a while he is in need physically. He knows a God who will continue to provide all he needs. He feels no need to 'speak in regard to need.' In all his letters the only time he asks for anything for himself is when he requests that Timothy would bring him his cloak, some books and some parchments.7 He would not necessarily have been wrong to have made his needs known, but there alone with God in his cell, he is confidently assured that God will provide for him.

NO 'QUICK FIX'

But Paul's contentment has not come by a 'quick fix'. The apostle shares that he has 'learned' this contentment over time experientially. It did not come in a flash of inspiration, but by trusting God again and again. If it came naturally he would not have had to learn it. A baby does not need to be taught to breathe—that is natural and automatic—but does need to learn to walk and talk because they are things that can only be learned by experience and instruction over a period of time. So often, we want God's spiritual blessings in our lap 'now', but God tells us to walk in faith and obedience to Him and we will acquire them by His grace. Learning to be 'content' also comes by personal faith and loyal obedience to God and His Word. It is in the very temptation to be discontented that Paul experiences God's contentment and gain. He cannot go where others can. He cannot have what others have. He cannot do what others do. He cannot help where others can. He cannot see whom he wants. He cannot receive what he needs. He is unjustly imprisoned. How can he find any contentment in those circumstances? But that is the exact set of contrary circumstances, temptations, frustrations and fears that give way to an amazing contentment to the man whose heart and mind are being kept in the peace of his ever near risen Lord. He knows too that the *real* future is exceedingly bright for him in Christ. Bolstered by his confidence in his coming Saviour and his eternal home in heaven and the certainty of Christ's presence with him, he is content! Often because we are lulled by having so many things that we want, we lose our focus on the fact that real contentment is godly and deep. It can neither be repeated nor removed by what our passing world offers. The world offers a tune to whistle on the way to the funeral. Christ offers the eternal harmony of being in tune with the Son of God who loves us and died for us.

CONTENTMENT AND GODLINESS

Thus it is that Paul says to Timothy that '*Godliness* with contentment is great gain.'[8] Paul is no stranger to that gain, always spiritual and sometimes material, that flows from seeking God first in his life and thus making him 'content'. How different from a world that taught then, and still teaches today, that to have is more important than to be, and to put self first is more important than self-crucifixion in putting Jesus Christ and others first. Knowing that God is at your elbow feeds contentment in a way no lottery win or successfully accomplished task can do. Rejoicing in the imminent return of the One who eternally gives perfect peace and joy in its fullness makes the believer truly content. He will feature in God's final climactic blessing in history. It is the freedom from the penalty, power and (one day) presence of sin in knowing the indwelling Christ, and the glorious future certainty of the victory of His second coming that makes the Christian content. They are fixed and sure and benefit the Christian. As William Cowper wrote: 'Freedom has a thousand charms to show, That slaves, howe'er contented, never know.' Those contented temporarily with the physical and earthly, but enslaved to sin now and eternally, can never experience that contentment of knowing the 'Son' who sets us 'free' so that we shall be 'free indeed'![9] Final and perfect contentment can be seen in heaven. What is it? It is to be freed from the world, the flesh and the devil and to enjoy the sunshine of communion with God, through Christ, in a way that can never be spoiled by any shadow of worldliness, sin or satanic opposition. Contentment on earth gets deeper as those same elements are combated by a growing spiritual relationship with God. In fact, living close to Christ alone can produce even the taste of such contentment here below. That spiritual relationship and that living close to Christ *is* godliness. And Paul does enjoy that ever deepening communion with God as he lives close to Christ, which is why he says that '*godliness* with contentment is great gain.'

NO EXCEPTIONS

The wonder of this learning curve of grace, with its attendant sense of joy and fulfilment, is that it applies to each and every situation. Paul says he has learned 'in *whatever state* I am' to be content: no trial too difficult; no bereavement too sad; no disappointment too overwhelming; no suffering too hard; no want too great; no sin too powerful; no failure too final; no fear too gripping. In all circumstances, he trusts His ever-present Saviour and anticipates His triumphant return to right all wrongs, to bless His people and to glorify God's holy name. There is no 'no go' area for God! In the same way as Romans 8:37 tells us that '*in all these things* we are more than conquerors through Him who loved us,' and that '*all things* work together for good to them that love God',[10] so all things here are an opportunity for Paul to learn more of the grace of God and from the God of grace. This is equally true for the Philippian Christians and for us today as God cannot have a set of principles that applies for one dedicated saint and not for another.

4:12 Satisfaction—learning in plenty and in poverty

12 I know how to be abased, and I know how to abound. Everywhere and in all things I have learned both to be full and to be hungry, both to abound and to suffer need.

ABASED AND ABOUNDING

The sea of life heaves and falls for us all. It is the same for the church in Philippi and it is no different for their beloved apostle. Paul's vindication of his apostleship in 2 Corinthians 11 reminds us of the amazing hardships, trials, persecutions, sufferings and disappointments he suffered for the sake of Christ and His gospel. But he also knew times of great love and acceptance, of amazing rescue and provision. He could look back to points of great authority and acclaim from people in authority, as well as of being near to death at the hands of mobs. Spiritually, too, he admitted that he was near to giving in and giving up at times, yet to being wonderfully strengthened, used and helped at other times.[11] Ebb and flow are the conditions in which the Christian has to navigate the boat of his life under the Pilot's guidance. Solomon's wisdom is seen in his request, after having the greatest riches that the world could give to any man, when he asks God: 'Give me neither poverty nor riches … Feed me with the food allotted to me.' He does not want the temptations of too many riches any more, or the trials of just not having enough. He wants God to choose what he is to have. The Philippians will also experience the highs and lows of life. But abased or abounding, that contentment and knowledge that God is working not only for them but also in them, feeds their trust in Christ. No doubt we experience the same today. We should not be so unrealistic as to expect rose petals always when Christ's way was strewn with thorns. We are wrong to set our sights on material gain, as riches are probably a greater stumbling block to the Christian than poverty. But neither should we punish ourselves with the thought that God only wants to test us and try us and that he has no 'treats' arranged for us. He 'daily loads us with benefits'[12] and a loving Father not only disciplines but is also generous towards His own precious children. He also expects them to steward what they have honourably, prayerfully and kindly. If we are in the sunshine of His provision and care, thank God for it and humbly enjoy it. Are we in the valley? Keep crossing it and we will again rise up on the mountain. Does it seem dark? Patience! Light is coming ever nearer. Abased or abounding, our God is in control.

NO GEOGRAPHICAL LIMITS

We have already seen, from verse 11, that the 'all things' of verse 12 are an opportunity to learn and to know God's contentment. That must be an important point, because Paul makes it again now. We need to be told the same thing often and clearly, because we are so slow to grasp God's life-changing truths. But Paul now expands that principle geographically! The blessed learning experience is not only 'in all things' but also 'everywhere'. Do we have places we hate to visit? Are there situations at which we feel weak and insignificant and thus refuse to serve God? Are we scared of hospitals or funerals, returning to a lonely flat, visiting houses for Christ, or taking our place in witnessing for Christ in public places through open-air meetings? Are there countries opposed to the gospel, or where our lifestyle would be seriously changed, where we will not consider going to share Christ? Are there places, large or small, where we seriously doubt if God's grace in Christ will make any difference to us? Paul tells these believers that 'everywhere' he has been, which included being in the sea shipwrecked and in prison awaiting probable death, he has 'learned' that the seesaw of life was pivoting on the contentment of knowing Christ.

REAL NEED

In all these circumstances and places it is the contrast between excessive plenty and very real immediate needs that tests Paul. Perhaps it is harder to be moved from abundance into real need, than it is to learn to cope with need on an ongoing basis. Those with little do not miss what they never were able to have, but do miss the absent essentials of life. Having abounded underlines the poverty of the need that may follow that abundance soon after. Never more will this be felt than in the question of food and drink. Paul has been from feast to famine, from being full to being empty, but has learned to be content no matter what he consumes or does not consume. No grumbling here. No 'if onlys'. Never is the question put: 'Why don't Christians support God's workers more generously?' Although Satan will ensure that the temptation to despair is never too far away, we do not hear Paul saying: 'I'm sick of this: that's it!' He knows that it is a small thing for God to provide soon, and continuously if He so pleases, and give him the 'fat of the land'. Therefore he will contentedly trust Him when the larder is empty. In 2 Corinthians 5:7 Paul tells the Corinthian Christians that 'we walk by faith, not by sight.' It is this walk that enables Paul, with God's grace, to be content in excess or in deprivation. Not many of us are in the same league as William MacDonald in appreciating this, and still fewer of us attempt to live it out. Writing on that verse from 2 Corinthians, he says: 'To walk by sight means to have visible means of support, to have adequate resources for the future, to employ human cleverness in insuring against unseen risks. The walk of faith is the very opposite; it is a moment-by-moment reliance on God alone. It is a perpetual crisis of dependence on the Lord. The flesh shrinks from a position of complete dependence on an unseen God. It seeks to provide a cushion against possible losses. If it cannot see where it is going, it is apt to suffer complete nervous collapse. But faith steps forward in obedience to the Word of God, rises above circumstances, and trusts the Lord for the supply of all needs.'[13] In Paul's circumstances he had little other possibility of advancing, other than in the way that MacDonald describes. Even when wise provision can and should be made, however, we need to remind ourselves to trust in the God of provision, rather than in the provision of God. Circumstances can change, but He does not! But the willingness of men like Paul and William MacDonald is not an excuse for well-fed Western Christians to ignore their brothers in harder circumstances. Perhaps we should have more self-imposed emptiness from time to time in order that others might enjoy a little more from our 'abundance'.

4:13 Christ's strength for everything

[13] I can do all things through Christ who strengthens me.

EVERYTHING IS POSSIBLE

Everything that God wants Paul to do for Him is achievable by His grace. That is true for all Christians, past and present. We should not forget the 'I can do' of this verse. God never gives a task without His enabling. The 'I can do' is not a smug statement of self-sufficiency but a logical deduction to be made from knowing the Almighty God. In our own strength, of course, each of the Philippians (and we, too) would have to say, 'I cannot'. But possessed by Christ, through His Spirit and His Word, 'I can do' is a necessary part of the normal Christian life. Paul is not here talking about some unnecessary, dramatic miracle to make folks say, 'Wow!' From his prison, he is talking in the context of being in need after abundance, and of experiencing God's holy contentment in all circumstances and in all places.

It is the 'I can do' of faith that is as available to twenty-first century Christians as it was to Paul and the Philippians. The power of the risen Christ is at work in every Christian to make that 'I can do' a fact rather than an over-idealistic fantasy.[14] And there is no exception clause in this contract of grace! 'All things' means that God will give every faithful believing Christian all the strength and help needed for *each and every* testing and challenging situation through which duty dictates that the disciple must pass. The harder the challenge, the greater the potential experience of His strength, grace and help. Never forget that 'those who wait on the LORD shall renew their strength; they shall mount up with wings like eagles, they shall run and not be weary, they shall walk and not faint.'[15]

SAME SOURCE

There is one source: 'through Christ'. Salvation comes to the sinner 'through Christ'. With that salvation comes our assurance, fellowship, answered prayer, oneness as a spiritual family, and ongoing mercy, grace and peace. So it is hardly surprising that our strength to say, 'I can do'—and then to do it—also comes through our crucified and risen Saviour. There is no other name or source apart from Him. We either know Christ, and all the good things that the Father has given us in Him, or we know nothing at all of God, His mercies, His grace, and His strength. As someone succinctly put it: 'Know Christ, know blessing; no Christ, no blessing.' Just as we came into blessing by knowing Christ, so we continue in it by knowing Him better day by day.

GOD'S STRENGTH

What is the strength that Paul experiences? The present tense of the verse underlines that it is present strength we have 'through Christ'. It is strength now that Christ gives, for He is 'Christ who strengthens me'. Yesterday's strength was good for yesterday's challenges but it is strength for today that I need right now. Our Christian walk has to be current or we are not walking at all.

This strength is also personal strength. It is strength from 'Christ who strengthens *me*' so that Paul can say, '*I* can do all things'. It is not just for the church, the well-known speakers or missionaries, or the exceptionally gifted servants of God. It is for me! Paul's God is the Philippians' God, is Calvin's God, is Hudson Taylor's God, is Lloyd-Jones' God, is Wesley's God, is Bunyan's God, is Spurgeon's God, is *my* God. Just as salvation comes personally to all in the same basic way, so does God's strength. If I cast myself upon God and His Word, prayerfully seeking to honour Him in a holy life and in unstinting service, I have as much right to expect to experience God's strength as the so-called 'Christian greats' did and do! But someone may object that he or she does not feel strong, but is very much aware of a sense of feeling weak and inadequate. Good! That is how every person should feel in his or her own strength. Paul said elsewhere[16] 'when I am weak then am I strong'. That sense of weakness is a qualification, not a disqualification, for proving God's strength in our lives. It tells me just how much I really need 'Christ who strengthens me'. Let Hudson Taylor explain how he found strength in his Saviour, when in 'agony of soul' about his powerlessness and fears, and after he said, 'I prayed for faith, but it came not.' He continued: 'When my agony of soul was at its height, a sentence in a letter from dear McCarthy was used to remove the scales from my eyes, and the Spirit of God revealed the truth of *our oneness* with *Jesus* as I had never known it before. McCarthy, who had been much exercised by the same sense of failure, but saw the light before I did, wrote … "But how to get faith strengthened? Not by striving after faith, but by resting on the Faithful One." As I read I saw it all! "If we believe *not*, He abideth faithful." I looked to Jesus and saw (and when I saw, oh, how joy flowed!) that He had said, "*I* will never leave you." Ah, *there* is rest! I thought, "I have striven in vain to rest in Him. I'll strive no more. For has *He* not promised to abide with me—never to leave me, never to fail me?" And … *He never will!*'[17] There is no reason why you and I should not trust the promise and presence of the Saviour in the same way that the great missionary pioneer to China did. After all, we face the same inadequacy!

Notes

1 1 Corinthians 4:12; Acts 18:3.
2 1 Timothy 5:18.
3 James 1:17.

4 Habakkuk 3:17–19.

5 Acts 20:35.

6 2 Corinthians 9:7.

7 2 Timothy 4:13.

8 1 Timothy 6:6.

9 John 8:36.

10 Romans 8:28.

11 2 Corinthians 1:8–11.

12 Psalm 68:19.

13 William MacDonald, *True Discipleship* (STL), pages 39,40.

14 Colossians 2:12,13.

15 Isaiah 40:31.

16 2 Corinthians 12:10.

17 Dr and Mrs Howard Taylor, *Hudson Taylor and the China Inland Mission—The growth of a work for God* (Overseas Missionary Fellowship), page 175.

Mini-overview 4:14 to 4:19

Sharing and supply—

The threefold blessing of blessing others.

4:14 Sharing in distress

¹4 Nevertheless you have done well that you shared in my distress.

'NEVERTHELESS'

Paul has just made it very clear that He is enabled to meet any situation, with contentment, by the strength of his Saviour and Lord who is 'at hand.' Even though this verse reveals his distress caused by the combination of his great physical and financial need, his loneliness, and his concern for the church, he has 'learned' to get through 'Not somehow but triumphantly', as a Christian friend of mine, dying with cancer, stressed to me when he gave me a card displaying those four words. So, trusting God's strengthening grace and faithful provision, there is a sense in which he did not need the support of the saints at Philippi. But Paul does not claim to be an island! He is in fellowship with his beloved brothers there, and he has been encouraged by them. So, despite everything that God is and does, he says, 'Nevertheless you have done well.' In thanking God he is careful to applaud the human agency, too. We could turn that around to address our support of others. They, and we, know that 'God will supply all [their] needs according to His riches in glory by Christ Jesus', but that does not mean that we should be anything other than faithful and eager to support them financially and materially, as well as spiritually and socially. God who provides for them also provides for us and we should be always ready to share with others what He has so generously shared with us. Their faith and contentment should touch us no more than their distress and need. Spiritually minded servants of God deserve our support, 'nevertheless', in their faithful service for Him. With the Lord at hand to witness that, and with His coming hastening the day or our accountability, we would do well to remember that.

WHY SHARING HELPS

In Paul's distress, these Christians 'shared' with him. The word implies acting as his partner. One of the tenets of Partnership Law is that, unless there is another agreement, profits and losses are shared equally between the partners. God has blessed and prospered the Philippians and they want to share what they have with him. Sharing is good for a number of reasons, be it sharing money as discussed in verse 10, or sharing of time, prayer and self. But sharing with someone 'in distress', especially when that distress is suffered because of that person's faithfulness to the Lord, is doubly important. Even the world says that 'a friend in need is a friend indeed.' A man who is distressed can forget just how much people really care for him. He can turn in on himself and wrongly imagine that no one cares. The more he gives in to the distress, the more distressed he can become. Distress turns and breeds in a vicious circle. In that situation he becomes like a stray, straggling, wounded buffalo separated from the herd, easy fodder for a hunting lion or pack of wolves. When others share in his distress, it tells him that he is still in the 'herd' with them, and that others care for him and want to protect and help him. If that distressed person is himself an influential leader, experiencing a time of weakness and attack from Satan, such sharing support is also a capital investment for others. The struggling, but encouraged, Christian leader will be able to minister better to others after he has been helped himself in those circumstances. Paul knew how this works as he revealed to the Corinthians, when he said: 'Blessed be the God and Father of our Lord Jesus Christ, the Father of mercies and God of all comfort, who comforts us in all our tribulation, that we may be able to comfort those who are in any trouble, with the comfort with which we ourselves are comforted by God.'[1]

'WELL DONE'

Paul does not comment on how much better or worse they could have done, or challenge them as to whether more money could have been squeezed out, but he simply says 'you have done well'. It is good to commend when it is due, and he gratefully commends these believers. Perhaps two of the most welcome words in eternity to the hearty servant of God, despite his many sins and failures, will be 'Well done, good and faithful servant!'[2] Do we live our lives treasuring that commendation more than the world's popularity, wealth or applause? Others will say we are foolish for giving our money and time for something that cannot be seen immediately to benefit us materially: we should keep what we have for ourselves, according to them. Jim Elliot, the martyred American missionary, gives us the right answer to people like that with the challenge of his wise logic: 'He is no fool who gives what he cannot keep to gain what he cannot lose.'

4:15 At the beginning

15 Now you Philippians know also that in the beginning of the gospel, when I departed from Macedonia, no church shared with me concerning giving and receiving but you only.

THE FACTS

Paul appeals to what his Philippian friends already know. They recall that no one else was financially supportive of Paul when he started his missionary and evangelistic gospel work for God. He uses this knowledge to commend them. Perhaps their knowledge that no one else cared enough to share was one factor that intensified their generosity. Perhaps we should be more careful to direct our giving to people and works of God who do not catch the eye, or the purse strings, of the Christian public as much as certain others.

IN AT THE START

Many people want to see how a venture is going before they get involved. They do not want to 'back a loser'. The whole fashion industry testifies to this: there are few trendsetters, but many sheep-like followers. To find someone who will take the risk at the start in a big venture is rare, but the bigger the risk, the bigger the reward. So it is with the 'beginning of the gospel' at Philippi. These Christians were in at the start. There was no knowing how and where it might end, but because it was God's gospel, they fully supported Paul in his pioneer endeavours to make it known. If Paul and his gospel ventures failed, they would fail with him, but they would support him anyhow. No other church encouraged him by financial giving except them. Whilst wisdom is needed in new initiatives for God, to make sure that they are genuine works of God being run on biblical principles, wisely conceived and properly carried out, we should never underestimate the role of first encouragers and givers. Enough people will try to pour cold water on efforts of others that might challenge their indifference or demand their financial support. The great missionary pioneer to China, Hudson Taylor, was actively discouraged from missionary work by a board of older Christians, who may have been doctrinally sound but who also appear to have been evangelistically sound asleep! But God stirred him up to go and make a tremendous contribution to the work of Christ. When zeal is lacking around, the great Encourager is within and at hand, and how encouraged would He be at His return if He found us faithful in seeking, encouraging and financing new avenues for honourably sharing His changeless gospel with the lost?

GENEROSITY AND INDIFFERENCE

Just a word about generosity. God is generous: He 'so loved' that He 'gave' His best.[3] We have already noted that Jesus taught that to give was more blessed than to receive.[4] Here we see that this generous Philippian church was responsible in partnership with Paul for the spread of the gospel. Its generosity was an informed one: alone this fellowship communicated with Paul about 'giving and receiving'. They knew what they were being generous about and why. Why are some smaller poorer churches more generous than some bigger richer ones? Ask any full-time worker if that is not true. Much money is often spent on important but secondary things, whilst little goes directly to the work of the gospel at home and abroad. Some churches have unrealistic policies about visiting speakers' expenses and free-will donations. The better paid among them would never expect to be treated in the same way by their employers, but it seems that sometimes with some Christians anything goes for Christian workers and the works they represent. But surely, someone will insist that dedicated labourers for Christ should be willing to sacrifice, should they not? Yes! But so should we all, and manifest it in sacrificial giving, both as churches and as individuals. And we should not hide our mean attitudes and practices behind the self-giving of others. It seems sad that legacies to Christian causes seem to be the main means of keeping some works going, and even they are becoming fewer and farther between. Where is the joyful, sacrificial, systematic, regular giving of God's people? Why is it not reflected more often by the generous giving of some churches to pioneer gospel causes and missionaries?

LONELINESS

Self-pity is not in Paul's personal vocabulary, but the words 'but you only' perhaps do reveal a loneliness of leadership that a committed Christian can experience. It is not only the value of the gift, but the number of the givers that can encourage an afflicted worker. Perhaps the sum is paltry in this affluent world's eyes but significant to the giver in his, or her, personal circumstances. God knows! Just to know that a number of people and fellowships care enough to give at all is a great encouragement to a Christian worker. When Paul went out from Macedonia in those early gospel days to which he refers, he knew that God's grace and strength were sufficient for him. And he knew that one small church was praying for him, and how precious that would be to him. How much more could he have been encouraged by a real interest from others, manifested in monetary support? Does my church help to fight the loneliness of missionaries and Christian workers by financial support? Do I? And loneliness hits so many people. Elisabeth Elliot, the widow of Jim Elliot who was martyred by the head-hunting Auca Indians, confides: 'in the most unpremeditated ways, in the oddest places and for the most absurd reasons, as I'm going about my business, generally calm, even cheerful, that sudden tide sweeps in. Its called loneliness.' She adds later: 'Loneliness comes over us sometimes as a sudden tide. It is one of the terms of our humanness, and, in a sense, therefore, incurable. Yet I have found peace in my loneliest times not only through acceptance of the situation, but through making it an offering to God, who can transfigure it into something for the good of others.'[5] The Lord who is with us now spiritually, and also coming again in great power and glory, is our 'very present Help in trouble'[6] and that includes the trouble caused by loneliness.

4:16 Continuing the vision

[16] For even in Thessalonica you sent aid once and again for my necessities.

INCONVENIENT BUT DONE!

Without our facilities to move money easily and quickly around the world, it was difficult for the small company of those who loved the Lord in Philippi to send money to Thessalonica. It all had to be arranged in detail.

Excuses could have been made for not sending a gift: perhaps it would not get there; maybe bandits would take it; perhaps the courier might not make it? Yet 'even in Thessalonica' is a principle to teach us that we should master the difficulties, or excuses for not giving, and get on with it. They had encountered difficulties before, but sent their gifts repeatedly to Paul. We should be far more determined than most of us are to give repeatedly to needy Christian causes and people. Sometimes it may not be a lack of generosity that is our problem: if the person were in our own living room we might give very generously. Perhaps it is our laziness we need to deal with. Or could it be that we could spend half an hour exploring potentially very significant financial tax advantages to God's work by giving, under provisions which our government accords us. Let us give wisely and repeatedly, whether or not it is easy or simple to do so.

REPEATED ENCOURAGEMENT

Not only was their giving 'even in Thessalonica', but it was repeated often. Paul commends his Christian friends because they 'sent *aid* once and again.' Their encouraging support was shown in that it was not a flash in the pan, but something so real to them that it was a continuing priority. An occasional large gift may help to salve our consciences, but repeated giving to those who cannot respond and who need it is close to the heart of God. The logic of repeated and continual giving is overwhelming. How often do the missionaries or ministers of the gospel we support need to eat? How often do they need to pay their other bills? How often do they need to buy clothes or spend money on their children or the upkeep of their house? Do the running costs of their car carry on? Do the Bibles, leaflets and other resources that they use in their work renew themselves? Are they exempt from paying for postage and telephone use? Would they appreciate a special treat now and then? If they take a break on holiday, do they have to pay for that? The questions are simple, but very important. Their needs and expenses, both personal and in the gospel, are ongoing, and so should be our giving. This is especially so when we happen to know that a certain worker gets no, or very little, support from others. Ideally his, or her, church should shoulder the responsibility. But that happens so rarely that most Christian missionaries and workers need additional support from enlightened and concerned individuals also.

OTHERS' NECESSITIES

The repeated gifts had been sent for Paul's 'necessities'. Necessities, by definition, recur again and again and again. That is why the church in this Roman colony gave again and again and again. We should not miss the point that the money was given because Paul *needed* it. How often do we unthinkingly indulge our desire for luxuries and things which are of little use to us whilst others, with genuinely real needs, go without? When was the last time that you or I gave the equivalent of the cost of a holiday to support the needs of a person or organisation trying to present the gospel to men, women, young people, boys and girls who are lost and without hope? Remember, the Lord 'at our elbow' knows when we give, and the day of His appearing may find us gratefully generous or miserably mean. William MacDonald rightly says: 'our giving should be Spirit-directed in answer to earnest believing prayer. It also goes without saying that we should first give ourselves to the Lord, then our money (2 Corinthians 8:5)'. He then goes on to suggest that we should consider our own local church needs, then those labouring in the gospel to establish churches (at home and abroad, of course), then those whose lives are devoted to Christian service without financial remuneration or support. He could have added specific missionaries, specific gospel and literature projects at home and abroad, and those who seek to introduce the gospel through meeting physical needs as a bridge and opportunity for Christian love, such as medical missionaries and works in famine-torn areas. He also counsels wisdom in ensuring that you know where the money goes and that it will be well used in the gospel. Sound advice![7]

4:17 Selfless receiving

[17] Not that I seek the gift, but I seek the fruit that abounds to your account.

WHAT JESUS SAID

Remember! The indwelling Christ, who is the soon coming Lord, is the One who taught that giving was more blessed than receiving[8] and He who gave Himself utterly and sacrificially has, by that giving of Himself on the cross, been responsible for 'bringing many sons to glory'.[9] Naturally, receiving something for needs is a blessing and encouragement, but Paul, who has learned to be content with much or with little, seeks greater blessing for the givers in the form of fruit. He is not thanking them now as a back door way of asking for a gift.

NOT SELF-SEEKING

Paul, in fact, is asking for nothing for himself. He trusts God and will take what comes from His faithful Lord. Perhaps we should use wise discernment in considering support more readily for those workers who rarely, if ever, ask for money. There is obviously a place for sharing needs with Christian brethren and churches who have expressed a genuine interest in the work in which the Christian labourer is involved, and that cannot be wrong in principle. But there are some who, on principle, feel unable to do that. They see it as an article of personal faith and do not wish to be misunderstood for the sake of their consistent witness for Christ. They will know the temptation to hold that view in principle, but to put carefully guided and lightly veiled words in their prayer letters that in practice *are* an appeal for help financially. Far better to be 'up front' than to do that! But there are some faithful and needy brothers and sisters in Christ who will not even mention finance or personal needs, and they deserve to be supported just as much as others who will. To develop the trend of thought further, those inviting Christian workers or preachers to meetings and services should also be discerning and realistic. Do you honour God by paying *all* their expenses incurred in visiting you? Do you work it out carefully beforehand and place the gift in an envelope, so as to avoid embarrassment for your invitee? Do you always err on the generous side in reimbursing expenses, or is there a sense of grudging and paying as little as you have to? No one should seek to profit or lose out in all this. What is right and fair should be done. The servant of God should be prepared to lose out, but should not be expected to do so by those inviting him. Then, as a completely separate issue, do you also make a generous donation to the work in which the Christian worker is involved? That is good for his work, and for yours. Sometimes Christian churches, especially the richer ones, can be very thoughtless, mean or negligent. 'God loves a cheerful giver'[10] whether that giver is personal or corporate. The aim is not to seek to bring profit to ourselves, but to glorify God and bless others. This principle of denying self-seeking should permeate our lives, our service for God and our attitudes. It was a significant pivot in the life and ministry of C. H. Spurgeon. He had been kept waiting for an interview by the error of a forgetful maid who forgot to announce the young and then little-known preacher's presence to a Baptist College principal and an elder from a fashionable large Cambridge church, considering Spurgeon as their preacher/pastor. Spurgeon said nothing after he left without his awaited and expected interview or expenses. The men were cross with him for not turning up! In the book *Travel with C. H. Spurgeon* the story is taken up: 'Leaving the house Spurgeon walked across Midsummer Common in Cambridge confused, but he thought he heard a voice clearly say to him: "Seekest thou great things for thyself? Seek them not." (Jeremiah 45:5) Taking it as a word from God he returned to pastoral work.'[11] Spurgeon did not know what plans his God had for his life and ministry and how going to Cambridge at that time might have frustrated them. God knew! The 'prince of preachers' to be learned an invaluable lesson that day, to seek God's glory and not what was in the possible opening for himself. Always in the realm of finance in Christian work we should seek the good of others and not 'great things' for ourselves.

SEEKING FRUIT

The fruit Paul seeks for the Christians in Philippi will 'abound to [their] account'! He wants them to be immeasurably and spiritually productive and rich! In our selfish world, men seek riches by accumulating and investing, and are often disappointed. In the kingdom of the coming King, who already lives and rules in the Christian's heart, real spiritual riches come from giving and distributing! Generous giving of money, time, praise and service is the seed corn from which a great and fruitful harvest of blessing will result both to the giver and to those he blesses with his gifts. It is the sowing/reaping principle. Sow sparingly and reap sparingly. Sow generously and reap generously. Note that Paul says this fruit '*abounds*' to their account. No stock market slumps here! This principle has a wide application, but it does include money. Imagine the fruit stalls in an open market! How good to see, smell and handle those colourful, varied and pleasing fruits. They came through sowing or planting, and through painstaking work, nurture and care. So Paul's work for the Philippian church involves his sowing the seed of the Word and planting churches. He labours for this, and in the nurture and care of the converts and their churches. Just to see their stand for Christ and growth in Him is the fruit Paul seeks. But he also seeks that they too will have the pleasure of bearing fruit, as he does. His life is invested in that. That means more, so much more, to him than any gift of money, however appropriate and welcome that may be in his needy circumstances. His priority is right: seek permanent spiritual fruit for others, not passing selfish money for himself! The Philippians' account in the Bank of Heaven is measured in spiritual fruit, not in material gain. We have an account there too. Is it in credit or debit?

4:18 Paul is full and God is pleased

18 Indeed I have all and abound. I am full, having received from Epaphroditus the things sent from you, a sweet-smelling aroma, an acceptable sacrifice, well pleasing to God.

HAVING 'ALL' AND BEING 'FULL'

How can Paul say, 'I have all and abound'? He is imprisoned and not surrounded by material comforts and pleasures. What does he mean by 'all' and how can he possibly be said to 'abound'? He underlines these thoughts by stating 'I am full'. Has he got a secret hoard of wealth? Does he know something we do not know about his prosperity? How is he 'full', why does he claim to have 'all', and in what sense does he 'abound'?

'ENOUGH IS AS GOOD AS A FEAST'

Paul has already declared that he is content and that through his knowledge of Christ he can do whatever he has to do. 'Enough is as good as a feast' is an old saying with modern relevance. Paul's 'all' means 'all that I need physically'. It also means 'all I need in Christ spiritually'. His fullness implies also that his needs are met. He is 'full' of contentment. He is being filled with God's Spirit as he trusts his Lord each day. He abounds not in worldly wealth or political prospects. His abundance is in gratitude for God's grace, love, presence and help. His treasure is located elsewhere, but he knows it abounds there. He envies no one. His 'all', his abounding and his being 'full' are because of his close walk with Christ.

He will receive more, abound more and know God's fullness more both in the remainder of his uncertain earthly life, and then in heaven itself. He is spiritually full, possessed of every blessing in Christ that a repentant and trusting sinner can have. But for now he is physically full too. The money sent to him probably bought him food, as part of the necessities that his Philippian brothers and sisters sought to supply. And because he is 'full' he says that he now knows what it is to 'abound'. He is not greedy and does not seek to accumulate. His needs have been more than adequately met and he sees that as abundance. Perhaps that is why he is 'content' in different circumstances. His expectations are neither selfish nor greedy, neither excessive nor unrealistic. So he is content with the abundance of 'enough'. What a lesson to those Christians in Philippi and also to us today. Contrast that with the world in which the Christian testimony of contentment must shine brightly. Jerome K. Jerome said, 'If you are foolish enough to be contented, don't show it, but grumble with the rest.' The world takes an admission of being happy with 'enough' as a strange sign of weakness, because it may prevent you getting more than enough! How wonderful to be of millionaire status spiritually and eternally, starting from the moment we trusted Christ, and to view enough as sufficient whilst passing through on this very short road ending in eternity.

SENDING GIFTS

We noted before the difficulty in sending the gifts to Paul, without twenty-first century communications and financial facilities. In fact, dear self-effacing Epaphroditus was the trusted messenger and courier. The church could trust him and it did: and he delivered, in more ways than one! How sensible in sending gifts to needy causes, especially when we are not a hundred per cent sure about all their credentials, to use a trusted Christian when one is available. We should check before giving to any cause or charity for the relief of poverty or famine, or for helping persecuted Christians, that they are scrupulously honest, biblically sound, well recommended by knowledgeable and reliable Christians, and single-minded in their work. Some organisations or charities can never meet a spiritual need because they have no gospel to proclaim and no Saviour to honour. In circumstances like that, often a trusted Christian missionary society, church or organisation may be able to find you a like-minded 'Epaphroditus' whom you know you can trust and with whom you share the desire to make Christ known.

PLEASING GOD AND BLESSING OTHERS

The loving gifts sent to Paul via Epaphroditus are compared with sweet smelling Old Testament sacrifices which spoke of worship and love for God. The aroma of that gracious generosity not only pleased Paul, but its pleasing scent drifted up into heaven itself and was also 'pleasing to God'. He loves cheerful givers.[12] He delights to see some children in His family showing love and concern for others. This is also a witness to the world and a sure sign that we 'have passed from death to life, because we love the brethren'.[13] Just think: a few simple gifts to a needy servant of God can please the God who made and owns the whole of creation! If we know His indwelling presence and blessing, we will want to please Him. If we are here when Christ returns, what a joy it will be to go up to meet Him in that cloud, and see His smile of pleasure and approval!

4:19 Supply line from heaven

[19] And my God shall supply all your need according to His riches in glory by Christ Jesus.

THE PERSONAL PRONOUNS

The personal pronouns in this verse are striking: '*my* God', '*your* need', '*His* riches.' Paul addresses the Philippians with the same confidence as a child would display to his friend in need about his father, who he knows will help him. He says: '*my*' God. Then, as we have seen, Paul's concern is not with his own necessities. He concentrates on what is good for the Philippian church when he says '*your*' need. He links the two, in full assurance of the measureless love, power and bounty of God, by highlighting '*His*' riches in glory by Christ Jesus. This sentence characterises Paul's life. The things that count for him are his relationship with God, the needs of others at every level, and the fact that God can meet those needs, by and in Christ.

THE UNSOUGHT SPIN-OFF

Selfless giving, by definition, seeks nothing for self! Yet the spin-off from the Philippians' generous God ensures that the greater blessing of giving will include the meeting of all their need! If they had given just in order that their need could be met, that would not have been the spirit of giving that pleases God. Such a self-seeking investment would have failed. But they have given because they love their Lord and His servant, Paul, and want to bless their apostle friend. The response to selfless giving, though not sought by it, is 'God shall supply all your needs'. A dear old Christian lady from Yorkshire once told me, 'Don't expect cream cakes, Love, when He only promised daily bread! But be ready for Him to give you cream cakes as well!' God's promise is to meet our needs, but remember that He is also the One who 'daily loads us with benefits'[14] just by His grace. He *often* gives more than He promised and *always* gives a lot more than we ever deserve.

THE MEASURE OF BLESSING

In fact, be it daily bread or cream cakes or both, the measure of blessing is an inexhaustible supply of top quality. Quantity and quality could not be better in God's inventory of blessing. Our need will be met 'according to His riches in glory'! Now, God's 'riches in glory' surpass, by infinitely larger numbers, all the wealth of all the earth's sources time and time again. We need never fear that His store to meet our needs (not necessarily our wants) will ever run out, or even run low. Be it the spiritual, moral, mental, physical, or emotional needs of an honouring and generous Christian, God will meet them from His heavenly store of 'riches in glory.' No matter what lavish wealth has been hoarded in the most sumptuous and richest places owned by rulers, pharaohs, popes, dictators or successful entrepreneurs, they are *nothing* compared to God's 'riches in glory.' Their wealth is passing and impersonal, and engenders more problems than solutions. God's 'riches in glory' are eternal, personal to every one of His saved ones, and given by the same grace that has solved the greatest problem anyone could have—that of having his sin forgiven and coming to know God. And God's riches include remembered rewards to His servants who have faithfully served Him. 'God is not unjust to forget your work and labour of love which you have shown towards His name, in that you have ministered to the saints and do minister,' was God's message to the scattered and persecuted Hebrew Christians.[15] He has the provision, wants to give you it, and will not forget you! Riches often cause more problems than they solve in this materialistic, money-grabbing world. That is why Francis Bacon said, 'Riches are a good handmaid, but the worst mistress.' And this world's passing riches are what Martin Luther referred to as the 'worldling's pleasure' and called them 'gilded toys of dust'. But God's glorious riches in Christ are eternal, intrinsically valuable, and the possession of the poorest of sinners who casts himself, or herself, on a God who is 'rich in mercy.'[16]

THE SAME SOURCE AGAIN

Such provision for our needs from His glorious richness is 'by Christ Jesus'. Everything we have of blessing and value is by Him. Our salvation, our sanctification, our strength, our joy, our peace, our fellowship—in fact everything—is 'by Christ Jesus'. Only by faith in Christ Jesus is a sinner saved, forgiven, cleansed, restored, renewed, helped, blessed, used and kept. How fitting that God's divine Source of blessing to us, the Lord Jesus Christ, should end this part of the chapter where we learn so much in the light of His coming and indwelling. Living in our lives, He enriches us now to meet our temporal needs. Coming back as King of kings, He will enrich us then with a richness that gloriously surpasses all and any needs. All needs will be banished when Jesus reigns then! We shall join in His riches in heaven itself, but be more taken up with Him than even what He gives to us!

Notes

1   2 Corinthians 1:3.
2   Matthew 25:21, 23.
3   John 3:16.
4   Acts 20:35.
5   **Elisabeth Elliot,** *Loneliness* (Nelson).
6   Psalm 46:1.
7   **William MacDonald,** *True Discipleship* (STL), pages 83,84.

8 Acts 20:35.

9 Hebrews 2:10.

10 2 Corinthians 9:7.

11 Clive Anderson, *Travel with C.H. Spurgeon* (Day One), page 33.

12 2 Corinthians 9:7.

13 1 John 3:14.

14 Psalm 68:19.

15 Hebrews 6:10.

16 Ephesians 2:4.

Mini-overview 4:20 to 4:23

Greetings and grace.

How to say 'goodbye' on the very best of terms!

4:20 The real 'mission statement'

²⁰ Now to our God and Father be glory for ever and ever. Amen.

OUR COMMON FATHER

Paul has treated the Philippians as family members both in his manner and in the content of what he says. This is right since they have all become redeemed children of God by faith in Christ.[1] So it is only fitting that his concluding greetings start with an acknowledgement that God is their common Father. He it is who brought us into His family by the new birth.[2] He alone watches over His children as a father, and pities and cares for them. He loves us enough to exercise a father's discipline when we need it.[3] He is the head of our Christian family. To have a loving, caring and good human father is a great privilege. Many do not have that privilege today, and the situation worsens as God's pattern of a settled family under the care and authority of a faithfully married man and his wife has been so diluted and diverted by modern standards of immorality and sin. Derek Prime hits the nail on the head when he says: 'The title "Father", therefore, is not as appealing and as meaningful as it ought to be. We may sadly transfer unhappy feelings about our human father to God.'[4] But to have an infinitely loving, caring and good Father—our Heavenly Father—and to know that He will be there for us to glorify 'for ever and ever', is (literally!) infinitely better. He is holy and untainted by sin.[5] It is sad when a family is deprived, by death, of its loved and loving father. But our heavenly Father is 'the everlasting Father'[6] and is eternal and changeless in character. I like the fictitious tale about the somewhat 'superior' and very intellectual young man who had just been awarded a Ph.D. in Theology at Bible College and was preaching at a down-to-earth rural church. His opening prayer sounded like the syllabus in theology, recently successfully negotiated by him. After many long words and flowery phrases, he finally prayed: 'Oh Thou Omniscient, Omnipresent, Omnipotent, Immanent and

Transcendent One, in Whom eternality and essence cohabit—what shall we call Thee?' At that stage a godly old man in the church had suffered enough! He stood up and called out: 'Call Him, "Father," lad!'

What a privilege that, whether we understand the long words or not, we can call Him 'Father' and know we are His blood-bought children! Like Paul, we need to remember that we share the benefits of that Fatherhood with every other blood-bought child of God and thus should treat each one with the love and concern we would want to show to our nearest human family.

THE GOAL OF GLORIFYING HIM

The tenets of the Reformation—which we could call 'The "Sola" System'—are 'Sola Scriptura' (Scripture alone), 'Sola Fide' (faith alone), 'Sola Gratia' (grace alone), 'Solus Christus' (Christ alone), and 'Soli Deo Gloria' (Glory to God alone). Here we see Paul's concurrence with the last tenet: he wants to see God glorified. He says 'to our God and Father *be glory* forever and ever'. Like a golden canopy over all his desires to make the gospel known, to see the church established, to promote oneness in the body of believers, and for his personal holiness and walk with God, is a single aim and goal, summarised by blind but far-seeing Fanny Crosby in the content and title of her triumphant hymn, *To God be the glory*. If that motivates the church after Paul has passed on, it will be blessed and effective. If that is our aim today, how much heartache and misunderstanding will be taken out of our relationships with others, both Christian and unconverted! If the Lord Jesus was concerned to glorify His Father,[7] then so should we be.

EVERLASTING

We can easily miss those words 'forever and ever'. The need to glorify God is an everlasting one. That means it should start *now* and never stop in eternity. God is eternal.[8] We too will live for ever. We had been on the road to everlasting punishment and ruin because of our sins[9] but, having repented and trusted Christ, we are now recipients of eternal life and look forward to being everlastingly with Christ in heaven.[10] Our gospel produces everlasting results.[11] So it is right that the aim of those ransomed by Christ's blood should be 'to our God and Father be glory forever and ever. Amen.' How different is our eternal future compared with a life out of fellowship with God lived for time alone, and with eternity to regret it. As we think of glorifying God for ever and ever, let us make every effort we can to reach with the gospel those whose eternity is a lost one. But let us also rejoice in our eternal state and blessings and glorify God now in anticipation of glorifying Him perfectly then. The theme of everlastingly glorifying God carries through to the book of Revelation. I can do no better than to conclude with passages from Revelation 4[12] and Revelation 5.[13]

'Whenever the living creatures give glory and honor and thanks to Him who sits on the throne, *who lives for ever and ever*, the twenty-four elders fall down before Him who sits on the throne and worship Him *who lives for ever and ever*, and cast their crowns before the throne, saying: "You are worthy, O Lord, to receive glory and honor and power; for You created all things, and by Your will they exist and were created."'

'And every creature which is in heaven and on the earth and under the earth and such as are in the sea, and all that are in them, I heard saying: "Blessing and honor and glory and power be to Him who sits on the throne, and to the Lamb, *for ever and ever*!" Then the four living creatures said, "Amen!" And the twenty-four elders fell down and worshiped Him *who lives for ever and ever*.'

4:21 Saluting the saints

[21] Greet every saint in Christ Jesus. The brethren who are with me greet you.

EVERY SAINT

Final impressions are as important as first impressions. You only have to watch people who love each other saying goodbye at an airport or railway station to realise that! It is interesting to note that this last section of the last chapter of the book begins in the same spirit as the first section of the first chapter of it. There, verse 1 confirms that Paul's letter is addressed to 'all the saints'. Indeed the whole letter has always been for them all, and so now it is no surprise that he asks the church to 'Greet every saint in Christ Jesus'. May we have, and continue in, that same love and concern for all who are in God's family. God loves 'every saint', Christ died for 'every saint', and we should not be selective in our Christian love either. It is interesting to see the depth of the meaning of the Greek word for 'greet' in *Strong's Concordance*: 'to enfold the arms' … 'to salute' … 'to welcome; embrace, greet, salute, take leave.'[14] Christian greetings were not a nod of the head in the street, but a loving family involvement. And it is to be for 'every saint'. Do we have some ground to make up in rediscovering the preciousness of our family ties in Christ with all who are truly born again into His family?

PAUL'S BROTHERS IN CHRIST

Paul's example catches on! His brothers in Christ, no doubt those visiting him and in Caesar's household as well as those physically with him in captivity, join in his greetings to the Philippian church, even though some will never have met them. It is good to be concerned for Christians we do not know, as well as those we do, and to pray for and support them. More than one missionary has been encouraged by a communal tape recording, or a 'round robin' letter sent from home which includes messages from people they have not yet met. We should not underestimate the blessing a greeting can bring, whether by letter, telephone, e-mail, or fax; it is hugely disproportionate to the amount of effort and expense in sending it. Anyone doubting that should start writing to missionaries, or begin encouraging hard working labourers in the gospel. Generally speaking, today communications are fast, effective and cheap. How much does an e-mail cost? How long does it take to send? Most missionaries have e-mail or e-mail access. The cost of international telephone calls has come down a lot, with the advance of technology. It means so much to our missionaries to *hear the voice* at the other end, and it should mean a lot to us to hear them also. But for those who prefer to write or send a parcel, with the advantage of being able to enclose photographs or some small treat, your hour or so spent in doing that is well worth it to those to whom you write. With how many missionaries are you meaningfully in contact? May these closing verses spur you on to be a blessing to lonely missionaries and other servants of God!

4:22 The multiplication of fellowship

22 All the saints greet you, but especially those who are of Caesar's household.

IN IT TOGETHER

Just as Paul wishes to include all the saints at Philippi among the recipients, he is eager to include all the saints with him in the sending of these Christian greetings. Fellowship multiplies quickly in an atmosphere of concerned selflessness. No doubt those in prison would be at least as blessed in sending greetings as the Philippians would be encouraged to receive them. Those engaged in correspondence to and from prisoners know that it means a lot to a man or woman not only to hear from 'the outside' but to be able to contact a friendly non prisoner also. That is why a wonderful opportunity exists to share the gospel in such exchange of letters. Also, it is an excellent thing to bring together two God-honouring churches or fellowships separated by miles in greetings, prayer and sharing. Everyone is encouraged thereby. How good to involve as many Christians in that as possible. Paul is the motivator here for inter-church fellowship. We can all follow his example.

FOUNDED OR FOUND?

The main parties in this greeting are, extremely encouragingly, those of 'Caesar's household'. Right there in the household of potentially the most powerful force in the world against the gospel are blood-bought brothers and sisters in Christ. And they know that their allegiance to the family of God is more important to them than their allegiance to their national leader, who has the power to have them 'snuffed out' physically. But who are these Christians in Caesar's 'back yard'? Was the church there *founded* by Paul or *found* by him? The answer is probably that he found it, but helped to shape it and added to it, by God's grace, through his own personal witness and teaching of God's Word. That household could include: those from among Caesar's family; those in high position in politics, law, the army and court life; those involved in administration and skilled support—whom we would call 'professionals' today; people from the many aspects of personal and domestic services necessary for such a high dignitary; tradesmen attached to his court; and, no doubt, many others whom we would call 'hangers on'. The converts amongst these folks could have heard the gospel from travellers and merchants visiting Israel, meeting Christian converts on their own business trips, and from the church in Rome itself. To their number, no doubt, would be added those who were converted through Paul whilst being inmates, employees or visitors, including some of those soldiers who were chained to their prisoner. A close friend of mine, converted in prison and recently released, told me of a prison officer who has just come to faith in Christ. Some of the spiritual input into that man was when he was handcuffed to my witnessing friend on his way to court! That is wonderful! But just imagine being a non-Christian soldier chained to the zealous, wise, knowledgeable, experienced and compassionate apostle! Confronted by the gospel as 'the power of God unto salvation',[15] the grace of God, the convicting power of the Holy Spirit, the prayers of those upholding Paul and his witness, and Paul's determination that he should 'become all things to all men, that [he] might by all means save some',[16] what chance would an even half-honest and half open-minded pagan soldier, or anyone else, have? The 'whole palace guard' as well as 'all the rest' certainly heard, as we saw in chapter 1:13! The man who saw each stumbling block as a stepping stone for the gospel, and each setback as a springboard, surely rejoices in the church in 'Caesar's household', whether found by him or founded by him. God will receive the glory from him, in either case. He is the God who saves sinners from all backgrounds, beliefs, ethnic origins, intellectual abilities, financial resources, abilities and social standings. One commentator has asked: 'May we not see in this union of members of the most alien races a striking illustration of the new bond which the Gospel had woven amongst men? There was a Jew standing in the midst between Macedonian Greeks and proud Roman citizens, including members of that usually most heartless and arrogant of all classes, the lackeys of a profligate court, and they are all clasping one another's hands in true brotherly love. Society was falling to pieces. We know the tragic spectacle that the empire presented then. Amidst universal decay of all that held men together, here was a new uniting principle; everywhere else dissolution was at work; here was again crystallising. A flower was opening its petals though it grew on a dunghill. What was it that drew slaves and patricians, the Pharisee of Tarsus, rude Lycaonians, the "barbarous" people of Melita, the Aeropogite of Athens, the citizens of Rome into one loving family? How came Lydia and her slave girl, Onesimus and his master, the praetorian guard and his prisoner, the courtier in Nero's golden house and the jailer at Philippi into one great fellowship of love? They were all one in Christ Jesus.'[17] Are we not privileged as Christians to belong to such a diverse family and to have such a wonderful Saviour! And we need to remind ourselves again that this Saviour is 'at hand'. He is in us and with us *now*, and He is coming again *soon*!

4:23 Still grace

23 The grace of our Lord Jesus Christ be with you all. Amen.

A TRIPLE REMINDER OF PRIORITIES

Three of the important recurring themes of the letter feature in the last full sentence of the letter. Again 'you all' are Paul's concern. One of the important reasons for writing to them is to encourage them into one-mindedness by having the mind of Christ governing their conduct and relationships. So it is fitting that the last two words (translated into English) apart from the 'Amen' are those words 'you all.' No more needs to be said about that! Then he reminds his readers again about 'grace'. Paul cannot miss that word from his greetings, but it is no mere habitual repetition. Nothing has been, is being, will be, or can be achieved for God and His kingdom without His 'grace'. We either tread the path of Christ's grace to salvation, sanctification and blessing, or we will remain strangers from Him, now and in eternity. Either grace governs our relationships, or they collapse. We rely on that grace for daily living and for our gospel witness, or our lives become inconsistent and our witness ineffective. It is good to be reminded of that grace in this last verse. We all need His grace always and everywhere for everything we seek to do or to be. And, completely consistent with Paul's life, evangelism, worship, letters, and particularly this Philippian letter, the last name on which he focuses is 'our Lord Jesus Christ'. Jesus is in the first verse and the last, and permeates the whole letter, as he does the whole Bible and the liberated, but imprisoned, apostle's life. What a reminder and example for us! Where would we be without the Lord Jesus Christ? What would we have to offer? To whom else could we go for forgiveness and help? Paul's co-apostle, Peter, gave us the test of a converted and committed Christian: 'Therefore, to you who believe, He is precious.'[18] May He be more precious to writer and reader alike as a result of having considered this letter together!

'AMEN'

There are sixty-six books in the Bible. Although I have never counted them, my Online Bible shows that there are twenty-two 'Amens' in the Old Testament and forty-four in the New Testament, also totalling sixty-six! It seems entirely appropriate that twice as many come after the birth of Christ than before the everlasting Son of God took upon Himself the flesh of our humanity. Philippians has two 'Amens', one in verse 20, and one here as the last word in the last verse of the letter. As one gifted and leading Bible teacher has said: 'Amen' is a 'confessional affirmation that underscores the preceding truth'.[19] Put more simply it is a heartfelt 'Yes—I agree!' Paul underlines the need for Christ's grace to be with all his beloved Philippians with that word 'Amen.' We need that grace too! May we add our 'Amen' too to his prayer, as well! With a confident, complete and joyful confidence in the inspired words of God's revealed Word, the Bible, we can heartily endorse Paul's 'Amen'. That prayer for grace should be the petition and the aspiration of every truly saved person who seeks God's glory and kingdom, and to please his, or her, Lord and Saviour. May we not merely say, 'Amen!' as a final punctuation mark to close a prayer and a book of the Bible. May our hearts be in that prayer, far more than our lips. May our lives, minds, wills and efforts re-echo Paul's 'Amen' to see God glorified, biblical truth upheld, the gospel preached, sin forgiven, Satan vanquished, souls saved, disciples made, and Christians encouraged to honour 'our Lord Jesus Christ' every day. May this mind be in us!

Notes

1 John 1:12.
2 John 1:13.
3 Hebrews 12:6.
4 **Derek Prime,** *The Lord's Prayer for today* (Day One), page 22.
5 John 17:11.
6 Isaiah 9:6.
7 John 12:28.
8 Romans 1:20; 1 Timothy 1:17.
9 Matthew 18:8; 25:46; 2 Thessalonians 1:19.

10 John 3:16; Matthew 25:46; John 5:24.

11 2 Timothy 1:10.

12 Revelation 4:9–11.

13 Revelation 5:13,14.

14 James Strong, *The New Strong's Exhaustive Concordance of the Bible* (Nelson), page 16 of Greek Dictionary of the New Testament, (under reference 782).

15 Romans 1:16.

16 1 Corinthians 9:22.

17 Alexander MacLaren, Expositions of Holy Scripture, Volume XIV (Eerdmans), page 79.

18 1 Peter 2:7.

19 John MacArthur (author of commentary/notes and general editor), *The MacArthur Study Bible, NKJV* (Word Bibles), note on Philippians 4:23, page 1829.

Check-out

Questions on each verse to consider or discuss personally, or in Bible studies, study groups, or one-to-one discipleship training

Philippians chapter 1

Verse 1
(a) In what ways should a Christian be a slave to Christ? Why is this liberating?
(b) Consider the principles of how a church should be run, based on the description of the church at Philippi, given in this verse.

Verse 2
(a) What is grace and what blessings come because of it?
(b) How are (i) Jesus and (ii) the gospel linked with peace in the New Testament?

Verse 3
(a) In what ways do you benefit if you are habitually thankful to God?
(b) What advantages are there in telling people you thank God when you remember them?

Verse 4
(a) What is the difference between legalistic bondage and godly habits?
(b) What part should joy play in Christian living and fellowship?

Verse 5
(a) How can you contribute to and be helped by fellowship?
(b) Why can fellowship in the gospel produce deeper links still?

Verse 6
(a) How does the knowledge that God started and continued His saving work in me give confidence (i) to me and (ii) to others?
(b) What is 'the day of Jesus Christ' in this context?

Verse 7
(a) How and why does Paul have the Philippian Christians in his heart?
(b) How can we be 'partakers of grace' with others?

Verse 8
(a) How would my conduct differ practically if I were more conscious that 'God is my witness'?
(b) What can we do to promote a greater affection for fellow Christians?

Verse 9
(a) Consider the blend and balance needed of love, knowledge and discernment. Why is this so?
(b) How can I co-operate with God to see my love for Him and for others increase constantly?

Verse 10
(a) Practically, what can I do to help me to 'approve things that are excellent'? In what way is the pursuit of excellence right or wrong?
(b) What part does sincerity play in a successful Christian life?

Verse 11
(a) What seeds should

we be sowing to produce the 'fruits of righteousness'?

Is it true that, in a sense, we determine how 'filled' our lives shall be with those fruits?

(b) In how many ways does 'righteousness' feature in the life of the Christian? Compare our righteousness with that of Jesus Christ.

Verse 12

(a) Consider the benefits of openly sharing your news with other Christians. Should there be any limits or caution about this? If so, what should they be and why?

(b) Think back to when unwanted events in your life, or the life of your church or fellowship, led to the 'furtherance of the gospel'. What lessons do such events teach you in the light of Scripture?

Verse 13

(a) Why does Paul say, 'my chains are in Christ'? What positive effects can result from a faithful Christian being imprisoned for his faith? How should we view Christians whose liberty has been taken from them for the sake of Christ?

(b) Think about how the gospel can spread to many as a result of one person hearing it. What examples from the Bible and from life can you recall?

Verse 14

(a) Consider the subject of 'confidence'. What helps our confidence in our Christian lives? What confidence comes 'direct' from God, and what comes via other Christians? How does verse 14 relate to this?

(b) What part should boldness play in our witness, and how do we get it?

Verse 15

(a) How many reasons can you think of why we should preach the gospel with 'good will'?

(b) What dangers are there in envying others? How can we deal with those dangers?

Verse 16

(a) How can selfish ambition be combated in the life of a Christian, and what will happen if it is not dealt with?

(b) What can de done to avoid insincerity in Christian service?

Verse 17

(a) How does your view of yourself as a Christian soldier appointed by God, rather than a pathetic victim of circumstances, fashion and help your attitude in the service of Christ?

(b) What does preaching 'out of love' entail?

Verse 18

(a) What part do circumstances and what part does resolution play in rejoicing?

(b) What main characteristics of Paul's own life do you see in this verse?

Verse 19

(a) What role, in the Bible and in your experience, have the prayers of others played in helping other Christians in need?

(b) In how many ways is the 'supply of the Spirit of Jesus Christ' essential to all those who know Christ? How can He help?

Verse 20

(a) Why do we act sometimes as if we are ashamed of the gospel of Christ? Why, sometimes, are we bold in our stand?

How can Paul's words in this verse help us?

(b) Consider continuance in Christian discipleship in the light of the phrase 'as always, so now also'.

Verse 21

(a) What do you think Paul means by 'for to me to live is Christ'?

(b) In what ways is it a gain to die? Given that dying is a gain for the Christian, why carry on living?

Verse 22

(a) Relate fruitfulness to labour. What part does God play and what part does the Christian labourer have to play?

(b) What elements of thinking do you think Paul balances when he says 'yet what I shall choose I cannot tell'?

Verse 23

(a) Why is Paul hard-pressed?

(b) In how many ways will it be 'far better' to be with Christ than to stay on earth? How should this affect us as we face up to our own death and the death of loved ones?

Verse 24

(a) What needs of the Philippian Christians do you think Paul had in mind? Are you willing and able to meet some of those kinds of needs, with God's help, in the lives of others? If so, how will you do it?

(b) What would be the 'downside' for Paul to 'remain in the flesh'?

Verse 25

(a) What is your view on why Paul now expresses his confidence that he will 'remain and continue with' the church at Philippi. On what should our confidence be based today?

(b) How and why are 'progress' and 'joy' linked? Can you think of any other biblical examples?

Verse 26

(a) Consider the causes of and hindrances to 'selfless rejoicing' for others.

(b) How can you add to the rejoicing of others when you meet with them in Christian fellowship?

Verse 27

(a) Why do we have the tendency to do things to be seen by others? How can we combat that so that we will carry on living for Christ, irrespective of the presence or absence of those we would like to impress?

(b) What does being of one mind in Christ involve, in a church or fellowship? Does it mean we should always agree with other Christians on every point?

Verse 28

(a) How can your testimony helpfully be a signpost to believers and to unbelievers? Why do they read the signpost differently?

(b) Are you ever frightened of what those who oppose the gospel may do or say to you or to your church members? If so, how can you deal with it? What is Paul's comment on it here and elsewhere?

Verse 29

(a) Meditate upon suffering as a gift, in the light of this verse. What positive and what negative aspects can you see? Is it inevitable or desirable?

(b) 'For His sake'. How should that principle affect

suffering, specifically, and the whole of your Christian life, generally?

Verse 30

(a) What components of the 'conflict' do you think weighed most heavily with Paul, on the one hand, and the Philippian church, on the other hand? Which would you find hardest to accept as God's gift, and why?

(b) Consider how our fellowship with God and with other Christians is affected by knowing that we face the same problems as they do.

Philippians chapter 2

Verse 1

(a) Can you think of other instances in the Bible where you come across the benefits to the Christian mentioned in verse 1?

(b) How true do you think it is that God always equips you for what He asks you to do? Can you think of examples in Scripture, or instances in your life?

Verse 2

(a) What can we do legitimately to complete the joy of other

Christians? What is likely to hinder their joy being fulfilled in us?

(b) How do the four concepts interact, and what is the part that love plays in all of this?

Verse 3

(a) In how many ways do you think that selfish ambition and conceit can spoil God's work in and through a Christian? How do they stop lowly mindedness?

(b) Consider practical ways that we can esteem others better than ourselves.

Verse 4

(a) How can we best organise our Christian lives so that we legitimately look after our own interests without spending an illegitimate amount of time on them?

(b) In how many ways can we look out for the interests of others?

Verse 5

(a) What especially impresses you about the 'mind which was also in Christ Jesus'? Consider biblical instances to show how Jesus thought.

(b) Consider the suggested steps to help

us to establish the mind of Christ within. Which of these do you need to reinforce, and why?

Verse 6

(a) How many evidences can you find from the Bible which underline that Jesus is God?

(b) As you consider the Man, Christ Jesus, how many attributes and prerogatives of deity do you see Him exercising in His earthly ministry?

Verse 7

(a) From your observation from the Scriptures, in how many ways do you think Christ emptied Himself in the exercise of the prerogatives of His deity, (a) completely and (b) partially?

(b) Consider slavery. In what ways was Jesus a slave, and why? In what ways should we be slaves? To what should we not become enslaved?

Verse 8

(a) What are the real hallmarks of the humility of Jesus, and how can we cultivate true humility in our lives?

(b) Consider what the

cross meant to Jesus, and what (a) His cross, and (b) our cross should mean to us.

Verse 9

(a) Consider the relationship between humility and spiritual blessing. How did Jesus demonstrate the principle? How will it work for us?

(b) Consider the names 'Jesus' and 'Emmanuel'. How much doctrine is included in those two names? How are the names linked?

Verse 10

(a) Think about why the different classes of beings should bow the knee to Jesus at His coming: angels, the dead in Christ, living Christians, non-Christians, and demons.

(b) Why do not more people bow the knee to the Lord Jesus Christ *now?*

Verse 11

(a) Imagine the scene. What strikes you most, in prospect, at the universal affirmation of the Lordship of the Lord Jesus Christ?

(b) In what way do you think all this will be 'to the glory of God the Father'?

Verse 12

(a) How should our knowledge that God is always with us, as Christians, be a challenge as well as a comfort?

(b) Why do we not always 'work out' our salvation as we should? What can we do about it to put that right?

Verse 13

(a) Consider God's spiritual input into your life. What practical changes can you make to encourage that input and to limit things that hinder it?

(b) Give careful thought to the relationship between being willing, doing, and pleasing God.

Verse 14

(a) What are the basic problems with people who easily complain? Why should Christians not complain?

(b) What disruptions to Christian fellowship does 'disputing' cause? How can it be avoided and overcome?

Verse 15

(a) In what way is Jesus 'the light of the world'? In what way should Christians, as lights, be to the world what He would be, if He were here physically?

(b) Consider 'blameless', 'harmless' and 'without fault' as serious Christian goals. How do we make progress in achieving those goals, and what hinders our progress, and why?

Verse 16

(a) In what ways can we hold fast to the 'word of life' and hold it forth to others? Why is the gospel referred to as 'the word of life'?

(b) Consider the relationship between building and rejoicing, and running and rejoicing, as pictures of the Christian life. What does 'in vain' mean in this context?

Verse 17

(a) How and why was Paul being 'poured out' for the Philippians? What could that mean in the future?

(b) What strikes you most about the reason and the fact of Paul's gladness and rejoicing? What can we learn from it?

Verse 18

(a) What 'same reason' do Paul and the Philippian Christians have for rejoicing?

(b) Consider Christian joy in the light of (i) bereavement; (ii) martyrdom; and (iii) persecution or imprisonment.

Verse 19

(a) Why should we 'trust in the Lord Jesus' for things other than our eternal salvation? What benefits are there in so doing?

(b) What added burdens, to his personal Christian duties and his normal leadership role, do you think Timothy would need to bear as Paul's representative to the Philippian church?

Verse 20

(a) Why do you think Paul has only Timothy who is 'like-minded'? Whose fault is it? What echoes of this do you hear today?

(b) What is involved in sincere caring for the state of other Christians? Why should we do it? How can God help us?

Verse 21

(a) Why are we Christians so selfish, and what can we do to combat it?

(b) What are the most important 'things which are of Jesus Christ' that we ought to seek?

Verse 22

(a) What reasons do you think the Bible would give for making a young convert wait for a position of leadership until he is of 'proven character'? Why do we sometimes ignore this?

(b) How can younger and older Christians cultivate a father/son relationship in the gospel. What factors hinder this being promoted? What can we do about them?

Verse 23

(a) When is urgency right and when is it wrong for the Christian? Consider any instances from the Bible where, on the one hand, it was right to wait before acting and, on the other hand, it was right to act immediately.

(b) What part do circumstances play in guidance for Paul, and for you? How do you balance believing prayer with acceptance of circumstances?

Verse 24

(a) Look back over chapter 1 and chapter 2:1–24, and consider in how many ways, and for how many things, does Paul 'trust in the Lord'?

(b) Consider Paul's enthusiasm for seeing and helping the Philippians. How can we apply the same principles and concerns in the lives of our churches?

Verse 25

(a) How should a twenty-first century Christian blend his roles as a brother, worker, soldier, messenger and carer? Can all these aspects be fulfilled in one person and, if so, how?

(b) What qualities did Paul find in Epaphroditus that made him so confident that he could send him in his place? Do you have those qualities?

Verse 26

(a) How do you think Epaphroditus developed a longing for the Christians at Philippi, and of what did it consist?

(b) Compare the church's concern for Epaphroditus with his concern for it.

Verse 27

(a) Why does God allow some Christian servants to recover from serious illness, whilst calling others home?

(b) How can the recovery of a very sick brother and fellow-worker encourage his companion in the gospel? How much of this is just normal 'humanity' and how much of it is directly attributable to God's grace?

Verse 28

(a) What part does eagerness play in Paul's work for God? Illustrate from this letter to the Philippians.

(b) In what things should a Christian rejoice? How many can you think of from the Bible?

Verse 29

(a) How can you receive someone 'in the Lord'?

(b) Why should we hold spiritual warriors in 'high esteem' and why is it that we often do not do that in practice? How can that be remedied?

Verse 30

(a) Was Epaphroditus commended for 'not regarding his life', or was he criticised for it? How do our modern standards of sacrifice compare with his?

(b) In what ways can we burden others by failing to support God's work and workers as we should? How can we support when we (i) live nearby, or, (ii) do not live nearby?

Philippians chapter 3

Verse 1

(a) Is the ability to 'rejoice' simply an emotion or is it an exercise of the will? If the latter, why should we rejoice, and in what should we rejoice?

(b) What is the point of telling someone the same thing more than once? Why is it necessary, and how should it be done?

Verse 2

(a) In what circumstances should the Christian leader be blunt about warning those to whom he ministers about harmful influences and people?

(b) Why is it considered 'evil' here to seek to persuade people to a different view and practice?

Verse 3

(a) How does putting no confidence in yourself for salvation conflict with popular thoughts about self-esteem?

(b) How is true worship in the Spirit affected if I do not centre upon the Lord Jesus Christ? How is my faith in Him affected if I have confidence in myself?

Verse 4

(a) How do you answer someone who says that Paul is beginning to boast?

(b) Why do some people still think that what they do can make them acceptable to God? What is their basic misunderstanding?

Verse 5

(a) What do you know about Paul's religious pedigree? What does it show us?

(b) What do you know, from the Bible, is commendable about the Pharisees? What about them is against the principles of God's grace and truth?

Verse 6

(a) How was Saul's zeal misplaced? How can our zeal be misplaced?

(b) Are there differences between righteousness coming from legal observance and that coming from God in salvation? What are the sources and effects of each?

Verse 7

(a) How do you account for such a change of attitude and priorities in Paul?

(b) What is the significance and application of the words 'for Christ'?

Verse 8

(a) Does this verse mean we have to despise everything we prized prior to conversion? If not, what should we count as 'loss', and why?

(b) Is Paul trying to 'gain' what he already has? What does he mean?

Verse 9

(a) How can a lost sinner be 'found' in Christ? What does it mean to be 'in Christ'?

(b) How did Paul get Christ's righteousness? Did he mean that he was now perfectly righteous in the way he lived? Or did he mean something more important than that?

Verse 10

(a) Why does Paul 'spoil' a good prayer by introducing suffering? Or is it essential to having the other two parts of the prayer answered? If so, why?

(b) In what sense should a Christian be conformed to the death of Christ? How do we get there and stay there?

Verse 11

(a) Did Paul think he might not be raised again if he failed as a Christian, or is the context of 'resurrection' here, more in the spiritual context of a daily crucifixion of self? Consider how death to self and resurrection interrelate.

(b) What is the meaning and application of the phrase 'by any means'? What 'means' do you and I have to be helped to live a 'resurrection life'?

Verse 12

(a) Why do you think that Paul freely admits he has not yet 'arrived' as a Christian?

(b) How should we treat our admission of failure to have 'arrived'? What should our attitude be?

Verse 13

(a) Paul, ready to face death, says he does one thing. How does his priority compare with modern teaching on Christian priorities?

(b) To what extent is our attitude to our past a help or hindrance to our continuation with Christ in our spiritual lives?

Verse 14

(a) To what extent is Paul's gradual 'reaching forward' in the future dependent upon his present 'pressing on'? Why? Can I 'reach forward' spiritually if my current commitment is less than wholehearted?

(b) What can 'the prize of the upward call of God in Christ Jesus' mean? What do you think it means in the context of the letter to the Philippians?

Verse 15

(a) What does Christian 'maturity' mean? What does it not mean?

(b) How does God normally reveal things to His children when they are not following His mind?

Verse 16

(a) How can past

attainment be used to help my present walk and my future goals for Christ? What biblical precedents do we have?

(b) Using the description of a 'walk' as 'a repetition of a step' how many things in the Christian life help our walk by being repeated on a daily or weekly basis?

Verse 17

(a) Consider the advantages and disadvantages of following the example of other Christians.

(b) How can a more mature Christian be a helpful pattern of godliness to a younger or weaker Christian?

Verse 18

(a) When is it appropriate for a person walking with Christ to shed tears?

(b) Is it right to tell anyone something 'often'? If so, why? If not, why not?

Verse 19

(a) What are the consequences in society, in families, and in individuals of making other gods beside the Lord God Almighty?

(b) How can we combat the temptation to cultivate an earthly mindset?

Verse 20

(a) Consider the Christian's privileges and duties as a citizen of heaven.

(b) How should eagerness for Christ's second coming be blended with a careful attempt to look at it biblically?

Verse 21

(a) What differences and similarities between our present bodies and our future resurrection bodies do you anticipate from the teaching of the Bible.

(b) Consider the phrase 'He is able' both in this immediate context and in the wider context of God's Word and dealings.

Philippians chapter 4

Verse 1

(a) Why should the lessons of chapter 3 lead Paul to say, 'Therefore ... stand fast in the Lord'? What is the link?

(b) What balance should there be between having Christian affection and stirred emotions for

fellow Christians, on the one hand, and insisting that they stand fast for Christ, on the other hand?

Verse 2

(a) Consider the importance and best way of imploring—i.e. urging, appealing to—those whom you feel really need to change.

(b) How can Christians who disagree on issues or facts be 'of the same mind in the Lord'? How does the indwelling 'mind of Christ' help?

Verse 3

(a) How does Paul seek to get help for those working hard for God in presenting the gospel? Is his method valid for us today? Should we do the same?

(b) Why does the fact that a Christian's name is written in the 'Book of Life' not make that Christian complacent but rather urge him, or her, to labour for Christ?

Verse 4

(a) Consider the link between emotion and rejoicing. Why is rejoicing far more than a question of 'feelings'?

(b) When is it right to

press a point to the point of repetition?

Verse 5A

(a) Consider 'gentleness' as a sign of strength, rather than weakness. What evidence of it do you see in the lives of Jesus Christ, the apostle Paul, and yourself?

(b) How can we make our gentleness known to all? What hinders that?

Verse 5B

(a) Consider 'The Lord is at hand'. Do you think it refers *primarily* to Christ's presence with the Christian now, or to His second coming? Why?

(b) How should my life be lived in the light of the second half of verse 5?

Verse 6

(a) How did Paul demonstrate in his life that 'nothing' meant 'nothing' and that 'everything' meant 'everything'? Do you put reservations on the limits of your anxieties? Why?

(b) Consider the effect that thanksgiving can have upon anxious care and upon prayer.

Verse 7

(a) Why does God's peace astound human understanding?

(b) Consider how hearts and minds are guarded by that peace. Who is responsible for that?

Verse 8

(a) Find examples in the New Testament of commands and principles urging negative restraint, and of those encouraging a positive seeking for holiness. How should they be blended in the Christian life? How does this relate to this verse?

(b) What is the difference between popular 'meditation' and biblical meditation?

Verse 9

(a) What is the purpose of learning, receiving and observing the examples of godly people? What should all this lead to? How?

(b) How are the 'peace of God' (chapter 4:7) and 'the God of peace' (this verse) linked?

Verse 10

(a) Apart from his relationship with the living God, what else makes Paul rejoice? Why?

(b) How did the Philippian Christians make the most of their opportunity to care for God's servant? How can we act in a similar way? Why do we often fail to do that?

Verse 11

(a) How does the world at large view the interaction of need and contentment? How does Paul view it?

(b) Explore the words 'I have learned'. What can they teach us?

Verse 12

(a) What and how does Paul learn from being abased and from abounding?

(b) Which is the greatest threat to a Christian's spiritual walk: poverty or plenty? Why?

Verse 13

(a) From the letter to the Philippians, look at some of the 'all things' Christ has enabled Paul to do, that would be difficult or impossible without His help and grace.

(b) Consider how God strengthens Christians. What part do we have in that?

Verse 14

(a) What part does open commendation have in Paul's dealings with the Philippian church? How can you be encouragingly commending without being dishonestly flattering or turning a blind eye to the truth?

(b) How does sharing help to alleviate the distress of Christians in difficult circumstances?

Verse 15

(a) Why does Paul have a special place in his heart for these people? How slow are you to encourage at the start of a venture for Christ? How should enthusiasm for His work be tempered by wisdom and objective thought?

(b) List the reasons, legitimate and illegitimate, that a church can give for not supporting a particular Christian worker.

Verse 16

(a) What part should the necessities of others play in the allocation of a Christian's finance? How do you avoid being disconcerted by the many needs around? What principles should you employ to direct your giving?

(b) Consider the difference between giving a very big donation once, and giving repeatedly over a period of time without receiving any reminders to give.

Verse 17

(a) Is it wrong to expect something back when I give to God's work? What can be included in the 'fruit that abounds to [my] account' and why?

(b) How would you advise a Christian worker to avoid seeking financial gifts for himself or herself? How, do you think, is the balance struck between making needs known and having a wrong motivation?

Verse 18

(a) What part does Epaphroditus play? Is there a parallel in Christian work today?

(b) What pleases God here, and why?

Verse 19

(a) What are the limits of God's generosity to the Philippians and to Christians today?

(b) In what way does God supply 'by Christ Jesus'? But for Him, would we have a right to expect receiving anything?

Verse 20

(a) How is God revealed as the Father of Paul and the Philippian Christians in this letter? What does the Fatherhood of God mean to you?

(b) Why should the motivation to glorify God permeate all we are and do for Him?

Verse 21

(a) Why is every Christian important to Paul? Do you exclude any from your circle of 'fellowship'?

(b) What blessings come when Christians greet each other?

Verse 22

(a) From this letter, recap what the word 'saint' means. How should a saint live?

(b) Reflect on and conjecture what it meant to the Christians working in 'Caesar's household' to have Paul as Christian leader in their midst.

Verse 23

(a) Ponder on the

benefits we see in this letter, and especially in this chapter, which come from the grace of God.

(b) Consider the direct references to the Lord Jesus Christ, both in this chapter and also throughout the letter to the Philippians. Note, from this letter, what He has done for us and given to us.